THE TIMES AND TEMPORALITIES OF INTERNATIONAL HUMAN RIGHTS LAW

This collection brings together a range of international contributors to stimulate discussions on time and international human rights law, a topic that has been given little attention to date. The book explores how time and its diverse forms can be understood to operate on, and in, this area of law; how time manifests in the theory and practice of human rights law internationally; and how specific areas of human rights can be understood via temporal analyses.

A range of temporal ideas and their connection to this area of law are investigated. These include: collective memory; ideas of past, present and future; emergency time; the times of environmental change; linearity and non-linearity; multiplicitous time; and the connections between time and space or materiality. Rather than a purely abstract or theoretical endeavour, this dedicated attention to the times and temporalities of international human rights law will assist in better understanding this law, its development, and its operation in the present. What emerges from the collection is a future – or, more precisely, futures – for time as a vehicle of analysis for those working within human rights law internationally.

Volume 27: Human Rights Law in Perspective

Human Rights Law in Perspective

General Editor: Colin Harvey
Professor of Human Rights Law
School of Law
Queen's University Belfast

The language of human rights figures prominently in legal and political debates at the national, regional and international levels. In the UK the Human Rights Act 1998 has generated considerable interest in the law of human rights. It will continue to provoke much debate in the legal community and the search for original insights and new materials will intensify.

The aim of this series is to provide a forum for scholarly reflection on all aspects of the law of human rights. The series will encourage work which engages with the theoretical, comparative and international dimensions of human rights law. The primary aim is to publish over time books which offer an insight into human rights law in its contextual setting. The objective is to promote an understanding of the nature and impact of human rights law. The series is inclusive, in the sense that all perspectives in legal scholarship are welcome. It will incorporate the work of new and established scholars.

Human Rights Law in Perspective is not confined to consideration of the UK. It will strive to reflect comparative, regional and international perspectives. Work which focuses on human rights law in other states will therefore be included in this series. The intention is to offer an inclusive intellectual home for significant scholarly contributions to human rights law.

Recent titles in this series

Gender Equality in Law: Uncovering the Legacies of Czech State Socialism
Barbara Havelkova

Investment and Human Rights in Armed Conflict: Charting an Elusive Intersection
Daria Davitti

Specifying and Securing a Social Minimum in the Battle Against Poverty
Toomas Kotkas, Ingrid Leijten and Frans Pennings

Protecting Human Rights and Building Peace in Post-Violence Societies
Nasia Hadjigeorgiou

Collective Trauma and the Armenian Genocide: Armenian, Turkish, and Azerbaijani Relations since 1839
Pamela Steiner

The Times and Temporalities of International Human Rights Law
Edited by Kathryn McNeilly and Ben Warwick

For the complete list of titles in this series, see 'Human Rights Law in Perspective' link at www.bloomsbury.com/uk/series/human-rights-law-in-perspective/

The Times and Temporalities of International Human Rights Law

Edited by
Kathryn McNeilly
and
Ben Warwick

• HART •
OXFORD • LONDON • NEW YORK • NEW DELHI • SYDNEY

HART PUBLISHING

Bloomsbury Publishing Plc

Kemp House, Chawley Park, Cumnor Hill, Oxford, OX2 9PH, UK

1385 Broadway, New York, NY 10018, USA

29 Earlsfort Terrace, Dublin 2, Ireland

First published in Great Britain 2022

A catalogue record for this book is available from the British Library.

Library of Congress Cataloging-in-Publication data

Library of Congress Control Number: 2021950752

ISBN: HB: 978-1-50994-990-8
ePDF: 978-1-50994-992-2
ePub: 978-1-50994-991-5

Typeset by Compuscript Ltd, Shannon
Printed and bound in Great Britain

Foreword: Thoughts for the Times of Human Rights

LYNDSEY STONEBRIDGE

In an essay written in 1949, the psychoanalyst, DW Winnicott argued that the reason why the experience of birth is traumatic is that the baby is in the total grip of external forces which, because she has no sense of time – and thus no sense of an ending – she cannot know is not permanent. It was an experience, he remarked, that was not unlike that of recent camp prisoners in the war, crushed, deprived of all agency, and without a sense that the experience would ever end.[1]

To be born into time, as Augustine taught, is to be human. To be deliberately and instrumentally, or casually and carelessly, deprived of time, it might follow, is to be subject to an inhuman act: banished not only from the world, but thrown back into timelessness – of trauma without end.

Unlike the baby, we know that time exists, that it begins and ends, and that some of us live on the 'right' side of time, able to move through it, to use it, even luxuriate in it, whilst others do not. To Winnicott's prisoners in temporal limbo we can add many people who are deprived of the right to time: the stateless trapped in territories and camps; the refugees and migrants stranded at sea and on borders; the sick without healthcare; slave labourers; those living on poisoned land; those under siege, etc. By contrast, to hold time is to hold power. Every torturer knows that time is one of their most effective instruments; the progenitors of slow violence exert their control by dialling up or dialling down on dread and hope alike.

In the origin stories of the West the bargain was that the law, as an instrument of the modern sovereign state, would keep the timelessness of endless struggle, violence, and suffering at bay by putting in place some rules to ensure that everyone at least inhabited something like the same temporal jurisdiction. Timelessness was replaced by collective narratives of time, such as that of the nation-state, with its forever lost and about to be re-found tales of unity; or the 'thinner grammar of time'[2] of the state itself (so thin that now it is difficult to

[1] DW Winnicott, 'Birth Memories, Birth Trauma, and Anxiety' (1949) in L Caldwell and H Taylor Robinson (eds), *The Collected Works of D.W. Winnicott: Volume 3, 1946–1951* (OUP, 2016) 201–20.

[2] I Baucom, 'Afterword: States of Time' (2008) 49(4) *Contemporary Literature* 713.

imagine a time before or beyond it); or the qualified international sharing-out of sovereignty between otherwise endlessly warring nation-states for the sake of future peace.

It was always an imperfect deal. In the context of the essays in this collection, however, it is notable that the development of international human rights law in the early twentieth century coincided quite precisely with the historical, political, and philosophical recognition that Western modernity had not after all vanquished the timelessness of human brutishness and suffering, but had merely displaced and appropriated it.

Writing in Vienna during World War I, Sigmund Freud wrote of how the war 'exceeded all limitations instituted in peacetime and known as international law'. As it challenged international law, the war also crashed over Europe's temporal order, overwhelming 'with blind rage, anything that stands in its way, as though there were to be no future and no peace afterwards'. 'We had expected', Freud despaired, 'the world-dominating peoples of the white race' to do better, to keep moral progress moving. For all his ethnocentrism, Freud hadn't really expected the dominating people of the white race to do much better. His point was not that the war was ending European civilisation, but that it was ending the illusion that Europe was a morally-progressive civilisation. The truth was that its people had always been happy to off-load their own 'primitivism' onto other races and nations, and get distant others to do the dying and suffering for them. As for the European metropoles now at war, the capitalist modern state had not vanquished the deadening timelessness of violence, he argued, but 'monopolised' it, just as it had the 'sugar and tobacco', and human labour, of its colonies.[3]

Freud's essay was called 'Thoughts for the Times on War and Death' – *Zeitgemäßes über Krieg und Tod*. As Samuel Weber has pointed out, the English translation mutes Freud's deliberate connection of his timely thoughts (*Zeitgemäßes*) to Nietzsche's *Untimely Meditations* – *Unzeitgemaße Betrachtungen* – of some 40 years earlier.[4] There Nietzsche debunked confident narratives about the onward march of German history. What others saw as progress, Nietzsche wrote, 'I try to understand as damage, breakage, and deficiency of the time [*Schaden, Gebreste und Mangel der Zeit*].'[5] By describing his thoughts as timely, Freud was arguing both that Nietzsche was right – that there was a recurrent, dark, complex *chronos* pulsing against western ideologies of history as progress – and declaring that in 1915 the philosopher's sense of

[3] S Freud, 'Thoughts for the Times on War and Death' (1915) in J Stratchey (ed), *The Standard Edition of the Complete Works of Sigmund Freud, Volume 14, (1914–1916)* (Hogarth Press, 1957) 274–300.

[4] S Weber, 'Wartime' in H des Vries and S Weber (eds), *Violence, Identity, and Self-Determination* (Stanford University Press, 1997) 91.

[5] Nietzsche's famous passage reads: 'Unzeitgemäß ist auch diese Betrachtung, weil ich etwas, worauf die Zeit mit Recht stolz ist, ihre historische Bildung, hier einmal als Schaden, Gebreste und Mangel der Zeit zu verstehen versuche, weil ich sogar glaube, daß wir alle an einem verzehrenden historischen Fieber leiden und mindestens erkennen sollten, daß wir daran leiden,' in M Holzinger (ed), *Unzeitgemaße Betrachtungen* (Create Space, Berlin, 2013) 209. This translation cited by Weber (n 4) 91.

untimeliness was now making itself present in the world. Nietzsche's untimeliness, in other words, had just become timely.

In the years between Nietzsche's and Freud's meditations, the scaffolding of modern international humanitarian and human rights law also began to be put into place. In 1899, the First Hague Peace Conference was convened, followed by the Second in 1907, which established the International Court of Arbitration. The Third, scheduled optimistically for 1915, did not take place – it was already wartime. The Carnegie-funded Hague Palace of Peace opened officially in August 1913, but no sooner had the bronze sculptures from around the world been heaved onto their plinths, the Palace fell quiet as Europe hurtled towards war in the summer of 1914. Determined to try again for a peaceable and more humane world, in 1922 the League of Nations set up the Permanent Court of International Justice. Determined to try yet again, the United Nations set up the International Court of Justice in 1946.

One argument is that the history of modern human rights has always had to catch-up with its own mission to improve the world like this; that although their progress is often impeded, human rights are basically characterised by their utopianism and forward drive. By contrast, in different ways the contributors to this volume all suggest that modern human rights might be intrinsically untimely in the sense that Freud and Nietzsche recognised, and indeed, that this untimeliness might be the source of their strength as well as their weakness.

The problem with the catch-up narrative, as with complaints that human rights are either dismally anachronistic or hopelessly utopian, is that it disguises the deep political and historical nature of this untimeliness. Born out of the ruins of colonialism, imperialism, total war and genocide, human rights were responding to the end of an illusion about western civilisation: the question was always going to be to what extent that end was acknowledged.

The human rights project of the second half of the 1940s was in part a reparative project to seize back time from chaos, and to keep the illusion intact. The belief was that you could recover moral progress through a revived and international commitment to human rights and positive law. Whilst some, including anti-colonialists, feminists and socialists, boldly imagined new political and existential times during this period, in the higher echelons of humanitarian power there was little impulse to re-imagine what human time itself might be. Rather, the move was to restore the rules of sovereign power by keeping the old temporal narratives of progressive beneficent political morality in place.

Just as Freud wrote back to Nietzsche, showing how the latter's untimely thoughts had become timely, the essays which follow speak to the history of human rights from our present. Two things become clear: first, that the story in which timeless suffering without end is banished by legislating for moral progress, development, etc, has long lost its piquancy in a world where inequality is the dominant economic model and where the rhythms and needs of human and natural life are pitted against the apparently forever times of accumulation. The illusion has, finally, been broken. Secondly, however, and precisely as a consequence of this failure, the terrain upon which rights are staked and claimed in reality consists of a plurality of modalities of temporal human and species being. The untimeliness that once rocked Freud's generation, has been superseded by a multi-temporal world.

This is what TWAIL, feminist, and environmental scholars, among others, have been telling us for quite some time: that it simply does not make sense to talk of human rights as though one dominant temporal jurisdiction could ever hope to gather up all the damage, breakage and deficiency without doing more damage by its efforts. That it makes more sense to think instead about how we might ensure rights to different modes of time – human, national, indigenous, political, economic, species, planetary etc. That instead of rescuing people from innumerable, and preventable, crises, we might pay more attention to the long times of trauma and despair, their causes and their remedies. That what we now need is not simply a more beneficent human rights regime, but a re-distribution of both rights and time.

Few post-war writers chronicled the existential and political agonies of being placed out of time with more attention than the Palestinian poet, the late Mahmoud Darwish. In his poem, *Jidariyya*, written in 1999 while he was recovering from heart surgery, and translated into English by Rema Hammami and John Berger in 2009 as *Mural*, Darwish writes of how the historical and political dislocations of place mean that he cannot find his existential place in human time even as he faces his death:

> Where am I?
> In this no-here …
> no-time and nothingness
>
> As if I had died already
> I know this story
> I know that I go towards what I don't know
> Perhaps I'm still alive somewhere
> Aware of what I want …[6]

'Where am I? In this no-here … no-time and nothingness'? Am I dead already? These are questions asked daily by the rightless who, denied a place from which to speak and be recognised – as the case of Palestine demonstrates most starkly – are also denied the right to time. But Darwish's poetry is also about uncertainty, about alternative futures and alternative presents: 'I know that I go towards what I don't know …. Perhaps I'm still alive somewhere, aware of what I want.' We know that we go towards what we do not know for sure will be the outcome of our work: I cannot think of a better way of describing the impulse of those committed to forging new times for international human rights law today.

[6] M Darwish, *Mural* (2000), trans Rema Hammami and John Berger (Verso, 2009).

Acknowledgements

THIS COLLECTION BEGAN in a very early stage with a workshop of the same title hosted in July 2018 at Queen's University Belfast, supported by small grant funding from the UK Socio-Legal Studies Association and the Queen's University Belfast AHSS Faculty Research Initiatives Fund. We extend thanks to all those who participated in and contributed to this workshop, including co-host Dr Mark Hanna, as well as to other contributors to the collection who joined the project subsequently and extended our discussions further to produce the present collection. We would also like to thank Sinead Moloney and all at Hart for their support and guidance throughout the production process.

Kathryn McNeilly
Ben Warwick

Contents

Contributors

Frederick Cowell is a Lecturer at Birkbeck Department of Law, University of London.

Fadia Dakka is a Senior Research Fellow at CSPACE, in the Faculty of Health, Education and Life Sciences, Birmingham City University.

Daria Davitti is an Associate Professor at the Faculty of Law, Lund University.

Julia Dehm is a Senior Lecturer at the La Trobe Law School, La Trobe University.

Mary Hansel is a Lecturer and Acting Director of the International Justice Clinic at the University of California, Irvine School of Law.

Kay Lalor is a Reader in Human Rights Law at Manchester Law School, Manchester Metropolitan University.

Anthony Langlois is an Associate Professor in International Relations in the College of Business, Government and Law at Flinders University.

Christos Marneros is a Lecturer at Kent Law School, University of Kent and Visiting Lecturer in Legal Philosophy at Riga Graduate School of Law, Latvia.

Kathryn McNeilly is a Senior Lecturer in the School of Law, Queen's University Belfast.

Samuel Moyn is Henry R. Luce Professor of Jurisprudence at Yale Law School and Professor of History at Yale University.

Paul O'Connell is a Reader in Law at the School of Law, SOAS University of London.

Lyndsey Stonebridge is Professor of Humanities and Human Rights at the University of Birmingham.

Michele Tedeschini is a Residential Fellow at the Institute for Global Law and Policy at Harvard Law School, Harvard University.

Stephen Young is a Senior Lecturer in Law at the Faculty of Law, University of Otago.

Ben Warwick is a Reader in Human Rights Law, Birmingham Law School, University of Birmingham.

Introduction

KATHRYN McNEILLY AND BEN WARWICK

I. INTERNATIONAL HUMAN RIGHTS LAW'S TIMEPIECES, AND PIECES OF TIME

TIME IS AN everyday experience, one that is central to our individual and social lives as well as the institutions and structures around us. We encounter time in the cycles of nature, the force of time's linear arrow, and in periods of disruption, transition or break. We practice time through the use of objects such as calendars and clocks,[1] in personal, professional and public spaces, in navigating the micro and macro elements of our existence, and in relation with others. Given its widespread and everyday significance, it should come as no surprise that time is also relevant to law. Similar to its role in everyday social life,[2] however, time in law is often invisible or taken for granted. Seeking to address this, the connection between law and time is a topic that has been of growing interest to legal scholars in recent years. Exploring law via temporal lenses has emerged through this work as one way to encounter new or deeper legal understandings. Adjudication, precedent, the operation of legal institutions, legislation, legal objects, and the connection between law and change are just some of the topics that have been explored by law and time scholars.[3] Time emerges through this work as inherently caught up with law in diverse ways, both as a discourse and via its daily activity or operation. Importantly, law can be understood as not just existing in time, but as creating and sustaining temporal ideas through diverse legal practices.[4] These ideas have wide significance within and beyond law itself. From the clock on the court building, to the work of time bars or limitation periods, the future-binding, or reversibility, of precedent, and the ability of law to speak to pasts, presents and shape futures, the temporal life of law comes into view as rich and complex.

[1] K Birth, *Objects of Time: How Things Shape Temporality* (Palgrave, 2012).

[2] B Adam, *Time and Social Theory* (Polity, 1994) 3.

[3] eg R French, 'Time in Law' (2001) 72 *Colorado Law Review* 663; R Tur, 'Time and Law' (2002) 22 *Oxford Journal of Legal Studies* 463; L Khan, 'Temporality of Law' (2009) 40 *McGeorge Law Review* 55; E Grabham, *Brewing Legal Times: Things, Form, and the Enactment of Law* (University of Toronto Press, 2016); S Beynon-Jones and E Grabham (eds), *Law and Time* (Routledge, 2019); S Ranchordás and Y Roznai (eds), *Time, Law, and Change: An Interdisciplinary Study* (Hart Publishing, 2020); T Chowdhury, *Time, Temporality and Legal Judgment* (Routledge, 2020).

[4] C Greenhouse, 'Just in Time: Temporality and the Cultural Legitimation of Law' (1989) 98 *The Yale Law Journal* 1631.

This body of thinking on law and time offers much potential for human rights lawyers operating in various national jurisdictions. It facilitates consideration of the temporal movements encountered in human rights adjudication, in the formal positing of human rights norms in law, and of how human rights fit with the temporal ontology of the legal systems they operate in more generally,[5] for example. What of those, though, who are interested in human rights law internationally? The majority of law and time work to date has focused on domestic law and legal systems. Accordingly, much remains to be known about the temporal nature of international law. At the international legal level time-focused exploration is detectable, but has not been expansive.[6] International human rights law appears as the subset where law and time analysis has begun to emerge most explicitly.[7] Yet, thinking in this vein still remains in its infancy. Space exists to build on these foundations and move toward a fuller, more substantive understanding of the various temporal elements and connections that exist within the unique features of this legal system. It is this work that the current collection seeks to begin.

For international human rights lawyers not yet familiar with thinking in this vein, time is nevertheless an important part of what is known about this area of law. Human rights are frequently understood via temporal ideas and rhythms. These can be apprehended, we argue as the 'timepieces' of human rights law internationally, guiding how its time is recognised and measured. Progress, for example, is often considered to be central to rights work and the overarching purpose of realising international human rights standards and protections.[8] Forward-moving progress is an intuitive temporal impulse for regional and United Nations (UN) human rights bodies, for non-governmental organisations and advocates on the ground, and scholars alike in navigating rights obligations and processes. This is evident in a focus on indicators, target setting, action planning, and related practices whereby linear movement from present to future is an underpinning assumption.[9] Calendar time is also often a frequent

[5] On the temporal ontology of the common law see R Mawani, 'The Times of Law' (2015) 40 *Law and Social Inquiry* 253.

[6] R Higgins, 'Time and the Law: International Perspectives on an Old Problem' (1997) 46 *International and Comparative Law Quarterly* 501; K Knop and A Riles, 'Space, Time, and Historical Injustice: A Feminist Conflict-Of-Laws Approach to the "Comfort Women" Agreement' (2016) 102 *Cornell Law Review* 853; S Wheatley, 'Revisiting the Doctrine of Intertemporal Law' (2021) 41 *Oxford Journal of Legal Studies* 484.

[7] F Johns, 'The Temporal Rivalries of Human Rights' (2016) 23 *Indiana Journal of Global Legal Studies* 39; K McNeilly, 'Are Rights Out of Time? International Human Rights Law, Temporality, and Radical Social Change' (2019) 28 *Social and Legal Studies* 817; B Warwick, 'Unwinding Retrogression: Examining the Practice of the Committee on Economic, Social and Cultural Rights' (2019) 19 *Human Rights Law Review* 467; K Young, 'Waiting for Rights: Progressive Realization and Lost Time' in K Young and A Sen (eds), *The Future of Economic and Social Rights* (CUP, 2019).

[8] J Donnelly, 'Progress in Human Rights' in E Adler and B Crawford (eds), *Progress in Postwar International Relations* (Columbia University Press, 1991).

[9] G de Beco, 'Human Rights Indicators: From Theoretical Debate to Practical Application' (2013) 5 *Journal of Human Rights Practice* 380; T Landman, 'Measuring Human Rights: Principle,

timepiece given the strong – albeit diverse – narratives surrounding the origins and development of human rights internationally. Scholars and practitioners have a robust sense of the past of human rights and their chronological expansion against calendar time, evidenced in the recent 'turn to history' in the field.[10] International human rights lawyers may additionally be familiar with temporal flows of cyclicality given the focus on cyclical monitoring mechanisms and practices which form a significant part of everyday work in this area.[11] The cycle is a common temporal frame for states, stakeholders and human rights bodies at both international and national levels. Alongside progress, calendar time and cyclicality, finally, urgency frequently appears. The human rights system is thought as both working within contexts of urgency to respond to emerging situations of concern, and also as a driver of urgency drawing attention to rights violations across the globe.[12] These timepieces offer a starting point for deeper temporal analysis. They are important to highlight and consider more consciously. In offering a starting point, however, they do not represent the end of the discussions that may be undertaken. Temporal analysis of the ways in which time intersects with and shapes this area of law can expand much further.

It is such an exploration of the times and temporalities of international human rights law that the present collection undertakes. In doing so, it starts with three questions that are designed to guide discussion and analysis throughout: First, how is it possible to understand time and its diverse forms of operation in, and on, this area of law? Secondly, how does temporality manifest in the theory and practice of international human rights law? Thirdly, how can specific areas of human rights be understood via temporal analyses? Examination of these interconnected questions is designed to offer a foothold for new understandings of the relationship between international human rights law and time, both as an overarching system, and within specific thematic areas of rights provision or other case studies. For those working with human rights internationally, these questions offer the means to approach existing understandings of time in this area in different ways and to connect with wider temporal rhythms and ideas which have been less visible to date. At this point, the reader may be considering why such analysis is necessary or useful, what it brings to the study or practice

Practice, and Policy' (2004) 26 *Human Rights Quarterly* 906; A Chalabi, 'The Nature and Scope of States' Obligation to Adopt a National Human Rights Action Plan' (2014) 18 *International Journal of Human Rights* 391.

[10] For an overview see S Moyn, 'Substance, Scale, and Salience: The Recent Historiography of Human Rights' (2012) 8 *Annual Review of Law and Social Science* 123; P Alston, 'Does the Past Matter? On the Origins of Human Rights' (2012) 126 *Harvard Law Review* 2043.

[11] See eg H Charlesworth and E Larking (eds), *Human Rights and the Universal Periodic Review: Rituals and Ritualism* (CUP, 2014); H Keller and G Ulfstein (eds), *UN Human Rights Treaty Bodies: Law and Legitimacy* (CUP, 2012).

[12] eg K Zwaan and E Rieter (eds), *Urgency and Human Rights: The Protective Potential and Legitimacy of Interim Measures* (Springer, 2020); H Jorem, 'Protecting Human Rights in Cases of Urgency: Interim Measures and the Right of Individual Application Under Article 34 ECHR' (2012) 30 *Nordic Journal of Human Rights* 404.

of human rights. It is important to note at the outset that a specific purpose underpins the asking of these questions and work towards new temporal analyses. Rather than a purely abstract or theoretical endeavour, we argue that this investigation assists in better understanding this area of law, its development, and its operation in the present. In other words, time can help enrich our knowledge as international human rights lawyers, scholars or practitioners of the legal system we study or work within. Let us explain more of what we mean by this.

This assertion is multifaceted. First, bringing temporal analyses to bear on international human rights law can help to better contextualise this law and its functioning as a discourse. Human rights take place in the context of wider, macro ideas of time. These include, significantly, the linearity which has characterised modern time and its progressively connected concepts of past, present and future.[13] Human rights are accordingly understood in ways that fit with time's arrow.[14] Alongside this, other temporal concepts provide important contexts, differing at various historical points and junctures. Experiences of global transition, the temporal significance of the digital age,[15] the temporalities of environmental change,[16] and the presence of temporal rhythms which transcend or complicate linear conceptions of time are also highly significant and influence the frames within which human rights take place.[17] Taking account of these broader temporal contexts and their waxing or waning is central to deepening our understanding of human rights internationally, their development, and how they are engaged around the world today as legal concepts. These contexts, however, are never purely pre-existing, external backdrops. Rather, it is possible to see the legal system in focus as in an active relationship with these temporal contexts, responding to them, in tension with them, or bolstering them in various ways.

Secondly, temporal analyses can also help to further our understandings of how international human rights operate on a daily basis. This includes how temporal rhythms and movements characterise their practice, and to what effects. As part of this work the precise ways in which every day human rights processes or mechanisms rely on or create rhythms and movements of time can be brought into view. To date the work of UN treaty monitoring bodies and

[13] R Koselleck, *Futures Past: On the Semantics of Historical Time* trans K Tribe (Columbia University Press, 2004).

[14] This has included linear movement toward future utopias: see, most notably, S Moyn, *The Last Utopia: Human Rights in History* (Harvard University Press, 2010). See also wider historical analyses, for example, M Ishay, *The History of Human Rights: From Ancient Times to the Globalization Era* (University of California Press, 2004).

[15] S Ranchordas and Y Roznai *Time, Law and Change* (Hart Publishing, 2019) 291–347.

[16] A Grear, 'Anthropocene "Time"? A Reflection on Temporalities in the "New Age of the Human"' in A Philippopoulos-Mihalopoulos (ed), *The Routledge Handbook of Law and Theory* (Routledge, 2019).

[17] For discussion of some of these issues see P Alston and F Mégret, 'Introduction' in P Alston and F Mégret (eds), *Human Rights at the United Nations: A Critical Appraisal* (OUP, 2020) 8–11.

the UN Human Rights Council's Universal Periodic Review are two sites that have been approached in such a way.[18] This has revealed temporalities of retrogression, linearity, cyclicality, discontinuity and duration to be integral parts of international human rights law's functioning, and has provoked opportunities to use these temporalities as lenses through which to better read these bodies and processes. Through standing back and considering temporal phenomena in the everyday operation of human rights, we are encouraged to approach this operation with fresh eyes, to understand how it is assisted or facilitated via temporal activity, to gain enhanced insight into what this area of law does, alongside what it says it does, and as a result to understand its function and mechanisms of activity anew.

Together with these benefits for contextualisation and insights into the system's everyday operation, third, thinking with and through time also holds potential to enhance apprehension of the relationship between this area of law and the social. Law and time thinking at the domestic legal level encourages a view of time as at heart a social concept, one that is central to how the world – including legal institutions and processes – is organised and navigated.[19] Law both contributes to social understandings of time, shaping how we understand the world around us, and draws from temporal understandings that exist in social life more broadly. Bringing this insight to international human rights law assists in further encountering or being attentive to the social effects of the norms and processes operating at this level.[20] In this respect, it is important to explore time not only in individualised or institutionalised ways – from the perspective of the individual human rights holder or international human rights institutions – but to examine the time of international human rights as having a fundamentally social character. Through this temporal analysis scholars and practitioners can add another thread to their understanding of this law's intricate connections to the social.

From the layers of deeper understanding signalled towards above, there is much to be said for reflecting on time and temporality more fully. In this work, as we have suggested, the starting point is the traditional timepieces of international human rights law: progress, calendar time, cyclicality, and urgency, among the most notable. The journey, however, must also include adding to these timepieces, being attentive to how these most obvious or overt temporalities do not exhaust the intersections between this area of law and time. Through this process,

[18] Warwick (n 7); K McNeilly, 'The Temporal Ontology of the Human Rights Council's Universal Periodic Review' (2021) 21 *Human Rights Law Review* 1.

[19] Greenhouse (n 4). For wider discussion on time and society see, for example, B Adam, *Timewatch: The Social Analysis of Time* (Polity, 1995).

[20] For socio-legal writing on international human rights law more generally see eg S Engle Merry, *Human Rights and Gender Violence: Translating International Law into Local Justice* (University of Chicago Press, 2006); S Greer, 'Towards a Socio-legal Analysis of the European Convention on Human Rights' in M Rash Maden and G Verschraegen (eds), *Making Human Rights Intelligible: Towards a Sociology of Human Rights* (Hart Publishing, 2013).

other connections to time can come into view. These may be less visible or well known, but hold potential to emerge as equally central to the everyday work of human rights. We can apprehend these times as diverse in nature, extending to include those that are bitty and mundane,[21] concrete and material,[22] non-linear, fragmented and overlapping, rather than smooth, continuous and predictable, for example. The remit of temporal investigation and analysis which stands to be undertaken resultantly emerges as multifaceted. Through approaching time in this way it is possible to encounter international human rights law via other timepieces or, perhaps more accurately, pieces of time. In identifying and thinking through these diverse pieces, our knowledge of the context, operation and social connections of the system grows.

II. COLLECTING INTERNATIONAL HUMAN RIGHTS LAW'S TIMES AND TEMPORALITIES

In the chapters to follow, reflections have been collected responding to the three overarching questions identified above. These emerge from examination of international human rights law as an overarching global discourse (O'Connell), as a specifically legal and/or adjudicable discourse (Cowell, Marneros, Hansel), as a practice (McNeilly), as an area for scholarly discussion (Tedeschini), and as relevant to specific thematic areas, subjects and/or harms (Young, Dehm, Lalor, Dakka and Davitti, Langlois). These contributions reveal a range of temporal ideas, rhythms and flows which may be further considered and attended to. Among these are temporalities which will be familiar to the international human rights reader and cohere or intersect with some of the traditional timepieces we have noted. For example, in his contribution Frederick Cowell explores the concept of collective memory in establishing and maintaining the authority of the European Court of Human Rights in the twentieth and twenty-first centuries. Here the past's ongoing significance in the present is reflected on as well as the potential 'vanishing point' for this past. Alongside this discussion of the past, the concept of the present also appears in the chapters to follow. In his reflections on the 'temporal trap' of human rights, Stephen Young elaborates on the 'permanent contest for the present' that he sees as defining international human rights law and the subjects constructed within it. This is explored via investigation of jurisdictional conflicts between tribal peoples, the state, and international human rights. In addition to the past and present, the future is also a subject of analysis for contributors. Paul O'Connell considers the possibilities for human rights futures, in particular in the context of the temporalities of global capitalism, considering 'what would need to be done to realise a future

[21] Grabham *Brewing Legal Times* (n 3) 11.

[22] See, ibid; S Keenan, 'Property as Governance: Time, Space and Belonging in Australia's Northern Territory Intervention' (2013) 76 *Modern Law Review* 464.

in which the interests associated with human rights are meaningfully protected'. In his chapter, Michele Tedeschini takes a different approach, analysing the discourse of futurity in human rights scholarship in the post-1989 period following the 'End of History'. Exploring a range of work in this area, Tedeschini considers how human rights have been evaluated as futural-facing concepts in this period, and to what effect.

Other familiar temporalities that emerge in the collection include Mary Hansel's analysis of crisis in international human rights law. Drawing from work on the close connection between international law and crisis,[23] for Hansel, the focus on crisis which is detectable in the human rights element of the international legal system holds potential to marginalise economic, social and cultural rights and a focus on the everyday which feminist thought in particular draws attention to. Investigating *jus cogens* norms, she examines the 'emergency time' approach which appears to be dominant and contrasts this to alternative temporal approaches, in particular that of repetition, which holds potential to better foreground the everyday. Alongside crisis, the times of nature and environmental change are considered in Julia Dehm's contribution on environmental rights. Such times are central to this subset of human rights, where temporal-focused thinking is common.[24] In this chapter, Dehm elaborates that 'environmental rights, arguably more so than other rights, have had to grapple with questions of intergenerational justice, and the way in which actions in the present have harmful future effects'.[25] She highlights the tension between the temporalities of international human rights and the environmental harms which such rights seek to respond to, as well as investigating the conceptions of the future produced by environmental rights, both in terms of linearity and possibilities for rupture.

In addition to these temporalities which may be familiar to the reader, wider temporal lenses appear as guiding analysis. These include those that are non-linear and that break with forward-moving progress. For example, Anthony Langlois draws attention to non-linear temporalities in his exploration of lesbian, gay, bisexual, transgender, intersex and queer (LGBTIQ) rights. In reflecting on the history and present degree of protection of LGBTIQ rights, Langlois argues for the importance and significance of 'feeling backwards' and remembering a time before these rights became a part of the international legal system. Beyond non-linear time, other contributors employ ideas of time as multitudinous, capable of holding different temporal rhythms and movements together at once. In this way of apprehending time, ideas of past, present and future do not progress in a linear way, but coexist with one another.[26] Writing in the context of women's rights, Kay Lalor suggests that thinking new

[23] H Charlesworth, 'International Law: A Discipline of Crisis' (2002) 65 *Modern Law Review* 377.

[24] See eg R Hiskes, *The Human Right to a Green Future: Environmental Rights and Intergenerational Justice* (CUP, 2009).

[25] See further, literature on long and slow time. eg, M Bjornerud, *Timefulness: How Thinking Like a Geologist Can Help Save the World* (Princeton University Press, 2018).

[26] eg G Deleuze, *Difference and Repetition* trans P Patton (The Athlone Press, 1994).

futures in this area requires engagement with the interconnected nature of past, present and future. She examines how a 'non-linear and multiplicitous temporal perspective opens up new possibilities' for our current understandings of gender and human rights. Christos Marneros in his contribution also understands time as multitudinous, characterised by 'pure becoming and never-ending variation and change'. Engaging with European Court of Human Rights jurisprudence on the right to life, he examines how this temporal approach – what he terms 'a becoming-chaotic of time' – may assist our thinking on human rights and our relation to them. These contributions offer a view of international human rights law as connected to, or holding potential to be thought via, conceptions of time that we may not be so closely acquainted with, encouraging us to consider the consequences and the potential such analyses may offer.

Finally, contributions in the collection draw attention to the material or physical nature of time in international human rights law. Here the concrete or tangible nature of time is brought into view. This includes Kathryn McNeilly's exploration of the role of documents as objects, artefacts and things in human rights monitoring processes.[27] McNeilly examines the central role of documents in creating temporal ideas of past, present and future across monitoring mechanisms and processes alongside human actors, providing tools to understand micro instances and practices of time creation in international legal processes. In a different vein, Fadia Dakka and Daria Davitti focus on the connection between time and space. Engaging the concept of rhythmanalysis, they examine how the temporal life of human rights is more than just discursive alone in the context of search and rescue at sea. In particular, Dakka and Davitti demonstrate how attending to the connection between time and space can assist in understanding jurisdiction in international human rights law in new ways. Through these contributions the time of human rights comes into view as more than discursive alone, encouraging us to consider its material construction and form.

Taken together, these contributions represent the times and temporalities of international human rights law as plural, multifaceted and vibrant, capable of being explored from a range of angles and perspectives. They each represent pieces of time which may be taken up to help create a picture of the times of human rights and the legal practices, processes and discourses that support them. Collectively they offer an insight into what we currently know, and do not know, about the times that make up this area of law, leading the reader to a point from which to reflect and think more consciously, rendering time visible and of significance. Through this collecting of time and its pieces it is possible to extend our horizons of temporal understanding and begin to measure time in new ways.

[27] See more generally, J Hohmann and D Joyce, *International Law's Objects* (OUP, 2019).

III. FUTURES FOR THE TIMES AND TEMPORALITIES OF INTERNATIONAL HUMAN RIGHTS LAW

What emerges from the collaborative contributions to this edited collection is a future – or, to be more precise, futures – for time as a vehicle of analysis in the field of international human rights law. It is possible to begin to see new points of departure or understanding and to approach this law from different angles. We do not submit, however, that these futures have been fully realised or achieved through the discussion undertaken in the chapters to follow. A number of issues appear as outstanding and open to further investigation. These include, first, enhanced attention to understandings of international human rights law, time and the relationship between the two that emerge from locations, structures and experiences beyond the Global North. Contributors in the present collection are primarily based in the Global North and offer reflections on the UN or European human rights systems. We do not propose that these reflections are comprehensive or capable of capturing all connections between time and human rights internationally. Space exists to broaden our conversations, the temporal tools used, and the global sites where these tools are employed. Expanding further in this way is essential in working towards full and vibrant conceptions of time, human rights and their combined reach.

More generally in pursuing futures for temporal analysis, the ideas and rhythms of time engaged in discussion must not be understood as exhaustive of the times and temporalities of international human rights law. Many other temporal tools and concepts stand to be taken up to stimulate new observations as well as forge new paths and routes of analysis. These include, for example, wider ideas of past, present and future; digital time;[28] engagement with timescapes[29] or chronotopes;[30] and additional temporalities of history and history making,[31] just to name a few. These ways of conceptualising or approaching time may hold productive insights and assist in contextualising or concretising international human rights law in ways which add to the analyses offered in this collection. These conceptions of time stand to be engaged in additional theoretical or doctrinal analyses using methodological approaches demonstrated in this collection and those which are not. Embracing this openness and a wide understanding of time is an essential part of adopting a more conscious and always curious approach to the temporal life of human rights.

[28] A Kaun, C Pentzold and C Lohmeier (eds), *Making Time for Digital Lives: Beyond Chronotopia* (Rowman and Littlefield, 2020).

[29] B Adam, *Timescapes of Modernity: The Environment and Invisible Hazards* (Routledge, 1989); B Adam, *Time* (Polity, 2004); K Goetz and J Meyer-Sahling (eds), *The EU Timescape* (Routledge, 2012).

[30] M Valverde, *Chronotopes of Law: Jurisdiction, Scale and Governance* (Routledge, 2015).

[31] D Edelstein, S Geroulanos and N Wheatley (eds), *Power and Time: Temporalities in Conflict and the Making of History* (University of Chicago Press, 2020). For further discussion in the context of international law, see N Wheatley, 'Law and the Time of Angels: International Law's Method Wars and the Affective Life of Disciplines' (2021) 60 *History and Theory* 311.

Alongside advocating for further images and ideas of time to be added, finally, it is also important to investigate further human rights mechanisms, processes or case studies which may be brought into contact with temporal analyses. It is impossible to cover all possible locations ripe for temporal analysis within one edited collection. Further engagement with international human rights jurisprudence and adjudication, with institutions such as the UN Human Rights Council or work of the Office of the High Commissioner for Human Rights, with activities such as human rights action planning, and with other thematic rights areas or case studies might be undertaken. It is a testament of the flexibility and fluidity of temporal analyses to say that all of these additional phenomena may be read through the lens of time and that understanding of them stands to be enhanced through deployment of such a lens.

Overall, therefore, to facilitate further development of law and time work within this subset of international law and take up the paths forged in this collection, we call for ongoing plurality in scholarship and thinking. We see the collection as holding the key to open a wide number of conversations. It does not, however, set the limits or remit of these conversations and the scholarly approaches or conceptions of time that they might be driven by. The futures for time which emerge from the work collected here have only just begun. Like time itself, these futures may be unexpected, non-linear and take us in directions that differ from those we anticipate. As international human rights lawyers, scholars or practitioners it is essential to continue to get to know the legal system we work with better, to explore its operation from new perspectives, and expand the tools we can use to do so. We show that time is one way to do this, and that law and time thinking should not be regarded as the purview of lawyers at the domestic level alone. The international legal system too is a location ripe for temporal analysis and discussion. The pieces of time and related reflections presented in this collection commence this more dedicated analysis and discussion. They provide both means to add to our knowledge and an invitation to ongoing and increased investigation of the connection between international human rights law and time. This work is important. Through this more conscious approach to measuring time in, and the time of, this legal system we work not only towards new futures for time as a vehicle of analysis in human rights work but, through the deeper knowledge we subsequently gain, towards wider future discussions more generally.

1

The Temporality of Memory and the Authority of the European Court of Human Rights

FREDERICK COWELL

I. INTRODUCTION

DURING THE UK's 1975 referendum on membership of the European Economic Community, arguments about the role of European unity preserving the peace after World War II were generally well received and had widespread common currency.[1] A generation later in the 2016 referendum on Brexit, David Cameron's reference to the European Union's role in preventing the outbreak of conflict was widely ridiculed. But the 1975 referendum was closer in time to the start of World War I than the 2016 referendum was to the end of the World War II. Leaders of both Yes and No campaigns in the 1975 referendum had fought in the Second and First World Wars, whereas in 2016 the youngest veterans were in their late eighties. The passage of time had led to collective memories fragmenting. The sociologist Maurice Halbwachs described collective memory as a social endeavour which reconstructed 'an image of the past' which accorded with the '"predominant thoughts" of that society'.[2] Halbwachs did not invent the concept of societal collective memory, but he did explain the temporality of collective memory and how the past could be constructed into a communal identity and shared, so that it became a self-sustaining explanation of how a society functioned.[3]

Collective memories are an important but sometimes under considered part of international human rights law.[4] They are often articulated as the source

[1] R Saunders, *Yes to Europe!* (Cambridge University Press (CUP), 2019) 10–12.

[2] M Halbwachs, *On Collective Memory* (University of Chicago Press Trans Lewis Coser, 1992) 40.

[3] N Russell, 'Collective Memory before and after Halbwachs' (2006) 79 *The French Review* 792.

[4] For leading studies in this field see D Levy and N Sznaider, *Human Rights and Memory* (University of Pennsylvania Press, 2010); L David, *The Past Can't Heal Us: The Dangers of Mandating Memory in the Name of Human Rights* (CUP, 2020).

of a human rights instrument's authority. For example the African Charter of Human and Peoples' Rights in its preamble refers to 'the virtues of [African state's] historical tradition and the values of African civilization' as well as the 'the total liberation of Africa' as the shared values on which the state parties to the Charter agreed upon, forming the basis of its authority.[5] Positioning human rights as a remedy to colonialism was a major feature in thinking about the African Charter on Human and Peoples' Rights as a distinct system of human rights.[6] Decisions of the African Commission on Human and Peoples' Rights such as *SEARC v Nigeria*,[7] specifically referenced colonialism in its interpretation of Article 21 of the Charter (the right to natural resources) when they concluded that the right existed because of 'colonialism … during which the human and material resources of Africa were largely exploited for the benefit of outside powers' and because of this the drafters of the Charter 'wanted to remind African governments of the continent's painful legacy'. The collective memory of colonialism among African states provided a foundational consensus on what human rights were for, which was important both for the creation of the African Charter and for the ensuing legitimacy of its interpretative and enforcement bodies.

As this chapter argues with reference to the European Convention on Human Rights (ECHR), the collective memory which forms its foundational legitimating consensus was a memory of totalitarianism, situated in the early Cold War, to which human rights was positioned as a remedy. This basic consensus on the role of human rights was the dominant assumption amongst the Convention's drafters in 1949–50, and as the first part of the chapter sets out this consensus is a necessary feature of the European Court of Human Rights' (ECtHR) authority in interpreting the ECHR. The focus on the ECtHR in this chapter is in part because it is the world's oldest and most powerful international human rights body. As a consequence, literature on compliance with human rights law often discusses it in the context of protecting human rights or the judicialisation of human rights protection.[8] As this chapter demonstrates, one of the reasons for this has been the relatively strong consensus surrounding the ECtHR's role linked to the political climate of its foundation in the late 1940s and early 1950s, which cemented a strong interstate consensus on the importance of human

[5] Preamble, African Charter of Human and Peoples' Rights (adopted 27 June 1981, entry into force 21 October 1986) 218 UNTS 1520.

[6] For accounts referencing colonialism see RN Kiwanuka, 'The Meaning of "People" in the African Charter on Human and Peoples' Rights' (1988) 82 *American Journal of International Law* (*AJIL*) 80.

[7] *Social and Economic Rights Action Center (SERAC) and Center for Economic and Social Rights (CESR) v Nigeria* (2002) Comm No. 155/66, para 56.

[8] JC Sims, 'Compliance without remands: the experience under the European Convention on Human Rights' (2004) 36 *Arizona State Law Journal* 639; C Hillebrecht, 'Rethinking compliance: the challenges and prospects of measuring compliance with International Human Rights Tribunals' (2009) 1 *Journal of Human Rights Practice* 362.

rights protection as a remedy to the threat of totalitarianism.[9] Methodologically this is known as historical institutionalism – an analytic lens for examining international institutions which stresses the temporal properties of concepts and emphasises processes and mechanisms that impact the origin, stability and change of institutions over time.[10] But as this chapter argues as time passes – in a linear sense as the present gets further away from the early Cold War context of the ECHR's origins – challenges are created for the legitimacy of the ECtHR. In part this is because the way in which a foundational consensus based on forms of politically constructed shared memory operates can be temporally contingent, linked to particular places and times, and making a historically intuitionist explanation of organisational authority open to contest by those whom it exercises authority over.

II. CONSENSUS AND AUTHORITY: HOW AN INTERNATIONAL HUMAN RIGHTS REGIME MAINTAINS ITS AUTHORITY

The literature in the area of compliance with human rights law is vast, but for the purposes of this chapter it is important to focus on the role of a collective interstate consensus, within that literature. This form of consensus serves both as a mechanism for the internal and external maintenance of a legal regime's authority. Authority, as Joseph Raz points out, is different from coercion, in that authority claims that following the commands of another agent is appropriate because that agent has legitimacy.[11] International human rights law, and the bodies created to enforce it, for the most part lack direct coercive powers. In so far as there is coercion, or the threat of coercion, on a state in relation to human rights compliance it is in the field of reputation cost.[12] Yet, the specific type of reputation affected by non-compliance with international human rights law is either indirect or existential and the potential impact, and fear on a state's part, of reputation damage is too unpredictable and uncertain to create a lasting basis for a court's authority. Therefore in order for a human rights body to function and to issue decisions in relation to the protection of human rights, whether they are judicial decisions (in the form of cases that the country wins or loses) or decisions that are declarative (such as those produced in the concluding observations of treaty bodies) it is necessary for it to develop a

[9] A Moravcsik, 'The origins of human rights regimes: Democratic delegation in Postwar Europe' (2000) 54 *International Organization* 217; AWB Simpson, 'Britain and the European Convention' (2001) 34 *Cornell Journal of International Law* 523.

[10] O Fioretos, 'Institutions and Time in International Relations' in O Fioretos (eds), *International Politics and Institutions in Time* (Oxford University Press (OUP), 2017) 12.

[11] J Raz, 'Introduction' In J Raz (ed), *Authority* (NYU Press, 1990) 3.

[12] See A Geisinger and MA Stein, 'Rational choice, reputation, and human rights treaties' (2017) 106 *Michigan Law Review* 1129; A Guzman, 'Reputation and international law' (2005) 34 *Georgia Journal of International and Comparative Law* 379.

form of content independent legitimacy.[13] This then makes compliance and the reasons to comply with a particular decision of that body the default presumption, or more specifically an expectation arises among state officials in favour of compliance.[14] Shai Dothan in relation to ECtHR compliance has noted that one of things that has encouraged compliance with relatively high cost decisions is that the Court has constructed its legitimacy upon a series of predictable and relatively low-cost decisions.[15]

At this point it is important to emphasise the conceptual distinction between normative and sociological legitimacy – the former form of legitimate authority may be signified by the capacity of the body itself, the rights it adjudicates or its procedural legitimacy,[16] whereas the latter describes the socio-political reasons behind a tribunal or review body's legitimacy.[17] Whilst distinct, the two are often practically interrelated; for example the literature on the spiral model of human rights change sees social pressure within states interacting with external agents, such as human rights bodies, in order to generate human rights reforms within states.[18] This requires an institution to have both normative legitimacy and to have a broader sociological legitimacy. Courtney Hilebrecht's study of the Inter-American Court of human rights identified how the interaction between regional human rights institutions and political actors in countries, both grassroots activists as well as government officials, was vital for giving an organisation as a whole legitimacy.[19] Liberal explanations of compliance with international human rights law also point towards the existence of an inter-state consensus about the utility of human rights. For instance in in the case of the ECHR the desire among member states of the Council of Europe to lock in democratic forms of government was a key component of the consensus which underpins compliance with the Convention and its organs.[20] 'Consensus' in these arguments refers to a form of elite level socialisation of the leaders of state governments leading to the political internalisation of human rights norms among political elites which is an essential precursor to the implementation of a

[13] In A Føllesdal, J Schaffer and G Ulfstein et al (eds), *The Legitimacy of International Human Rights Regimes: Legal, Political and Philosophical Perspectives* (CUP, 2014).

[14] B Çali, *The Authority of International Law Obedience, Respect, and Rebuttal* (OUP, 2015) 11.

[15] S Dothan, 'Judicial Tactics in the European Court of Human Rights' (2012) 12 *Chicago Journal of International Law* 116.

[16] N Grossman, 'The Normative Legitimacy of International Courts' (2013) 86 *Temple Law Review* 61.

[17] S Besson, 'The legitimate authority of international human rights bodies' in Føllesdal et al (n 13).

[18] For the theory see T Risse, and K Sikkink, 'The Socialisation of human rights norms into domestic practices: introduction' in T Risse-Kappen, T Risse, SC Ropp and K Sikkink (eds), *The Power of Human Rights: International Norms and Domestic Change* (CUP, 1999).

[19] C Hillebrecht, *Domestic politics and international human rights tribunals: the problem of compliance* (CUP, 2014).

[20] Moravcsik (n 9).

human rights body's decisions becoming the default position.[21] This is different from, but related to, the use of 'European consensus' as a tool by the ECtHR in relation to the interpretation of a particular right, where the Court examines practice from around Europe to identify a trend or common practice across member states in relation to the implementation or restriction of that right.[22] In these cases consensus is more commonly used to describe the policy of states in the present rather 'than the' foundations of an institution's authority in the past, but as will be shown below the two can intersect.

To understand the authority of an institution, it is necessary to look beyond Raz's work on the construction of normative authority, which is premised on distinguishing power and right, and bring in Jacques Derrida's work on the foundations of law's authority.[23] In 'The Mystical Foundation of Authority' Derrida argues that law has a mythical foundation of violence that can be separated from the functional or reinforcing violence that law uses to maintain its power.[24] This draws on the work of Walter Benjamin who distinguished two kinds of force at work in the law: the force creating law and the force maintaining law.[25] The latter form of force is exercised by the police or other state security forces, the former form of force occurs in different ways. Benjamin specifies wars as an example of foundational force as the conclusion of wars often leads to treaties or peace agreements, which found a legal order that then becomes a subsequent basis for further law-making.[26] Most studies of international law's authority seek to sidestep violence and take as a given that compliance with the law operates in the absence of force compelling obedience to the law.[27] In fact as Jean 'd'Aspremont argues, debates about authority in international law are often characterised by their self-referentiality as they refer to authority inwardly, by cross referencing existing sources of law.[28] Self-referentiality is a structural way of avoiding the foundational question in international law, by focusing on its

[21] For this argument see H Hongju Koh, 'How is international human rights law enforced' (1998) 74 *Indiana International Law Journal* 1397.

[22] For the definitive study on the subject see K Dzehtsiarou, *European Consensus and the Legitimacy of the European Court of Human Rights* (CUP, 2015) 9–36.

[23] For clarity on Raz's work on this point, see J Raz, 'The Problem of Authority: Revisiting the Service Conception' (2006) 90 *Minnesota Law Review* 1003.

[24] J Derrida, 'Force of Law: The "Mystical Foundation of Authority"' from D Cornell, M Rosenfeld and DG Carlson (eds), *Deconstruction and the Possibility of Justice* (Routledge, 2001) 3–67.

[25] M Mahlmann, 'Law and force: 20th century radical legal philosophy, post-modernism and the foundations of law' (2003) 9 *Res Publica* 19.

[26] See W Benjamin, *One-Way Street and Other Writings* (Penguin, trans JA Underwood, 2009) 1–29.

[27] TM Franck, 'Legitimacy in the International System' (1980) 82 *AJIL* 705; D Bodansky, 'The Legitimacy of International Governance: A coming challenge for international environmental law' (1999) 93 *AJIL* 596.

[28] J d'Aspremont, 'Bypassing the Authority of International Law: The Virtue of Modern Self-Referentiality' in G Hernández and G Jokubauskaite (eds), *Constructing Authority in International Law* (2018) available at papers.ssrn.com/sol3/papers.cfm?abstract_id=3040975.

sources rather than the forces which brought the law into being and lie behind the law. What Derrida seeks to do is show how law cannot disavow the mystical foundations of its authority as law's 'generalised violence' is connected with the bringing to bear of the law in a particular instance which references the violence of its foundations.[29]

It may seem somewhat unusual to be talking of violence in connection with the ECHR which was a treaty that was at the heart of a regional organisation designed to promote democracy but, as shown in section III, at the time of the ECHR's creation human rights were seen as a means of countering the violence of fascism or a takeover by authoritarian communism. As Andreas Huyssen notes, memory and the law interact in complex ways but the collective memory of violence and the dead from that violence underpins the claims made by human rights instruments.[30] Methodologically speaking this is not a collective memory but what Wulf Kansteiner describes as a collected memory – an 'aggregate of individual memories' which is constructed through a 'focus on acts of memorialization'.[31] This can be through a formal legal construction which references the historical past or by the inference of a set of collected memories as a justification for the exercise of authority, in either event the act of construction differs from a collective sense of memory which is more communal and bottom-up in its formation.[32] It therefore makes sense to use the term 'collected memory' as this better describes the nature of construction of memory in an international human rights instrument.

A collected memory can generate or create a sense of shared identity, and the act of memorialisation and of asking subjects to remember helps make identity concrete. As Jan Assmann puts it, collected memories 'preserves the store of knowledge from which a group derives an awareness of its unity and peculiarity'.[33] To do this, however, requires fixing a memory, or set of memories, at a particular in time, to give a sense of beginning to the political community to which a legal instrument belongs.[34] Those working on the sociology of memory, such as Barbra Misztal, have argued that memory and temporality cannot be detached from one another because collective memory is an important socially accepted currency since what is remembered is always a 'memory of an

[29] P Gehring, 'Force and "Mystical Foundation" of Law: How Jacques Derrida Addresses Legal Discourse' (2005) 6 *German Law Journal* 151.

[30] A Huyssen, 'International Human Rights and The Politics of Memory Limits and Challenges' (2011) 43 *Criticism* 607.

[31] W Kansteiner, 'Finding Meaning in Memory: A Methodological Critique of Collective Memory Studies' (2002) 41 *History and Theory* 179, 186.

[32] B Misztal, 'Memory and the Construction of Temporality, Meaning and Attachment' (2005) 149 *Sociological Review* 31.

[33] J Assmann and J Czaplicka, 'Collective Memory and Cultural Identity' (1995) 65 *New German Critique* 125, 130.

[34] The making of the past requires a fixed point or punctuation point of history or pre-history: E Zerubavel, *Time Maps: Collective Memory and the Social Shape of the Past* (University of Chicago Press, 2012) 8–9.

intersubjective past, of past time lived in relation to others'.[35] The formation of national identity is often portrayed as a temporal process which can knit together a fragmented past into a unified whole, using it as the basis for legitimating the operation of a nation state's institutions.[36] A collected memory works by building a past which can then be remembered in the present, both temporally punctuating the past but also creating controlled ways for collected memory to manifest itself in the present. In the ECHR's case a threat-remedy model of human rights was constructed, with human rights being positioned as a remedy to the threat of authoritarianism which was then enshrined into the structure of the ECHR, acting as a form of foundational authority for its application by the ECtHR. Collected memories can also act as a form of identity confirmation. As Rafael Narvaez argues, collective memory involves a politics of identity, objects and concepts 'unfold[ing] from the past unto the present, [which] can also be records of the past .... helping the group see from within': in this way memory can help fashion contemporary identity.[37] The ECHR did not explicitly aim to create a unified European national identity, but it did seek to create a consensus as to what a western European state was, or ought to be, as an international identity and in so doing created a foundational consensus for the ECtHR's authority.

III. THE HISTORICAL CONSENSUS OF THE EUROPEAN COURT OF HUMAN RIGHTS

Contrary to popular myth, the formation of the Council of Europe was not a product of the end of World War II but born out of the early stages of the Cold War. Popular myth can seem a somewhat pejorative term, but so many descriptions of the ECHR's formation situate it as taking place at or adjacent to World War II in similar terms to the UN Charter.[38] In fact, a number of historians have subsequently identified the early Cold War as being more influential in the shaping of the ECHR.[39] In August 1949 the delegates of the Consultative Assembly of the Council of Europe assembled at the University of Strasbourg, where according to the British Conservative lawyer David Maxwell-Fyfe 'most of the leading figures of Free Europe' were present.[40] Entirely coincidently that same

[35] B Misztal, *Theories of Social Remembering* (Open University Press, 2003) 6.

[36] T Edensor, 'Reconsidering National Temporalities Institutional Times, Everyday Routines, Serial Spaces and Synchronicities' (2006) 9 *European Journal of Social Theory* 525, 527–28.

[37] R Narvaez, 'Embodiment, Collective Memory and Time' (2006) 13 *Body & Society* 51, 64–65.

[38] These competing historical narratives in the history of human rights law are analysed in GD Cohen, 'The Holocaust and the "Human Rights Revolution": A Reassessment' in A Iriye (ed), *The Human Rights Revolution: An International History* (OUP, 2012). Michael Ignatieff more generally makes this case about international human rights law in general: M Ignatieff, *Human Rights as Politics and Ideology* (Princeton University Press, 2003) 4–5.

[39] Simpson (n 9); F Baudet, '"A statement against the totalitarian countries of Europe": human rights and the early Cold War' (2016) 16 *Cold War History* 125.

[40] E Bates, *The Evolution of the European Convention on Human Rights* (OUP, 2010) 51–61.

day the Soviet Union detonated its first atomic bomb. The omnipresent nature of the Cold War threat was neatly captured in some of the strident comments of delegates. Pierre-Henri Teitgen, a French lawyer and government minister, warned the Consultative Assembly of the Council of Europe to guard against 'Caesarism and Nazism'.[41] Fascism and 'Hitlerism', Teitgen continued, had 'tainted European public opinion' infiltrating 'doctrines of death … into our countries' allowing Communist forces to 'take advantage of disorder'.[42]

The British delegate to the Consultative Assembly, Lord MacNally, warned that any human rights instrument developed by the Council of Europe must be capable of resisting 'attempts to undermine our democratic way of life from within or without' and that such an instrument would have to 'give Western Europe as a whole greater political stability'.[43] The solution to the existential threat of communism was, as Teitgen argued, for states to 'bind themselves by the observance of the guarantee by an international Convention signed in the name of Europe … and then create a guaranteeing organ namely a European Court of Human Rights'.[44] Western powers, particularly the British and French delegations, saw the ECHR not just as a mechanism for preventing a totalitarian takeover, but also as a useful value statement to juxtapose communism and western democracy.[45] As Ed Bates notes, however, this did not mean they were convinced of the need for a human rights court; Henri Rolin, who would go onto become the President of ECtHR argued in 1949 that a court was not necessary for a collective pact against totalitarianism.[46] The legacy of those who viewed the Convention as an anti-totalitarian instrument can be found in the reference in the preamble to 'the foundation of justice and peace' being secured through an 'effective political democracy', clearly defining and demarcating the identity of parties to the ECHR.[47] It also can be seen in the framing of a number of the substantive rights to prohibit the arbitrary exercise of legal power (see Articles 5, 6 and 13) and Article 17, a rights abuse clause, which was aimed at preventing fascist or communist political movements using Convention rights to advance their political aims and in so doing undermine other rights.[48]

[41] Collected Edition of the 'Travaux Preparatoires of the European Convention on Human Rights' Vol. I 'Preparatory commission of the Council of Europe committee of Ministers Consultative Assembly 11 May – 8 September 1949' (The Hague, 1975) 41.

[42] ibid.

[43] ibid 30.

[44] ibid 76.

[45] A Deighton, 'The British in Strasbourg: negotiating the European Convention on Human Rights, 1950' in R Mariager, K Molin and K Brathagen, *Human Rights in Europe during the Cold War* (Routledge, 2014).

[46] Bates (n 40) 71.

[47] European Convention on Human Rights (ECH) ETS 5 1950, Preamble.

[48] ECHR Art 17. For the link between this and the history see H Cannie and D Voorhoof, 'The abuse clause and freedom of expression in the European Human Rights convention: an added Value for Democracy and Human Rights Protection?' (2011) 29 *Netherlands Quarterly of Human Rights* (*NQHR*) 54; F Cowell 'Anti-Totalitarian Memory: Explaining the Presence of Rights Abuse Clauses in International Human Rights Law' (2018) 6 *Birkbeck Law Review* 35.

There were, however, other ideas about what the ECHR was for; some delegates to the Consultative Assembly chose to explain the need for a human rights instrument in terms of representing a common heritage rooted in European traditions. The Swedish delegate said that the 'genius of Europe' was not just the 'belief in the existence of human rights' but that 'western civilisation' was embedded in the culture of European countries.[49] Similar culturally deterministic arguments were made by the Greek delegate who noted the role that classical Greek culture had played in the creation of human rights. There was another side to this story as the ECHR was also premised on the idea of constructing a forward-looking European identity. The European movement in 1948 had sought to construct broader pan-European cooperation on a whole range of different areas, including economic growth and patent protection. Writing for an American audience in 1956 William Coblentz and Robert Warshaw described the ECHR as ranking alongside the 'Marshall Plan, NATO ... the Schuman plan' in the remaking of European unity.[50] Polys Modinos writing in 1962 described the ECtHR as a 'revolutionary' development 'for the revival of our outworn institutions'.[51] Other sources between 1955 and 1968 also seem to describe the ECtHR in distinctly prospective terms, as part of a new European future based on international institutions.[52] The Convention's preamble also reflected these ideas with references to 'European countries which are like-minded and have a common heritage of political traditions, ideals' but this paragraph specifically linked these values to the 'collective enforcement' of rights, meaning that whilst the ECHR was an expression of a values based community, the enforcement of those.[53] In *Austria v Italy*, an early interstate case, the Commission described the ECHR as a statute to create 'a common public order of the free democracies of Europe' that was intended to safeguard 'their common heritage of political traditions' as well as protect the 'freedom and the rule of law' of states in Europe.[54]

The idea of the ECHR as a statement of values was ultimately secondary to the broader idea that ECHR membership, and by implication ECtHR compliance, was necessary to tackle an external threat. As Mikael Madsen notes, in a comparison of the European human rights system and the UN human rights system, the relative like-mindedness of states in the European system meant that it achieved a relatively high degree of institutional stability, but this

[49] ibid 82.

[50] W Coblentz and Ro Warshaw, 'European Convention for the Protection of Human Rights and Fundamental Freedoms' (1956) 44 *California Law Review* 94.

[51] P Modinos, 'Effects and Repercussions of the European Convention on Human Rights' (1962) 11 *International and Comparative Law Quarterly* (*ICLQ*) 1097, 1098.

[52] For examples see GL Weil, 'The Evolution of the European Convention on Human Rights' (1963) 57 *AJIL* 804; K Vasak, 'The European Convention of Human Rights beyond the Frontiers of Europe' (1963) 12 *ICLQ* 1206.

[53] ECHR Preamble.

[54] *Austria v Italy* App no. 788/60 (ECHR 11 January 1961) p 18.

like-mindedness was contingent upon seeing European human rights as 'mainly a measure against an external threat'.[55] Additionally, the substantive rights that the Convention protected were small 'L' liberal freedoms and were often interpreted in such a manner by the ECtHR – for example rulings on the right to property under Article 1 Protocol 1 were often distinctly liberal in character.[56] This was in part a reflection of the founding forces of the ECHR which, as Marco Duranti, has argued aimed to protect traditionally conservative western European societies and their constitutional orders.[57] Yet in spite of the presence of an external threat, scepticism over broader intervention by European institutions in domestic affairs remained a difficult obstacle to overcome. When European states were contemplating the draft European Political Community (EPC) Treaty in 1954, the French government strongly objected to powers that would allow the putative EPC being able to intervene in violations of rights by member states.[58] In 1957 when the Treaty of Rome created the European Economic Community there was no direct commitment to human rights in the treaty.[59] It wasn't until 1959 that the European Court of Human Rights became operational and its caseload during the 1960s and 1970s was minimal.[60] In the 1980s the ECtHR was prepared to rule against governments in cases involving national security and the freedom of the individual, in a manner which could be highly controversial, but this could be broadly accepted because of the European human rights system's role in providing a broader protection against totalitarianism.

The end of the Cold War seemingly rendered this imperative moot. Instead, there was a reinvention of the nature of the external threat as a form of positive role model, making it almost inevitable that newly democratising states in Eastern Europe would join the Council of Europe.[61] In the 1950s when the ECHR was opened for signature there was, as Susan Marks put it, a 'bold line' that distinguished 'the democratic "we"' who were signatories of the ECHR from the 'totalitarian "they"' who were not.[62] Following the end of the Cold War in the 1990s, eastern European states moved from being a 'they' into being

[55] MR Madsen, 'From Cold War Instrument to Supreme European Court: The European Court of Human Rights at the Crossroads of International and National Law and Politics' (2007) 32 *Law & Social Inquiry* 137, 140.

[56] T Allen, 'Liberalism, Social Democracy and the Value of Property under the European Convention on Human Rights' (2010) 59 *ICLQ* 1055.

[57] M Duranti, *The Conservative Human Rights Revolution: European Identity, Transnational Politics and the Origins of the European Convention* (OUP, 2016).

[58] KK Patel, *Project Europe: A History* (CUP, 2018) 150–51.

[59] ibid.

[60] For data on this point see S Greer, *The European Convention on Human Rights: Achievements, Problems and Prospects* (CUP, 2005) 33–38.

[61] Y Stivachtis and M Habegger, 'The Council of Europe: The Institutional Limits of Contemporary European International Society?' in Y Stivachtis and M Webber, *Europe after Enlargement* (Routledge, 2017) 59, 60.

[62] S Marks, 'The European Convention on Human Rights and its Democratic Society' (1996) 66 *British Yearbook of International Law* 209, 210.

part of the 'we'. As some historians noted, the post-Cold War democratic transition of these states led to their greater integration within Europe and European institutions, as Spain and Portugal had done a generation earlier following their transition from fascist dictatorship in the 1970s.[63] There was a reconfiguration of the ECHR's foundational consensus which unified the idea of the ECHR as an instrument with a teleological vision of a European future and the idea of it as an anti-totalitarian instrument into one.[64] This can be seen in some of the literature on the ECHR and transitional justice describing the cases coming from the newly democratising states in eastern Europe.[65] The idea of a memory being shared by new entrants into the system may seem odd, but forms of memory construction are, as some theorists of memory point out, elite constructs, using official forms controlled and curated by political and legal power structures.[66] The ECHR's foundational collected memory, which saw human rights as a remedy for totalitarianism, gained its elastic character in part because of the social structure in which the participants (i.e. state parties) operated. The ECHR relied on an induction of the political elites heading governments and sitting in the parliamentary assembly of the Council of Europe into participating and acknowledging a form of collected memory, and then used this to serve as the foundational consensus for the ECHR and the ECtHR's operation.

IV. COLLECTED MEMORY AND BACKLASH TO THE EUROPEAN COURT OF HUMAN RIGHTS

References to European consensus as a dynamic formulation in ECtHR judgments are an attempt to both make the Court responsive to changing social conditions but also to give it a source of authority as representative of broader European public opinion.[67] Yet, in order to issue decisions against states, and maintain its authority to do so, the ECtHR also relies on a form of foundational consensus as outlined in section I of this chapter. This, as discussed above in section III, is built on the collected memory of the threat of totalitarianism and the ability of human rights to operate as a remedial mechanism towards that threat. The study of collective memory or collected memory, as Jeffery Olick

[63] See I Kershaw, *Roller-Coaster: Europe, 1950–2017* (Allen Lane, 2018) 299–307.

[64] See Levy and Sznaider (n 4) 124–28.

[65] See A Gross, 'Reinforcing the New Democracies: The European Convention on Human Rights and the Former Communist Countries – A Study of the Case Law' (1996) 7 *European Journal of International Law* (*EJIL*) 89.

[66] For an example see P Nora, 'General Introduction: Between Memory and History' in L Kritzman (ed), *Realms of Memory: Rethinking the French Past, vol. 1* (Columbia University Press, 1996).

[67] See Dzehtsiarou (n 22) ch 6. See also O Bassok, 'The European Consensus Doctrine and the ECtHR Quest for Public Confidence' in P Kapotas and VP Tzevelekos (eds), *Building Consensus on European Consensus: Judicial Interpretation of Human Rights in Europe and Beyond* (CUP, 2018) 238–44.

argues, can be seen as part of the 'field of political culture research insofar as it is concerned with the cultural constitution of political identities and activities'.[68] The collected memory that provides the ECtHR's foundational consensus is a political identity that both appeals to states as an identity worth associating with and as a justificatory mechanism for the Court's operation underpinning a state's formal legal obligation to comply with the Court.

However, compliance can break down with states refusing to implement ECtHR decisions in certain cases which in turn can lead to more systemic forms of non-compliance. The idea that international human rights law and international tribunals are suffering from a crisis of authority has received a lot of scholarly attention, usually in the context of what is sometimes referred to as backlash.[69] Wayne Sandholtz, Yining Bei and Kayla Caldwell draw distinction between 'resistance' to an international court, which would include 'criticism of specific judgments' or 'failure to comply with a specific judgment', and 'backlash' to a court which they argue involves states ceasing to 'cooperate or comply with the court', 'withdrawal' or some form of reform to limit or terminate the court.[70] However, rather than being two distinct categories it is often more appropriate to think of backlash as existing as a continuum of state behaviour with lower-level incidents of non-compliance escalating into more severe forms of backlash.[71] Even when a state eventually complies with a decision that they once opposed, a court's authority can be weakened by backlash and concerns have been raised in the context of the ECtHR about how individual cases of backlash can have wider knock on effects on its authority.[72] Although there has been some analysis of backlash in the context of wider political trends, the temporal nature of some of the causes of backlash towards the ECtHR has been under examined.

The linear passing of time since the ECHR's creation in the early 1950s, has led to the relationship between the collected memories underpinning Convention and the authority of the Court starting to fracture. For a collected memory to provide a foundational legitimating function of the sort described in section II it needs to, in the words of Peter Novick, have 'no sense of the passage of time'

[68] J Olick, *The Politics of Regret: On Collective Memory and Historical Responsibility* (Routledge, 2013) 22.

[69] See eg E Posner, 'Liberal Internationalism and the Populist Backlash' (2017) 49 *Arizona State Law Journal* 795; G John Ikenberry, 'The end of liberal international order?' (2018) 94 *International Affairs* 7.

[70] W Sandholtz, Y Bei and K Caldwell, 'Backlash and international human rights courts' in A Brysk and M Stohl (eds), *Contracting Human Rights: Crisis, Accountability, and Opportunity* (Edward Elgar, 2018) 160.

[71] MR Madsen, Pa Cebulak and M Wiebusch, 'Backlash against international courts: explaining the forms and patterns of resistance to international court' (2018) 14 *International Journal of Law in Context* 197.

[72] N Muižnieks 'Non-implementation of the Court's judgments: our shared responsibility' Council of Europe 28 August 2016, www.coe.int/en/web/commissioner/-/non-implementation-of-the-court-s-judgments-our-shared-responsibility.

denying 'pastness' and insisting on certain concepts as having a continuing presence.[73] Novick was writing about collective, bottom-up memories which he described as conveying some 'eternal or essential truth about the group' but this equally applies to the construction of a collected memory by an instrument like the ECHR.[74] Collective memories underpinning the Convention can punctuate the past and explain the ongoing authority of the Court in the present, because as Halbwachs observed, memory is not history but serves as a function of explaining the present.[75] But the ECHR's collected memory has increasingly struggled to fulfil the function of legitimising authority and has instead become associated with the idea of 'pastness' which is one of the factors behind instances of backlash and leads to suggestions that the Court needs to reform or adapt to meet the new needs of states. To understand how this emerges it is important to first look at how the interpretation of the ECHR by the ECtHR has used its foundational consensus and then at how that feeds into backlash to the ECtHR.

A. Evolutionary Interpretation of the ECHR and the Passage of Time

Evolutive interpretation of the ECHR by the ECtHR treats the Convention as a 'living instrument', which can be interpreted in a manner which evolves with changing understandings of concepts and meanings. The 'living instrument' metaphor has been applied to the interpretation of a variety of different law-making international treaties, such as the 1994 Marrakesh Agreement Establishing the World Trade Organisation, as well as other more diverse treaties such as the 1840 Waitangi Treaty, establishing the rights of the British Crown and the Maori people in the founding of New Zealand.[76] Since 1978 the ECtHR has interpreted the ECHR in this fashion holding in *Marckx v Belgium* that the Convention must be 'interpreted in the light of present day conditions'.[77] In this case the state party was defending a set of laws that distinguished between legitimate and illegitimate children in adoption procedures. The Court conceded the state's contention that at the time the Convention was drafted in the 1950s 'it was regarded as permissible and normal in many European countries to draw a distinction in this area between the "illegitimate" and the "legitimate" family', but held that the Convention needed to be interpreted in light of 'present-day conditions'.[78] Evolutive interpretation relies on seeing an instrument as not

[73] P Novick, *That Noble Dream: The 'Objectivity Question' and the American Historical Profession* (CUP, 1988) 4.

[74] ibid. see also J Wertsch, 'Collective Memory and Narrative Templates' (2008) 7 *Social Research: An International Quarterly* 133, 147–48.

[75] Hawlbachs (n 2).

[76] D Moeckli and N White, 'NigelTreaties as Living Instruments' in D Kritsiotis and M Bowman, *Conceptual and Contextual Perspectives on the Modern Law of Treaties* (CUP, 2018).

[77] *Marckx v Belgium* App No. 6833/74 (1979) 2 EHRR 330.

[78] ibid para 41.

being fixed in the temporal moment of its signing and ratification. On the one hand this allows an instrument to adapt to changing circumstances and especially in relation to a human rights instruments makes them relevant to the present, asserting what Fleur Johns calls the 'timelessness' of human rights.[79] Yet on the other hand, an evolutive interpretation can lead states to question whether when they ratified a treaty they envisaged a particular interpretation of a right, leading the doctrine to come into conflict with the doctrine of state consent.[80] Political and legal institutions in the domestic sphere make evolutive interpretations regularly but they do not suffer from the same political difficulties that international bodies do when interpreting legal instruments.[81]

Literature on backlash to the ECtHR identifies criticism of evolutive interpretation as a core feature behind backlash from states.[82] This is in part because of the nature of the specific judgment which has triggered backlash, and also due to the structural form of evolutionary interpretation which implies a teleological progress towards a future that is determined by an external judicial institution.[83] The ECtHR as an institution is therefore caught maintaining two temporal positions regarding evolutive interpretation: first it maintains that it is a necessity in order for rights to reflect the contemporary needs of society and developing understandings of rights. For example, in *Soering v UK* the extradition of an individual to the United States to face the death penalty was held to be a violation of Article 3 of the ECHR (the prohibition of torture and inhuman and degrading treatment); the Court's application of the 'living instrument' doctrine was influenced by current 'developments and commonly accepted standards in the penal policy' in European states.[84] But in order to maintain its authority to issue such rulings it relied on the second temporal position; maintaining that as a Court it was justified in making rulings against states, using an evolutive interpretation of rights, because of the collected memory of totalitarianism and the Court's role in responding to the threat within that collected memory. In *Soering* it did this explicitly by referring to the 'common heritage' of the Convention, reasoning it would hardly be compatible with that heritage for a state to extradite someone where there were 'substantial grounds for believing that he would be in danger of being subjected to torture'.[85] In the early period of the Court's operation, this temporal element was not explicit, but World War II

[79] F Johns, 'The Temporal Rivalries of Human Rights' (2016) 23 *Indiana Journal of Global Legal Studies* 39, 44.

[80] This argument is explored in K Dzehtsiarou, 'European consensus and the evolutive interpretation of the European Convention on Human Rights' (2011) 12 *German Law Journal* 1730, 1734–37.

[81] K Dzehtsiarou and DK Coffey, 'Legitimacy and Independence of International Tribunals: An Analysis of the European Court of Human Rights' (2014) 37 *Hastings International and Comparative Law Review* 271.

[82] See C Draghici, 'The Strasbourg Court between European and Local Consensus: Anti-Democratic or Guardian of Democratic Process?' (2017) *Public Law* 11.

[83] Madsen et al (n 71).

[84] *Soering v United Kingdom* [1989] 11 EHRR 439, 102.

[85] ibid para 88.

was very recent, many of the heads of government of ECHR state parties had fought in it, and the Cold War was at its height. In early cases the Convention's origins were quite literally in the minds of some of the leading judges; one of the judges sitting in the Grand Chamber in *Tyrer v UK*,[86] who with the majority of judges agreed that the Convention was a 'living instrument', was Pierre-Henri Teitgen, one of the Convention's drafters who as noted above had envisaged it as a bulwark against 'Nazism'.[87]

The Court's development of the living instrument doctrine in the 1970s and 1980s also came at a time when states were still willing to use the ECHR as a foreign policy tool, as interstate cases against Turkey and Greece illustrated.[88] As the Council of Europe's membership expanded in the 1990s, however, the Convention's usefulness as a foreign policy tool receded and more attention began to be paid to the Court's role in social policy decisions. Decisions made about the evolution of the Convention's meaning could then be positioned as being anti-democratic because they went against what a state had decided domestically on the matter. Although often framed as a problem of interpretation in some of the literature, the ageing of the ECHR's original foundational consensus meant it could no longer automatically assume it had the authority it once did.[89] By the 2010s, after two decades of increasing democratisation in most Council of Europe member states, there was a widespread desire for the interpretation of the ECHR to be more concentrated in national institutions.[90] Reforms to the ECtHR were an ongoing process, but the increasing language of sovereignty preservation in the 2010s, often cited as a reaction to the evolving nature of the Court's power, was also at a deeper level a reflection of changing perceptions of the foundational consensus on which the Court's authority rested.[91]

B. Originalism – The ECtHR's Departure from a True Ideal

The argument over the implementation of *Hirst v UK* – which held that the UK's blanket ban on prisoner voting was a disproportionate restriction of the right to

[86] *Tyrer v UK* App. no. 5856/72 (1978) 2 EHRR 1.
[87] R Spano, 'The European Court of Human Rights and National Courts: A Constructive Conversation or a Dialogue of Disrespect?' (2015) 33 *Nordic Journal of Human Rights* 1.
[88] MR Madsen, 'The challenging authority of the European Court of Human Rights: from Cold War legal diplomacy to the Brighton Declaration and backlash' (2016) 79 *Law & Contemporary Problems* 141.
[89] For an example see T Kleinlein, 'Consensus and Contestability: The ECtHR and the Combined Potential of European Consensus and Procedural Rationality Control' (2017) 28 *EJIL* 871.
[90] B Cali, 'Coping with Crisis: Whither the Variable Geometry in the Jurisprudence of the European Court of Human Rights' (2017) 35 *Wisconsin International Law Journal* 237.
[91] See GF Ferrari and O Pollicino, 'The Impact of Supranational Laws on the National Sovereignty of Member States, with Particular Regard to the Judicial Reaction of UK and Italy to the New Aggressive Approach of the European Court of Human Rights' (2011) 2 *Comparative Law Review* 1.

participate in elections – showcased a particular kind of argument against the evolutive interpretation of the ECHR – originalism.[92] In many ways originalism was an explicit counter to the living instrument doctrine.[93] Originalism was buried in a broader critique of the ECtHR, but much like its American counterpart, originalist thinking on the ECHR maintained that there existed a true or original interpretation of the Convention in line with its founders' thinking. In the debate in the UK Parliament on implementing *Hirst*, a number of Members of Parliament (MPs) criticised the ECtHR for interfering with the UK's sovereignty by making such a decision.[94] The substance of the backlash soon evolved, as Helen Hardman notes, away from the specific question of prisoners voting and the principle of democracy, towards one of the legitimacy of an international court limiting executive power.[95] As one former judge at the ECtHR noted, many countries react badly to decisions against them and occasionally there are muted threats to withdraw from the country concerned.[96] Some of the backlash in the UK to *Hirst*, however, began to focus on the legitimacy of the ECtHR's interpretation of the ECHR as a departure from its original or true purpose. In 2013 the then UK Justice Secretary Chris Grayling MP criticised the ECtHR, saying that his 'concern' was with the Court not the Convention because 'the way in which [the ECHR] is being interpreted … has moved a long way away from the intentions of the people who drafted it in the first place'.[97] Other critics of the ECHR seized on both *Hirst* and *Vinter* – to make the case that the Court was moving away from the 'original words of the convention' towards its own form of judicial activism.[98] Perhaps the most high profile example of this originalist line of criticism came in 2012 when the then Prime Minister David Cameron delivered a speech to the Council of Europe which celebrated the UK's contribution in creating the ECHR after World War II but warned that the ECtHR's interpretative role was causing 'the very concept of rights' to be in danger of 'slipping from something noble to something discredited'.[99] This originalist line of argumentation, in the UK context, traces its intellectual pedigree back to

[92] *Hirst v United Kingdom (No 2)* (2005) ECHR 681.

[93] See Spano (n 87).

[94] D Nicol, 'Legitimacy of the Commons debate on prisoner voting' (2011) *Public Law* 681.

[95] H Hardman, 'Prisoner voting rights: the conflict between the government and the courts was really about executive power' LSE British Politics and Policy 20 June 2019, https://blogs.lse.ac.uk/politicsandpolicy/prisoner-voting-rights/.

[96] E Myjer, 'Why much of the criticism of the European Court of Human Rights is Unfounded' in S Flogaitis, T Zwart and J Fraser (eds), *The European Court of Human Rights and Its Discontents: Turning Criticism into Strength* (Edward Elgar, 2013).

[97] HC Debate 17 December 2013 Vol.572. Col. 598.

[98] *Vinter & Ors v UK* [2013] ECHR 645. See Christopher Chope HC Debate 30 June 2015 Vol 597. Col 420.

[99] D Cameron, 'Cameron's speech on the European court of human rights in full' reproduced in *The Guardian* (25 January 2012) www.theguardian.com/law/2012/jan/25/cameron-speech-european-court-human-rights-full.

Lord Hoffmann's claim in 2009 that when the ECHR was created the original member states had not 'agreed to uniformity of the application of those abstract rights in each of their countries, still less in the 47 states which now belong'.[100]

From historical and legal perspectives there are a number of different arguments against the idea that ECtHR interpretation was never contemplated by the original 10 parties to the Convention, but this argument is in fact a proxy much larger point of contention concerning the temporality of the original legitimating consensus of the ECHR. Arguments about a treaty's original meaning invoke its foundational consensus into the present by asking, through the process of interpretation, what the original intentions of the parties were and then moving forwards in time to assess how this applies in the present.[101] This approach to interpretation is supported by Martin Dawidowicz, who concludes in an examination of the Vienna Convention on the Law of Treaties, that the determination of whether or not the meaning of a treaty term has evolved can only be made by reference to its meaning at the time a treaty was concluded.[102] For law making treaties such as the ECHR which create rights and obligations for people living within state parties to treaty in the present, harking back to the past can be a way of privileging the original foundational consensus of an instrument rather than contemporary rights abuses, especially when the historical consensus privileged a particular ideology of rights. Historians such as Duranti have shown the Convention's goal was to protect conservative constitutionalism of western Europe.[103] Originalism's goal is to confine the ECHR to that world. Equally, originalism privileges a particular group of states, namely the states which created the ECHR. It is not entirely coincidental that reforms to the Convention, such as Protocol 15, have had the effect of privileging certain states with more established domestic institutions who are better placed to argue that those institutions are able to balance limitations and restrictions of rights in the ECHR.[104] In this case the past provided a means of envisaging a different role for the Court, whether that described the reality of how the Court previously functioned is another matter altogether; originalism in an ECHR context was a means of opposing the living instrument doctrine and of reasserting a set of privileges for certain states. Yet, to do that required imbibing the collected memory underpinning the ECHR with a distinct sense of 'pastness',

[100] Lord Hoffmann, 'The Universality of Human Rights' Judicial Studies Board Annual Lecture 19 March 2009 www.judiciary.uk/wp-content/uploads/2014/12/Hoffmann_2009_JSB_Annual_Lecture_Universality_of_Human_Rights.pdf.

[101] See J Wyatt, *Intertemporal Linguistics in International Law: Beyond Contemporaneous and Evolutionary Treaty Interpretation* (Bloomsbury Publishing, 2019).

[102] M Dawidowicz, 'The Effect of the Passage of Time on the Interpretation of Treaties: Some Reflections on Costa Rica v. Nicaragua' (2011) 24 *Foundation of the Leiden Journal of International Law* 201, 208.

[103] Duranti (n 57).

[104] For evidence of this see Ø Stiansen and E Voeten, 'Backlash and Judicial Restraint: Evidence from the European Court of Human Rights' (2018) available at ecpr.eu/Filestore/PaperProposal/f99b79f8-cd8d-444b-985a-4a9dd5ac02b7.pdf.

weakening its capacity to provide what Wertsch called an 'essential truth' about the present.[105] Weakening is the appropriate term to use here because as Johns argues, international human rights law succeeds as a form of law which makes universal claims by being temporally 'ever-present'.[106] Situating the true concern of rights as being in the past, or associated with a sense of 'pastness' as originalism does, is a means of weakening its authority to deal with the present.

C. The Re-imagination of External Threats and the Temporality of Consensus

One of the issues with the ECHR's foundational legitimating consensus being based on a threat-remedy conception of totalitarianism is that the threat is temporally located in a particular time, in this case the late 1940s and 1950s. As the political circumstances that constituted a threat in that era changed, it became possible for governments to suggest that there were different contemporary external threats facing European states. In *Ilias and Ahmed v Hungary* before the Grand Chamber of the ECtHR, the Hungarian government argued that the 'practical impossibility of removing undocumented migrants who were not entitled to international protection had rendered immigration uncontrollable'.[107] As a consequence the Hungarian government argued this was creating a form of 'social tension, a feeling of powerlessness and a sense of loss of sovereignty in affected States'.[108] When the Grand Chamber found that there had been no violation of the Article 5 rights of the claimants, there was some criticism of the way that this decision had been reached.[109] The applicants were migrants who had been detained in the Röszke transit zone on the border between Hungary and Serbia, where the Chamber ruled there had been a violation of their Article 5 rights because they had been held without 'any formal decision of the authorities and solely by virtue of an elastically interpreted general provision of the law'.[110] Their detention was the result of a series of policies authorised by Hungarian Prime Minister Viktor Orbán to deter migrants, who had been crossing the Mediterranean in large numbers since 2013, from entering into the country.[111] The Grand Chamber's decision can be understood as part of a wider

[105] Wertsch (n 74) 418.
[106] Johns (n 79) 54.
[107] *Ilias and Ahmed v Hungary* app. no. 47287/15 (ECHR 21 November 2019) para 109.
[108] ibid.
[109] V Stoyanova, 'The Grand Chamber Judgment in *Ilias and Ahmed v Hungary:* Immigration Detention and how the Ground beneath our Feet Continues to Erode' *Strasbourg Observer* (23 December 2019) strasbourgobservers.com/2019/12/23/the-grand-chamber-judgment-in-ilias-and-ahmed-v-hungary-immigration-detention-and-how-the-ground-beneath-our-feet-continues-to-erode/.
[110] *Ilias and Ahmed v Hungary* Application no. 47287/15 (ECHR 14 March 2017) para 68.
[111] C Cantata and PK Rajaram, 'The Politics of the Refugee Crisis in Hungary: Bordering and Ordering the Nation and its Others' in C Menjívar, M Ruiz and I Ness, *The Oxford Handbook of Migration Crises* (OUP, 2019) 181, 186.

trend in ECtHR jurisprudence where the reasoning of governments for detaining immigrants goes under-scrutinised and deference is given to governments claiming that they are dealing with a migrant crisis.[112] It can also be read in context of a wider trend toward the reconceptualisation of immigration as a form of external threat facing the European order, setting up the prevention of migration from external sources as an alternate threat to the foundational consensus which the ECtHR and other European institutions need to acknowledge. Migration began to be constructed as a threat within Hungary where the government alleged that migrants were inferior: 'racialised "others"' who they argued posed a 'threat to order' and the 'imagined sameness' of society.[113] In March 2017, speaking at the European People's Party's annual congress in Malta, Orbán said that the ECtHR was fast becoming a 'threat to the security of EU people' because its decisions were an 'invitation for migrants'.[114]

Attacks on EU policies and the ECtHR were used interchangeably by the Hungarian government to suggest that not only the migrants themselves but also the policy agenda of the EU in relation to immigration, was a threat to national sovereignty.[115] The progressive interpretation of migration as an external threat happened across the course of the 2000s with the literature on the subject showing how discussions of migration interacted with concerns about security and terrorism.[116] This fused together two issues which had previously not necessarily been automatically connected, as literature on immigration cases at the ECtHR in the 1990s showed.[117] Historically, the ECHR had been relatively silent on the rights of migrants, in the original text the main references to migration were framed in terms of restricting the political activity of non-citizens with a relatively clear Cold War context in mind.[118] Decisions in the mid-1990s about the treatment of immigrants and their access to social benefits, such as *Gaygusuz v Austria*, showed how the Convention system could be used to protect migrant rights.[119]

[112] C Costello, 'Immigration Detention: The Grounds Beneath Our Feet' (2015) 68 *Current Legal Problems* 143.

[113] C Thorleifsson, 'Disposable strangers: far-right securitisation of forced migration in Hungary' (2017) 25 *Social Anthropology* 318, 319.

[114] S Michalopoulos, 'Orban attacks the European Court of Human Rights' EURACTIV.com (30 March 2017) www.euractiv.com/section/global-europe/news/orban-attacks-the-european-court-of-human-rights-at-epp-congress/.

[115] L Bustikova and P Guasti, 'The Illiberal Turn or Swerve in Central Europe?' (2017) 5 *Politics and Governance* 166.

[116] D Bonner 'Porus Borders, terrorism and Migration Policy' in *Irregular Migration And Human Rights: Theoretical, European And International Perspectives* (Martinus Nijhoff Publishers, 2004); J Carling, 'The European Paradox of Unwanted Immigration' in JP Burges and S Gutwirth (eds), *A Threat Against Europe? Security, Migration and Integration* (VUB Press, 2011).

[117] For examples of this literature see K Marie-Whitney, 'Does the European Convention on Human Rights Protect Refugees from Safe Countries' (1996) 26 *Georgia Journal of International and Comparative Law* 375; K Groenendijk, 'Long-term immigrants and the Council of Europe' (1999) 1 *European Journal of Migration & Law* 275.

[118] M-B Dembour, *When Humans Become Migrants: Study of the European Court of Human Rights with an Inter-American Counterpoint* (OUP, 2015) 35–55.

[119] *Gaygusuz v Austria* (1997) 23 EHRR 364.

By the early 2010s high-profile cases in countries such as Denmark and Belgium involving the rights of non-nationals not only triggered backlash in the domestic sphere, but also served to cement the idea that the ECtHR favoured or was giving rights to migrants.[120] Domestic politics in many countries shaped the perception of migration as a threat, which as research by Madsen showed was sufficient to weaken the institutional commitment of states to the Court.[121] In popular political imagination the ECtHR ignored the supposed threat to European states from migrants, by finding that domestic policies restricting the rights of migrants were Convention violations. Although the data about the precise scale and strength of these political sentiments in European countries has been questioned, their impact was to weaken the elite consensus surrounding the Court's authority leading either towards acts of backlash or to reforms designed to make the Court more responsive to the position of state parties.[122] More broadly, responses to immigration cases were symptomatic of the ECHR's original collected memory lacking the justificatory power it once had, with the passage of time allowing for new and competing ideas about the threats European states faced.

V. CONCLUSION: THE VANISHING POINT OF COLLECTED MEMORY

If the linear passage of time corrodes and fractures the capacity of a collected memory to act as a foundational form of authority for an international instrument, is it possible that a vanishing point is reached where a collected memory is fully relegated to the past? In section I noted when looking at the two UK referendums, in both cases politicians appealed to the collected memory underpinning the legal process of European integration. In the latter case, however, collected memory no longer served the same legitimating function for international institutions. A vanishing point had been reached where a collected memory belonged decisively to the past. The French anthropologist Émile Durkheim observed that the notion of time was in a sense a collective endeavour requiring a societal wide appreciation of both its units of measure but also a clear understanding of what constituted the past.[123] Collected memories' capacity to authorise the present

[120] J Hartmann, 'A Danish Crusade for the Reform of the European Court of Human Rights' (*EJIL: talk!*, 14 November 2017) www.ejiltalk.org/a-danish-crusade-for-the-reform-of-the-european-court-of-human-rights/; M Bossuyt, 'Judges on Thin Ice: The European Court of Human Rights and the Treatment of Asylum Seekers' (2010) 3 *Inter-American & European Human Rights Journal* 2.

[121] MR Madsen, 'Two-level politics and the backlash against international courts: Evidence from the politicisation of the European court of human rights' (2020) *The British Journal of Politics and International Relations* published online doi.org/10.1177/1369148120948180.

[122] ibid. On questioning the evidence see J Hartmann and S White, 'The Alleged Backlash Against Human Rights: Evidence From Denmark and the UK' in KMcCall-Smith, A Birdsall and E Casanas Adam (eds), *Human Rights in Times of Transition: Liberal Democracies and Challenges of National Security* (Edward Elgar, 2020).

[123] É Durkheim, *The Elementary Forms of Religious Life* (OUP, trans Carol Cosman, 2008) 11–13.

depends on it not being relegated to the past but instead punctuating, providing a basis for legitimating the operation of the present. As Rosalyn Higgins described it, the horizontality of the international legal system works when the shared belief that the legal act of state consent which happened in a 'then' is relevant to and governs the 'now'.[124]

It is possible a point is reached where a collected memory no longer serves the same function it once did, and a historical institutionalist account of an institution's authority loses its salience. Whilst legal obligations would remain, and there may well be another basis for an international tribunal's authority, its foundational consensus has been eroded. The analogy of a vanishing point has its limitations: as section III of this chapter indicates, the corrosion of collected memory is a gradual process. Arguments about the authority of the Court and the passage of time are a component of much wider instances of backlash against the ECtHR, rooted in response to specific cases or the politics of certain countries. Nevertheless, the fact that instruments creating legal obligations to protect human rights can rest on a consensus that is temporally contingent, illustrates just how fragile the foundations of international human rights law actually are.

[124] R Higgins 'Time and the Law: International Perspectives on an Old Problem' (1997) 46 *ICLQ* 501, 501.

2

The Temporalities of Environmental Human Rights

JULIA DEHM

I. INTRODUCTION

TEMPORAL CONCEPTS AND terminology saturate ecological discourses, and thus those of environmental politics, environmental law and environmental human rights. These contain frequent invocations of the cyclical rhythms of nature, warnings that we are living through the 'great acceleration', demands for prevention, precaution and mitigation and the growing awareness that we have entered a new geological epoch, the 'Anthropocene'. This chapter starts from the premise that such temporal rhythms are not an external background to the environmental crisis but rather that 'the environmental crisis is also a crisis in the way we imagine time'.[1] Moreover, because time is not neutral but rather an 'immense but unstable tool of power' the pursuit of environmental justice also requires the pursuit of temporal justice.[2] Environmental human rights, therefore, perhaps more so than other human rights, have unavoidably had to engage with questions of time and temporality. Although environmental human rights have made important temporal innovations, this chapter suggests that environmental human rights remain unable to address to the temporal dissonance that is an underlying cause of ecological harms, that they are limited in their ability to respond to the complex temporalities of how ecological harms unfold and finally that they produce a temporal ontology for themselves that is inadequate, and arguably counterproductive, for working toward ecologically just futures.

In order to explore these different facets of the relationship between environmental human rights and time and temporality, this chapter first outlines three different ways in which ecological debates engage temporal problems: temporal dissonance as an underlying cause of ecological harms, the complex

[1] P Huebener, *Nature's Broken Clocks: Reimagining Time in the Face of the Environmental Crisis* (University of Regina Press, 2020).

[2] ibid.

temporalities of how ecological harms unfold and the temporal impacts of the way we respond to ecological harms. It then moves to show how these temporal dynamics play out in the context of environmental human rights, by exploring first the temporalising effect of the dominant narratives told about environmental human rights. Such accounts are structured by narratives of progress, where the recognition of a global right to a safe, clean, healthy and sustainable environment is presented as the telos that affirms underlying assumptions of progress in and through law. Problematically, the narrative power that such accounts hold prevents more critical and nuanced accounts that interrogate the practical effects of environmental rights and their relationship with political economy and power. Section IV turns to consider how frameworks and discourses of environmental human rights have exhibited 'temporal unfitness'[3] in responding to the complex temporalities through which environmental change unfolds. Environmental rights, arguably more so than other rights, have had to grapple with questions of intergenerational justice, and the way in which actions in the present have harmful future effects as well as how historical actions constrain future possibilities and give rise to reparative obligations in the present. Yet, despite important innovations and the fact environmental human rights are temporally ambitious, they remain inadequate to respond to the temporal challenges that ecological harms present. Finally, drawing on a growing body of scholarship looking at how law produces conceptions of time, this chapter turns to consider the 'temporal ontology'[4] of environmental human rights, specifically the way in which they construct different visions of and different relations to, the future. It suggests that environmental human rights produce two different visions of and ways of relating to the future and that this 'hetrerochrony'[5] endows them with much of their animating force. The first of these visions is characterised by linearity and the pursuit of sustainable development while the latter is marked by a more radical rupture, openness to the new and the possibility of 'alternative futures' and 'future worlds in waiting'.[6] However, the analysis shows that both these different 'temporal ontologies' are inadequate, and arguably even counterproductive, for the task of building ecologically just futures. Therefore, the conclusion then turns to thinking about what other temporal tools might help us live together well in the Anthropocene.

[3] F Johns, 'The Temporal Rivalries of Human Rights' (2016) 23 *Indiana Journal of Global Legal Studies* 39, 41.

[4] K McNeilly, 'The Temporal Ontology of the Human Rights Council's Universal Periodic Review' (2021) 21 *Human Rights Law Review* 1.

[5] D Edelstein, S Geroulanos and N Wheatley, 'Chronocenosis: An Introduction to Power and Time' in *Power and Time* (University of Chicago Press, 2020).

[6] A Grear and LJ Kotzé, 'An Invitation to Fellow Epistemic Travellers–towards Future Worlds in Waiting: Human Rights and the Environment in the Twenty-First Century' in *Research Handbook on Human Rights and the Environment* (Edward Elgar, 2015).

II. THE COMPLEX TEMPORALITIES OF ENVIRONMENTAL CHANGE

Ecological debates engage multiple distinct but interrelated temporal issues or problems. First, the timescales of the natural world – the cyclical pattern of the seasons, the patterns of growth, death and renewal, the slow accretional processes of adaptation and evolution, the long timescales of 'deep time' through which geological change folds – exist in tension with the standardising and accelerating temporal dynamics of modernity and capital. Indeed, Lucia Reisch has suggested that the ecological crisis can be understood precisely as 'a clash of different timescales' between the 'timescale of modernity – with the acceleration of technological innovations' and the 'timescales that govern life and earth'.[7] Similarly, Benjamin Richardson highlights how '[m]odern economic systems and their governance are moored in the present and immediate, at odds with nature's stretching across expansive time frames from the distant past to the long-term future'.[8] Time has been, he writes, 'detach[ed] from its organic cycles and sequences', producing 'time-distorted decay and damage' in nature.[9] Barbara Adam writes about how the complex temporalities of ecological change and 'contextual, irreversible temporalities of life and the multiple rhythmicities of nature' too often come into conflict with the dominant conceptions of 'clock time', linear causality and the principles of abstraction, rationalisation and objectivity on which this is based.[10] This clash is not innate, but a product of how the specific modern idea of standardised 'clock time' was gradually consolidated and imposed across the world as part of the process of colonisation. As Geoff Gordon has shown, the development of standardised time and transnational law was co-constitutive and the ongoing maintenance of standardised time 'undergrids transnational networks predicated on the transactional and contractual engagements', which are fundamental to relations of property and security and has 'played a role in enabling the global expansion of liberal-capitalist orders'.[11] In addition, as Anna Grear has shown, the imposition of standardised time was 'operatively fundamental to the colonial (capitalist) foundations of the Anthropocene crisis'.[12] Alongside the standardisation of time, the 'work of synchronization' has sought to make the multiple temporalities of the world appear to be synchronised, uniform and universal.[13] Jordheim and

[7] LA Reisch, 'Time and Wealth' (2001) 10 *Time & Society* 367, 372.

[8] BJ Richardson, *Time and Environmental Law: Telling Nature's Time* (CUP, 2017) 2.

[9] ibid.

[10] B Adam, *Timescapes of Modernity: The Environment and Invisible Hazards* (Routledge, 2005) 8.

[11] G Gordon, 'Railway Clocks' in J Hohmann and D Joyce (eds), *International Law's Objects* (OUP, 2018) 396–97.

[12] A Grear, '"Anthropocene 'Time'?" – A Reflection on Temporalities in the "New Age of the Human"' in A Philippopoulos-Mihalopoulos (ed), *Routledge Handbook of Law and Theory* (Routledge, 2019) 305.

[13] H Jordheim, 'Synchronizing the World: Synchronism as Historiographical Practice, Then and Now' (2017) 7 *History of the Present* 59; H Jordheim and E Wigen, 'Conceptual Synchronisation: From Progress to Crisis' (2018) 46 *Millennium* 421, 426.

Wigen argue that for the past two centuries the concept of progress and the 'idea of a homogenous, linear, global movement towards a common, unspecified, ever-receding goal' has been the key concept that has been used to synchronise multiple temporalities.[14] Supplementing the ideational account with a materialist one, Marxist scholars have shown how the world market works to synchronise the temporal gaps between different modes of production by imposing the discipline of socially-necessary labour-time.[15] The growing complexity and geographical reach of disaggregated supply chains has directed increased attention to 'temporal sequencing and coordination'[16] between different places and ever greater synchronisation of plural times and temporalities. The accelerationist tendencies of capital[17] mean that the 'lack of symmetry between human and nature timescales … is widening'[18] and thus the 'contradictory and non-harmonic relationship' between the times of capital, of politics and that of ecology is becoming more pronounced.[19] Therefore many scholars have highlighted the urgent need to 'bring these diverse temporalities into a less conflictual relation',[20] to 'align human affairs with Earth's timescales'[21] and address the 'disjunctures between the temporalities of capital and of bodily rhythms and seasons; tensions between the wider rhythms and variegated beats of the living order and the striated times of technological system'.[22]

The political problems raised by discordant temporalities have become more acute in the so-called 'Anthropocene'. The suggestion that we have entered a new 'geological epoch', namely that of the 'Anthropocene'[23] – itself a 'intrinsically a spatio-temporal-material phenomenon'[24] – has prompted renewed attention to temporal questions, given the term suggests both the collapse of traditional nature/society boundaries[25] as well as of traditional spatial and temporal boundaries.[26] One particularly politicised debate pertains to its

[14] Jordheim and Wigen (n 13) 425.

[15] M Tomba, *Marx's Temporalities* (Brill, 2012).

[16] Johns (n 3) 49; D Cowen, *The Deadly Life of Logistics* (University of Minnesota Press, 2014).

[17] See NM Perrone, 'Speed, Law and the Global Economy: How Economic Acceleration Contributes to Inequality and Precarity' (2020) 33 *Leiden Journal of International Law* 557.

[18] B Richardson, 'Doing Time – The Temporalities of Environmental Law' in LJ Kotzé (ed), *Environmental Law and Governance for the Anthropocene* (Hart Publishing, 2017) 56.

[19] JM Antentas, 'Daniel Bensaid, Melancholic Strategist' (2016) 24 *Historical Materialism* 51, 65.

[20] B Adam et al, 'Time for the Environment: The Tutzing Time Ecology Project' (1997) 6 *Time & Society* 73.

[21] Richardson (n 8) 6.

[22] Grear (n 12) 307.

[23] PJ Crutzen, 'The "Anthropocene"' in E Ehlers and T Krafft (eds), *Earth System Science in the Anthropocene: Emerging Issues and Problems* (Springer, 2006); M Subramanian, 'Anthropocene Now: Influential Panel Votes to Recognize Earth's New Epoch' [2019] *Nature*.

[24] Grear (n 12) 300.

[25] B Latour, 'Fourth Lecture: The Anthropocene and the Destruction of (the Image of) the Globe' in *Facing Gaia: Eight Lectures on the New Climatic Regime* (John Wiley & Sons 2017); Jedediah Purdy, *After Nature: A Politics for the Anthropocene* (Harvard University Press, 2015).

[26] Grear (n 12) 300.

periodisation, whether its origins lie concurrent with European colonialism,[27] the 'great acceleration' of the mid-twentieth century, or whether it is indeed a 'time-transgressive Anthropocene with multiple beginnings rather than a single moment of origin'.[28] Additionally, the recognition of humans as a 'geological force'[29] has directed attention to different scales of Earth history or 'deep history'.[30] However, the most fundamental challenge possibly lies in the way in which 'environmental transformation mangles conventional temporalities' to produce 'interwoven geological and artificial temporalities' and how the climate crisis in particular produces a 'warping of time' and reflects a 'messy mix-up of time scales'.[31] Similarly, Grear identifies how in the epoch that has been designated the 'Anthropocene' there is an ever greater sense of how 'temporalities collide, inter-penetrate'[32] due to a 'overall sense of velocity, intensification, of temporalities folding in on each'.[33] Others have suggested that living in the present moment of ecological crisis, arguably gives rise to what has been called 'shadow time': 'the feeling of living in two distinctly different timescales simultaneously'.[34]

Secondly, ecological phenomena are characterised by an inescapable indeterminacy, requiring an engagement with questions of risk, probability, uncertainty, reflexivity and awareness of unintended consequences and an attentiveness to the complex, non-linear and discontinuous ways in which ecological harms unfold. Thus, grappling with ecological concerns requires a sophisticated 'time literacy': Barbara Adam warns that '[w]ithout a deep knowledge of this temporal complexity … environmental action and policy is bound to run aground, unable to lift itself from the spatial deadend of its own making'.[35] Environmental hazards are marked by a 'spatio-temporal unboundedness' and 'time-space distantiation' resulting in harmful effects often being spatially and temporally dispersed from the actions that caused them. There is thus often great complexity involved in the establishment of causal chains – or attribution of causal responsibility – when harms are characterised by non-linear, discontinuous connections and environmental hazards with long periods of latency which may 'work invisibly below the surface until they materialise as symptoms'.[36]

[27] H Davis and Z Todd, 'On the Importance of a Date, or Decolonizing the Anthropocene' (2017) 16 *ACME: An International E-Journal for Critical Geographies* 763–74.
[28] Subramanian (n 23).
[29] D Chakrabarty, 'The Climate of History: Four Theses' (2009) 35 *Critical Inquiry* 197, 201.
[30] D Chakrabarty, 'Anthropocene Time' (2018) 57 *History and Theory* 5, 6; see also M Bjornerud, *Timefulness: How Thinking like a Geologist Can Help Save the World* (Princeton University Press, 2018).
[31] Edelstein, Geroulanos and Wheatley (n 5) 22; the final quote is from A Malm, *Fossil Capital: The Rise of Steam Power and the Roots of Global Warming* (Verso Books, 2016) 187.
[32] Grear (n 12) 308.
[33] ibid.
[34] 'Shadow time' in *The Bureau of Linguistical Reality*, see bureauoflinguisticalreality.com/portfolio/shadowtime/.
[35] Adam (n 10) 8.
[36] ibid 9.

The reality of environmental harms is that they often manifest through forms of what literary theorist Rob Nixon has described as 'slow violence' which is 'neither specular nor instantaneous, but rather incremental and accretive, its calamitous repercussions playing out across a range of temporal scales'.[37] These dynamics mean that decision makers need to contend with uncertainty in deciding what – if any – regulatory actions to take.[38] They also, as Ben Richardson argues, 'complicat[e] managing those impacts' as people might be unwilling to take action now in the interest of future benefits, or to remedy historical harms and thus a 'mismatch can thus arise between awareness and action, and between who incurs the costs and who receives the benefits of action'.[39] A further implication is that past actions continue to have effects in the present and constrain further possibilities. For example, the historical accumulation of anthropogenic greenhouse gas emissions in the atmosphere means that even if the future is not fully fixed, the conditions under which it will be collectively made have already been determined by past actions.[40] Unavoidably therefore, a sensitivity to the 'interpenetration of past, present and future in any one moment of analysis' is needed.[41]

Finally, the modes of describing, regulating or responding to environmental threats have embedded in them specific temporal assumptions and produce their own temporalities. Environmental politics frequently gains impetus from quasi-apocalyptical accounts of future catastrophes, whether the prospect of a 'silent spring',[42] 'limits to growth',[43] the explosion of a 'population bomb'[44] or the depletion of resources or the extinction of species.[45] Activists and advocates often seek to fuel a sense of urgency through representations such as the metaphorical doomsday clock 100 seconds from midnight[46] or warmings that we have less than a decade to prevent runaway climate change.[47] The language of 'crisis' or 'emergency' used to generate a sense of urgency enacts its own temporal logics, in ways that may risk further marginalising the historical and

[37] R Nixon, *Slow Violence and the Environmentalism of the Poor* (Harvard University Press, 2011) 2.

[38] Richardson (n 8) 49.

[39] ibid 47.

[40] J Dehm, 'International Law, Temporalities and Narratives of the Climate Crisis' (2016) 4 *London Review of International Law* 167, 168.

[41] Adam (n 10) 205.

[42] R Carson, *Silent Spring* (40th anniversary, A Mariner Book, Houghton Mifflin Company, 2002).

[43] D Meadows et al, *The Limits to Growth* (Universe Books, 1972).

[44] PR Ehrlich, DR Parnell and A Silbowitz, *The Population Bomb*, vol 68 (Ballantine books, 1971).

[45] E Kolbert, *The Sixth Extinction: An Unnatural History* (A&C Black, 2014); A Dawson, *Extinction: A Radical History* (Or Books, 2016).

[46] J Mecklin, 'Closer than Ever: It is 100 seconds to midnight – 2020 Doomsday Clock Statement', *Bulletin of the Atomic Scientists* (23 January 2020) thebulletin.org/doomsday-clock/current-time/.

[47] Intergovernmental Panel on Climate Change, *Global Warming of 1.5° C: An IPCC Special Report on the Impacts of Global Warming of 1.5° C Above Pre-Industrial Levels and Related Global Greenhouse Gas Emission Pathways, in the Context of Strengthening the Global Response to the Threat of Climate Change, Sustainable Development, and Efforts to Eradicate Poverty* (Intergovernmental Panel on Climate Change, 2018).

structural causes that have produced the need for action.[48] Similarly, apocalyptic imaginaries have complex impacts. They may give rise to apathy, indifference or bitter cynicism due to a belief that disaster is inevitable,[49] produce a sense of despair that 'the game is over, it's too late, there's no sense trying to make anything any better',[50] or generate feelings of grief for 'lost futures'[51] and the 'slow cancelation of the future'.[52] In other strands of environmental thought, fears of a catastrophic future give rise to a nostalgic affective relationship with the past sentimentally envisioned as 'beautiful, harmonious, and self-sustaining' that has been corrupted by the modern world and a sense of regret, mourning, and melancholy.[53] Yet most mainstream environmental politics is generally premised upon a future-orientation, and paradoxically it often reinforces rather than unsettles the narratives of development and progress that have constituted modernity. Principles of 'progression' and 'non-regression' are gaining increased recognition in international environmental law,[54] and there are constant extortions to the international community about the need to 'not backtrack' from commitments made, the ability to recover from 'setbacks' or the dangers of 'insufficient progress'.[55] Ecological modernisation approaches often place hope in technological innovation and 'comic faith in technofixes, whether secular or religious',[56] even though some of the technological solutions proposed – such as geoengineering – impel lives, livelihoods and futures.[57] The paradigm of 'sustainable development' calls for the exercise of forward-orientated prudential self-management in the present in the interest of the future,[58] and a rejection of dominant economic growth models that promote 'near-sighted behaviour' where the 'future is discounted into irrelevance'.[59] The logic and language of

[48] On temporality of crisis and emergency see M Hansel in this volume, see also B Anderson and others, 'Slow Emergencies: Temporality and the Racialized Biopolitics of Emergency Governance' (2020) 44 *Progress in Human Geography* 621.

[49] See M Hulme, *Why We Disagree about Climate Change: Understanding Controversy, Inaction and Opportunity* (CUP, 2009).

[50] DJ Haraway, *Staying with the Trouble: Making Kin in the Chthulucene* (Duke University Press, 2016) 3.

[51] M Fisher, *Ghosts of My Life: Writings on Depression, Hauntology and Lost Futures* (John Hunt Publishing, 2014).

[52] F Berardi, *After the Future* (AK Press, 2011).

[53] UK Heise, *Imagining Extinction: The Cultural Meanings of Endangered Species* (University of Chicago Press, 2016) 7.

[54] L Rajamani and E Guérin, 'Central Concepts in the Paris Agreement and How They Evolved' in D Klein and others (eds), *The Paris Agreement on climate change: Analysis and commentary* (OUP, 2017). See also UN Environment Programme, 'Principle of non-regression', globalpact.informea.org/glossary/principle-non-regression, especially 'Need for non-regression in environmental law and policy' WCC-2012-Res-128-EN and 'Reinforcing the principle of non-regression in environmental law and policy' WCC-2016-Res-074-EN.

[55] The Future We Want, UNGA Res 66/288 (11 September 2012) UN Docs A/RES/66/288, para 20.

[56] Haraway (n 50) 3.

[57] See J Baskin, *Geoengineering, the Anthropocene and the End of Nature* (Springer, 2019).

[58] Brundtland Commission Report, *Our Common Future World Commission on Environment and Development* (CUP, 1987).

[59] Richardson (n 8) 6; see also N Stern, 'Ethics, Equity and the Economics of Climate Change' [2012] Centre for Climate Change Economics and Policy Working Paper 80.

anticipatory action infuses environmental law, governance and politics: the need for 'precautionary'[60] action, the promotion of 'adaptive' forms of management that are responsive to changing conditions, as well as the growing emphasis on developing 'technologies of preparedness'[61] and building 'resilience' for anticipated catastrophes.[62] Unavoidably therefore, ecological discourses and legal and regulatory frameworks are actively involved in the production of futures. However, between different strands of ecological politics there are crucial differences in the way in which the future is known, rendered actionable, related to and the different forms of action in the present – with different political and ethical stakes – this enlivens. The following sections will explore how the different temporal dynamics ecological debates give rise to play out in the context of environmental human rights.

III. TEMPORALISING NARRATIVES ABOUT ENVIRONMENTAL HUMAN RIGHTS

The way in which narratives about environmental human rights are structured and narrated have clear temporalising effects and produce specific temporal relations.[63] The dominant narratives told about environmental human rights adopt a clear temporal structure, marked by gradual, but inevitable, progress towards the telos of the international recognition of a right to a safe, clean, healthy and sustainable environment. In such accounts the international recognition of environmental human rights is presented as a necessary evolution in the field of human rights to address new challenges and 'adapt to new circumstances without betraying its principles'.[64] The relationship between the environment and human rights is generally described as one that has 'evolved rapidly over the past two decades', and although it is recognised that 'much more remains to be done to clarify and implement'[65] environmental rights, the clear assumption is that this relationship 'will continue to develop and evolve for many years to come'.[66] Despite 'conceptual complexity, legal uncertainty, and ethical quandaries'[67] most accounts assume there will be gradual resolution of conceptual

[60] J Peel, *The Precautionary Principle in Practice: Environmental Decision-Making and Scientific Uncertainty* (Federation Press, 2005).

[61] M Dunn Cavelty, M Kaufmann and K Søby Kristensen, 'Resilience and (in) Security: Practices, Subjects, Temporalities' (2015) 46 *Security Dialogue* 3, 7.

[62] RM Schott, 'Resilience, Normativity and Vulnerability' (2013) 1 *Resilience* 210, 213.

[63] See Dehm (n 40).

[64] JH Knox, 'Climate Ethics and Human Rights' (2014) 5 *Journal of Human Rights and the Environment* 22, 23.

[65] UNHRC 'Report of the Special Rapporteur on the issue of human rights obligations relating to the enjoyment of a safe, clean, healthy and sustainable environment' (24 January 2018) UN Doc A/HRC/37/59, para 17.

[66] UNHRSP, 'Framework Principles on Human Rights and the Environment' (2018), p 3.

[67] K Conca, *An Unfinished Foundation: The United Nations and Global Environmental Governance* (OUP, 2015) 123.

issues and further clarification and elaboration of environmental rights as part of an inevitable 'evolution'[68] towards greater 'uniformity and certainty in the understanding of human rights obligations relating to the environment'.[69] Prior to the international recognition of the right to a safe, clean, healthy and sustainable environment, advocates treated its eventual recognition as almost inevitable, pointing to progress towards universal recognition, including the adoption of environmental rights by a number of regional instruments[70] and in the Constitutions of over 110 states,[71] as well as the protection of procedural rights in a number of international environmental law treaties.[72] The optimism of such accounts was also sustained by evidence of the 'greening' of human rights as well as growing acceptance of the fact that a healthy environment is a necessary enabling condition for the full enjoyment of human rights, that environmental degradation interferes with human rights and that measures to protect the environment must be rights compliant.[73] Although, recognition of a right to a safe, clean and healthy environmental at the international level was a 'long time coming',[74] advocates kept insisting that it was 'past time to codify this recognition in the form of a human right to a healthy environment'.[75] Environmental rights are, they proclaimed, 'an idea whose time is here'[76] and that '#TheTimeIsNow'[77] for universal recognition of the right to a safe, clean, healthy and sustainable environment. On 8 October 2021 in a historical

[68] D Ryland, 'The Evolution of Environmental Human Rights in Europe' [2005] *Managerial Law*.

[69] UNHRC (n 65) para 9.

[70] See African Charter of Human and Peoples' Rights adopted 27 June 1981, entered into force 21 October 1986) (1982) 21 ILM 58, art 24; Additional Protocol to the American Convention on Human Rights in the Area of Economic, Social and Cultural Rights (Protocol of San Salvador) (entered into force 16 November 1999) OAS Treaty Series No 69 (1988) reprinted in Basic Documents Pertaining to Human Rights in the InterAmerican System OEA/Ser L V/II.82 Doc 6 Rev 1 at 67 (1992), art 11; League of Arab States, 'Arab Charter of Human Rights' (2008), art 38; Association of Southeast Asian Nations, 'Human Rights Declaration' (2012), para 28(f).

[71] D Boyd, J Knox and M Limon, '#TheTimeIsNow: The Case for Universal Recognition of the Right to a Safe, Clean, Healthy and Sustainable Environment' (Universal Rights Group, 2021) 8; see also DR Boyd, *The Environmental Rights Revolution: A Global Study of Constitutions, Human Rights, and the Environment* (UBC Press, 2011); JR May and E Daly, *Global Environmental Constitutionalism* (CUP, 2015).

[72] See United Nations Economic Commission for Europe, Convention on Access to Information, Public Participation in Decision-Making and Access to Justice in Environmental Matters, 25 June 1998 (known as 'the Aarhus Convention'), in force 21 October 2001, 2161 UNTS 447; Economic Commission for Latin America and the Caribbean, Regional Agreement on Access to Information, Public Participation and Justice in Environmental Matters in Latin America and the Caribbean (known as 'the Escazú Agreement'), 4 March 2018, in force 22 April 2021.

[73] For an overview see UNGA 'Human rights obligations relating to the enjoyment of a safe, clean, healthy and sustainable environment' (19 July 2018) UN Doc A/73/188, paras 12–27.

[74] OW Pedersen, 'European Environmental Human Rights and Environmental Rights: A Long Time Coming' (2008) 21 *Geo. Int'l Envtl. L. Rev.* 73.

[75] JH Knox and R Pejan, 'Introduction' in JH Knox and R Pejan (eds), *The Human Right to a Healthy Environment* (CUP, 2018) 16.

[76] UNHCR (n 65) para 20.

[77] Boyd, Knox and Limon (n 71).

resolution the UN Human Rights Council recognised the right to a safe, clean, healthy and sustainable environment.[78]

Environmental human rights are often seen as arriving 'late': they were not included in the Universal Declaration on Human Rights or either of the two Covenants. Rather, the notion of environmental human rights first arose as part of a so-called 'third generation' of human rights that address 'planetary concerns' and are predicated on 'solidarity' and were intertwined with visions for a more equitable international economic order.[79] The 1972 Stockholm Declaration, which in principle 1 affirmed that '[m]an (sic) has the fundamental right to freedom, equality and adequate conditions of life, in an environment of a quality that permits a life of dignity and well-being, and he (sic) bears a solemn responsibility to protect and improve the environment for present and future generations',[80] was for a long time seen by many as the 'instrument that comes the closest' to recognising a human right to a healthy environment.[81] Some commentators have characterised the two decades post 1972 as reflecting 'not just a lack of progress but an actual step backward for the idea of environmental human rights':[82] while the 1987 World Commission on Environment and Development report declared that 'all human beings have the fundamental right to an environment adequate for their health and well-being'[83] the 1992 Rio Earth Summit outcomes failed to mention 'human rights' or 'environmental human rights' and affirmed only a much weaker notion of an entitlement 'to a healthy and productive life in harmony with nature'.[84] In the late 1980s the United Nations Sub-Commission on Prevention of Discrimination and Protection of Minorities appointed a Special Rapporteur, Fatma Zohra Ksentini, to prepare a study on the relationship between the environment and human rights, which prompted the Commission on Human Rights to address the relationship between environment and human rights for the first time in a 1990 resolution.[85] Ksentini's final report in 1994 included some 'Draft Principles on

[78] UNHRC Res 48/13 (2021), UN Doc A/HRC/RES/48/13.

[79] SP Marks, 'Emerging Human Rights: A New Generation for the 1980s' (1980) 33 *Rutgers L. Rev.* 435; C Wellman, 'Solidarity, the Individual and Human Rights' (2000) 22 *Hum. Rts. Q.* 639; P Alston, 'A Third Generation of Solidarity Rights: Progressive Development or Obfuscation of International Human Rights Law?' (1982) 29 *Netherlands International Law Review* 307.

[80] Declaration of the United Nations Conference on the Human Environment, UN Doc A/Conf.48/14/Rev. 1 (1973), principle 1.

[81] UNHRC, 'Report of the independent expert on the issue of human rights obligations relating to the enjoyment of a safe, clean, healthy and sustainable environment, John H. Knox' (24 December 2012) UN Doc A/HRC/22/43, para 14.

[82] Conca (n 67) 121.

[83] UNGA, 'Report of the World Commission on Environment and Development' (4 August 1987) UN Doc A/42/427.

[84] Rio Declaration on Environment and Development in Report of the United Nations Conference on Environment and Development (Vol 1), Rio de Janeiro, 3–14 June 1992 (12 August 1992) UN Doc A/CONF.151/26, principle 1.

[85] UNCHR Res 41 (1990) UN Doc E/CN.4/RES/1990/41.

Human Rights and the Environment'[86] which affirmed that '[h]uman rights, an ecologically sound environment, sustainable development and peace are interdependent and indivisible' and that '[a]ll persons have the right to a secure, healthy and ecologically sound environment'. Although the Draft Principles were seen by scholars as a 'progression from earlier discussion[s]',[87] the Commission on Human Rights deferred proper consideration of this report for a decade and declined to adopt or endorse these draft principles.[88] There was a long institutional hiatus until 2012 when the Human Rights Council established a mandate and appointed an independent expert, John Knox, to study the human rights obligations relating to the enjoyment of a safe, clean, healthy and sustainable environment and identify best practices on how human rights obligations can inform environmental policy making.[89] Throughout his mandate, Knox emphasised the 'interdependent' nature of environmental protection and human rights such that a safe, clean, healthy and sustainable environment is necessary for the full enjoyment of a vast range of human rights, whilst human right are vital for the protection of the environment.[90] In his final report in January 2018 John Knox proposed 16 'framework principles' on human rights and the environment that affirm the mutual reinforcing nature of environmental protection and human rights promotion.[91] Knox stressed that these principles do not create new obligations, but 'provide practical guidance on how human rights obligations should be implemented in the environmental context'.[92] He also recommended that the Human Rights Council consider supporting the recognition of the right in a global instrument.[93] During 2020 momentum built for the recognition of such a right, with the High Commission in July declaring that 'It is time for global recognition of the human right to a healthy environment'.[94] In September 2020 Costa Rica, the Maldives, Morocco, Slovenia and Switzerland put out a joint statement which committed them to bringing a resolution that would declare universal recognition of the right to a safe, clean, healthy and sustainable environment. Concurrently, a letter from almost 1,000 civil society organisations

[86] UNCHR, 'Review of further developments in fields with which the sub-commission has been concerned – human rights and the environment: final report prepared by Mrs. Fatma Zohra Ksentini, special rapporteur' (6 July 1994) UN Doc E/CN.4/Sub.2/1994/9.

[87] NAF Popovic, 'In Pursuit of Environmental Human Rights: Commentary on the Draft Declaration of Principles on Human Rights and the Environment' (1995) 27 *Colum. Hum. Rts. L. Rev.* 487, 493.

[88] For a detailed overview see 'Environmental Rights Report: Human Rights and the Environment – Materials for the 61st Session of the United Nations Commission on Human Rights, Geneva, March 14 – April 22, 2005' (EarthJustice 2005). See also UNHRC (n 81) para 16.

[89] UNHRC Res 19/10 (2012) UN Doc A/HRC/RES/19/10.

[90] UNHRC (n 81).

[91] UNHRC (n 65).

[92] JH Knox, 'The United Nations Mandate on Human Rights and the Environment' (2018) 2 *Chinese Journal of Environmental Law* 83, 88. See also UNHRC (n 65) para 8.

[93] UNHRC (n 65) para 14.

[94] 'Statement by Michelle Bachelet, UN High Commissioner for Human Rights' (1 July 2020) www.ohchr.org/EN/NewsEvents/Pages/DisplayNews.aspx?NewsID=26022&LangID=E.

urged the Council to 'recognise without delay the human right to a safe, clean, healthy and sustainable environment'.[95] The right to a safe, clean, healthy and sustainable environment was recognised at the international level just prior to this chapter going to print.

These dominant accounts are all structured by a temporalising narrative where the recognition of environmental human rights is presented as a telos and the gradual movement towards this objective depicted as evidence of underlying assumptions of progress in and though law.[96] These narratives of environmental human rights thus reflect a 'progressive temporality marked out in human rights terms',[97] where the gradual realisation of environmental human rights is cast as part of an inevitable arc towards greater global justice. Arguably the linearity and progressive temporality that characterises the way human rights are dominantly narrated[98] is even more pronounced in discussions of environmental human rights, given such rights were so recently recognised at the global level, and thus there is still a greater sense of the promise and potentiality of more right-compliant futures. Yet such teleological accounts of the progressive realisation of environmental human rights constrain our capacity to critically analyse the operation of environmental human rights and pose uncomfortable questions about the 'manifold divergences and the potential for profound conceptual conflict' between environmental and human rights discourses[99] or about political contestation between stakeholders over the role, scope and content or rights.[100] Moreover, such progressive accounts are unable to reckon with how human rights are implicated in discourses of development and economic growth that are driving environmental destruction and how rights frameworks have been 'ideologically porous .... to the very same globalised neo-liberal ideology so profoundly implicated in the production of not only intense human suffering, particularly in the global South, but also of environmental destruction caused by irresponsible corporate exploitation of the living order'.[101] In the face of a steadily worsening ecological crisis, such narratives of progress in and through law feel jarringly disconnected to the reality of rapid biodiversity loss, the continued growth in greenhouse gas emissions and breached planetary boundaries which are all leading to a 'ghastly future'.[102] Indeed, the continual reproduction of such

[95] Boyd, Knox and Limon (n 71) 5.

[96] For a discussion of narratives of progress and international law see T Skouteris, *The Notion of Progress in International Law Discourse* (TMC Asser Press, 2010).

[97] Johns (n 3) 56.

[98] K McNeilly, 'Are Rights out of Time? International Human Rights Law, Temporality, and Radical Social Change' (2019) 28 *Social & Legal Studies* 817.

[99] A Grear, 'Where Discourses Meet' (2010) 1 *Journal of Human Rights and the Environment* 1, 1 and 5.

[100] G Blouin Genest and S Paquerot, 'Environmental Human Rights as a Battlefield: A Grammar of Political Confrontation' (2016) 7 *Journal of Human Rights and the Environment* 132.

[101] A Grear, 'The Vulnerable Living Order: Human Rights and the Environment in a Critical and Philosophical Perspective' (2011) 2 *Journal of Human Rights and the Environment* 23, 35.

[102] I take this term from CJA Bradshaw and others, 'Underestimating the Challenges of Avoiding a Ghastly Future' (2021) 1 *Frontiers in Conservation Science* 9 although I concur with the important

myths of progress presents a barrier to producing viable solutions to increasing inequality and environmental destruction,[103] or interrogating the role of law in enabling and authorising ecological harms.[104] Instead of a celebratory teleological account, environmental justice is better served by a sober political economy analysis of the extent to which environmental human rights can disrupt and contest the root causes of and powerful structural forces driving environmental exploitation, given the limitations of their anthropocentric nature and individualistic, liberal-legalist form,[105] alongside a situated interrogation of why and how in specific contexts environmental rights have contested or tacitly allowed the underlying structural dynamics driving ecological destruction.

IV. THE TEMPORAL UNFITNESS OF ENVIRONMENTAL HUMAN RIGHTS

This section explores the ways in which environmental human rights have attempted to, but been unable to fully address, the complex temporalities that environmental issues raise. Due to the complex temporal dynamics that both contribute to and result from environmental harms, it is unsurprising that environmental human rights have, perhaps more than other human rights, unavoidably had to grapple with questions of intergenerational justice, and the way in which actions in the present have harmful future effects, and how historical actions both constrain future possibilities and give rise to reparative obligations in the present. The claims arising from environmental harms frequently 'posit a virtual, elongated ethical temporality often coexisting antagonistically with the time of politics'.[106] While environmental human rights have sought to respond to such 'elongated' ethical demands, they have not been able to overcome the structural constraints of the human rights form that assumes an individual, autonomous, presently-existing and anthropocentric subject suffering a contemporaneously-caused harm. As such, although they have been temporally ambitious, environmental rights remain 'temporally unfit' to deliver temporal justice in the face of temporally transgressive environmental harms.[107]

critiques of this analysis raised in J Bluwstein et al, 'Commentary: Underestimating the Challenges of Avoiding a Ghastly Future' (2021) 2 *Frontiers in Conservation Science* 15.

[103] U Natarajan and J Dehm, 'Where is the environment? Locating Nature in International Law' *Third World Approach to International Law Review* (30 August 2019), twailr.com/where-is-the-environment-locating-nature-in-international-law/.

[104] J Dehm, 'Reflections on Paris: Thoughts towards a Critical Approach to Climate Law' (2018) 1 *Revue québécoise de droit international* 61, 171; U Natarajan and K Khody, 'Locating Nature: Making and Unmaking International Law' (2014) 27 *Leiden Journal of International Law* 573–93 at 592.

[105] PD Burdon, 'Environmental Human Rights: A Constructive Critique' in A Grear and L Kotzé (eds), *Research Handbook on Human Rights and the Environment* (Edward Elgar, 2015).

[106] Edelstein, Geroulanos and Wheatley (n 5) 21.

[107] Johns (n 3) 41.

Questions of intergenerational justice infuse the field of environmental politics and the formulation of sustainable development:[108] environmental summits from Stockholm (in 1972) to Rio +20 (in 2012) pronounced the 'solemn responsibility' humanity bears to 'protect and improve the environment for present and future generations',[109] to 'equitably meet developmental and environmental needs of present and future generations'[110] and 'promot[e] intergenerational solidarity for the achievement of sustainable development, taking into account future generations'.[111] Additionally, there are references to the rights of future generations in a wide range of environmental treaties and agreements,[112] as well as to 'intergenerational equity' in the preamble to the Paris Agreement.[113] Unavoidably, environmental justice raises complex questions of intergenerational obligations and 'presumes a connection with and a concern for the claims of future persons'[114] who either will be the beneficiaries of decisions we make now or 'face exclusively bad choices'[115] if current unsustainable modes of production are not transformed. More so than other rights domains, environmental rights pose critical questions about how present-day obligations may be owed to the not-yet born and the responsibilities we bear to future people who constitute 'an indefinite population of virtual humans, a cast of projected "anthro-potentialities"'.[116] In order to address the imperatives of intergenerational justice, advocates have sought to give an intertemporal dimension to rights claims by positioning future actors as legally present rights-holders by according rights to yet-unborn 'future generations'. Although philosophical debates continue about whether it is possible to 'assign moral significance to non-existing beings', whether future persons, who do not yet exist, can have rights and whether such rights can give rise to correlating legal duties,[117] this

[108] The formulation of sustainable development as development that 'meets the needs of the present without compromising the ability of future generations to meet their own needs' necessarily foreground the interests and considerations of the not-yet-born: Brundtland Commission Report (n 58).

[109] Declaration of the United Nations Conference on the Human Environment (n 80) principle 1.

[110] UNGA, 'Rio Declaration on Environment and Development' (12 August 1992) UN Doc A/CONF.151/26 (Vol. 1), principle 3.

[111] The Future We Want (n 55) para 86.

[112] For a list see UNGA, 'Intergenerational Solidarity and the needs of future generations: Report of the Secretary-General' (5 August 2013) UN Doc A/68/322, paras 34–35.

[113] Paris Agreement on Climate Change (opened for signature on 22 April 2016, entered into force 4 November 2016) UNTS XXVII.7.d, preambular recital 11.

[114] RD Hiskes and RP Hiskes, *The Human Right to a Green Future: Environmental Rights and Intergenerational Justice* (CUP, 2009) 5.

[115] H Shue, 'Changing Images of Climate Change: Human Rights and Future Generations' (2014) 5 *Journal of Human Rights and the Environment* 50, 63.

[116] Edelstein, Geroulanos and Wheatley (n 5) 21.

[117] Some of these arguments are canvassed in UNGA (n 112), see also B Lewis, 'Human Rights Duties towards Future Generations and the Potential for Achieving Climate Justice' (2016) 34 *Netherlands Quarterly of Human Rights* 206, 208 for a rebuttal of these arguments.

focus on the rights of future generations, is one distinct contribution environmental rights thinking could make to change the temporal orientation of the broader human rights field.[118] However, the radical implications of such intertemporal rights claims have not (to date) been properly realised. The right of '[e]ach generation … to receive the planet in no worse condition than that of previous generations'[119] and the correlating obligation on those alive today to 'to conserve this fragile planet Earth and its human cultural legacy for future generations',[120] articulated by Edith Brown Weiss, has primarily been taken up rhetorically, rather than as a juridically actionable right. While in 1994, Ksentini's final report noted the 'right to a satisfactory environment is also a right to the "conservation" of nature for the benefit of future generations'[121] the 2018 Framework Principles do not mention 'future generations' or even the 'future'. While the growing focus on rights of children to be able to live in a healthy environment throughout their lives would arguably also implicitly consider the rights of the not-yet-born,[122] to date, despite the specific vulnerability of future generations to environmental harms and especially climate change, they have been under noticed in human rights analysis of the climate regime and the Paris Agreement in particular.[123] Perhaps the most concrete manifestation of such obligations was the ruling by the Supreme Court of the Philippines in the 1993 '*Children's Case*' which famously granted standing to a group of young people to both 'defend their generation's right to a sound environment and to perform their obligation to preserve that right for future generations'.[124] Numerous countries have included a reference to future generations in their Constitutions[125] and others have established Commissioners, Ombudsmen or other national institutional arrangements to investigate and protect the rights of future generations,[126] although no progress has been made on calls to institute a High Commissioner for Future Generations at the global level.[127]

[118] JH Knox, 'Constructing the Human Right to a Healthy Environment' (2020) 16 *Annual Review of Law and Social Science* 79, 92.

[119] E Brown Weiss, 'In Fairness to Future Generations' (1990) 32 *Environment: Science and Policy for Sustainable Development* 6, 10.

[120] ibid 7.

[121] UNCHR (n 86) para 256.

[122] Knox (n 118) 92. There is growing focus on children's rights and the right to a healthy environment, see 'Decision adopted by the Committee on the Rights of the Child under the Optional Protocol to the Convention on the Rights of the Child on a communications procedure in respect of Communication No 104/2019' (8 October 2021) UN Doc CRC/C/88/D/104/2019; *Juliana v United States*, 947 F.3d 1159 (9th Cir. 2020); *Sharma by her litigation representative Sister Marie Brigid Arthur v Minister for the Environment* [2021] FCA 560.

[123] B Lewis, 'The Rights of Future Generations within the Post-Paris Climate Regime' (2018) 7 *Transnational Environmental Law* 69.

[124] *Minors Oposa v Secretary of the Department of Environment and Natural Resources*, 33 I.L.M. 173 (1994); T Allen, 'The Philippine Children's Case: Recognizing Legal Standing for Future Generations' (1993) 6 *Geo. Int'l Envtl. L. Rev.* 713, 713.

[125] UNGA (n 112) para 37.

[126] ibid paras 39–48.

[127] ibid paras 53–61.

Yet, the vexed problem of intergenerational justice and obligations to future beings will unavoidably continue to make unsettling demands and disrupt any attempts to impose temporal closure on environmental human rights, even as the legal form of rights remains inadequate to properly respond to such complex inter-temporal justice claims.

Even as environmental human rights have gestured towards, but not enacted or realised, the rights of future generations and obligations to those who come after us, it has also struggled to take up questions about the obligations that the past imposes on the present.[128] The persistence of historical injustices 'saturates' many environmental issues, and especially that of climate change.[129] The 'historical legacies of uneven use of fossil fuels and exploitation of raw materials' have enabled 'uneven and persistent patterns of eco-imperialism and "ecological debt"'.[130] As Carmen Gonzales has highlighted '[t]he roots of contemporary environmental injustice lie in colonialism'[131] and North-South environmental conflicts are 'inextricably intertwined with colonialism and with post-colonial trade, aid, finance, and investment policies that impoverished Southern nations and enabled the North to exploit the South's resources while externalizing the social and environmental costs'.[132] These historical ecological injustices remain unrepaired and continue to cause harm in the present, and therefore give rise to urgent demands for compensative and reparative justice.[133] However, as Gonzales shows, human rights law 'may be ill-equipped to handle the North's ecological debt to the South for centuries of colonial exploitation (including slavery) and decades of "modernization" and "development"'.[134] Moreover, 'the redress mechanisms of the international human rights system may be unwilling or unable to provide reparations for systemic injustices such as slavery, colonialism and the North's ecological debt to the South'.[135] Although the Framework Principles make no explicit mention of obligations arising out of past ecological injustice, ecological and temporal justice demand a deep reckoning with historical responsibilities and the remediation or reparation of historical harms.

[128] For a discussion of human rights obligations in relation to reparations for racial discrimination rooted in slavery and colonisation, see UNGA 'Contemporary forms of racism, racial discrimination, xenophobia and racial intolerance' (21 August 2019) UN Doc A/74/321.

[129] S Humphreys, 'Climate Justice: The Claim of the Past' (2014) 5 *Journal of Human Rights and the Environment* 134.

[130] P Chatterton, D Featherstone and P Routledge, 'Articulating Climate Justice in Copenhagen: Antagonism, the Commons, and Solidarity' (2013) 45 *Antipode* 602, 606.

[131] CG Gonzalez, 'Environmental Justice, Human Rights, and the Global South' (2015) 13 *Santa Clara J. Int'l L.* 151, 159.

[132] ibid 158.

[133] S Mason-Case and J Dehm, 'Redressing Historical Responsibility for the Unjust Precarities of Climate Change in the Present' in B Mayer and A Zahar (eds), *Debating Climate Law* (CUP, 2021).

[134] Gonzalez (n 131) 187.

[135] ibid 190.

V. THE TEMPORALISING EFFECTS OF ENVIRONMENTAL HUMAN RIGHTS

This final substantive section explores the constructive role played by environmental human rights in the 'shaping of time' and how they contribute to the production of specific forms of temporal ordering and participate in the creation of specific temporal ontologies.[136] A growing body of scholarship has started to explore how law does not just exist in time, but actively produces and constructs ideas of time.[137] Law plays a fundamental, constitutive role in constructing not just visions of the future, but the way in which the past, present and future relate to one another and the way in which we experience, relate to and act in relation to the future. Futures are, as Barbara Adam reminds us, 'created continuously' including by legal performative and enacting practices.[138] Moreover, there are, as Ben Anderson writes, always 'various ways in which "the future" comes to be "at stake" – socially, culturally, technologically, economically, politically – and that it can be oriented to, invested in, performed and made material'.[139] Jens Beckert has shown how the making of imagined futures and the temporal disposition of economic actors towards the future is key to capitalist dynamics, because fictional expectations shape behaviour, and thereby help bring certain futures into being.[140] Law plays a key role in facilitating the social communication of future expectations, allowing expectations to be secured as stable over time and in guiding action in relation to certain expectations.[141] Human rights have a close relation with futurity: there have been extensive scholarly discussions about the future of human rights,[142] the future-orientation of human rights,[143] and the futures imagined by human rights given how their utopian dimension is animated by 'the image of another, better world of dignity and respect that underlies their appeal'.[144] Additionally, the key international human rights texts were drafted during a period when the future, which for several centuries had

[136] E Grabham and SM Beynon-Jones, 'Introduction' in E Grabham and SM Beynon-Jones (eds), *Law and Time* (Routledge, 2020) 2.

[137] McNeilly (n 98); E Grabham, *Brewing Legal Times: Things, Form, and the Enactment of Law* (University of Toronto Press, 2016); Grabham and Beynon-Jones (n 136); CJ Greenhouse, 'Just in Time: Temporality and the Cultural Legitimation of Law' (1989) 98 *The Yale Law Journal* 1631.

[138] B Adam, 'Futures in the Making: Contemporary Practices and Sociological Challenges' (conference presentation American Sociological Association, 16 August 2005) 1.

[139] R Coleman and R Tutton, 'Introduction to Special Issue of Sociological Review on "Futures in Question: Theories, Methods, Practices"' (2017) 65 *The Sociological Review* 440, 445.

[140] J Beckert, *Imagined Futures* (Harvard University Press, 2016).

[141] N Luhmann, *Law as a Social System* (Klaus A Ziegert tr, Oxford University Press, 2004) 142–46. See also J Dehm, 'Law and the "value" of future expectations: climate change, stranded assets and capitalist dynamics' (*Verfassungsblog*, 6 March 2020) verfassungsblog.de/law-and-the-value-of-future-expectations-climate-change-stranded-assets-and-capitalist-dynamics/.

[142] U Baxi, *The Future of Human Rights*, 2nd edn (OUP, 2002); KG Young (ed), *The Future of Economic and Social Rights* (CUP, 2019).

[143] See P O'Connell in this volume.

[144] S Moyn, *The Last Utopia: Human Rights in History* (Harvard University Press, 2012) 4.

been a moral and philosophical category, 'became an object of social science'.[145] In the post-World War II era the future came to be seen as something that 'could be rendered visible and hence inherently governable'[146] and the new fields of study of futurology, futurism, and future studies gave rise to forms of future expertise, methods, and technologies.[147] This new interest in the futurity thus turned the future into a 'veritable battleground'[148] between competing visions of the future, different approaches to how the future could be 'known' and how predictions of the future could 'be used to control or protest certain futures'.[149]

Environmental human rights are a particularly pertinent site to investigate the way human rights produces specific orientation to, relationships with and ways of relating to the future for two reasons. First, environmental human rights are perhaps the context where the utopian future promised by human rights appears most illusionary. Environmental human rights promise a virtuous cycle, where 'sustainable development and the protection of the environment, including ecosystems, contribute to human well-being and to the enjoyment of human rights', yet, they are persistently haunted by the very real, converse possibility, namely that 'environmental damage can have negative implications, both direct and indirect, for the effective enjoyment of all human rights'.[150] Resolutions note how 'the impact of climate change, the unsustainable management and use of natural resources, the unsound management of chemicals and waste, the resulting loss of biodiversity and the decline in services provided by ecosystems may interfere with the enjoyment of a safe, clean, healthy and sustainable environment'.[151] In all these domains current projections are grim: the World Meteorological organisation warms of temperature increases of 3–5 degrees Celsius, each year 242 million tons of plastic waste and 400 million ton of hazardous waste are produced, and currently 27,000 species vanish annually with one million species facing extinction.[152] Thus, while 'first generational' civil and political rights are sustained by a convoluted and 'dialectical temporality of tautology and teleology'[153] that posits the human personality as both

[145] J Andersson, *The Future of the World: Futurology, Futurists, and the Struggle for the Post Cold War Imagination* (OUP, 2018) 3.

[146] ibid.

[147] ibid 6.

[148] J Andersson, 'The Great Future Debate and the Struggle for the World' (2012) 117 *The American Historical Review* 1411, 1412.

[149] ibid.

[150] UNHRC Res 37/8 (2018) UN Doc A/HRC/RES/37/8.

[151] ibid.

[152] SA Atapattu, CG Gonzalez and SL Seck, 'Intersections of Environmental Justice and Sustainable Development: Framing the Issues' in SA Atapattu, CG Gonzalez and SL Seck (eds), *The Cambridge Handbook of Environmental Justice and Sustainable Development* (CUP, 2021) 1–2.

[153] JR Slaughter, *Human Rights, Inc.: The World Novel, Narrative Form, and International Law* (Fordham University Press, 2009) 246.

their 'natural premise and their positive promise', and 'second generational' economic and social rights are structured by the promise of 'progressive realisation', 'third generational' environmental rights are animated by an impossible promise – of inhabiting a safe, clean, healthy and sustainable environment – that arguably has already been foreclosed. The damage that has already been done to the natural world is such that even a (very necessary) radical transformation of economic, political and social systems that govern our lives will probably lead only to a 'less-ravaged future' – certain climatic impacts are already locked in and unavoidable, many extinctions have already occurred.[154]

Secondly, although environmental human rights discourses and frameworks present both the protection of human rights as an enabling condition for a healthy environment and conversely a healthy environment as an enabling condition for the realisation of human rights, there is no clear sense of the causal connections that would lead to this mutually co-constitutive relationship.[155] Despite this evasive circularity, I suggest environmental human rights produce (at least) two very different ways in which the past, present and future relate to one another, and thus modes of relating to the future in the present. On one hand, environmental human rights, due to the way in which they are intertwined with notions of sustainable development, work to produce and stabilise a linear temporality and a relationship to a future that is imagined as a predictable progression from the present. On the other, environmental human rights gesture towards 'alternative futures' and 'future worlds in waiting',[156] thereby producing a temporality of rupture and discontinuity, a sense of a contingent and unknown future and an openness and embrace of the new. On one level these two distinct but co-existing temporal ontologies are conflictual, yet this 'hetrerochrony' also gives environmental human rights much of their animating force. In practice, these two temporal ontologies operate to mutually reenforce each other, paralleling the way in which the 'symbolic valence' of human rights is produced by how the 'regulatory' dimension of rights is supplemented by a more 'emancipatory' or 'political' dimension reflected in the persistent gap between human rights norms 'on the books' and their 'imaginative appeal'.[157] The next sections explore each of these temporal ontologies produced by environmental human rights and demonstrate the various problems arising from and limitations inherent in both these modes of describing the relationship between the past, present and future.

[154] I take this term from Bradshaw and others (n 102); although see critique of this analysis in Bluwstein et al (n 102).
[155] UNHRSP (n 66).
[156] Grear and Kotzé (n 6).
[157] S Pahuja, 'Rights as Regulation: The Integration of Development and Human Rights' in B Morgan (ed), *The Intersection of Rights and Regulation* (Ashgate, 2007) 168.

A. Environmental Human Rights, Sustainable Development and Market Environmentalism

The first way in which environmental human rights produce a specific account of the future is through the assumptions of linear temporality, where the future is seen as a telos towards which the present is heading. Through a focus on how environmental human rights are achieved through and intimately intertwined with the process of sustainable development, environmental human rights have the 'effect of instantiating an orientation to a constructed past, present or future in linear or teleological form'.[158] Both the 1992 Rio Declaration on Environment and Development and the 1993 Vienna Declaration explicitly recognise that the 'right to development must be fulfilled so as to equitably meet developmental and environmental needs of present and future generations' (something that has been reiterated in Commission and Council resolutions subsequently[159]) and that 'environmental protection shall constitute an integral part of the development process'.[160] In her 1994 report, Ksentini described the 'intrinsic link that exists between the preservation of the environment, development and the promotion of human rights'.[161] The various Commission resolutions between 1994–96 on environmental human rights are marked by a tension between an emphasis on socio-economic development and on environmental protection.[162] Thereafter, the Commission's interest in environmental human rights waned. In 1995 the Expert Group on Identification of Principles of International Law for Sustainable Development consolidated this link between environmental human rights and sustainable development, declaring that 'the right to a healthy environment provides a focus to guide the integration of environment and development' and moreover that '[d]evelopment is sustainable where it advances or realizes the right to a healthy environment'.[163] When the Commission re-engaged with environmental human rights, around the time of the 2002 World Summit on Sustainable Development (WSSD), the title of the draft resolutions added five words to now read, 'Human rights and the environment as part of sustainable development', a 'small but highly symbolic shift' as a concession to large developing states.[164] Although the Johannesburg Declaration on Sustainable Development did not include any reference to rights,[165] in 2005 the

[158] Grabham and Beynon-Jones (n 136) 19.
[159] See eg UNHRC Res 16/11 (12 April 2011) UN Doc A/HRC/RES/16/11.
[160] Vienna Declaration and Programme of Action (1993), principle 11; UNGA (n 110) principles 3 & 4.
[161] UNCHR (n 86) para 238.
[162] Boyd, Knox and Limon (n 71) 12.
[163] 'Report of the Expert Group Meeting on Identification of Principles of International Law for Sustainable Development', Geneva, Switzerland, 26–28 September 1995, para 31.
[164] Boyd, Knox and Limon (n 71) 13.
[165] UN, 'Report of the World Summit on Sustainable Development: Johannesburg, South Africa, 26 August–4 September 2002' UN Doc A/CONF.199/20.

Secretary-General prepared a report on 'human rights and the environment as part of sustainable development' documenting the growing recognition of the connection of human rights and the environment since the WSSD.[166] When after a further pause, the Commission again engaged with the issue of environmental rights in 2011, Resolution 16/11 recalled relevant principles of sustainable development and noted in a preambular paragraph that 'sustainable development and the protection of the environment can contribute to human well-being and the enjoyment of human rights'.[167] The Framework Principles also articulate a close relationship between environmental rights and sustainable development, stating in its opening paragraph that 'Environmental harm interferes with the enjoyment of human rights, and the exercise of human rights helps to protect the environment and to promote sustainable development.'[168] It also asserts that '[s]tates should respect, protect and fulfil human rights in the actions they take to address environmental challenges and pursue sustainable development'.[169] Thus, although the push by some states to 'place the mutually dependent goals of promoting human rights and protecting the environment within the wider framework of (sustainable) development'[170] has been strongly resisted by other states, a close association has arisen between environmental human rights and the process of sustainable development. This has been reenforced by greater attention to the social pillar of sustainable development: sustainable development is widely understood, requiring interconnections between economic development, environmental protection and human rights,[171] especially given how the 'social pillar' of sustainable development intersects with human rights.[172]

The close intertwining of sustainable development and environmental human rights imposes a specific temporality on environmental human rights, namely a form of linearity, which 'can be violently excluding of those who do not or cannot fit within the historico-development project'.[173] The language and framework of development, even when accompanied by the adjective 'sustainable', brings with it certain ways of understanding, invoking and imagining time and temporality.[174] As Uma Kothari writes, 'because development is embodied in notions of modernity and progress, the idea that particular linear changes take place in linear time is reproduced'.[175] Development discourse constructs

[166] UNCHR, 'Human rights and the environment as part of sustainable development' (19 January 2005) UN Doc E/CN.4/2005/96.

[167] UNHRC Res 16/11 (12 April 2011) UN Doc A/HRC/RES/16/11.

[168] UNHRSP (n 66) para 1.

[169] ibid principle 16.

[170] Boyd, Knox and Limon (n 71) 13.

[171] S Giorgetta, 'The Right to a Healthy Environment, Human Rights and Sustainable Development' (2002) 2 *International Environmental Agreements* 171, 174.

[172] Atapattu, Gonzalez and Seck (n 152) 4.

[173] Grabham and Beynon-Jones (n 136) 4.

[174] U Kothari, 'History, Time and Temporality in Development Discourse' in CA Bayly et al (eds), *History, Historians and Development Policy: A Necessary Dialogue* (Manchester University Press, 2011) 65.

[175] ibid 66.

economic hierarchies and geographical distinctions between the 'developed' and the 'underdeveloped' world, but also produces a temporal division, where the 'underdeveloped' is imagined as a backward and traditional past while the 'developed' world is imagined 'the (global) future'.[176] Because development implies both a trajectory of change from the latter to the former, and a normative vision of such an outcome, it involves 'projections of where we are, where we should be going, and how we move from one set of circumstances to another are predetermined in ways that foreclose the future'.[177]

The linear temporal ontology of environmental human rights in their more 'regulatory' mode thus reproduces violent hierarchies, exclusions and marginalisations, whilst also positing an implausible vision of how an ecologically just future can be reached. Problematically, it assumes that a linear progression from the present, and the continuation of current models of development and economic growth can lead to a sustainable future, when it is precisely these underlying drivers of ecological destruction that require radical contestation. Sustainable development has long been critiqued as an 'oxymoron'[178] that fails to resolve the inherent contradictions between ecological limits and 'capitalist economy [that] requires systematic environmental degradation and toxic pollution to achieve sustained economic growth and allocative efficiency'.[179] These tensions between limits and growth are even more pronounced in more recent human rights texts that advocate for a 'growth model of economic development as the vehicle for securing environmental human rights' and promote 'green growth'.[180] A report prepared for the 2012 Rio +20 Summit promoted the integration of human rights and environmental action as key to developing a 'green economy',[181] even though scholars have described 'green growth' as a 'misguided objective'[182] and environmental justice advocates have critiqued the concept of the 'green economy' as promoting the further commodification, marketisation and financialisation of the environment and the conceptual transformation of the 'environment' into 'natural capital' and 'ecosystem services'.[183]

[176] ibid 68.

[177] ibid.

[178] W Sachs, 'Sustainable Development and the Crisis of Nature: On the Political Anatomy of an Oxymoron' in M Hajer and F Fischer (eds), *Living with Nature: Environmental Politics as Cultural Discourse* (Oxford University Press, 1999).

[179] J Hancock, *Environmental Human Rights: Power, Ethics and Law* (Routledge, 2019).

[180] Burdon (n 105) 76.

[181] Human Rights and the Environment – Rio+20: Joint Report OHCHR and UNEP (Office of the High Commission of Human Rights and United Nations Environment Programme, 2012), see Part II.

[182] J Hickel and G Kallis, 'Is Green Growth Possible?' (2020) 25 *New Political Economy* 469.

[183] D Brockington, 'A Radically Conservative Vision? The Challenge of UNEP's Towards a Green Economy' (2012) 43 *Development and Change* 409; N Bullard and T Müller, 'Beyond the "Green Economy": System Change, Not Climate Change?' (2012) 55 *Development* 54; J Boehnert, 'The Green Economy: Reconceptualizing the Natural Commons as Natural Capital' (2016) 10 *Environmental Communication* 395.

B. Environmental Human Rights, Contingent Futures and Scenario Planning

In addition to their work in constructing and stabilising a sense of a linear, predictable, progressive future, environmental human rights also promise, and help construct a relationship to, a much more transformative vision of 'alternative "environmental" futures' and a '"not yet" beyond the "now"'.[184] In this sense they help create a 'conception of the future that is unknown, non-linear and more open to embrace of the new',[185] and enact an optimism about an 'unknown future that does not follow progressively from the past' and of 'the social as an endless becoming open to transformation'.[186] Yet, there is something dangerously seductive about such promises of contingent, open futures enabled by rights when the stark ecological reality is that historical actions have already constrained future possibilities. This section therefore suggests that this open future promised by environmental rights is marked by both 'false contingency' and 'false necessity':[187] the vision of an ecologically just future ignores the existing limits, pressures and tendencies that shape future ecological possibilities (described above), while simultaneously treating as self-evident that human rights are the primary, indispensable and necessary tool for creating an ecologically just future. It is a vision marked by the problem of 'false contingency' because it does not account for the structural factors that determine the range of future possibilities.[188] However, this vision also succumbs to the problem of 'false necessity' by treating human rights as an unavoidable, indispensable and self-evident tool for creating such an ecologically just future. Although the utopian, ideational aspect of environmental human rights produces a sense of the potentiality of alternative worlds, this openness is constantly foreclosed by the more 'regulatory' dimensions of rights. As Ben Golder has shown, the imagined potentiality of rights and the continued faith that they might be able to 'animate vibrant and dissent political projects' nonetheless is always constrained by the 'exclusions and circumscriptions of the human rights form, particularly as it functions in the context of a global capitalist economy'.[189] Human rights frameworks have at best been powerless to contest, and at worst complicit in the rise of neoliberalism, and are thus an inadequate tool to mount a structural critique of neoliberal capitalism.[190] Paralleling how rights have been unable to

[184] Grear and Kotzé (n 6) 2.
[185] McNeilly (n 98) 822.
[186] ibid 833–34.
[187] S Marks, 'False Contingency' (2009) 62 *Current Legal Problems* 1.
[188] ibid.
[189] B Golder, 'Beyond Redemption? Problematising the Critique of Human Rights in Contemporary International Legal Thought' (2014) 2 *London Review of International Law* 77, 96 emphasis in original.
[190] S Moyn, 'A Powerless Companion: Human Rights in the Age of Neoliberalism' (2014) 77 *Law and Contemporary Problems* 147; J Whyte, 'Powerless Companions or Fellow Travellers?: Human Rights and the Neoliberal Assault on Post-Colonial Economic Justice' (2018) 2 *Radical Philosophy* 13. See also PD Burdon 'Environmental protection and the limits of rights talk' (*Right Now*, 10 August 2012) rightnow.org.au/opinion-3/environmental-protection-and-the-limits-of-rights-talk/.

impose a 'ceiling' on economic inequality, in the environmental context they have been unable to place structural limits on how the 'capitalist economy requires systematic environmental degradation and toxic pollution to achieve sustained economic growth and allocative efficiency'.[191] Peter Burdon has therefore raised serious concerns that a human rights model cannot address the 'root causes'[192] of environmental exploitation because rights frameworks are unavoidably anthropocentric, individualistic and involve 'acceptance of the political and economic system of liberal democratic capitalism'.[193] He thus argues that a form of rights orientated towards the protection of a market-based individual is inadequate to contest the rapturous capitalist growth model that is driving environmental destruction.[194] While Burdon sees the use of human rights arguments by the marginalised as 'strategically necessary' in certain contexts, he cautions that environmental human rights are not a 'transformational discourse' but rather 'represent a liberal reformist project that avoids confrontation with the underlying negative hierarchies perpetuating environmental exploitation'.[195] Therefore, he finds that the ideational promise that animates environmental human rights that they can prefigure an open, unknown future, is nonetheless always constrained, given that rights offer only a 'liberal democratic form of utopianism that is predicted on the abandonment of alternative political formations and the vision of human emancipation they contain'.[196] Even as environmental human rights create a sense of an open contingent future, they simultaneously reimpose limits and constraints.

In order to better illuminate the problems with this temporal ontology, I suggest that the promise of an open, contingent future that animates environmental human rights creates a relationship to the future that is analogical to that produced by the methodology of scenario planning, a future technology that has become ubiquitous in strategic planning spaces, and especially in the context of strategic natural resources and environmental planning.[197] This section draws out some parallels between the temporal work done by environmental human rights in positing open contingent futures and the work done by 'scenario planning' as a technology and methodology, in that the temporality of both

[191] Hancock (n 179).

[192] S Marks, 'Human Rights and Root Causes' (2011) 74 *The Modern Law Review* 57; see also Burdon (nn 105 and 190).

[193] Burdon (n 105) 72.

[194] Burdon (n 190).

[195] Burdon (n 105) 72–73.

[196] ibid 72. See also P O'Connell (in this volume) arguing that 'past, present and future are not infinitely open, but, rather, constrained by concrete regulative tendencies that are characteristic of the capitalist mode of production'.

[197] See generally M Cooper, 'Turbulent Worlds: Financial Markets and Environmental Crisis' (2010) 27 *Theory, Culture and Society* 167; in climate change governance L Rickards and others, 'Opening and Closing the Future: Climate Change, Adaptation, and Scenario Planning' (2014) 32 *Environment and Planning C: Government and Policy* 587; and by oil companies J Andersson, 'Ghost in a Shell: The Scenario Tool and the World Making of Royal Dutch Shell' (2020) 94 *Business History Review* 729.

is characterised by a 'double movement of promised freedom and (sometimes not so) subtle re-inscription'.[198] The analysis below provides an examination of 'scenario planning' as a future technology, its history and the way it cultivates a specific relationship with the future, to show that it produces a temporality that 'work[s] in the service of dominant interests by expending our horizon into a set of imaginary possibilities that, though their unstated assumptions and omissions, simultaneously limits how we think about present and future possibilities'.[199]

Scenario planning is a 'forecasting technique which attempts to divine not this or that aspect of the future but the multiple future worlds attendant on alternative actions in the present'.[200] The techniques of scenario planning have come to inform strategic planning in a number of domains including military, corporate, political and environmental planning, making it 'perhaps the most ubiquitous and most consequential of epistemologies in contemporary politics'.[201] This technique arose out of concerns within the field of futurology about how to engage with problems of non-linearity, and questions of complexity of interlocking systems, the impact of feedback loops and unintended consequences of specific actions.[202] Unlike technologies of prediction, which forecast probable future outcomes based on projections or extrapolations of the past, scenario planning sets out multiple 'plausible alternatives views about how the future may develop'[203] which are all understood as 'equally potential and … nonexclusive'.[204] It thus departs from the deterministic approach of 'classical' forecasting models that assume 'structural stability'[205] and rather, 'develops a semantics of counterfactual propositions, opening onto a pluriverse of event-contingent worlds'.[206] Rather than projecting through deterministic and quantitative methods a future that is imagined as singular and certain, based on past developments, it posits in narrative form a plurality of possible futures that could be actively and creatively brought about within dynamic, evolving social structures and relationships.[207] The methodology of scenario planning is not concerned with questions of risk, which remain within the realm of the calculable, but rather the 'radical uncertainty of unknowable contingencies' and how to foster decision-making under such conditions.[208] Scenarios are

[198] S Orpana, 'Freedom 2044? The Temporality of Financialization and Scenario Planning in Looper' in P Huebener (ed), *Time, Globalization and Human Experience: Interdisciplinary Explorations* (Routledge, 2017) 72.
[199] ibid 83.
[200] Cooper (n 197) 170.
[201] ibid 171.
[202] Andersson (n 148) 1415.
[203] National Intelligence Council cited in Cooper (n 197) 173.
[204] RJ Williams, 'World Futures' (2016) 42 *Critical Inquiry* 473, 473.
[205] Ml Godet, 'From Forecasting to "La Prospective" A New Way of Looking at Futures' (1982) 1 *Journal of Forecasting* 293, 294.
[206] Cooper (n 197) 173.
[207] Godet (n 205) 298; Williams (n 204) 473.
[208] Cooper (n 197) 173.

not focused on the probable, but rather refer to the contingently possible: as such they 'belong to the ontology of possible worlds and to the psychology and epistemology of counterfactuals and thought experiments'[209] and rely on the 'grammatical constructions of the conditional or the subjective'.[210] However, although the methodology of scenario planning is ostensibly based on a recognition that '[s]tructual changes, resistance and discontinuities are part of the future' and an ideological commitment to the plural futures and 'freedom for human action',[211] and thus on a surface level aligns with a radical – and potentially disruptive – embrace of the new, scholars have suggested that this future methodology has in practice 'functioned as a pluralistic layover on the way to a metaphysical, corporate singularity' of global capitalism.[212] Simon Orpana argues that although multiple futures are envisioned in scenario planning, such scenarios paradoxically have the effect of 'narrowing visions of what is possible', because the multiplicity of futures envisioned all 'presuppose[e] certain, historically contingent facts (like the persistence of capitalism) as constant across all the possible worlds under consideration'.[213]

The power of scenario planning lies in the way the practice of envisioning different futures actually operates as a means of 'making futures present … based on acts of creative fabulation'.[214] Therefore, these methods of depicting the future are more than simply narratives but rather 'become means of world intervention' and 'tools for the actual shaping of future worlds and economic orders'.[215] As Simon Orpana's analysis shows, the pre-emptive temporality of scenario planning does not simply try and predict the future, but in fact 'actually steers toward or away from certain outcomes, creating the preconditions for future events under the guise of merely trying to anticipate them'.[216] These narrative techniques can endow possible futures with a real materiality that guides actions in the present, given that 'intense expectations mobilises resources, produces incentives, creates chains of obligations, silences (or at least sidelines) dissenting voices, justifies certain actions in preference of others and produces new networks'.[217] Additionally, the projection of certain future possibilities helps to cultivate specific modes of conducting oneself in relation to the future[218]

[209] P Dragos Aligica, 'The Challenge of the Future and the Institutionalization of Interdisciplinarity: Notes on Herman Kahn's Legacy' (2004) 36 *Futures* 67, 76.

[210] Cooper (n 197) 174.

[211] Godet (n 205) 296.

[212] Williams (n 204) 541.

[213] Orpana (n 198) 80.

[214] B Anderson, 'Preemption, Precaution, Preparedness: Anticipatory Action and Future Geographies' (2010) 34 *Progress in Human Geography* 777, 784.

[215] J Andersson, 'The Future of the Western World: The OECD and the Interfutures Project' (2019) 14 *Journal of Global History* 126, 129.

[216] Orpana (n 198) 80.

[217] Adam (n 138) 7.

[218] S O'Brien, '"We Thought the World Was Makeable": Scenario Planning and Postcolonial Fiction' (2016) 13 *Globalizations* 329, 333.

by shaping thinking and responses about the future in the present.[219] Given the real power such visions of the future have, significant material consequences arise from the fact that in practice the exercise invariably remains constrained by the duel problems of false necessity and false contingency: that is treating certain things that are actually contingent as fixed, while also treating things that are fixed as contingent. In particular, postcolonial critics have drawn attention to how the 'discourse of scenario planning elides history – specifically the intertwined processes of colonialism and capitalism'[220] giving future speculations a 'ludicrous quality' as they too often 'fail to take account of the historical violence that undergirds the present and, by extension, the place from which the speculation unfolds'.[221] Yet, the converse is also a problem. In the environmental context, scenario approaches too often underemphasise still existing political and structural possibilities for climate mitigation and instead focus on 'adapting as individual migrants to increasingly unadapted socioecological conditions' rather than 'the possibility of changing these very conditions'.[222]

The history of the adoption of scenario planning illuminates how this process of envisioning multiple, open and contingent futures remains implicitly constrained by these dual dynamics of false contingency and false necessity, and how these structural biases have served particular interests and agendas. The popularity of scenario planning grew in parallel with the 'declining credibility of long-term planning and prediction over the course of the twentieth century'[223] especially as neoliberal ideologies argued that the complexity of the social world made it impossible to 'acquire the full knowledge which would make mastery of events possible'.[224] Scenario planning was seen to have a number of benefits over traditional planning approaches. First, it drew attention to a larger range of possibilities that need to be considered in any strategic process,[225] given its purpose was precisely to 'stimulate and stretch the imagination'.[226] It also sought to overcome the biases that inform future modelling, and the tendency to ignore, or fail to even comprehend, potential future realities because they do not align with preconceived ideas or visions[227] and to provide a more holistic and interdisciplinary analysis than the more fragmented approach adopted in forecasting that tended to ignore interdependencies within a social system.[228] Most critically,

[219] S Lockie, 'Climate, Scenario-Building and Governance: Comprehending the Temporalities of Social-Ecological Change' in *The Routledge International Handbook of Social and Environmental Change* (Routledge, 2014) 95, 102.

[220] O'Brien (n 218) 331.

[221] ibid.

[222] R Felli and N Castree, 'Neoliberalising Adaptation to Environmental Change: Foresight or Foreclosure?' (2012) 44 *Environment and Planning* A 1, 4.

[223] Johns (n 3) 48.

[224] F Hayek, 'The Pretence of Knowledge', Lecture to the memory of Alfred Nobel, 11 December 1974; see also J Whyte, 'Calculation and Conflict' (2020) 119 *South Atlantic Quarterly* 31.

[225] Aligica (n 209) 76.

[226] ibid 73.

[227] Godet (n 205) 294–95.

[228] ibid 294.

however, it was a technology and methodology that provided a response to the growing sense that both the present and future were increasingly unfamiliar and rapidly changing.[229] Initially these new methods and methodologies arose in the context of Cold War defence planning. The RAND Corporation pioneered the development of the Delphi technique and the 'systems analysis' approach and Herman Kahn, who is widely recognised as the 'father' of scenario planning, was based first at the RAND Corporation before founding the conservative thinktank the Hudson Institute.[230] Although initially intended as a tool for public policy making, the scenario planning methodology was quickly picked up by the business community: in the wake of the oil crisis in the early 1970s 'the number of "adopters" of scenario planning almost doubled'[231] with a further 'surge of adoption' in the late 1970s in response to the more unpredictable political, economic and social environment that resulted from the decade's interlocking monetary, economic and energy crises.[232] Scenario planning was seen as a methodology particularly adapted to dealing with decision-making in the context of uncertainty, where the balance of power and 'rules of the game' were in flux,[233] and for conditions of crisis, because it allowed decision-makers to 'examin[e] possibilities which seem relatively unlikely but which would have very desirable – or catastrophic – consequences if they occurred' to not just 'plan for that which is more or less predictable' but also to be able to 'hedge against that which is uncertain, both to be able to exploit favorable events and to guard against the consequences of unfavorable ones'.[234] By the early 1980s, half of the US Fortune 1,000 industrial firms had incorporated scenario planning in their corporate strategies, and its popularity continued to grow in the 1990s, arguably because of growing turbulence and volatility in the business environment, and the 'rise of uncertainties, particularly in the realm of finance, environment, and security'.[235]

Unsurprisingly, therefore, the history and popularisation of scenario planning is intertwined with environmental questions, especially those of catastrophic risks as well as resource constraints and ecological limits. In particular it provided a critical tool for oil corporations that responded to their 'perceived need … to think in forward-orientated ways in order to protect their interests in the shakeup of global capitalism that occurred [between 1967 to 1976]'.[236] Resource corporations faced a duel threat during this period, with both Third

[229] Aligica (n 209) 76.

[230] R Bradfield et al, 'The Origins and Evolution of Scenario Techniques in Long Range Business Planning' (2005) 37 *Futures* 795, 798.

[231] ibid 803.

[232] ibid.

[233] Godet (n 205) 296.

[234] H Kahn, 'The alternative world futures approach' in F Tugwell (ed), *Search for Alternatives: Public Policy and the Study of the Future* (Witrop Publishers, 1973) cited in Aligica (n 209) 68.

[235] O'Brien (n 218) 332.

[236] Andersson (n 197) 729.

World claims to resource sovereignty articulated as part of demands for a New International Economic Order[237] and projections about ecological constraints – most famously in the 1972 Club of Rome Limits to Growth report[238] – both potentially threatening to impose limits on corporate extraction.[239] Arguably a big factor driving the take up of scenario planning during this period by Dutch Royal Shell – who is widely seen as the 'most celebrated corporate exponent of scenarios'[240] – was that 'their narrative structure allows scenarios to project images of a future beyond limits'.[241] Due to the declining utility of conventional forecasting for the oil industry, Shell, in 1969, initiated their 'Year 2000' project, which identified and utilised 'first generation scenarios' as part of their 1985 'Horizon Planning' exercise. In a remarkably precedent move, Shell formally adopted scenario planning as an ongoing strategy for the company in 1972–73 and thereby was able to identify a shortage of oil and spike in oil prices, prior to the 1973 oil crisis. Shell has continued to develop and update their scenarios. In 2018 Shell released its new 'Sky' scenario showing how the Paris Agreement goal to 'hol[d] the increase in the average global temperature to well below 2°C above pre-industrial levels'[242] could be achieved. In contrast to other 2°C models, Shell's scenario assumes a large increase in global energy demand and a future of continued 'fossil-fuelled development' where 'the push for economic and social development is coupled with the exploitation of abundant fossil fuel resources and the adoption of resource and energy intensive lifestyles around the world'.[243] While their scenario also assumes rapid scale-up of solar power, and increases in wind, bioenergy and nuclear power and the widespread adoption of a carbon price, key to achieving its climate targets is a heavy reliance on carbon capture and storage technologies, particularly bioenergy with carbon capture and storage (BECCS). BECCS have been described as a 'speculative technology' or 'technological imaginary'[244] or even 'climate unicorns'[245] as they exist predominately in the minds of modellers, and are unlikely to be feasible

[237] M Bedjaoui, *Towards a New International Economic Order* (United Nations Educational, Scientific and Cultural Organization, 1979); N Gilman, 'The New International Economic Order: A Reintroduction' (2015) 6 *Humanity: An International Journal of Human Rights, Humanitarianism, and Development* 1.

[238] Meadows et al (n 43).

[239] Andersson (n 197) 733.

[240] Bradfield et al (n 230) 800; for a detailed discussion see Andersson (n 197).

[241] Andersson (n 197) 733–34.

[242] Paris Agreement (n 113) art 2.1(a).

[243] S Evans, 'In depth: Is Shell's new climate scenario as 'radial' as it says?' (*Renew Economy*, 4 April 2018) reneweconomy.com.au/depth-shells-new-climate-scenario-radical-says-19102/.

[244] M Workman et al, 'Decision Making in Contexts of Deep Uncertainty-An Alternative Approach for Long-Term Climate Policy' (2020) 103 *Environmental Science & Policy* 77, 78.

[245] M McGrath, 'Caution urged over use of "carbon unicorns" to limit warming' *BBC News* (5 October 2018) www.bbc.com/news/science-environment-45742191; see also W Carton, 'Carbon Unicorns and Fossil Futures. Whose Emission Reduction Pathway Is the IPCC Performing?' in JP Sapinski, HJ Buck and A Malm (eds), *Has It Come to This?: The Promises and Perils of Geoengineering on the Brink* (Rutgers University Press, 2020).

at the scale envisioned by Shell's scenario. Shell's 'Sky scenario' was therefore strongly criticised for 'the risks of relying on what remains a relatively untested range of technologies and approaches – and the general moral hazard of assuming negative emissions will be possible'.[246] Shell's 2021 update of their scenario, which includes for the first time a scenario based on limiting warming to 1.5°C, remains 'strongly insistent on the need for continued extraction and burning of oil and gas'.[247] Despite scenario planning's focus on contingent, open futures, Ketan Joshi highlights how any changes to their core business is fundamentally unimaginable for Shell, even as their scenario treats the massive scale-up of unproven and untested speculative technologies for carbon removal and tree planting at a 'ludicrous scale' as 'required'.[248] He writes:

> This is where the imagination of Shell's modellers hits a brick wall: a reduction in the operation of their business within the next few decades is essentially unthinkable, and unmodeled. There is plenty of optimism about renewables, energy efficiency and electric vehicles, but there is also optimism about the continuation of their core business, to be cancelled out – eventually – through the operation of carbon removal.[249]

Thus, Shell's scenario is marked by both 'false necessity' by treating the continued extraction of fossil fuels as inevitable rather than mutable, contestable and changeable as well as 'false contingency' in that it treats a seductively easy mitigation method that remains untested and implausible as inevitable. Nonetheless, despite these problems, the scenario does real work to protect business interests of Shell – and other fossil fuel companies – in the present.

What is arguably even more concerning is that Shell is 'far from alone' in developing scenarios that rely on negative emissions technology in order to meet Paris Agreement targets.[250] Scenario planning has become a key tool in climate policy, where scenarios are seen as a 'tangible reference point' that 'bring[s] the future into the present' and thereby enables policymakers to 'estimate the impacts of expected climate change on people and ecosystems [and] also to debate responsibilities and mitigation measures'.[251] While such climate models were originally seen as a 'tool to explore hypotheticals' and envision certain future possibilities, they have since the IPCC Fifth Assessment Report increasingly been treated as prescriptive rather than simply descriptive.[252] Alarmingly, the overwhelming majority of scientific scenarios that limit warming to 2°C similarly rely on the large-scale use of BECCS 'to compensate for an overshoot

[246] Evans (n 243).
[247] K Joshi, 'Shell still has a long way to go before it's truly on board with climate action' (*Renew Economy*, 10 February 2021) reneweconomy.com.au/shell-still-has-a-long-way-to-go-before-its-truly-on-board-with-climate-action/.
[248] ibid.
[249] ibid.
[250] Evans (n 243).
[251] Lockie (n 219).
[252] Workman et al (n 244) 81.

of atmospheric CO_2 budgets'.[253] Wim Carson has shown that the introduction of such negative emission technologies into these models was seen as an 'economic necessity' by modellers due to hegemonic assumptions about the imperative of cost-optimisation. Such assumptions about cost-optimisation, he shows, have operated to close down political debate about climate futures and thereby 'enacts inertia as some kind of natural law, rather than a condition that is maintained and reproduced through historically-specific socio-economic structures and therefore responsible to political choice'.[254] He thus argues that it is 'time to start refusing to perform, through seemingly innocuous models, that kind of gradualism that has long-ago proven incapable of taking us out of this mess'.[255]

Building ecologically just futures requires a fundamental change in our politics and our sense of what is possible. Yet both scenario planning and environmental human rights produce a temporal ontology that performs and prefigures contingent futures that nonetheless remain constrained and limited by the very assumptions and structural economic, political and social relations that are the root causes of the current crisis. While environmental human rights continue to play a critical role in supporting ecological struggles, their temporal ontology is one that is inadequate, and arguably counterproductive, for actually building and materialising more ecologically just futures.

VI. ON UNCERTAIN FUTURES AND PLURAL TEMPORALITIES

In concluding, I want to return to the question of the possibilities that open up if we both eschew the utopianism of rights and acknowledge the stark ecological realities that will shape, to some degree, planetary futures. Such a stance does not represent defeatism, but can foster hopeful, concrete politics of building a more just and liveable world. Acknowledging that 'many worlds are closed to us, many futures are not in the becoming – too much damage has been done, too much lost, too many lifeways extinct or already living ghosts'[256] does not invite fatalism: indeed it only heightens the importance and stakes of struggles for an environment that is safer, cleaner, healthier, more sustainable. As ecologist Lesley Hughes says, 'The new mantra is that every fraction of a degree, every year and every choice matters'.[257] Recognising that the current challenge is building just futures on an already damaged planet forces us to grapple with 'the problem of

[253] Workman et al (n 244).
[254] Carton (n 245).
[255] ibid.
[256] N Osborne, 'For Still Possible Cities: A Politics of Failure for the Politically Depressed' (2019) 50 *Australian Geographer* 145, 148.
[257] G Readfearn and A Morton, '"Every choice matters": can we cling to hope of avoiding 1.5C heating?' *The Guardian* (3 April 2021) www.theguardian.com/environment/2021/apr/03/every-choice-matters-can-we-cling-to-hope-of-avoiding-15c-heating.

living despite economic and ecological ruination'[258] and to undertake the hard, and often slow, work of building 'still-possible worlds'.[259] This calls not for 'grandiose, superhero feats of saving' but rather a commitment to 'still possible futures' that advance more relational and environmentally conscious ways of living and being together and 'the work of imagining them, prefiguring them, breathing and singing life into them' as a praxis of care, grounded in place.[260]

Despite the utopian, impossibility of their promise, environmental rights have a concrete, material value in making it possible to name as a violation actions by states (and sometimes corporations) that make our environment less safe, less clean, less healthy and less sustainable. Indeed, although the Framework Principles are generally understood as laying the groundwork for the subsequent recognition of environmental rights, what they actually do is set the main human rights obligations relating to the environment and 'provide integrated and detailed guidance for the practical implementation of these obligations'.[261] In contrast to other rights, where lofty pronouncements of rights preceded subsequent debates about the obligations they give rise to, the process of formulating clear obligations prior to the recognition of a right appeared somewhat back-to-front. Yet, this focus on obligations is potentially even more valuable than the subsequent articulation of a right to a safe, clean, healthy and sustainable environment. Conceptually, the obligations that bind us to community and to place are normatively prior to – and have priority over – the articulations of rights. Although 'any talk of bonds, duties, obedience and obligations has largely lost its purchase on our collective legal and political imaginaries', Daniel Matthews proposes that responding to complex ecological entanglements calls for a 'renewed focus on the discrete labours of obligation as a primordial form of binding beings [which] can help re-order the old hierarchies that structure modernity's worldview'.[262] The obligations entailed with 'being-in-community' with lively and diverse human and non-human actants who unfold in a complex and dynamic set of relations and the forms of reciprocity and solidarity this demands, go beyond the state-centric obligations articulated in the Framework Principles.[263] However, a deeper reorientation to a register of 'obligations' could direct attention to the 'sensory and affective realities of associative life and the complex normative claims that it makes on us' and to 'the multiplicity of forces that ensure the habitability of place and community'.[264]

[258] A Lowenhaupt Tsing, *The Mushroom at the End of the World: On the Possibility of Life in Capitalist Ruins* (Princeton University Press, 2015) 19.

[259] Osborne (n 256) 148.

[260] ibid.

[261] UNHRC (n 65) annex, para 2.

[262] D Matthews, 'Law and Aesthetics in the Anthropocene: From the Rights of Nature to the Aesthesis of Obligations' [2019] *Law, Culture and the Humanities* 1743872119871830; see also K Birrell and J Dehm, 'International Law and the Humanities in the Anthropocene' in S Chalmers and S Pahuja (eds), *Routledge Handbook of International Law and the Humanities* (Routledge, 2021) 419–20.

[263] Matthews (n 262) 16.

[264] ibid.

Such a reorientation calls for attention to human and non-human needs, entailing attunement, sensitivity and a broader 'enlivening of the senses'.[265] In relation to the temporal questions that have been the focus of this chapter, it calls for greater attention to the plural temporalities of our 'inherently multi-temporal' world.[266] Perhaps as Anna Tsing suggests, 'what is needed to appreciate the multiple temporal rhythms and trajectories of the assemblage' is the sort of 'noticing' necessary to appropriate 'polyphonic' music where autonomous melodies intertwine.[267] Anna Grear similarly calls for openness to a 'multiplicity of overlapping, porously open spatio-temporalities' and the embrace of the 'materiality and the affective energies of multiple spatio-temporalities' in order to foster a 'spatial and temporal web of interspecies dependencies'.[268] Indeed, she suggest that such 'respect for the variegated spatio-temporalities is fundamental to countering the violent chrono-politics of neoliberal capitalism'.[269] The acknowledgment of temporal plurality is critical but insufficient. Given the close relationship between law and power, there is also a need to recognise the 'contrasts, oppositions, conflicts, and struggles involved in structuring, regulating, and synchronizing time'[270] and to find ways of 'thinking politically temporal diversities'.[271] In particular, in order to embrace and enact an openness to multiple temporalities it is necessary to disrupt and resist both the tendency of the world market to flatten 'hetrerochrony' by synchronising temporalities and the tendency of law to 'aspir[e] to assimilate and absorb other temporalities'.[272] Innovative work in human ecology is demonstrating how responding to and adapting to climate requires also a reconceptualisation of the notion of time as 'unique, flexible and relational' in order to better anticipate climate variation and synchronise activities with the ecological context.[273] The notion of an 'ecological calendar' is a 'dynamic, experimental framework' to give meaning to time in situated contexts that is embedded in the relationship of people and ecosystems.[274] Given that environmental human rights and their 'traditional role, nature, objectives and construction'[275] need to be radically rethought in the

[265] ibid.
[266] Jordheim and Wigen (n 13) 426.
[267] Tsing (n 258) 23–4.
[268] Grear (n 12) 310–12.
[269] ibid 310.
[270] H Jordheim, 'Introduction: Multiple Times and the Work of Synchronization' (2014) 53 *History and Theory* 498, 51.
[271] Tomba (n 15) xiii.
[272] R Mawani, 'Law as Temporality: Colonial Politics and Indian Settlers' (2014) 4 *UC Irvine L. Rev.* 65, 71.
[273] K-AS Kassam et al, 'Anticipating Climatic Variability: The Potential of Ecological Calendars' (2018) 46 *Human Ecology* 249, 250.
[274] ibid.
[275] LJ Kotzé, 'Human Rights and the Environment in the Anthropocene' (2014) 1 *The Anthropocene Review* 252, 254.

Anthropocene, such models of time as situated, relational and embedded, might indeed prove to be an inspiration for new types of legal frameworks 'in which the human is entangled and thrown in the midst of a lively materiality – rather than assumed to be the masterful, knowing centre, or the pivot around which everything else turns'.[276]

[276] A Grear, 'It's wrongheaded to protect nature with human-style rights' (*Aeon*, 19 March 2019) aeon.co/ideas/its-wrongheaded-to-protect-nature-with-human-style-rights.

3

The Temporal Trap of Human Rights

STEPHEN M YOUNG

I. INTRODUCTION

THIS CHAPTER ARGUES that international human rights discourse produces a temporal trap. The temporal traps provide the appearance that human rights are temporally flexible and can reflect subjects' own temporalities, but constructs subjects in a permanent contest for the present. I begin from the position that legal jurisdiction is a spoken power to deliver a judgment or an authority, as well as a territorial and spatial delineation.[1] Where legal jurisdictions constitute particular spaces (legal territories), jurisdictions also constitute the time and temporalities of its subjects – even if, and especially when, subjects invoke a law of that jurisdiction to contest those spaces, times, temporalities and subject-formation. When two jurisdictions clash or conflict, for example, when there are struggles over territory or who has authority over that territory or space, it is possible to appreciate and evaluate the collision of legal temporalities.[2] This chapter investigates temporalities arising from jurisdictional conflicts between tribal peoples',[3] state's, and international human rights.[4] Examining clashes between these types of legal jurisdictions reveals that international human rights produce a temporal trap – a permanent contest for the present.

[1] S Dorsett and S McVeigh, *Jurisdiction* (Routledge, 2012) 4–5.

[2] K Knop and A Riles 'Space, Time, and Historical Injustice: A Feminist Conflict-of-Laws Approach to the "Comfort Women" Agreement' (2017) 102 *Cornell Law Review* 853, 893–96; Dorsett and McVeigh (n 1) ch 6.

[3] This chapter uses the term 'Indigenous peoples' to signify a subjectivity that is related to international legal discourse and distinguish it from 'tribal' or 'tribal peoples' own legalities. See S Young, *Indigenous Peoples, Consent and Rights: Troubling Subjects* (Routledge, 2020) 9–10.

[4] CJ Winter, 'Does Time Colonise Intergenerational Environmental Justice Theory?' (2019) 29 *Environmental Politics* 278; JB Richland, 'Jurisdictions of Significance: Narrating Time-Space in a Hopi-US Tribal Consultation' (2018) 45 *American Ethnologist* 268, 274–78; T Love and E Tilley, 'Temporal Discourse and the News Media Representation of Indigenous–Non-Indigenous

To make this argument, I draw from critical theorists and scholars to consider human rights temporalities through a performative approach to legality. A central claim made by theorists of performativity is that all utterances and performatives have re-citational slippage and, hence, unknown consequences.[5] Despite unknown consequences arising, not everything is radically contestable or entirely inexplicable because 'the past shapes the possibilities of the present'.[6] To draw attention to this 'shaping', the performative approach I employ highlights the effects of disciplinary powers.[7] Discipline or disciplinary power helps specify the practices that make and produce particularly modern subjects,[8] those who are structured and associated with the temporalities of the modern state.[9] It also helps specify the practices of scholars, advocates, rights-claimants, and others that make and produce individuals and communities as disciplined subjects of international human rights discourse. Disciplined subjects, including those who reproduce human rights discourse (rights-claimants, scholars, advocates and others), are not only docile, useful, agentic and productive,[10] they are also are temporally structured in a way that is associated with the universal jurisdiction of international legal discourse. Unlike disciplined subjects of modern states who are associated with a delineated spatial jurisdiction, those who invoke universal jurisdiction produce a universalised temporal discipline: it appears in all times and always. Where states reproduce 'modern' jurisdictions, universal human rights produce a 'postmodern' jurisdiction.[11] This universal temporality appears a-temporal, an aspect of the temporal trap.

Through an exploration of conflicting legal jurisdictions, it is apparent that many tribal peoples have their own temporalities and place-based legalities that are involved in contesting the state. Additionally, we will see that some tribal

Relations: A Case Study From Aotearoa New Zealand' (2013) 149 *Media International Australia* 174, 176–77.

[5] JL Austin, [1962] *How to Do Things With Words: The William James Lectures delivered at Harvard University in 1955* (OUP, 2011) 15–19, 105–07; 110 at n 2; J Butler, *Excitable Speech: A Politics of the Performative* (Routledge, 1997) 149–51. For examples of scholars that use performativity in a rights-based context, see K Zivi, *Making Rights Claims: A Practice of Democratic Citizenship* (OUP, 2012) 26–27, 46–51, 116; K McNeilly, *Human Rights and Radical Social Transformation: Futurity, Alterity, Power* (Routledge, 2018) 35–39.

[6] S Marks, 'False Contingency' (2009) 62 *Current Legal Problems* 1.

[7] M Foucault, *Discipline and Punish: The Birth of the Prison* (Pantheon, 1978); M Foucault, *The History of Sexuality* (Pantheon, 1978) vol 1, 139 and Pt 5 generally; J Butler, *Gender Trouble: Feminism and the Subversion of Identity* (Routledge, 1990) 2–3.

[8] E Freeman, *Beside You in Time: Sense Methods & Queer Sociabilities in the American 19th Century* (Duke University Press, 2019) 2; A Allen, 'The Anti-Subjective Hypothesis: Michel Foucault and the Death of the Subject' (2000) 31 *Philosophical Forum* 113, 121–26; B Golder and P Fitzpatrick, *Foucault's Law* (Routledge, 2009) 19–20.

[9] The modern state is temporalized, see RS Parfitt, 'Newer is Truer: Time, Space, and Subjectivity at the Bandung Conference' in L Eslava, M Fakhri and V Nesiah (eds), *Bandung, Global History, and International Law: Critical Pasts and Pending Futures* (CUP, 2017) 53.

[10] M Foucault, 'The Subject and Power' (1982) 8 *Critical Inquiry* 777, 790.

[11] F Jameson, 'The End of Temporality' (2003) 29 *Critical Inquiry* 695, 699–707; F Jameson, 'The Aesthetics of Singularity' (2015) 92 *New Left Review* 101, 120.

peoples become identifiable Indigenous peoples through claiming international human rights.[12] Although claiming human rights to support a position in a contest is potentially helpful, becoming Indigenous peoples through invoking universal international human rights, disciplined acts, produces the a-temporal appearance that they have always been Indigenous peoples and subjects of international human rights law. When this occurs, as we will see, scholars, advocates and others, including rights-claimants, who are involved in the reproduction of human rights discourse may be unwittingly and unintentionally constructing tribal peoples as Indigenous peoples and, therein, re-writing unique laws and temporalities for human rights and international legal purposes. Inscribing and re-citing international legal discourse for Indigenous peoples may disrupt 'business as usual', generate controversies stemming from historical wrongs and even contest the temporality of the modern state.[13] However, as a performative approach indicates, claiming human rights as Indigenous peoples never fully stabilises a resolution or completely ends political controversies.[14] Those who enter into these contests with states are required to engage in permanent contests in the present and for the present through a discourse that universalises, as it contests, the spatiality of the state. Additionally, where tribal peoples claim ownership over international human right discourse – as though their subject-status as Indigenous peoples pre-exists the discourse, rather than international legal discourse pre-existing their subject-status – the a-temporal temporality of international legal discourse suggests that they are already, always have been, and always will be involved in disputes with states. These are features of the temporal trap.

This chapter has three main sections. Each examines conflicts between types of legal jurisdictions – those pertaining to tribal laws, states laws and international human rights laws. While the conflicts are ostensibly about the authority over particular spaces, each involves temporal conflicts. Section II considers two examples of conflicts between tribal peoples and modern states. Neither of those conflicts involves, at an initial stage, international human rights claims. However, reviewing those conflicts establishes that tribal peoples have their own legalities and temporalities and, in those contests, states attempt to reconcile tribal peoples into its discourse about modernity, a progressive and linear temporality.[15]

Section III considers conflicts between tribal peoples' legalities and international human rights law. It explores how some tribal peoples have argued that

[12] Young (n 3).

[13] F Johns, 'The Temporal Rivalries of Human Rights' (2016) 23 *Indiana Journal of Global Legal Studies* 39, 56.

[14] Butler (n 7) 14; Zivi (n 5) 26–27, 46–51, 116; R Birla, 'Performativity Between Logos and Nomos: Law, Temporality and the "Non-Economic Analysis of Power"' (2012) 21(2) *Columbia Journal of Gender and Law* 90, 101; J Butler, *Bodies That Matter: On the Discursive Limits of 'Sex'* (Routledge, 1993) 218–22.

[15] Johns (n 13) 56.

international human rights law perverts their legalities and ways of living.[16] It also examines how some tribal peoples performatively enact international human rights discipline and become Indigenous peoples by invoking rights recognised in the United Nations Declaration on the Rights of Indigenous Peoples (2007) (UNDRIP). Because human rights are universal and they appear applicable everywhere and in all times, statements arise like 'Indigenous peoples have been entitled to a right of self-determination since time immemorial'.[17] The temporality in this statement produces the view that those who claim human rights are pre-legal natural subjects of international law and need international legal discourse for their disputes, instead of tribal peoples who became Indigenous peoples when they performatively inscribe international legal discourse into their ways of life.[18] The effects and the temporal trap of human rights become more apparent when Indigenous peoples claim human rights to contest the uneven and inequitable development of modern states.

Section IV returns to the two conflicts introduced in section II. It evaluates how claimants, as well as scholars and advocates, have introduced international human rights into those contests to alter the terrain and temporalities of those contests. It reveals that not only do tribal peoples who become Indigenous peoples through claiming human rights re-invest in the state's spatial discourse of property rights, but the a-temporal temporality suggests that tribal peoples have already been entered into permanent contests without their approval, acknowledgement or consent.

II. TEMPORAL CONFLICTS BETWEEN TRIBAL AND STATE LAWS

This section examines conflicting temporalities in tribal and state legal conflicts through two examples that do not involve international human rights at the stage discussed here. These conflicts shows that tribal and state temporalities are involved in legal conflicts over spaces and authorities. I chose these examples because international human rights law has been subsequently invoked.

The first conflict considered here is between Gitksan and Wet'suwet'en people and Canada. In 1984, the Gitksan and Wet'suwet'en peoples initiated legal proceedings against the Crown on the basis that British Columbia refused to negotiate and uphold their title to land. According to Ryan Hartigan, the

[16] N Tomas, (2001) 'Locating Human Rights in the South Pacific: A Korero about Human Rights' in S Garkawe, L Kelly and W Fisher (eds), *Indigenous Human Rights* (Sydney Institute of Criminology Monograph Series No 14, 2001) 128; I Watson, *Aboriginal Peoples, Colonialism and International Law: Raw Law* (Routledge, 2015) 39.

[17] See eg E-I Daes, 'The UN Declaration on the Rights of Indigenous Peoples: Background and Appraisal' in S Allen and A Xanthaki (eds), *Reflections on the UN Declaration on the Rights of Indigenous Peoples* (Hart Publishing, 2011) 37.

[18] Young (n 3) 22, 32.

1991 trial opinion in *Delgamuukw v British Columbia*[19] was 'a meeting point of performative and written culture, of Indigenous memory and Anglo-derived juridical practices, and of law and performance'.[20] Gitksan peoples presented 'sacred memories of ancestors, histories, and territory,' while Wet'suwet'en peoples offered 'spiritual songs, dances and performances'.[21] Notably, the Gitksan and Wet'suwet'en peoples 'self-consciously introduced multiple, disjunctive temporalities into the courtroom'.[22] Although these performances invoked a citational-chain that temporally linked them to their land through their law, McEachern CJ declared, '[t]his is a trial, not a performance!'.[23] In short, he refused to consider their laws as relevant evidence. McEachern CJ's judicial declarative established 'the courtroom's disciplining of temporality and history through confronting performative testimony with its own performative enactments'.[24] The conflict enabled McEachern to performatively re-assert the state's modern temporality – a racialised, hierarchical and civilising discourse.[25] For example, McEachern wrote:[26]

> … it would not be accurate to assume that even pre-contact existence in the territory was in the least bit idyllic. The plaintiffs' ancestors had no written language, no horses or wheeled vehicles, slavery and starvation were not uncommon, wars with neighbouring peoples were common, and there is no doubt, to quote Hobbs, that aboriginal life in the territory was, at best, 'nasty, brutish and short'.

The Court performatively reconstructs 'a specifically framed regulation of temporality, evaluating the claimants in terms of what McEachern considered was an appropriate level of civilization located in modernity, which he denied was presented in the Gitksan and Wet'suwet'en peoples'.[27] McEachern's opinion re-enacts the temporal discipline of modern state law,[28] a linear, progressive and teleological temporality that excludes the plaintiffs from modernity and includes them in its temporalisation as pre-civilised. It was an overtly hierarchical and racist opinion.

The Gitksan and Wet'suwet'en were successful in their appeal to the Canadian Supreme Court.[29] In their success, however, the Supreme Court re-asserted modernity, a progressive temporality and a corrected modern legal discipline that minimised McEachern's overtly racialised and hierarchical temporality in

[19] *Delgamuukw v British Columbia*, 79 DLR (4th) 185, [1991] 3 WWR 97 (BCSC) [Cited to DLR].
[20] R Hartigan, '"This Is a Trial, Not a Performance!" Staging the Time of the Law' in A Sarat, L Douglas and M Merrill Umphrey (eds), *Law and Performance* (University of Massachusetts Press, 2018) 71.
[21] ibid 69.
[22] ibid 81.
[23] ibid 70.
[24] ibid.
[25] Parfitt (n 9) 53–54; Love and Tilley (n 4) 175–77.
[26] *Delgamuukw v British Columbia* (n 19) para 208.
[27] Hartigan (n 20) 73.
[28] ibid.
[29] *Delgamuukw v British Columbia* [1997] 3 SCR 1010, 153 DLR (4th) 193 [Cited to SCR].

finding that the trial judge had not complied with the evidentiary principles articulated elsewhere.[30] It reduced Gitksan and Wet'suwet'en laws and assertions of authority to evidence – which courts would treat as equal to written evidence[31] – to reconcile 'the prior occupation of North America by distinctive aboriginal societies with the assertion of Crown sovereignty over Canadian territory'.[32] Far from upholding Gitksan and Wet'suwet'en authority, it maintained a modern, progressive and linear temporalisation when it clarified that an Aboriginal societies' 'prior occupation' and title is a 'burden' on otherwise perfected Crown sovereignty.[33] *Delgamuukw* was a win for the Gitksan and Wet'suwet'en claimants, but it reasserted the state's temporality and perpetuated tribal subjection to Canadian law in less racialised tones. Importantly, when compared to McEachern's opinion, the Supreme Court's opinion appears to make progress.

The second conflict considered here arises between several Māori iwi – Ngāi Tūhoe and Whanganui iwi – and New Zealand. New Zealand passed the Te Urewera Act in 2014 and the Te Awa Tupua Act 2017. Both Acts reconstituted spaces, the Te Urewera National Park and the Whanganui river-system, as legal persons. Despite claims that these new legal persons are 'ground-breaking'[34] – perhaps a well-intentioned idiom that reveals a deeper ambivalence – both Acts are compromises that temporarily stabilise unresolved disputes about whether Māori or Crown have authority over those spaces.[35] However, as unequal compromises, both Acts subject Māori to New Zealand's temporality. For instance, at one level, to understand the Te Awa Tupua Act, what it does and does not do, requires historicising the Whanganui River with reference to New Zealand's colonial history and the construction of the modern state.

The legal colonial history of New Zealand conventionally begins with the signing of the Treaty of Waitangi in 1840. Though there are differing Māori and English discourses regarding the Treaty texts, the Crown relied on the Treaty to assert its acquisition of sovereignty.[36] As more settlers arrived and tensions flared, New Zealand's Chief Judge later declared the Treaty 'a simple nullity'.[37] Even before that, Māori lands and resources were being sold, taken, stolen and appropriated. Regarding the Acts at issue, in 1954, New Zealand designated Te Urewera a national park, and in 1987, the Whanganui National Park opened.[38]

[30] ibid paras 78–84.
[31] ibid paras 87 and 107.
[32] ibid para 81.
[33] ibid para 145.
[34] E Macpherson, E O'Donnell and F Clavijo Ospina, 'Meet the River People: Who Speaks For the Rivers?' (*Stuff*, 2 April 2018) www.stuff.co.nz/environment/102741097/meet-the-river-people-who-speaks-for-the-rivers.
[35] A Geddis and J Ruru, 'Places as Persons: Creating a New Framework for Māori-Crown Relations' in JNE Varuhas and S Wilson Stark (eds), *The Frontiers of Public Law* (Hart Publishing, 2020) 255.
[36] ibid 258. The following is not a comprehensively detailed history.
[37] *Wi Parata v Bishop of Wellington* (1877) 3 NZ Jur (NS) 72 (SC), para 78.
[38] Geddis and Ruru (n 35) 259.

Throughout this time, Māori persistently alleged that the Crown breached the Treaty of Waitangi, and, in 1975, New Zealand created the Waitangi Tribunal to hear those allegations. In 1990, Whanganui iwi lodged a claim with the Waitangi Tribunal arguing that the creation of the Whanganui National Park and other uses of the river breached the Treaty.[39] The Tribunal largely agreed, so the government began negotiating with Whanganui iwi to resolve their allegations. An unresolved issue that arose was who had authority over the river, which they agreed to avoid by treating it as a legal person in 2017.[40] Even though the creation of that legal personality is novel, the Act does not significantly alter how state legal regulations apply to that new legal person.

Regarding temporalities, these Acts are the result of Treaty settlements, and 'a settlement' according to Christine Jill Winter, 'implies a temporal full stop, redolent with connotations of time ending, of a finality and fixedness'.[41] Despite the appearance of finality, Winter argues that settlements are never fully finalised or fixed, which is consistent with a performative approach. As such, she posits that these Acts potentially enable and facilitate Māori temporalities – cyclical, concentric or spiral senses of time.[42] That is possible, but state legality creates disciplined subjects to give effect to that law and it is not temporally neutral. Settling with settler-states reconciles and temporarily stabilises a particular contest for the re-assertion of modernity (which is always contested and re-asserted as it is contested). As Andrew Geddis and Jacinta Ruru argue 'Parliament has mandated that Te Urewera retain a particular teleology, which then defines the sort of "person" it is'.[43] Legal personhood may enable a 'governance arrangement that reflects Māori understandings', but passing legislation to create and subject it to other state laws integrates them within its linear view and, ostensibly, with a progressive approach to law.[44] It provides the impression that New Zealand sets a standard for other states to follow.[45]

In the two conflicts discussed here, the disputes involve who has authority over various spaces. The disputes also involve clashing temporalities. Tribal peoples have their own temporalities and legalities, which are not necessarily commensurate with a progressive, linear temporality. Modern states attempt to stabilise a racialised, hierarchical view of civilisation through the presentation of a linear, progressive and teleological temporality.[46] This linear and progressive temporality

[39] ibid 262.
[40] ibid 263.
[41] Winter (n 4) 8.
[42] ibid 8–13.
[43] Geddis and Ruru (n 35) 265.
[44] ibid 269.
[45] K Warne, 'A Voice of Nature' (*National Geographic*, April 2019) www.nationalgeographic.com/culture/2019/04/maori-river-in-new-zealand-is-a-legal-person; K Evans, 'The New Zealand River That Became a Legal Person' (*BBC*, 20 March 2020) www.bbc.com/travel/story/20200319-the-new-zealand-river-that-became-a-legal-person; E Ainge Roy, 'New Zealand River Granted Same Legal Rights as Human Being' *The Guardian* (London, 16 March 2017) www.theguardian.com/world/2017/mar/16/new-zealand-river-granted-same-legal-rights-as-human-being.
[46] Parfitt (n 9) 53–54.

has typically excluded tribal peoples from development (alternatively, it has been used to subject them to development discourses) by categorising them as pre-modern.[47] The ability of any individual or community, including tribal peoples, who have personal or idiosyncratic rhythms to contest state authority and enter into the modern state's 'real historical time', requires their reconciliation with a 'linear teleology of history'.[48] When states categorise some as pre-modern, those individuals can contest that categorisation and become contributors to a modern state when they performatively enact their self-discipline and normalise themselves as subjects of discourse. That does not mean they entirely give up or abandon their own rhythms or temporalities. But their own temporalities are irrelevant when they use state-sanctioned means of contesting the state and move in concert with state temporalities for, at least, the duration of that contest. Given the uneven development and distribution of resources throughout a modern state's population, which modern states (re)produce and justify through its racialised and hierarchical approach to civilisation, it remains possible to use state law as well as human rights to contest state development projects. These avenues for contestation produce the appearance of progress.

III. TEMPORAL CONFLICTS BETWEEN TRIBAL AND INTERNATIONAL HUMAN RIGHTS LAWS

This section examines conflicts between tribal laws and international human rights laws. It explores how some tribal peoples have argued against international human rights law, claiming that it perverts their legalities and ways of living.[49] It also examines how some tribal peoples performatively enact as Indigenous peoples by invoking rights recognised in UNDRIP. My assertion that tribal peoples become Indigenous peoples when claiming human rights might appear 'wrong' or counter-intuitive, which is a product of the a-temporal temporality of international human rights.

Human rights can usefully draw attention to the harmful and problematic ways that modern states develop and reproduce hierarchical and racial inequalities because international human rights discourse re-cites the terminology of international legal decolonisation, particularly self-determination.[50] In re-iterating the terms of decolonisation through a rights-based discourse, human

[47] See A Escobar, (1995) *Encountering Development: The Making and Unmaking of the Third World* (Princeton University Press, 1995) 3–4, discussing the US Truman Doctrine; see also RA Williams, *Savage Anxieties: The Invention of Western Civilization* (Palgrave Macmillan, 2012).

[48] Parfitt (n 9) 54.

[49] Tomas (n 16); Watson (n 16).

[50] Jameson, 'The End of Temporality' (n 11) 700–01. Due to slippage in re-citational acts, the meaning of 'self-determination' as well as 'decolonisation' changes within human rights discourse, see M Davis, 'Indigenous Struggles in Standard-Setting: The United Nations Declaration on the Rights of Indigenous Peoples' (2008) 9 *Melbourne Journal of International Law* 439, 458–59; G Christie, 'Implementation of UNDRIP within Canadian and Indigenous Law: Assessing

rights create a citational-chain to decolonisation through the performative enactment of discipline that has a non-modern, non-linear temporality. That is because the formal international legal processes of decolonisation universalised the form of the modern state to create post-colonial states.[51] In universalising the form of the modern state's spatial and temporal constructs, decolonisation increased 'space over time' so that a 'new dominant of postmodernity was to be found in space itself, [with] the temporal sinking to a subordinate feature of space as such'.[52] While disciplinary power is typically associated with the development of modern states, the discipline associated with a universalised human rights discourse provides the appearance of an a-temporal and a-historical temporality. The universalised temporality of human rights enables human rights claimants to appear in any time without regard for state-based temporalities or histories: the temporality of human rights appears a-temporal, plastic and useful at any time by anyone.

As such, and even if they are useful, human rights can conflict with tribal peoples' legalities and temporalities. Nin Tomas writes that[53]

> Many Indigenous commentators from the South Pacific view human 'rights' as inappropriate language to describe the kinds of relationships that we consider to be fundamental to our existence as humans. … Furthermore, the language of 'human rights' is seen as part of the language of 'law', meaning western law. … A major barrier to our success is the legal definitional process which slices through our Indigenous institutions, dismembering the collective products of our concentricity.

Similarly, speaking from an Aboriginal First Nation's perspective, Irene Watson argues that 'the UNDRIP positions Indigenous Peoples as domestic subjects of the various colonial states and thereby fails to enable the future development of a framework'.[54] For Tomas and Watson, international legal discourse abstracts their legalities and temporalities from their ways of being. The discipline of human rights shapes their projects and threatens their futures.

Despite this concern, the a-temporal temporality of human rights might provide the appearance that there is no conflict between international and tribal legalities. For instance, former chairperson of the UN Working Group on Indigenous Populations (WGIP), Erica-Irene Daes said that 'Indigenous peoples have been entitled to a right of self-determination since time immemorial'.[55] This statement appears simple, intuitive and transparent. It could mean that all Indigenous peoples have self-governed since as long as anyone remembers and they are still rightfully entitled to do so. That statement also involves incredibly

Challenges' in *UNDRIP Implementation: More Reflections on the Braiding of International, Domestic and Indigenous Laws* (Centre for International Governance Innovation, 2018) 26, 30–31.

[51] M Åhrén, *Indigenous Peoples' Status in the International Legal System* (OUP, 2016) 34.

[52] Jameson, 'The Aesthetics of Singularity' (n 11) 105.

[53] Thomas (n 16) 128.

[54] Watson (n 16) ibid 39.

[55] Daes (n 17) ibid 37.

abstract and disciplinary temporal complexities. It presupposes that Indigenous peoples pre-exist international legal discourse and are somehow naturally and universally identifiable as 'Indigenous peoples' without regard for the construction of tribes, First Nations, states, empires, international legal discourse or any legal discourse. As spatially commodious, and without regard for previously constructed boundaries (whether state, tribal or otherwise), there is no concern with when or how tribal peoples become identifiable or constituted as Indigenous peoples. It is a-temporal and a-historical. However, temporalising Daes' statement makes it appear as either a legal claim or anachronistic.

As I have discussed elsewhere, the term 'Indigenous peoples' is a subject-status that emerged from international legal discourse in the early 1980s.[56] Self-determination is also an international legal concept associated with decolonisation that gained legal and political significance after the mid-20th century,[57] and 'time immemorial' is a legal term connected to common law traditions.[58] After 1980, those who performatively enact their subjectivity as Indigenous peoples can invoke international human rights law, like self-determination. Claiming that Indigenous peoples had self-determination significantly before 1980 is anachronistic (even where tribal peoples self-governed long before the formation of states, empires or international law).[59] That is a temporal and historical argument. Due to the a-temporal temporality of human rights, concerns for temporality may fall away or be dismissed as not real problems. In this way, international legal discourse appears to solve conflicts between tribal peoples and Indigenous peoples before they appear. Put simply, international human rights discourse provides the view that tribal peoples have always been Indigenous peoples. That is an aspect of the temporal trap.

If all tribal peoples are already Indigenous peoples for human rights purposes, then their unique histories, pasts, and identifiers are a-temporally dissolved and aggregated for purposes of international legal discourse. It is then difficult to see how tribal and international legal discourses differ. As an example, in the WGIP, Moana Jackson expressed concerns 'about attempts to limit the concept of self-determination to the conduct of internal affairs … [because it] was not primarily a post-Second World War concept but had existed since time immemorial and was not dependent exclusively on international law for its.[60] Jackson's statement depends on and is simultaneously distrustful of international legal discourse.

[56] Young (n 3) 3, 22, ch 2.

[57] International Covenant on Civil and Political Rights (New York, 16 December 1966) 999 UNTS 171 (entered into force 23 March 1976), art 1; International Covenant on Economic, Social and Cultural Rights (New York, 16 December 1966) 993 UNTS 3 (entered into force 3 January 1976), art 1.

[58] See S Dorsett, '"Since Time Immemorial": A Story of Common Law Jurisdiction, Native Title and the Case of Tanistry' (2002) 26 *Melbourne University Law Review* 32.

[59] S Young, 'Re-historicising Dissolved Identities: Deskaheh, the League of Nations, and International Legal Discourse on Indigenous Peoples' (2019) 7 *London Review of International Law* 377.

[60] Commission on Human Rights, Sub-Commission on Prevention of Discrimination and Protection of Minorities, 'Report of the Working Group on Indigenous Populations on Its Eleventh Session' 45 E/CN4/Sub2/1993/29 (23 August 1993), para 56. For commentary, see Young (n 3) 62–63.

As a simple and intuitive statement, Jackson is attempting to enliven decolonisation in a way that is unbounded by international law.[61] Doing so, however, as a re-citation of international legal discourse is not amenable to wilful acts in a non-contested manner because performative re-citations 'precede and exceed the momentary occasion of its enunciation'.[62] Even though a benefit of Indigenous peoples' international human rights is in perpetuating and re-citing decolonisation, because human rights ostensibly have universal jurisdiction,[63] which can be cited and re-cited in numerous ways from numerous places, problems arise from the production of a seemingly a-temporal and a-historical subject.

At one level, where decolonisation reproduced the form of the modern state for former colonies, international human rights universalise the spatiality and temporality of that discourse. In contests with modern states, examined below, it appears natural that Indigenous peoples re-cite international legal discourse to assert authority over spaces and territories in the state-sanctioned terminology of property rights. When Indigenous peoples assert rights in the spatial terms of the modern state, states can agree to uphold those rights and treat them as it treats other property rights in its jurisdiction. Of course, Indigenous peoples can then re-contest that infringement as inconsistent with their authorities and legalities and, in re-citing the terms of the state, enter into a 'permanent site of contest'.[64] This constant and repeated self-making to contest modern states is the temporal trap of international human rights. It seems even more intractable because, if international human rights law is temporally a-temporal, then those who claim human rights as Indigenous peoples are already and always involved in permanent contestation with states.

The temporal trap can arise in another way. Because international legal discourse produces a seemingly a-temporal and a-historical subject, scholars, advocates and others who are engaged in the discipline of human rights might assume that all tribal peoples are and have always been Indigenous peoples and, therefore, subjects of international human rights law. That is, scholars, activists or others might assume that tribal peoples are de facto instead of de jure Indigenous peoples, and claim human rights (and universalised property concepts) on behalf of tribes while advancing the centrality of international legal discourse. To see this at work, consider how the international legal discourse becomes part of the legal conflicts between tribes and states.

[61] Certainly, decolonisation is not limited to international law. See E Tuck and KW Yang, 'Decolonization Is Not a Metaphor' (2012) 1(1) *Decolonisation: Indigeneity, Education & Society* 1. International legal discourse of decolonisation remains a hurdle that contests and supports that view.

[62] J Butler, *Notes Towards a Performative Theory of Assembly* (Harvard University Press, 2015) 176.

[63] A Anghie, 'Finding the Peripheries: Sovereignty and Colonialism in Nineteenth-Century International Law' (1999) 40 *Harvard International Law Journal* 1, 80; Human Rights Watch, 'Basic Facts on Universal Jurisdiction' (19 October 2009) www.hrw.org/news/2009/10/19/basic-facts-universal-jurisdiction; D Hawkins, 'Universal Jurisdiction for Human Rights: From Legal Principle to Limited Reality' (2003) 9 *Global Governance* 347, 347–65.

[64] J Butler, *Bodies That Matter: On the Discursive Limits of 'Sex'* (Routledge, 1993) 221–22.

IV. TEMPORAL CONFLICTS BETWEEN STATE AND INTERNATIONAL HUMAN RIGHTS LAWS

This section returns to the two conflicts introduced in section II. It evaluates how claimants, as well as scholars and advocates, have introduced international human rights into those contests. It reveals that those tribal peoples who claim international human rights begin to defend their territories in the spatial terms of modern states. Furthermore, where this a-temporal temporality arises, other subjects may have already entered tribal peoples into those contests by invoking international human rights on their behalf.

The Canadian Supreme Court's *Delgamuukw* case established that the Gitksan and Wet'suwet'en might have unextinguished Aboriginal title.[65] However, in some circumstances, Canadian law can justifiably infringe Aboriginal rights that might exist, including when the government has fulfilled its legal duty to consult and accommodate Aboriginal interests.[66] Doing so progresses 'reconciliation of the pre-existence of aboriginal societies within the sovereignty of the Crown',[67] which maintains as it re-asserts the progressive and linear temporality of the state. This is relevant because in 2014 Coastal GasLink sought to construct a pipeline across Wet'suwet'en territory. Accordingly, British Columbia sought to fulfil the government's duty to consult and accommodate through consultation with five Wet'suwet'en Band Councils and 12 of 13 of its Hereditary Houses.[68] After these consultations, the Band Councils approved the pipeline's construction while the Hereditary Houses opposed it.[69] The difference between Hereditary Houses and Band Councils is that Hereditary Houses are organised under tribal law while Band Councils are constituted by Canada's Indian Act 1876, which sought to modernise tribes. To prevent further construction of the pipeline, several hereditary groups including the Unist'ot'en refused to engage in additional consultation, blockaded their territory and hung a sign stating 'NO ACCESS WITHOUT CONSENT' to 'administer a "free, prior and informed consent protocol" to individuals seeking access'.[70] Importantly, they claim free, prior and informed consent (FPIC), a human right of Indigenous peoples recognised in UNDRIP. The Unist'ot'en claimed human rights and asserted control over their borders, which reproduces state-based approaches for their borders.

Nearly simultaneously, the British Columbia Supreme Court granted Coastal GasLink an injunction to prevent Unist'ot'en from opposing the pipeline in this

[65] *Delgamuukw* (n 29). In speaking of Canadian law I use the term from s 35 of the Constitution Act 1982: 'Aboriginal' or 'Aboriginal peoples'.

[66] *R v Sparrow* [1990] 1 SCR 1075, 70 DLR (4th) 385 [Cited to SCR] paras 1108–11.

[67] *Haida Nation v British Columbia (Minister of Forests)* 2004 SCC 73, [2004] 3 SCR 511, para 17, citing *Delgamuukw*(n 29) para 186.

[68] *Coastal GasLink Pipeline Ltd v Huson* 2019 BCSC 2264 (available on CanLII) paras 57–58.

[69] ibid paras 60–68.

[70] ibid paras 18–19.

way.[71] In doing so, the Court ignored FPIC and tribal legality and held that the Hereditary groups 'are entirely aware that the legal rights claimed by them remain outstanding and are at odds with the permits and authorizations granted to [Coastal GasLink]' for pipeline construction.[72] In applying Canadian law, the Court reduced Wet'suwet'en legality to 'fact evidence' because it can only treat their legality as an 'effectual part' of Canadian law when recognised through previously established state legal processes.[73] In finding that the Unist'ot'en refused further consultations and that their blockade amounted to a self-help remedy, the Court enjoined and criminalised how they defended their territory.[74]

Although it has since been reported that Canada, British Columbia and Wet'suwet'en have negotiated an agreement that will recognise their aboriginal title,[75] this scenario is even more remarkable because British Columbia was the first former English colony to pass a UNDRIP implementation bill.[76] Sheryl Lightfoot proclaims that it is 'groundbreaking provincial legislation to implement global standards for upholding the rights of Indigenous peoples'. However, that legislation was not applied in *Coastal GasLink* because British Columbia has not yet implemented it in an applicable manner. The Unist'ot'en website explains its significance:[77]

> At a time when the Province of British Columbia is celebrated for adopting the UN Declaration on the Rights of Indigenous Peoples (UNDRIP), the Wet'suwet'en people are actively denied the protections of UNDRIP on our own lands. When we enforced our own laws and required that industry seek Free, Prior, and Informed Consent for development on our lands, we faced a brutal display of militaristic police violence and an ongoing police occupation of our territories.

In short, Unist'ot'en invoke international legal discourse, specifically FPIC, as their legality to defend their land.[78] They are not wrong to invoke international legal discourse as their law, but it has disciplinary effects. The a-temporality of international legal discourse produces the appearance that Wet'suwet'en have always defended their lives and territories in those terms and in those ways. It makes it difficult to see they have become intelligible to an international audience as a result of re-citing international legal discourse. It then looks natural

[71] ibid para 223.
[72] ibid para 152.
[73] ibid paras 127–28, 137–38.
[74] ibid paras 71–74, 157–58.
[75] C Bellrichard, 'Wet'suwet'en, B.C. and Canada Sign MOU on Negotiations for Legal Recognition of Title' (*CBC News*, 14 May 2020) www.cbc.ca/amp/1.5570128.
[76] S Lightfoot, 'B.C. Take Historic Steps Towards the Rights of Indigenous Peoples, but the Hard Work Is Yet to Come' (*The Conversation*, 14 November 2019) theconversation.com/b-c-takes-historic-steps-towards-the-rights-of-indigenous-peoples-but-the-hard-work-is-yet-to-come-126311.
[77] 'Wet'suwet'en Hereditary Chiefs Reject the BC Supreme Court Decision to Criminalize Wet'suwet'en Law' (*Unist'ot'en*, 31 December 2019) unistoten.camp/wetsuweten-hereditary-chiefs-reject-the-bc-supreme-court-decision-to-criminalize-wetsuweten-law/.
[78] Unist'ot'en (n.d.) 'Free Prior and Informed Consent Protocol' unistoten.camp/come-to-camp/fpic/.

that the terminology they use to defend their territory is the spatiality of state legal discourse: their FPIC protocol is 'like a border crossing',[79] they seek to prevent 'trespassers',[80] while, after the verdict, the Unist'ot'en issued an 'eviction notice' to Coastal Gaslink.[81] While it may help defend their territory, re-citing national and international legal discourse is not under their (sole) control or able to be used how they want for their benefit.

One benefit arising from performatively enacting as subjects of international legal discourse is that it enables others to identify them and support them as Indigenous peoples. For instance, the UN Committee on the Elimination of Racial Discrimination 2019 called upon Canada to 'halt [pipeline] construction and suspend all permits' until the Wet'suwet'en people 'grant their free, prior and informed consent, following the full and adequate discharge of the duty to consult'.[82] The British Columbia Commissioner for Human Rights then echoed that message, affirming that 'we have obligations to ensure [FPIC] exists for all impacted Indigenous groups'.[83] While potentially promising for the Wet'suwet'en, the Commissioner continues, 'Canada cannot simultaneously vie for a seat at the Security Council while ignoring their obligations'. While potentially troubling for the state, it provides Canada an opportunity to re-assert modernity and progress.

Those hereditary groups pre-date international legal discourse, but they do not pre-date international legal discourse as identifiable Indigenous peoples. Hence, even if they adopt FPIC into their laws, the meaning of FPIC exceeds their uses. They can assert their uses and meanings of FPIC while urging British Columbia to implement UNDRIP, and British Columbia can implement UNDRIP as it sees fit. Any contest about the meaning of those terms provides the state with the opportunity to re-assert modernity in the following problematic ways. For example, if Canada or British Columbia accept the Wet'suwet'en claims without contesting them, it will then begin formally delineating Wet'suwet'en boundaries as a recognised nation (and in the terms of state-based property, 'aboriginal title') within the state.[84] Alternatively, British Columbia could implement UNDRIP in consultation with all impacted Indigenous peoples, and do

[79] ibid.

[80] *Coastal GasLink* (n 68) para 86.

[81] 'Wet'suwet'en Hereditary Chiefs Evict Coastal GasLink From Territory' (*Unist'ot'en*, 4 January 2020) unistoten.camp/wetsuweten-hereditary-chiefs-evict-coastal-gaslink-from-territory/.

[82] Committee on the Elimination of Racial Discrimination (2019) 'Prevention of Racial Discrimination, Including Early Warning and Urgent Action Procedure' Decision 1 (100), Hundredth Session, 2801st Meeting (13 December 2019).

[83] K Govender, 'Statement from B.C.'s Human Rights Commissioner on UN CERD's Decision Statement' (British Columbia's Office of the Human Rights Commissioner, 10 January 2020) bchumanrights.ca/news/statement-from-bcs-human-rights-commissioner-on-un-cerds-decision-statement/.

[84] As mentioned above, it has been reported that Canada, British Columbia and the Wet'sewet'en have entered into an agreement (Bellrichard (n 75)). The details of that agreement have not been made public.

so in ways without substantively altering British Columbian or Canadian law. Article 32(2) of the UNDRIP requires states to 'consult and cooperate in good faith … in order to obtain their free and informed consent prior to the approval of any' large development projects, like pipelines. Minimally, it requires good faith consultation, but not necessarily obtaining FPIC. Canadian law already requires good faith consultation,[85] and, as *Coastal GasLink* demonstrates, the requirement that each party participate in 'good-faith consultation' can work against Hereditary House interests. The *Coastal GasLink* Court found that the developers held the necessary permits, which presumes that the government fulfilled its duty to consult and accommodate all potentially affected Aboriginal interests.[86] It then issued the injunction upon finding that the Uni'stot'en had refused the 'mutual obligation of aboriginal groups and the Crown to consult in good faith', which 'undermine the rule of law and the administration of justice'.[87]

In short, those who oppose the pipeline may continue to insist that their use and meaning of FPIC is the real, true, important and meaningful one. But where FPIC becomes domestic law, then Canadian courts can determine what FPIC means in law and, potentially, ascertain whether Wet'suwet'en peoples are exercising FPIC consistently with their 'traditional governance structures'.[88] FPIC and international human rights law may affect and transform how Wet'suwet'en, other First Nations, and Canadians think of themselves without substantively altering legal effects.

In the face of militarised police forces and a state legal regime that criminalises how the Wet'suwet'en defend their territory, human rights appear to be useful and progressive. However, it not only universalises the spatial discourse of the state (property), its universality enables others – like state actors, scholars, and advocates – to use and invoke that discourse in ways that appear progressive but may work against how those who claim human rights seek to use them.

To see the effects of international human rights discourse in another context, consider, again, the legal personhood of the Whanganui River. Geddis and Ruru argue that the Te Awa Tupua Act does not reflect a 'rights of nature' perspective that upholds 'legal personality primarily as a mechanism to improve the environmental protection afforded to those places'.[89] They claim that those approaches 'are at worst mistaken and at least are incomplete'.[90] Instead, they view the legislation as the result of a negotiated compromise between the

[85] *Haida Nation* (n 67) para 49.
[86] *Coastal GasLink* (n 68) paras 219–20. The Court found that the defendants did not challenge the validity of the permits and authorisations.
[87] *Coastal GasLink* (n 68) paras 157–58.
[88] ibid paras 134–35, 151.
[89] Geddis and Ruru (n 35) 256.
[90] ibid.

government and particular Māori who 'conceive of and relate to the particular places at issue'.[91] As a compromise, it 'returned the riverbed to the river itself, not to the iwi' so that the 'river itself no longer can be owned'.[92] As such, that Act may harmonise with *tikanga* Māori (Māori laws or ways of doing things) better than a rights-based discourse about 'property'. As contained in New Zealand law, this new, modern, and potentially progressive development has attracted international attention.[93] In the same way that the Act does not reflect a rights-of-nature perspective, it does not reflect international legal discourse on Indigenous peoples' human rights.

However, as no one can own or stabilise international legal discourse, others can invoke that discourse on behalf of Whanganui iwi even if Whanganui iwi did not. As an example, Toni Collins and Shea Esterling write that 'the Te Awa Tupua Act is about the acknowledgement of the significance of the River to the Indigenous peoples of Aotearoa New Zealand, the Māori, and in particular the Whanganui iwi who assert an important connection to it'.[94] Even if they intend to use the term 'Indigenous peoples' as a mere adjective, they uphold the Act for those subject to international legal discourse in New Zealand and then move from the universalised international legal subjectivity, Indigenous peoples, to state discourse, Māori, to a tribal signifier, Whanganui iwi. Then they reverse that movement and expropriate a dispute between Whanganui iwi and New Zealand over a place and authority for ostensibly universal benefit: '[t]he Te Awa Tupua Act reflects the unique relationship that many Indigenous peoples have with nature and their understanding of property'.[95] Whatever uniqueness and compromises the Whanganui iwi have made with the New Zealand government disappear in favour of international legal discourse.

With admirable intentions, Collins and Esterling invoke human rights on behalf of the Whanganui iwi (and all Indigenous peoples) to argue that the Crown should recognise Māori property rights in freshwater.[96] They carefully distinguish British conceptions of property from *tikanga* Māori, and then note that some Māori individuals and communities have asserted water ownership.[97] Then New Zealand's refusal to grant property and ownership rights to Whanganui iwi, and the ensuing compromise, appears backwards and non-progressive. In constructing the Whanganui iwi as Indigenous peoples, they

[91] ibid.

[92] B Williams, 'Reconceptualizing Entrenched Notions of Common Law Property Regimes: Māori Self-Determination and Environmental Protection Through Legal Personality for Natural Objects' (2019) 26 *Buffalo Environmental Law Journal* 163, 177–78.

[93] Warne (n 45); Evans (n 45); Ainge Roy (n 45).

[94] T Collins and S Esterling, 'Fluid Personality: Indigenous Rights and the Te Awa Tupua (Whanganui River Claims Settlement) Act 2017 in Aotearoa New Zealand' (2019) 20 *Melbourne Journal of International Law* 197, 204.

[95] ibid.

[96] Waitangi Tribunal (2019) The Stage 2 Report on the National Freshwater and Geothermal Resources Claims (Wai 2358), 58, 66–67, 103–08.

[97] Collins and Esterling (n 94) 14–17.

uphold the Inter-American Court of Human Right's jurisprudence as relevant examples of culturally appropriate approaches to property law for Indigenous peoples. They then claim that the Te Awa Tupua Act 'reflects the ethos of international human rights law including its recognition of the close relationship between the protection of culture and lands, territories and resources' but that it 'does not go beyond the recognition of this gloss'.[98] For them, the Act's focus on 'cultural aspects comes at the expense of claims to property and so fails to provide the real material gains that human rights law purports to offer Indigenous peoples'.[99] Therefore, 'the failure of the Crown to reference the UNDRIP within this settlement process begins to look like political resistance to international human rights law'.[100]

The Crown resisted granting ownership to Whanganui iwi and, arguably, it does not provide 'real material grains', but it is not clear that either negotiating party invoked international human rights. Furthermore, the Inter-American Court's jurisprudence on Indigenous peoples' property rights has had effects that may not help Whanganui iwi in any material manner.[101] Noting that Whanganui iwi and the claimants in the Inter-American Court of Human Rights involve 'Indigenous peoples' helps Indigenous peoples and proponents of international legal discourse more than it helps tribes with their unique disputes. Invoking international legal discourse on behalf of Whanganui iwi may generate some political pressure, and in time lead to freshwater property rights for Whanganui iwi, but that would require that they assert their claims in terms of property rights. Whanganui iwi might resist doing so on the grounds that it conflicts with their legality, but it would provide the government with a means of modernising itself and regulating Whanganui iwi according to its property regimes.

V. THE TEMPORAL TRAP

The temporal trap of human rights is produced by the a-temporal temporality of human rights. Tribal peoples have their own legalities and idiosyncratic temporalities, which can conflict with the a-temporal temporality of international human rights. In many cases, conflicts between tribal laws into international human rights law might be ignored. That is because the a-temporal temporality of international human rights law produces the view that Indigenous peoples are pre-legal natural subjects of international legal discourse, instead of tribal peoples (and others) who become intelligible Indigenous peoples when they performatively inscribe international legal discourse into their ways of life. If so, then scholars, advocates and others, including rights-claimants, who are involved

[98] ibid 5.
[99] ibid 21.
[100] ibid 23.
[101] Young (n 3) ch 6; JE Correia 'Adjudication and Its Aftereffects in Three Inter-American Court Cases Brought Against Paraguay: Indigenous Land Rights' (2018) 1 *Erasmus Law Review* 43.

in the reproduction of human rights discourse may be unwittingly constructing tribal peoples as Indigenous peoples and, therein, re-writing unique legalities and temporalities for human rights and international legal discourse purposes.

In looking at the Wet'suwet'en and Whangangui iwi contests, those are disputes about who has authority over certain spaces. Those contests also involve temporalities. In both, human rights have been claimed as a universalised legal discourse without concern for spatial borders or temporalities to contest the state, which may also conflict with tribal legalities. Assuming the Wet'suwet'en and the Whanganui iwi are Indigenous peoples does not mean that they lose their own laws, temporalities or forms of living. Nevertheless, if they are to claim human rights as Indigenous peoples, they will have to performatively re-cite that discourse. That requires some degree of re-writing and transformation. Those who use human rights to re-cite decolonisation can draw attention to the harmful and problematic ways that modern states develop and reproduce hierarchical and racial inequalities. Beneficially, it enables others to identify the claimants and support them as Indigenous peoples.

As those terms are re-cited, multiple and differing uses of those terms will arise in ways that no one can fully stabilise. Where decolonisation universalised the temporality and spatiality of the state, re-citing decolonisation through human rights re-asserts a spatial discourse associated with the modern state. Claiming human rights may perverts tribal peoples' legalities as it simultaneously enters them into a contest that presupposes the spatial discourse of the state. Indigenous peoples who claim rights and defend their territory in a recognisable and state-sanctioned language of property rights may work against how those who claim human rights seek or intend to use them: states can uphold and support the terms of that discourse, especially to the degree that claimants re-cite property-based claims, without adhering to how any claimant intends to use those terms. Indigenous peoples can always re-contest or provide specificity about their meaning for any terms, but in re-citing the terms of the state, they re-enter into a permanent contest for the present. Furthermore, from an a-temporal international human rights perspective, the temporal trap arises because those who enter into this a-temporal temporality have already entered into a permanent contest whether they approve or not.

4

Documents and Time in International Human Rights Law Monitoring: Artefacts, Objects, Things

KATHRYN McNEILLY*

I. INTRODUCTION

TIME IS AN ever-present part of international human rights law from the macro to the micro. It is central to the overarching narratives and conceptual ideas that define this area of law as well as to its everyday practice and implementation in localised settings. Across these various spaces and places, international human rights law can be understood as not just taking place against the backdrop of time, but as actively constructing temporal ideas, rhythms and flows in fundamental ways.[1] These ideas of time emerge in and drive its practice in both overt and subtle fashions. In this chapter I investigate the work of creating time in international human rights law with a focus on United Nations (UN) monitoring practice. This is activity aimed at examining states' implementation of their obligations and facilitating enhanced levels of compliance. Stemming from development of the first binding international human rights treaties,[2] monitoring has expanded substantially in the intervening decades. Today this work is undertaken by UN Charter bodies – including the Special Procedures of the Human Rights Council; the Universal Periodic Review (UPR); and the Human Rights Council Complaint Procedure – and Treaty Bodies attached to the nine core[3] human rights treaties.[4] Monitoring

* The research underpinning this article was facilitated by a Leverhulme Research Fellowship 2019–2020 (RF-2019-205).

[1] K McNeilly, 'Are Rights Out of Time? International Human Rights Law, Temporality, and Radical Social Change' (2019) 28 *Social and Legal Studies* 817. See more widely C Greenhouse, 'Just in Time: Temporality and the Cultural Legitimation of Law' (1989) 98 *Yale Law Journal* 1631; E Grabham, *Brewing Legal Time: Things, Form, and the Enactment of Law* (University of Toronto Press, 2016).

[2] N Rodley, 'The Role and Impact of Treaty Bodies' in D Shelton (ed), *The Oxford Handbook of International Human Rights Law* (OUP, 2013) 621–22.

[3] These are the Committee on the Elimination of Racial Discrimination; the Committee on Economic, Social and Cultural Rights; the Human Rights Committee; the Committee on the

accordingly involves a collection of diverse activities whereby states are reviewed in relation to their obligations usually by independent experts, but following creation of the UPR in 2006, also by their peers. The international human rights monitoring system has an overt time creating nature from the beginning by virtue of the fact that it creates either cyclical monitoring patterns – periodic reporting to Treaty Bodies and the UPR – or one-off interventions at a particular point in time to address an ongoing, urgent or unremedied situation of violation – the Special Procedures and Treaty Body Optional Protocol activity, for example. However, I wish to draw attention to the creation of time in less grand ways in monitoring, focusing on temporalities generated in more subtle, everyday ways by objects or things.[5]

On the face of it, this may seem puzzling for the reader. If we are to assume that temporal ideas are generated in monitoring practices, surely this is driven by humans – appointed experts, Secretariat staff, state delegates, civil society representatives, for example – who direct and oversee such activity? Indeed, when we think of international human rights law generally we are used to foregrounding humans, not only as the subject of such law but as the actors responsible for its everyday implementation.[6] I encourage the reader to put aside this commonsensical tendency and to approach objects with a new-found naivety which may uncover their nature and work in fresh ways.[7] To begin this investigation, I direct attention to one object only: the document. Documents are artefacts of central importance in the international human rights system and, especially, in its monitoring. Reports, factsheets, concluding observations, recommendations, lists of issues, for example, are at the heart of the review that monitoring practices undertake. I suggest that these documents can be observed as more than human-made artefacts possessing agency only at the behest of their human authors, readers or users. Rather than just inert tools, documents are objects with capacity to generate temporal ideas such as past, present and future. This is of course not to assert that they possess a full agency on a par with humans

Elimination of All Forms of Discrimination Against Women; the Committee Against Torture; the Committee on the Rights of the Child; the Committee on Migrant Workers; the Committee on the Rights of Persons with Disabilities; and the Committee on Enforced Disappearances which comprise the nine main treaties. The Subcommittee on Prevention of Torture also undertakes monitoring work, albeit the functions of this Committee differ.

[4] For discussion on monitoring see: A Nolan, R Fredman and T Murphy (eds), *The United Nations Special Procedures System* (Brill, 2017); N Rodley, 'United Nations Human Rights Treaty Bodies and Special Procedures of the Commission on Human Rights – Complementary or Competition? (2003) 25 *Human Rights Quarterly* 882; F Gaer, 'A Voice Not an Echo: Universal Periodic Review and the UN Treaty Body System' (2007) 7 *Human Rights Law Review* 109; A Nolan, L Grover and G Ulfstein (eds), *UN Human Rights Treaty Bodies: Law and Legitimacy* (CUP, 2012).

[5] For general discussion on nonhuman objects in international law broadly see J Hohmann and D Joyce (eds), *International Law's Objects* (OUP, 2018).

[6] This is a tendency across legal thinking more generally: H Yoon Kang and S Kendall, 'Legal Materiality' in S Stern, M Del Mar and B Meyler (eds), *The Oxford Handbook of Law and Humanities* (OUP, 2020) 22.

[7] J Bennett, *Vital Matter: A Political Ecology of Things* (Duke University Press, 2009) 121.

but – following insights of Actor Network Theory (ANT) – to recognise that there are 'many metaphysical states between full causality and sheer inexistence'[8] for them in the networks that make up monitoring practices. In these practices, documents operate alongside humans as objects with a time creating capacity which is effective and affective.

In addition, sometimes documents can be observed to act in monitoring processes in ways which demonstrate a more lively and dynamic power or agency with an enhanced distance from humans. Here documents move from apprehension as objects to 'objects as other', or things.[9] This is evident in how they can operate to elude the reader or author, how they can jar, stop humans in their tracks, or fundamentally change apprehensions in unforeseeable ways. Documents here demonstrate an ability to act in ways that are beyond human control and intention, evidencing a vitality of their own which may surprise.[10] When this is so, documents often serve not to create smooth ideas of time, such as those of past, present and future, but to interrupt smooth temporal rhythms. In other words, they create a jolt in time which disrupts. This livelier, 'thingly'[11] temporal work must also be considered as part of the time creating capacity of documents in monitoring processes. The result is that rather than just artefacts functioning as inputs or records in monitoring activity, documents operate both as objects, and as more unsettling, dynamic things at various points in their generation of time.

In undertaking this investigation, the chapter proceeds in four sections. First, in section II, the foundations for the assertion that documents may be understood as objects with time creating capacity are outlined. This encompasses writing in a range of disciplines which offers tools to think through the work of documents in international human rights law. Secondly, the temporal role of documents in the case study area of monitoring practice will be explored in section III. Examples across the Treaty Body system, the UPR, and the Special Procedures will be drawn upon to demonstrate how documents can serve to create temporalities of past, present and future in these activities. Thirdly, attention turns in section IV to examine occasions where documents exceed their role as objects and demonstrate themselves to have a thingly power which creates interruptive, jarring and unexpected temporalities in monitoring practices. Here the insights of Thing Theory and vital materialism are engaged and combined with an understanding of documents as creators of time. The chapter concludes in section V by encouraging this new perspective on monitoring documents as more than just artefacts to stimulate wider examinations of objects and time in international human rights law.

[8] B Latour, *Reassembling the Social: An Introduction to Actor-Network-Theory* (OUP, 2007) 72.
[9] B Brown, 'How to Do Things with Things' (A Toy Story)' (1998) 24 *Critical Inquiry* 935.
[10] Bennett (n 7).
[11] ibid xiii.

II. UNDERSTANDING THE TIME CREATING AGENCY OF DOCUMENTS

The study of documents as objects with significance is by no means new. Organisational and management studies, Science and Technology Studies (STS), sociology, anthropology, and legal studies are just some of the disciplines that have enriched our understanding of the work that documents do. One particularly influential body of literature traversing disciplinary boundaries in this area is ANT which has provided tools to understand the agentic work of objects. Developed in the field of STS by writers such as Bruno Latour,[12] Michel Callon,[13] John Law,[14] Annemarie Mol,[15] and Marilyn Strathern,[16] ANT advances an ontological symmetry which sees nonhuman objects – machines, tools, technical artifacts, animals, natural phenomena, material structures, texts, etc – as acting alongside humans in actor-networks. In Latour's language, both are actants.[17] ANT does not propose that the agency of objects is the same as humans, but it does reveal how objects are not purely passive: they can make a difference to the action of other agents,[18] and thus must be incorporated into our understandings of the world. As Latour elaborates, objects 'might authorize, allow, afford, encourage, permit, suggest, influence, block, render possible, forbid, and so on'.[19] In ANT studies, focused initially on exploring 'science in the making' but subsequently expanding further,[20] documents are often key actants which enable certain orders of meaning and action to emerge.[21] They work with humans in constructing meaning and the social. One instructive ANT investigation pertinent for lawyers to consider is Latour's study of the Counseil d'État where physical texts and files are understood as part of the actor-networks generating law and its creation of the social alongside judges, litigants, architecture, legal concepts, and wider everyday office objects.[22] For Latour, the physical

[12] B Latour and S Woolgar, *Laboratory Life: The Construction of Scientific Facts* (Princeton University Press, 1986); B Latour, *The Pasteurization of France* (trans A Sheridan and J Law, Harvard University Press, 1988).

[13] M Callon, 'Some Elements of a Sociology of Translation: Domestication of the Scallops and the Fishermen of St Brieuc Bay' in J Law (ed), *Power, Action and Belief: A New Sociology of Knowledge?* (Routledge, 1986) 196–223.

[14] J Law, *Organizing Modernity: Social Ordering and Social Theory* (Blackwell, 1993).

[15] A Mol, *The Body Multiple: Ontology in Medical Practice* (Duke University Press, 2003).

[16] M Strathern, 'Cutting the Network' (1996) 2 *Journal of the Royal Anthropological Institute* 517.

[17] B Latour, *The Politics of Nature: How to Bring the Sciences into Democracy* (trans C Porter, Harvard University Press, 2004) 75.

[18] Latour (n 8) 71.

[19] B Latour, 'Nonhumans' in S Harrison, S Pile and N Thrift (eds), *Patterned Ground: Entanglements of Nature and Culture* (Reakiton Books, 2004) 226.

[20] This includes law: E Cloatre, 'Law and ANT (and its Kin): Possibilities, Challenges, and Ways Forward' (2018) 45 *Journal of Law and Society* 646.

[21] B Latour, 'Visualisation and Cognition: Drawing Things Together' in H Kuklick and E Long (eds), *Knowledge and Society: Studies in the Sociology of Culture Past and Present* (JAI Press, 1985) 1–40.

[22] B Latour, *The Making of Law: An Ethnography of the Counseil D'État* (Polity, 2009). See also A Pottage, 'The Materiality of What?' (2012) 39 *Journal of Law and Society* 167; K McGee (ed), *Latour and the Passage of Law* (University of Edinburgh Press, 2015).

movement of documents, their filing and storage, their reading, and the intertextuality between them is essential to apprehension of the material, everyday practice of law.[23] These documents include legal reports, judgments, statutes, documentary evidence, and so on. ANT insights are particularly influential for the present analysis, allowing the capacity that documents possess to emerge.

Alongside ANT authors such as Latour, others have investigated documents. For example, situated in anthropology and accounting respectively, Marilyn Strathern and Michael Power have revealed documents as key objects in audit procedures.[24] Anthropologist Annelise Riles has explored documents as artifacts of modern knowledge practices',[25] drawing attention to how documents produce, stretch and abbreviate agency and elicit specific responses. In one study Riles investigates document drafting at the 1995 Beijing World Conference on Women, uncovering how document text stimulates powerful effects for human participants.[26] In doing so, Riles connects with the work of Richard Harper and his ethnography of documents in the International Monetary Fund.[27] In this work, Harper produces the concept of a 'document career'. This term captures the movement of documents throughout an organisation. For Harper, understanding the career of documents is crucial to understanding the life of an organisation more generally. Throughout their career documents do not function as passive objects at the whim of their human authors and readers. Rather, drawing from Dorothy Smith,[28] Harper stresses that 'the relationship between the user and text is always active and transformational'.[29] Documents, in other words, are generative and relational, working alongside, rather than just for, humans. Closer to home for the international human rights lawyer, legal scholars, in particular those interested in law's materiality,[30] have also drawn attention to documents and theorised their work in legal contexts. Victim application forms, files in patent practice, and land title registration documents are some examples that have been explored.[31] Cornelia Vismann has been a significant influence in this thinking, demonstrating at the intersection of legal history

[23] Latour ibid 70–106.

[24] M Strathern, *Audit Culture: Anthropological Studies in Accountability, Ethics and the Academy* (Routledge, 2000); M Power, *The Audit Society: Rituals of Verification* (OUP, 1997).

[25] A Riles, 'Introduction: In Response' in A Riles (ed), *Documents: Artifacts of Modern Knowledge* (University of Michigan Press, 2006) 7.

[26] Riles, '[Deadlines]' in ibid 71–94.

[27] R Harper, *Inside the IMF: An Ethnography of Documents, Technology and Organisational Action* (Academic Press, 1998).

[28] D Smith, *Text, Facts and Femininity: Exploring the Relations of Ruling* (Routledge, 1993).

[29] Harper (n 27) 43.

[30] Kang and Kendall (n 6).

[31] S Kendall, 'Archiving Victimhood: Practices of Inscription in International Criminal Law' in S Motha and H van Rijswijk (eds), *Law, Violence, Memory: Uncovering the Counter-Archive* (Routledge, 2015) 156–76; H Yoon Kang, 'Science Inside Law: The Making of a New Patent Class in the International Patent Classification' (2012) 25 *Science in Context* 551; B Bhandar, 'Title by Registration: Instituting Modern Property Law and Creating Racial Value in the Settler Colony' (2015) 42 *Journal of Law and Society* 253.

and media studies how documents and files are not just administrative tools, but play a role in constituting law and its authority.[32]

From the above, the work documents perform is brought into view. Where, however, does time fit in? In existing studies of documents, temporality often arises, either implicitly or explicitly. In the latter category, Riles outlines how documents drafted at international conferences and similar events have a history and also a future as part of a larger trajectory of action and intertextuality.[33] In exploring the drafting process for the Beijing Declaration and Platform for Action, she also reveals the temporal gridlock and sense of retrogression that was produced via the document text by the word 'gender' and its bracketing.[34] Time is likewise central to Harper's notion of the 'document career.' Documents are 'matrixed through time',[35] they have a past, present and future, and are a crucial part of how an organisation organises itself in time.[36] In this existing literature it is possible to get a glimpse of how documents may not just be located within or operate against pre-existing time, but how these objects might have time creating capacity: they may generate gridlock, retrogression, may facilitate a new future direction for an organisation, for example. In legal studies, documents have been explicitly understood as creating time. At the level of national law, reports, forms, and other documentation are apprehended as objects which serve, in the words of Emily Grabham, to 'brew legal time'.[37] For Grabham, drawing on ANT and wider object-orientated perspectives, across legal locations, institutions and spaces 'linear and other arrangements of time are … brewed through changing relationships of humans and material forms.'[38] Documents appear as one significant part of this material brewing of legal time.[39]

I take the work above as a starting point to think about documents and time in international human rights law. I argue that documents are objects in the legal field which help to shape the temporal rhythms produced in the sites and practices of this area of law too. Work is needed, however, to reflect on the precise ways in which this occurs. This is important, but also challenging, due to the fact that international human rights law often operates to inadvertently conceal the time creating work of documents through a focus on documentation as input or – reflecting what Vismann sees as a wider impulse common to modern administration in the West[40] – as record. This is especially so in monitoring practices. Due to expansion of monitoring mechanisms in recent decades, the volume of

[32] C Vismann, *Files: Law and Media Technology* (Stanford University Press, 2008).
[33] Riles (n 26) 80.
[34] ibid 82.
[35] Harper (n 27) 4.
[36] ibid 134.
[37] Grabham (n 1).
[38] ibid 14.
[39] See also I van Oorschot, 'Doing Times, Doing Truths: The Legal Case File as Folded Object' in E Grabham and S Benyon-Jones (eds), *Law and Time* (Routledge, 2019) 229–46.
[40] C Vismann, 'Out of File, Out of Mind' in W Hui Kyong Chun and T Keenan (eds), *New Media, Old Media: A History and Theory Reader* (Routledge, 2006) 97.

documentation attached to these practices has increased.[41] While their content, length and purpose of course varies, and they have increasingly moved from physical to electronic media,[42] documents occupy a central place across all monitoring activities. Documents can indeed be understood as the blood pumping around the body of this work. These observations will no doubt be familiar to anyone with knowledge of the monitoring system. Less familiar, however, is conscious reflection on the time creating function which also characterises these documents. Reports, recommendations, concluding observations, core common documents, factsheets, lists of issues, stakeholder submissions, agendas, etc are frequently regarded as tools at the disposal of human actors: inert resources transporting information between states, the UN, and civil society rather than active objects which help create time within international human rights law. On closer inspection, however, the temporalities underpinning monitoring processes appear, to a significant extent, as shaped by documents and the work they do. These temporalities are diverse. Below I focus on just three of the most obvious and recognisable temporalities which documents as objects help to generate: past, present, and future.

III. THE TIME CREATING AGENCY OF DOCUMENTS AS OBJECTS IN MONITORING

A. The Past

Temporal flows relating to the past are imperative in monitoring practices. While these practices are concerned with identifying present human rights challenges and future action, they are equally caught up with evaluation of the past and the extent to which states have adhered to their obligations in this past. This can involve review of a particular period of time in cyclical reporting – as with Treaty Bodies and the UPR – or examination of an alleged human rights violation which occurred (or is ongoing) over specified dates – as with the Special Procedures and Optional Protocol mechanisms. In monitoring activities, states, civil society stakeholders, non-governmental organisations (NGOs), National Human Rights Institutions (NHRIs) and sometimes individuals present documentation relating to the past. Depending on the monitoring mechanism in question, this takes the form of written reports, responses to communication from UN bodies, briefing documents, or complaints. This documentation does

[41] S Egan, 'Strengthening the United Nations Human Rights Treaty Body System' (2013) 13 *Human Rights Law Review* 209, 212.

[42] This reflects a wider change in medium for documents more generally: Vismann (n 32) 161–64; K Megill, *The Corporate Memory: Records and Information Management in the Electronic Age*, 2nd edn (KG Saur Verlag, 2005). This move contrasts with Latour's primarily physical encounter with texts and files in the Counseil d'État.

more than present experts or peer reviewers with information to assess. In such contexts, documents create temporal pasts in important ways. To illustrate this, let us turn to a concrete example: periodic reporting in the Treaty Body system.

A central function of Treaty Bodies is review of state reports.[43] States parties are required to submit an initial report upon ratification of the treaty, followed by subsequent reports at a periodicity usually between two to five years.[44] Each periodic report is submitted several months in advance of a scheduled public examination, commonly referred to as a 'constructive dialogue'. After receipt of the report, many Treaty Bodies prepare a 'list of issues'[45] which is submitted to the states party indicating the topics and concerns the dialogue will focus on. This in turn triggers creation of another document in which the states party responds to the list of issues. Following the constructive dialogue a concluding observations document is prepared commending and assessing the states party's record and making recommendations for action.[46] In this process, however, the state report and written response to the list of issues are not the only documents which inform the review. Treaty Bodies are empowered to consider information received from other sources, such as NGOs and NHRIs. In addition to being able to attend the public examination and often to orally brief Committee members,[47] NGOs and NHRIs can submit written documentation to the Committee. Often termed 'shadow reports', these documents provide additional information to that presented by the states party. Submitted electronically, and sometimes in hard copy, shadow reports travel from national offices and headquarters to the UN and present accounts of human rights obligations on the ground.[48]

I want to focus here on the shadow report and consider the work that this document does in relation to creation of the past. This has three elements. Shadow report documents, first of all, serve to construct conceptions of the past at the international level. These conceptions may contrast with those constructed by the state report.[49] Shadow reports can serve to bring additional experiences or accounts into view, engaging the reader in new perspectives on the obligations under review, the measures put in place at the national level, and the experience of everyday rights holders. Here the shadow report is doing more than just distributing alternative information. This document is bringing

[43] Rodley (n 2) 626.

[44] ibid 627.

[45] Following the lead of the Human Rights Committee, this is prepared by a special rapporteur or dedicated task force. See Rodley (n 4) 627.

[46] M O'Flaherty, 'The Concluding Observations of United Nations Human Rights Treaty Bodies' (2006) 6 *Human Rights Law Review* 27.

[47] A Clapham, 'UN Human Rights Reporting Procedures: An NGO Perspective' in P Alston and J Crawford (eds), *The Future of UN Human Rights Treaty Monitoring* (CUP, 2000) 175–98.

[48] These documents link into increasing participation by NGOs and NHRIs in reporting processes which 'has grown from a point where [these stakeholders] had no formal role at all to play in the process to one which has been aptly characterised as a "critical dependency" of that process': Egan (n 41) 227.

[49] F Gaer, 'Implementing International Human Rights Norms: UN Human Rights Treaty Bodies and NGOs' (2003) 2 *Journal of Human Rights* 339.

different pasts into being – making them visible and intelligible – at the international level in a way that may otherwise not happen. Shadow reports generate pasts through their very existence and capability of being read by Treaty Body Committee members and wider audiences. Without shadow report documents, these pasts would not be comprehensible to, or exist within, the treaty body system.[50] Related to this, secondly, these documents construct the past as multiple. Each shadow report submitted represents a different narrative about the past in the state being reviewed. Whether physically printed for Committee members or transmitted electronically as a folder of files, these documents visibly represent different experiences of the past. They remind that the past is not singular, consisting of multiple threads which need to be acknowledged and considered in the present of the monitoring process. Shadow report documents, therefore, help bring into being a past in treaty body monitoring that is multitudinous and thick. Thirdly, recalling Smith's conception of the 'active' nature of documents, shadow reports demonstrate agentic temporal work in the ways they construct affective pasts. In engaging with the shadow report, the reader's perception and understanding of the past, and the human rights issues arising in it, can be changed in an affective way. The narratives that are built by these documents may be surprising, upsetting, or educating and lead the reader to an engagement with the past which they otherwise would not have experienced.[51] In other words, shadow report documents work with human actors to not only bring pasts, and their multiple nature, into being in the treaty body system, but to stimulate affect in their networked relation with human experts and readers. From this, it is clear that when shadow reports are apprehended as objects – physical or electronic – they undertake temporal work which brings the past into being at the international level in various ways, rather than merely presenting information on pre-existing pasts.

B. The Present

In other contexts, documents work to create temporal presents. To consider this it is instructive to turn to another example: the UPR. A relatively recent addition to UN monitoring machinery,[52] the UPR was developed as a function of the new Human Rights Council in 2006. The mechanism was designed to review all states periodically across the full range of their human rights obligations

[50] The extent to which these pasts are effectively taken into account or acted upon in the system is a separate question for consideration.

[51] For wider work on documentation and affect in monitoring see J Billaud, 'Keepers of the Truth: Producing "Transparent" Documents for the UPR' in H Charlesworth and E Larking (eds), *Human Rights and the Universal Periodic Review: Rituals and Ritualism* (CUP, 2014) 63–84.

[52] Charlesworth and Larking ibid; E Domínguez Redondo, 'The Universal Periodic Review of the UN Human Rights Council: An Assessment of the First Session' (2008) 7 *Chinese Journal of International Law* 721.

and commitments, as well as applicable international humanitarian law,[53] and is unique in being based on peer – as opposed to expert – review.[54] The process begins with information gathering on the national human rights situation in the four-to-five-year period under review. Three documents contribute to this: a national report produced by the state under review (SuR); a summary of comments made by UN bodies compiled by the United Nations Office of the High Commissioner for Human Rights (OHCHR); and a summary of comments submitted by civil society stakeholders also compiled by the OHCHR. These documents form the basis of review by the UPR Working Group, made up of Human Rights Council member and observer states who examine the SuR's record in real time. An outcome report is produced from the Working Group meeting which includes, crucially, a list of all recommendations made to the SuR which must be either accepted or 'noted'.[55] While it may be natural, as in Treaty Body processes, to regard documents as information carriers or artefacts recording the UPR process and its outcome, I suggest that these objects in fact undertake additional work. In particular, they are important in creating and sustaining a present in the review.

In Harper's work,[56] expanded by others,[57] it is possible to see how documents have a present: moments when they are read, filled out, cited, and so on. Beyond this, Harper demonstrates how documents can, additionally, play an important role in creating presents: they bring people together for meetings, briefings, field missions, and other events.[58] In the UPR, documents demonstrate a similar present-creating activity. It is the three reports – from the SuR, civil society stakeholders, and UN bodies – that bring states together in the Working Group session to engage in interactive dialogue. These documents form the basis of the monitoring which happens in particular presents at the UN's European headquarters in Geneva, transmitted worldwide via webcast. However, it is important to note that once documents bring this present into being they do not fade into the background. In the UPR Working Group, documents are visibly an active part of the present. When viewing a Working Group session via webcast, it is possible to see that documents are printed out, opened on laptops, moved between members of state delegations and Secretariat staff via paper or on screens. These documents include pre-prepared statements which are read out by delegates and notes that are taken by actors in the room, among others. All of this activity happens in real time and sustains the Working Group session. Documents have a fluid and energetic physical presence in the review. They can

[53] UN Human Rights Council, *Resolution 5/1: Institution-building of the United Nations Human Rights Council* UN Doc. A/HRC/RES/5/1 (18 June 2007).

[54] For discussion see J Cowan and J Billaud, 'Between Learning and Schooling: The Politics of Human Rights Monitoring at the Universal Periodic Review' (2015) 36 *Human Rights Quarterly* 1175.

[55] UN Human Rights Council (n 53) para 32.

[56] Harper (n 27).

[57] For example, D Brenneis, 'Performing Promise' in Riles (n 25) 41–70.

[58] See Harper's discussion of an IMF mission to arcadia and his exploration of the use of a staff report.

be understood to do more than just bring humans into a room. Rather, they are the energy that bolsters the room and the networked assemblage[59] of the Working Group meeting in its present.

Beyond creating and sustaining presents in this energetic way, documents can also generate new temporal rhythms in the present, influencing how the present is understood and experienced. One example of this is urgent temporalities. An aspect of monitoring practice demonstrating this particularly well is the Human Rights Council Special Procedures. Described as the 'eyes and ears' of the UN human rights system,[60] Special Procedures stem from a competence accorded to the Commission on Human Rights and the Sub-Committee on the Prevention of Discrimination and Protection of Minorities to 'examine information relevant to gross violations of human rights and fundamental freedoms'.[61] This ad hoc power has evolved to create a system whereby independent experts – usually known as Special Rapporteurs – or Working Groups are granted mandates on either a geographic or thematic basis.[62] As of 2020, there are 79 mandate holders working across 44 thematic and 11 country mandates.[63] In addition to conducting country visits, convening consultations, and engaging in advisory and public awareness work,[64] an important function of the Special Procedures is sending written communications to states or, occasionally, other bodies. These communications take two forms: allegation letters, which relate to past human rights violations, and urgent appeals, which are regarding ongoing or potential violations.[65] Between December 2016 and May 2019 1,622 communications were sent, often joint between two or more Special Procedures.[66] The basis of communications is information received from individuals, NGOs or wider stakeholders, submitted to the relevant mandate-holder either online or by post.[67] It is at the discretion of the individual expert, in consultation with

[59] G Deleuze and F Guatarri, *A Thousand Plateaus: Capitalism and Schizophrenia* (University of Minnesota Press, 1987).

[60] United Nations, Secretary-General Urges Human Rights Council to Avoid Narrow Considerations, Selectivity; Supports Independence while Condemning 'Inflammatory Rhetoric' www.un.org/press/en/2011/sgsm13366.doc.htm.

[61] UN Economic and Social Council, *Resolution 1235 (XLII)* UN Doc. E/4393 (June 1967).

[62] E Dominguez-Redondo, 'The History of the Special Procedures: A "Learning-by-Doing" Approach to Human Rights Implementation' in Nolan, Freedman and Murphy (n 4) 11–52.

[63] UN Human Rights Council, *Facts and Figures with Regard to the Special Procedures in 2020* UN Doc. A/HRC/46/61/Add.1 (15 March 2021).

[64] See J Connors, 'Special Procedures: Independence and Impartiality' in Nolan, Freedman and Murphy (n 4) 64.

[65] M Limon and T Piccone, 'Human Rights Special Procedures: Determinants of Influence. Understanding and Strengthening the Effectiveness of the UN's Independent Human Rights Experts' (Universal Working Group, March 2014) 28.

[66] UN Human Rights Council, *Communications Report of Special Procedures*, UN Doc. A/HRC/42/65 (September 2019); A/HRC/41/56 (June 2019); A/HRC/40/79 (March 2019); A/HRC/39/27 (September 2018); A/HRC/38/54 (June 2018); A/HRC/37/80 (March 2018); A/HRC/36/25 (September 2017).

[67] While usually this takes a written form, more recently audio-visual material has been received: E McPherson and T Probert, 'Special Procedures in the Digital Age' in Nolan, Freedman and Murphy (n 4) 261–70.

criteria found in the Code of Conduct,[68] to determine whether information received will be acted on. Communications take the form of a formal letter sent via diplomatic channels, later made available publicly on the OHCHR website, asking for clarification, further information, and action from the state, or other party, involved. It is the second form of communication – urgent appeals – that I would like to consider.

In urgent appeals, Special Procedures aim to secure intervention to prevent or interrupt a pressing human rights situation. Examples include cases of imminent execution, arbitrary detention, and torture. Listing the details of the allegations received, reminding of the international human rights obligations engaged, and requesting a response to a list of matters, urgent communications follow a recognisable format. They also share the same function: to intervene in the present by creating a temporal urgency where the relevant human rights situation is brought into sharp relief.[69] Sometimes urgent appeals generate the desired preventative action from states, other times they do not. Whether successful or not in terms of outcome, these documents serve to generate urgent temporalities by virtue of the way in which they often draw public attention to a pressing issue or reframe it in new ways as a human rights violation. It is not just the content of the communication document which generates urgency, however, but also its speed. In contrast to many other monitoring documents produced by UN bodies, urgent appeal documentation is produced and dispatched in a swift, time-sensitive manner – essential for their preventative purpose – facilitated by a Quick Response Desk at the OHCHR.[70] Alongside content and speed, the unique nature of urgent appeal communication – both the document's form of delivery as a letter transmitted through formal diplomatic channels and its escalating nature – bring into being temporal rhythms of urgency in a way that few other monitoring documents do. Across all these elements, the urgent appeal document as object performs important temporal work shaping the present.

C. The Future

The time creating agency of documents as objects, thirdly, can be observed in how they serve to bring futures into being. Returning to the work of Harper and Riles, just as documents have a present, they also have a future. Riles's investigation of the drafting of the Beijing Declaration and Platform for Action discusses the trajectory that this document will have in relation to future conferences and

[68] UN Human Rights Council, *Resolution 5/2: Code of conduct of the Special Procedures mandate-holders of the Human Rights Council* UN Doc. A/HRC/RES/5/2 (18 June 2007).

[69] N Rodley, 'Urgent Action' in G Alfredsson, J Grimheden, B Ramcharan and A de Zayas (eds), *International Human Rights Monitoring Mechanisms: Essays in Honour of Jakob Th. Moeller*, 2nd edn (Martinus Nijhoff Publishers, 2009) 191–95.

[70] B Ramcharan, *The Protection Roles of UN Human Rights Special Procedures* (Martinus Nijhoff, 2009) 155.

international, as well as local, documentation.[71] In his work, Harper explores how documents help predict and determine future decision-making activities for organisations like the IMF.[72] Expanding these insights further, however, documents not only have futures and inform human decisions and actions pertaining to the future as inert tools, but may be key actants in creating and enacting futures themselves. The relationship that documents have with the future is powerful and generative in the actor-networks of monitoring. Again, it is possible to engage an example from monitoring practices to help demonstrate this.

This requires a return to the UPR, albeit to a different part of its process: the UPR pre-sessions which occur around a month before the Working Group meets. Following observation that the opportunity civil society actors have to inform the review is limited beyond the combined stakeholder report compiled by OHCHR, international NGO UPR Info initiated the pre-sessions in 2012.[73] These sessions have two aims: first, local actors, NGOs and NHRIs are enabled to orally brief states on the human rights situation in the SuR; secondly, state delegations are given the opportunity to ask questions and gather further information.[74] Through this, the pre-sessions seek to influence the process of recommendation drafting, ensuring that the recommendations made during the review are specific, up to date, and well-targeted.[75] The pre-sessions, therefore, are a multi-stakeholder advocacy opportunity, taking place outside the formal structures of the process but consciously designed to inform these structures.

Prior to the pre-sessions, UPR Info provides guidance to civil society participants on the best way to present information.[76] This guidance includes advice on the use of 'Advocacy Factsheets'.[77] First used by Mongolia in the 2015 pre-sessions, these factsheets are 'a collection of individual documents, each focusing on a particular human rights topic'.[78] UPR Info uploads factsheets, presentations, and statement documents from each pre-session to a dedicated page on their website.[79] These documents vary in content, format, and length: some present narrative summaries of progress/challenges and recommendations for action, some produce short bullet point summaries, while others provide slide presentations, for example. In addition to informing the present of the pre-session – as with documents in the UPR Working Group discussed above – these documents can also help create the future in important ways in this monitoring

[71] Riles (n 26) 80.
[72] Harper (n 27) 112, 156.
[73] UPR Info, *UPR Info Pre-sessions: Empowering Human Rights Voices From the Ground* (UPR Info, 2016).
[74] N Higgins, 'Creating Space for Indigenous Rights: The Universal Periodic Review as a Mechanism for Promoting the Rights of Indigenous Peoples' (2019) 23 *International Journal of Human Rights* 125, 130–31.
[75] UPR Info (n 73) 11.
[76] Higgins (n 74) 131.
[77] UPR Info (n 73) 28.
[78] ibid.
[79] UPR Info, Pre-Sessions, www.upr-info.org/en/upr-process/pre-sessions.

mechanism. In their presentation to state delegates at the pre-session, they help to shape the recommendations that will be made in the upcoming Working Group meeting.[80] They inform what this future session will look like and, ultimately, its outcomes which the SuR will have to work with, if the recommendations made are accepted, for the next four to five years. More than just informing the decision-making of the human actors that make up reviewing state delegations, factsheets and wider pre-session documents are part of creating these wider futures in their relationships with human actants. As a collection of objects, they are not just tools at the disposal of state delegates, but important actants within the actor-network of the recommendation drafting process and the futures this enacts. Pre-session documents influence what issues are drawn to the attention of state delegates, what facts they are aware of, and even the wording of recommendations. These documents hold the potential at the pre-session, therefore, to substantially shape the future of the Working Group session, and beyond. The futures that are enacted in the UPR would often look different without them.

This specific example of future creation in the UPR sits alongside the more general work of outcome reports across all monitoring practices – whether cyclical or one-off in nature – which seek by their very purpose not just to comment on the future, but to enact it. In particular, the futures which these documents aim to enact are those which are more human rights compliant and grounded in enhanced fulfilment of the rights obligations under review. The enactment of new laws and policies, moves to ratify new treaties or remove reservations are some of the futures that have been brought into being by monitoring outcome reports and their work in network with actors at the national level.[81]

IV. THE TIME CREATING AGENCY OF DOCUMENTS AS THINGS IN MONITORING

In discussion so far, documents have been apprehended as objects with the capacity to act alongside humans in ways that have time creating significance, bringing into being temporal flows such as past, present and future. In this respect they help to 'brew legal time'[82] in the diverse relational networks of international human rights law monitoring. As noted at the outset, however, sometimes documents demonstrate a more lively and dynamic power with implications for the temporalities they create. In these instances, documents create a jolt in time which causes a disruption. This moves their time creating work beyond the generation of smooth and expected temporal rhythms, including past, present

[80] For discussion on the impact of the pre-sessions, see UPR Info (n 73) 24–27.

[81] See, eg, J Krommendijk, 'The Domestic Effectiveness of International Human Rights Monitoring in Established Democracies. The Case of the UN Human Rights Treaty Bodies' (2015) 10 *The Review of International Organizations* 489.

[82] Grabham (n 1).

and future and a progressive connection between them. Here the temporalities created are more jarring. At this point in their work documents are no longer objects, they operate as things. As things, documents still act in relationships with humans but show an even greater degree of distance from their human interlocuters. This more 'thingly' element of documents and time in monitoring must also be considered.

To apprehend documents in this way it is necessary to turn to the insights of work that has become known as Thing Theory. Explaining the difference between objects and things, Bill Brown comments that while we look through objects, we can catch only a glimpse of things.[83] Things appear as what is excessive in objects, what appears when objects stop working, when they elude their human-designated function and utilisation. For Brown, this occurs when 'you cut your finger on a sheet of paper, you trip over some toy, you get bopped on the head by a falling nut'.[84] In this respect, the difference between objects and things can be described thus: 'objects are the way things appear to the subject – that is, with a name, an identity, a gestalt or stereotypical template … Things, on the other hand … [signal] the moment when the object becomes the Other, when the sardine can looks back, when the mute idol speaks, when the subject experiences the object as uncanny ….'[85] Developing thinking on things via what she terms 'vital materialism', Jane Bennett describes things as possessing a vitality, a liveliness, or a power which 'draws attention to an efficacy of objects in excess of the human meanings, designs, or purposes they express or serve'.[86] In this approach, things have an active vibrantness, producing dramatic and subtle effects,[87] and are 'not entirely reducible to the contexts in which human subjects set them'.[88] In her work Bennett explores many nonhuman entities – organic and inorganic – through this lens, including metal, rubbish, electricity and, interesting for the lawyer, the deodad.[89] In all these cases, she encourages the reader to see a vibrant effectivity of things which is independent from the human.

In human rights monitoring practices there are occasions when documents can be understood to act as things and demonstrate vitality in this way. Building on Brown and Bennett, I suggest that in this thingly existence documents can have temporal effects, creating ideas of time which are disruptive and surprising. This occurs when a document stalls or eludes human actors – demonstrating agency further beyond the control of their human authors, readers or users – creating temporal effects which are unpredicted and interruptive. One such instance is when a document becomes misplaced, corrupted or left behind.

[83] B Brown, 'Thing Theory' (2001) 28 *Critical Inquiry* 1, 4.
[84] ibid.
[85] WJT Mitchell, *What Do Pictures Want? The Lives and Loves of Images* (University of Chicago Press, 2005) 156–57.
[86] Bennett (n 7) 22.
[87] ibid 6.
[88] ibid 5.
[89] ibid 9.

For example, in the UPR process, a document may not be successfully transported between the pre-session and the permanent mission office, or between the latter location and the Working Group. Here the document causes a disruption as a physical object, a jarring to the present and, potentially, to the future of the UPR session in question. Electronically, documents may frequently become corrupted or have a broken link on the OHCHR website or UN extranet, rendering them inaccessible and leading to an interruption in the past or present of the monitoring process in question. A similar phenomenon also emerges when documents contain unintentionally inaccurate information. For example, a Treaty Body shadow report may inform a question or recommendation in periodic monitoring which has been surpassed by events that have followed the report's submission. Here the shadow report causes a jar, a blip in the process and potentially its future outcome. Documents may additionally demonstrate existence as things when they do not generate the effect or affect desired by their human author. The issues or experiences highlighted in a shadow report document may not be acted on by Treaty Body experts in periodic review or the UPR pre-session factsheet may not trigger a recommendation being made in the way that is hoped. Here the document frustrates the connection between past, present and future that its author envisaged and desired.

Some of the above may be unique to the experience of actors directly involved in international human rights monitoring – the transportation of documents by state delegates, for example – but those external to monitoring processes may also experience documents as things in this way – document links broken on United Nations webpages are a particular example. Across the various instances outlined, documents do not construct and sustain smooth and expected ideas of time – such as past, present and future explored above – rather, they interrupt, elude, jar and cause temporal effects which are unexpected as a result of their vitality and lively existences. Documents here create temporalities that step outside linear continuity and that stimulate discontinuity or a sense of break. As a party to any of the examples above, the human actor may be surprised by documents, disappointed by them, or inconvenienced by them. Their status as thing jumps out – asserts its presence[90] – and stops human actors in their temporal tracks. This is not to say that documents as objects cannot create disruptive temporal flows or ideas. We may think of occasions – including that of Special Procedure urgent appeal documentation above – where this may occur. Rather, what is distinct about the temporal life of documents as things is that the disruptive times they create are not as knowable or as expected by human actants. The temporal jolt, jar and interruption of things is distinct and emerges from the occasions when the space between humans and documents expands slightly and we experience the object as other. This too is part of the time creating power that documents have, albeit one which is livelier, is less easy to pinpoint, and is

[90] Brown (n 83) 4.

characterised by the inability of objects to be fully controlled in manners that we may not have considered.

V. CONCLUSION

Documents are in many ways the staple of the international human rights lawyer. They outline legal obligations, specify procedural rules, bring new institutions and bodies into existence, and contain goals and targets, to name just a few of their most familiar functions. When it comes to monitoring practices, the function of documents is particularly evident in this activity which seeks to examine the implementation of states' human rights obligations and make recommendations for the future. These processes require written documents to drive them and facilitate the review that they undertake. Documents are, in this respect, definitive artefacts of monitoring practices, commonly understood as inputs and outputs, or records, in the system. In this chapter I have encouraged the reader to explore beyond this familiar understanding and approach documents from a different view, as objects with a capacity to act alongside humans to create the ideas of time which drive monitoring practices, including past, present and future. More than this, documents in monitoring can frequently elude and appear as things, exceeding our expectations and intended usages of them. When this occurs, temporalities are generated which are disruptive, which jar and interrupt the smooth temporal flows that might be anticipated in monitoring practices.

In closing it is imperative to note, of course, that documents are not the only objects or things with time creating effects in human rights monitoring, or indeed in this area of law more widely. Computers, screens, microphones, badges, buildings, websites, business cards, tables, chairs, and a variety of other objects are also essential in the everyday activity of monitoring and also assist in generating important ideas of time within this activity.[91] In this respect, work to examine the complex networks of actants that contribute to creating time in law must extend beyond documentation alone and may lead to further avenues of exploration for international human rights lawyers interested in engaging with materiality and the temporal effects it generates. This may appear to be unfamiliar terrain, and yet it is also very familiar. It requires looking at the artefacts that lawyers know and work with on a daily basis anew. Understanding the temporal work that documents perform in monitoring practices offers a first step in widening analysis in this way, as well as in considering other facets of international human rights law where similar temporal networks and agencies are at play. There is much that remains to be discovered about the temporal life of human rights in international law, and work to this end continues.

[91] K McNeilly, 'How Time Matters in the Human Rights Council's Universal Periodic Review: Humans, Objects, and Time Creation' (2021) 34 *Leiden Journal of International Law* 607.

5

Gender, Temporality and International Human Rights Law: From Hidden Histories to Feminist Futures

KAY LALOR

I. INTRODUCTION

IN INTERNATIONAL HUMAN rights law, the relationship between gender and rights is often narrowly focused, closely aligned with a particular conception of 'women's' rights and structured through binaries of male/female and sex/gender.[1] This limited vision of gender and rights is vulnerable to marginalisation, depoliticisation and co-option into wider international legal institutions in a way that undermines the possibility of far reaching change.[2] Despite these challenges, feminist scholarship continues to engage with questions of gender and rights, seeking to imagine and practice 'visions of a better world'.[3] This chapter contributes to this feminist project by schematising the role played by time and temporality in thinking new futures of gender and international human rights law. Drawing upon a Deleuzian perspective, the chapter maps time not merely as the medium within which law unfolds, but as active, virtual, and multiplicitous. It argues that the repetition of human rights language and norms create grand narratives that seek, but inevitably fail, to bring order to the chaos of time's multidimensional flow. Gendered practices and gender-based rights both contribute to and undermine these temporal movements. As such, by attending to temporalities of gender in international human rights law, we are

[1] R Kapur, *Gender, Alterity and Human Rights: Freedom in a Fishbowl* (Edward Elgar, 2018) 89–95.

[2] S Kouvo and Z Pearson, 'Introduction' in S Kouvo and Z Pearson (eds), *Feminist Perspectives on International Law: Between Resistance and Compliance?* (Hart Publishing, 2014).

[3] D Otto and Anna Grear, 'International Law, Social Change and Resistance: A Conversation Between Professor Anna Grear (Cardiff) and Professorial Fellow Dianne Otto (Melbourne)' (2018) 26 *Feminist Legal Studies* 351, 352.

better equipped to bring about futures that are not bound by the limitations of 'ritualised incantations'[4] of gender and rights that have shaped past and present.

The temporal approach adopted here emphasises the multidimensionality of time in which past, present and future are all interconnected dimensions of each other. Thus, thinking new futures requires a careful engagement with legal presents and pasts. Informed by postcolonial and feminist legal analysis that centres the colonial encounter in the formation of the sovereign state and, eventually, the modern international human rights regime,[5] the chapter interrogates how gender is assembled within international legal doctrines and explores how these gendered dimensions of international legal history are habitually repeated in the present and projected into the future.

Beginning with an exploration of Deleuzian multidimensional temporalities, the chapter first explores how multidimensional time operates within international law and international human rights law. It then draws upon this theoretical framework to unpick the gendered dimensions of international human rights' pasts, presents and futures. In particular, it examines how the gendered dimensions of the colonial origins of international law have shaped the visible and invisible presence of gender in modern international human rights law. The chapter concludes by exploring how a different, non-linear and multiplicitous temporal perspective opens up new possibilities beyond the limitations of our current framework of gender and rights.

II. TIME'S MULTIDIMENSIONALITY AND THE CREATION OF THE STABLE SUBJECT

Viewing time as multidimensional foregrounds its capacity to both arrange and dissolve that which we normally think of as stable. For Rosi Braidotti:

> The monistic unity of the subject is also posited in terms of time. A subject is a genealogical entity, possessing his or her own counter-memory, which in turn is an expression of degrees of affectivity and interconnectedness. Viewed spatially, the poststructuralist subject may appear as fragmented and disunited; on a temporal scale, however, its unity is that of a continuing power to synchronize its recollections.[6]

Adapting Braidotti's argument to international human rights law requires acknowledgement that subjectivity in international law is 'variegated'.[7] States

[4] H Charlesworth, 'Talking to Ourselves? Feminist Scholarship in International Law' in Kouvo and Pearson (n 2) 23.

[5] A Anghie, *Imperialism, Sovereignty and the Making of International Law* (CUP, 2007); M do Mar Castro Varela, 'The Ethical State?' in D Cooper, N Dhawan and Janet Newman (eds), *Reimagining the State: Theoretical Challenges and Transformative Possibilities* (Routledge, 2020); Otto and Grear (n 3); Kapur (n 1).

[6] R Braidotti, *Transpositions* (Polity, 2006) 151.

[7] K Parlett, 'The Individual and Structural Change in the International Legal System' (2012) 1 *Cambridge Journal of International and Comparative Law* 60, 75.

are the traditional subjects of international law 'with a full range of rights, duties and attendant capacities'.[8] Individuals, while still subjects, protected by a range of international human rights treaties have 'much more limited capacity to engage in the international legal system'.[9] Nonetheless, both individual subject and sovereign state can be conceived as 'geographically exclusive, sovereign, bounded, [and] "thing-like"'[10] and simultaneously as plural, multifaceted and discontinuous.[11] Thus, the foundations of gender-based rights in international human rights law rest upon unstable and changing subjectivities, held together by the operation of time and memory.[12]

Significantly, a multidimensional approach to time does not deny the importance of linear time, but does insist upon the incompleteness of linear temporality.[13] For Deleuze, linear, historical time is 'Chronos', 'the oriented line of the present',[14] or a series of successive moments, in which unity, synchronicity and identity are possible – the time of the stable subject above. Yet Chronos is not the whole of time, it is complemented by Aion: 'the cyclical, dynamic and molecular time of becoming'.[15] If Chronos is the time of the living present, in which bodies act and are acted upon, Aion is the time in which the present is infinitely subdivided into past and future: the time where an action has always occurred, or is yet to occur, or the time of the infinite future and infinite, or pure, past.[16]

Thus, time cannot be reduced to a conscious experience, or to an interlocking series of moments: it is an active multiplicity of processes and syntheses. The past is not frozen as a fixed object, the future is not an unchanging 'immanent prolongation of present action'.[17] Through the interaction of Chronos and Aion, past, present and future operate as dimensions of each other.[18] Within Chronos, present and future are contracted as dimensions of the present, within Aion, present is infinitely subdivided into past and future. In this sense, we

[8] ibid.

[9] ibid 79.

[10] D Cooper, *Feeling Like a State: Desire, Denial, and the Recasting of Authority* (Duke University Press, 2019) 84.

[11] Thank you to Roussa Kasapidou for our conversations on this topic.

[12] D Otto, 'Lost in translation: re-scripting the sexed subjects of international human rights law' in A Orford (ed), *International Law and its Others* (CUP, 2006); G Heathcote, 'Security Council Resolution 2242 on Women, Peace and Security: Progressive Gains or Dangerous Development?' (2018) 32 *Global Society* 374.

[13] A Al-Saji, 'The Memory of Another Past: Bergson, Deleuze and a new theory of time' (2004) 37 *Continental Philosophy Review* 204.

[14] G Deleuze, *The Logic of Sense* (Continuum, 2004) 89.

[15] Braidotti (n 6) 154, see also Deleuze, ibid 89.

[16] RJ Johnson, 'On the Surface: The Deleuze-Stoicism Encounter' in RJ Johnson and AJ Greenstine (eds), *Contemporary Encounters with Ancient Metaphysics* (Edinburgh University Press, 2017); Deleuze (n 14) 74.

[17] Al-Saji (n 13) 205.

[18] J Williams, *Gilles Deleuze's Philosophy of Time: A Critical Introduction and Guide* (Edinburgh University Press, 2011).

cannot necessarily privilege past, present or future, only map their differential and multiplicitous interaction.

Thus, the non-chronological, non-material, 'virtual' time of Aion is as real as linear, chronological time experienced by living bodies and minds. Virtual time 'entails the coexistence of the present with the past, it also entails the continual elaboration of the new, the openness of things (including life) to what befalls them'.[19] Braidotti's quote above is illustrative of the fact that *where* in time a subject is located determines its unity or fragmentation. The state is simultaneously unified and hierarchical, and stable and fragmented, non-linear and discontinuous. The rights bearing subject is both the repository of legal protections and a discordant and constantly changing assemblage that subverts both the identity of the rights bearer and the mechanisms by which these rights might be protected. By viewing the subjectivity of both individuals and states as temporally disunifed, it is possible to regard the contradictory operation of gender-based rights as compatible rather than contradictory: they depend upon where in time (and space) we are located as we approach them. Section III explores the role of law within this process.

III. INTERNATIONAL LEGAL TEMPORALITY

This section views law's temporal rhythms through a Deleuzian reading of Bergsonian 'duration'. For Bergson, time – or duration – is 'ceaseless becoming'[20] encompassing all human and non-human lived experience.[21] Duration proceeds through self-differentiation in a multidirectional, multidimensional flow of 'bifurcations, divisions and dissociations'[22] in contrast with linear (or for Bergson, mathematical) time. In Deleuze's reading of Bergson, Bergson's theory of memory is central to understanding duration.[23] Duration is memory, but is virtual rather than psychological: the whole of memory – referred to as the pure past – is preserved in itself, distinct from the present. Thus:

> The past and the present do not denote two successive moments, but two elements which coexist: One is the present, which does not cease to pass, and the other is the past, which does not cease to be but through which all presents pass. It is in this sense that there is a pure past, a kind of "past in general": The past does not follow the present, but on the contrary, it is presupposed by it as the pure condition without which it would not pass.[24]

[19] E Grosz, 'Deleuze's Bergson: Duration, the Virtual and a Politics of the Future' in C Colebrook and I Buchanan (eds), *Deleuze and Feminist Theory* (Edinburgh University Press, 2000) 229.
[20] R Mawani, 'The Times of Law' (2015) 40 *Law and Social Inquiry* 253.
[21] G Deleuze, *Bergsonism* (Zone Books, 1991) 37.
[22] Grosz (n 19).
[23] Deleuze (n 21) 55.
[24] ibid 59.

The pure past coexists with the present at various levels of contraction and relaxation. This may pass unnoticed as we move habitually through linear time,[25] but is evident when the 'present makes an appeal'.[26] In such moments, we leap into the virtual past, which contracts and rotates according to the needs of the present. This process is the 'actualisation' of the pure past – the whole of time – according to the orientation of the present and 'the indeterminate, the unfolding emergence of the new.'[27] The actualisation of the pure past according to the needs of the present moment creates the conditions for difference, or the possibility of the present being other than itself. Thus, time is multidimensional – past, present and future are all intersecting dimensions of each other.

Law and jurisprudence can be approached through a Bergsonian metaphysics.[28] Law has particular temporal rhythms and routines – case law, precedent, statutory interpretation or treaty monitoring all constitute the legal past and can be viewed as a succession of moments that build progressively and logically from past, to present, to future. Law here is a series of 'snapshots of reality' within a constant flow of duration.[29] Yet while law can be viewed as a limited, logical progression, this is not the totality of law or legal action. Instead, law is also dynamic, non-linear, self-differentiating and multifaceted. The past and future of law are not fixed and static objects to be picked up and used in our legal present, but are dynamic, shifting and becoming.

From this perspective, law's temporality is multiplicitous, but produces a narrative of regularised temporal progression. Like the constant interplay of Chronos and Aion, there is a push and pull of an organising legal narrative, that also cannot escape (and indeed must contain) the whole of virtual time. As such, law's linearity is a grand narrative that can only be produced through the actualisation of the pure past in the present, or through the engagement with the dynamic time of duration. Law depends upon and denies time's multiplicity in order to maintain its coherence. Indeed, as Fleur Johns notes '[t]he temporalities of international law are thus multiple and misaligned. Just as there is no "general history", so there is no general temporality of international lawfulness'.[30]

The different legal-temporal horizons that emerge or are organised through law's functioning are not simply a result of law responding to external factors. Law as duration engages in its own internal movements, it differentiates itself from itself, bifurcates and divides to create different internal temporalities.[31]

[25] K Lalor, 'Encountering the Past: Grand Narratives, Fragmented Histories and LGBTI Rights "Progress"' (2019) 30 *Law and Critique* 21.

[26] Deleuze (n 21).

[27] ibid 229.

[28] A Lefebvre, *The Image of Law: Deleuze, Bergson, Spinoza* (Stanford University Press, 2008); J MacLean, 'Rhizomatics, the Becoming of Law, and Legal Institutions' in L de Sutter and K McGee (eds), *Deleuze and Law* (Edinburgh University Press, 2012); Mawani (n 20).

[29] Maclean ibid 160.

[30] F Johns, 'The Temporal Rivalries of Human Rights' (2016) 23 *Indiana Journal of Global Legal Studies* 39 44.

[31] Mawani (n 20).

International lawyers may seek a facsimile of coherence or linearity, but this can never represent the whole of law's memory.[32] Different jurisdictional arrangements, legal forms and articulations of legal problems, or even moments within a case bring different spatio-temporal horizons in to play. Moreover, temporal movement is not neutral – it is a series of conscious or unconscious actualisations of the pure past that either maintains or challenges present practice. A legal problem makes a demand of the pure past, which is actualised around those facts or circumstances in a way that brings certain space-times into contact, thickening and shaping particular processes and modes of action. Most often, this process is 'habitual', unnoticed and depoliticised – facilitating a particular temporal arrangement in which some elements within a legal assemblage are foregrounded and others ignored. Within the context of gender and human rights, Hilary Charlesworth has described this as the 'ritualised incantations' of feminist ideas within international institutions,[33] to the extent that the vocabulary 'feminism' or 'women's rights' is emptied of meaning, even while the inclusion of women is celebrated.[34]

A temporal analysis of rights is particularly useful here: ritualised repetitions of human rights language and norms bring both stability and frameworks for action. However, these repetitions exist simultaneously with the pure past, which both exposes the limitations of stable systems and maintains the possibility of difference and change. The remainder of the chapter explores this tension in the context of pasts, presents and futures of gender and rights. Beginning with the colonial encounter, which generated various modern legal doctrines including those of sovereign states and rights bearing subjects, the chapter explores linear, gendered 'incantations' of human rights and their destabilisation by the different temporalities that they inevitably contain and express.

IV. GENDERED DIMENSIONS OF HUMAN RIGHTS PASTS, PRESENTS AND FUTURES

The analysis above pushes back against the historicisation of law that fixes events and their effects in time and depoliticises mechanisms by which these events were produced. Indeed, law as duration is law that continuously internally reproduces – 'a moving forward but also a turning back'[35] – diving into the pure past and extending out into the unknown future. The sections that follow first present a relatively static or fixed narrative of gender and international human rights law before complicating this story by unmooring the past and future from their orientation within the present.

[32] Johns (n 30).
[33] Charlesworth (n 4) 23.
[34] BS Chimni, *International Law and World Order: A Critique of Contemporary Approaches*, 2nd edn (CUP, 2017) 384–85.
[35] Mawani (n 20) 260.

A. Linear Pasts: Gendered Dimensions of the Colonial Encounter

Balakrishnan Rajagopal notes that even when rights might hold emancipatory potential, 'the human rights discourse has also turned out to be a core part of hegemonic international law, reinforcing pre-existing imperial tendencies in world politics'.[36] This section argues that gender has been part of this paradox from the genesis of modern international law – and thus to understand gendered rights, we must understand gender and international law.

Cynthia Weber has written powerfully on the gendered dimensions of colonialism.[37] The Victorian image of the masculine, conquering state and man colonising the feminised colonial other resonated through the ontological, epistemological and legal orders of empire.[38] The division of the world into colonised and coloniser, and erasure of colonised knowledges as part of the imperial 'rage for order'[39] is well established. Of interest here, is the division of the world into a masculine/feminine dichotomy of power and submission within which women are the 'naturally' weaker half of the binary: dependent extensions of men rather than full subjects of law.[40] Simultaneously, the expansion of empire laid the foundations for the modern Western, bourgeois, heterosexual family.[41] The gendered division of labour, confinement of (middle and upper class) women to the private sphere and the industrialisation and globalisation of work create a new and totalising gendered order. As part of this process, other knowledges and practices beyond the gender binary were erased, as imperial legislators sought to impose Victorian moralities and structures of gender relations on those that they had colonised. These gendered subjectivities expanded beyond intersubjective practice, into state behaviour, and carry forward into the present. In particular, Weber, following Richard Ashley, argues that a particular vision of 'sovereign man' – modern enlightened and rational – exists as the necessary foundation of the modern state and is juxtaposed with the chaotic, barbarous and uncivilised 'other', who transgresses gendered norms in various ways.[42]

Logics that maintain a masculine/feminine binary but oscillate between intersubjective and interstate practice also inhere in imperial 'civilising missions'.

[36] B Rajagopal, 'Counter-hegemonic International Law: rethinking human rights and development as a Third World strategy' (2006) 27 *Third World Quarterly* 767, 768.

[37] C Weber, *Queer International Relations: Sovereignty, Sexuality and the Will to Knowledge* (OUP, 2016).

[38] ibid.

[39] L Benton and L Ford, *Rage for Order: The British Empire and the Origins of International Law 1800–1850* (Harvard University Press, 2016).

[40] D Otto, 'International Human Rights Law: Towards Rethiking Sex/Gender Dualism and Asymmetry' in M Davies and V Munro (eds), *A Research Companion to Feminist Legal Theory* (Routledge, 2013).

[41] A McClintock, *Imperial Leather: Race, Gender and Sexuality in the Colonial* Contest (Routledge, 1995).

[42] Weber (n 37) 35.

The denigration of colonised peoples was a mechanism for legitimising their conquest, repurposing the use of extreme violence that accompanied colonial conquest as the white man's burden, and thus a neutral or even benevolent project.[43] Most significant here is not only the gendered dynamics of state logics, but the extent to which gender – specifically the treatment of colonised women – became part of the logic by which the colonised man was proved to be barbaric and unable to govern. The gendered logic of the imperial saviour became that of 'white men saving brown women from brown men'.[44] Moreover, as Kapur notes, the civilisational discourse of empire has translated readily into modern international human rights discourses.[45] Thus, static and binary notions of gender are integral to various international human rights campaigns, including anti-trafficking and Gender, Peace and Security movements.[46] Not only does this reify 'woman' as weak and in need of protection from aggressive (usually non-Western) men, it recreates colonial, civilisational logics of empire, within modern international spaces, and strengthens regimes of carcerality and surveillance often doing little to help the most vulnerable.[47]

These gendered binaries sit in stark contrast with 'rich multiplicity of women's history'[48] and with feminist theoretical critiques that femininity cannot be thought simply as the 'other' of the rational male subject.[49] Moreover, class and colonial projects of empire were enthusiastically embraced by Western women – even at the time, the dynamics of dominance and control was more complex than a simple binary.[50] Indeed, a huge amount of work is done by this binary as it is continually repeated in different forms within different spatial and temporal horizons of different legal orders. The complexity of international legal histories means that the feminised subject of international human rights law must be constantly refreshed and reproduced anew in different circumstances (or temporal horizons) so that its masculine other can maintain the appearance of stability. Ironically – but unsurprisingly – the colonial drive for order and stability sits upon unstable ontological foundations. Significant here is the totalising, nature of the gendered, hierarchical state that is produced in this

[43] ibid; T Mahmud, 'Geography and International Law: Towards a Postcolonial Mapping' (2007) 5 *Santa Clara Journal of International Law* 525.

[44] G Chakravorty Spivak, '"Can the Subaltern Speak?" revised edition, from the "History" chapter of Critique of Postcolonial Reason' in RC Morris (ed), *Can the Subaltern Speak? Reflections on the History of an Idea* (Columbia University Press, 2010) 70.

[45] Kapur (n 1) 39.

[46] ibid ch 3.

[47] ibid.

[48] Kapur in Otto (n 12) 347.

[49] R Braidotti, *Nomadic Subjects: Embodiment and Sexual Difference* (Columbia University Press, 1994) 83. See also Otto (n 12).

[50] SM Rai, 'Reimagining the state: Marxism, feminism, postcolonialism' in D Cooper, N Dhawan and J Newman (eds), *Reimagining the State: Theoretical Challenges and Transformative Possibilities* (Routledge, 2020).

framework. The logics of imperial statecraft expand to fill all available space and in so doing stabilise and justify their own existence.

B. Gendered Repetitions of Coloniality in Modern Human Rights: From Linear Presents to Static Futures

The complex presence of gender in the colonial encounter and the genesis of international law has led to habitual unthinking repetitions of gendered dynamics in the postcolonial present. This means that it is particularly important to attend to how gender contributes to the memory of the present in different ways and how the interaction of gender and time is at once multiplicitous and unaware of its multiplicity. Returning to the gendered colonial divide, Anne McClintock notes that '[d]espite most anti-colonial nationalisms' investment in the rhetoric of popular unity, most have served more properly to institutionalize gender power.'[51] McClintock's intervention here makes clear the habitual repetition or incantation of gender in international law – the unthinking patterns of action and behaviour that maintain certain axioms over others. Ironically, each repetition of these patterns might be slightly different – as the foundational figuration of modern state and modern man is unstable, its ongoing repetition must adjust to account for this. Yet while patterns may differ in material terms, they repeat an unacknowledged axiom of the gendered organisation of international power.

The repetition of unacknowledged axioms of gender and law makes space for the distinct, but related acknowledged presence of gender in international human rights arenas. This 'history' of women's rights at the UN is captured by the Report of the Special Rapporteur on violence against women, its causes and consequences:

> Over the past 25 years, violence against women has come to be recognized as a violation of women's human rights and a form of gender-based discrimination. The struggle by the women's rights movement to persuade the international community to view discrimination against women and gender-based violence against women as human rights violations came about gradually and was reinforced by the evolution of the international legal framework on women's human rights and violence against women, including with regard to domestic violence, along with the growing role of independent expert mechanisms established to monitor its implementation, including the mandate of the Special Rapporteur, as well as other relevant United Nations and regional mechanisms that contributed to such developments.[52]

[51] A McClintock, 'The Angel of Progress: Pitfalls of the Term "Post-Colonialism"' (1992) 31/32 *Social Text* 84.

[52] UNHCR, 'Violence against women, its causes and consequences: Report of the Special Rapporteur on violence against women, its causes and consequences' (20 June 2019) UN Doc. A/HRC/41/42.

In this iteration, gender entered international human rights law in the late 1980s and early 1990s. Yet the flourishing of feminist international legal conversations during this era sat alongside the realisation of a tension in which feminists found themselves trapped between 'resistance and compliance' in which they were 'asked to be the "women's voice", but not to challenge the foundations of international law and its institutions'.[53] The tension here is not gender's invisibility but that its inclusion is often on very narrow terms that do little to challenge international law's foundations – which cohere around a self/other binary within which the 'other' is generally identified with the feminine. The result is the ongoing 'peripheralisation' of gender in international law.[54] The habitual or ritualised incantations of international law stabilise a female rights bearing subject, but their capacity for more radical change is limited.[55] Moreover, 'women' as half of the binary cannot capture the complexities of gendered lives beyond or alongside binarised gender as they are lived and embodied in different material contexts.[56]

Thus, a relatively coherent narrative of the stable rights bearing female subject and bounded state that secures these rights emerges through the habitual repetition of epistemological certainties that are rooted in the colonial encounter. This accompanies the literal repetition of human rights practices in the cyclical rhythms of international law's monitoring mechanisms such as the Convention on the Elimination of All Forms of Discrimination Against Women (CEDAW) and Universal Periodic Review (UPR) reporting cycles. Even those charter-based mechanisms with the capacity to act ad-hoc, such as the Special Rapporteur on Violence Against Women and Girls or the Independent Expert on Sexual Orientation and Gender Identity (SOGI), also have cyclical reporting responsibilities. These cyclical rhythms inveigh international human rights law with a series of ritualised processes (or incantations), by which gendered issues are iterated through formal languages that translate a myriad injustices into the overarching structures and languages of UN human rights.[57] The point here is not that there is no room for flexibility in international approaches to women's rights, but that the formal mechanisms through which these rights are known and administered at the highest levels follow particular temporal patterns.

Kathryn McNeilly notes that the cyclical monitoring of international treaties sits alongside a strong sense of linear time.[58] Indeed, repetition helps to ensure that the linearity or predictability of the international legal present

[53] Kouvo and Pearson (n 2).

[54] Charlesworth (n 4) 23.

[55] Kapur (n 1).

[56] See D Otto in in K McNeilly, 'Are Rights Out of Time? International Human Rights Law, Temporality, and Radical Social Change' (2018) 28 *Social & Legal Studies* 817, 831.

[57] J Mertus, 'Road Blocks, Blind Spots, Speed Bumps: A Feminist Look at the Post-9/11 Landscape for NGOs' in Kouvo and Pearson (n 2).

[58] McNeilly (n 56). This too has a colonial aspect. See CJ Greenhouse, 'Just in Time: Temporality and the Cultural Legitimation of Law' (1988–1989) 98 *The Yale Law Journal* 1631.

projects forwards into the future. In particular, and recalling the civilising mission of colonialism, there is an alignment of gender equality or women's rights with civilisation or 'progress'. One of the effects of this is the reproduction of imperial temporalities that require a separation between the barbaric 'other' – located temporally and spatially 'elsewhere' – and the civilized 'self'.[59] As such, 'progress' acts as a myth or an ideology: it is a standard to be met – measured by development goals, concluding observations and reports – and simultaneously, a goal that will remain continually out of reach. It is thus both unattainable but always visible and predictable.[60]

Various consequences emerge here. First, to maintain the myth of progress, law shapes time and temporalities, rendering certain aspects of gender visible or invisible in international human rights practice. The maintenance of these visibilities requires a simultaneous erasure of the colonial origins of both sovereign statehood and rights bearing subjectivity. The past is actualised in the present and then rendered invisible. It is necessary for international human rights law's authority and for directing the focus of international instruments, but remains unacknowledged as a source of that authority, even while parallels can be drawn between 'then' and 'now'.[61]

The second point that emerges is the tendency of habitual repetition to freeze us in a permanent, predicable present. The civilised self is in permanent opposition to the savage 'other' that exists as a marker of the past, but this duality emptied of the violence of colonial relations. Simultaneously, the cyclical mechanisms through which gender and human rights are administered render the present inert, habitual and predictable. Thus, in the linear temporal narrative outlined here (the time of Chronos), the past and future are dimensions of the present. Key objects of human rights law – the state, sovereignty and rights bearing subjectivity – remain static and fixed. There is no space for thinking of how they might exist differently. This resonates with Kapur's observation that there is little space for how the male/female binary might be otherwise in international human rights law. Nevertheless, constant renewal is needed to maintain this illusion of stability in the binary as it relates to statehood, sovereignty and rights: the sovereign state and sovereign man need very particular conditions to maintain themselves. The pure past and future infinitives of Aion are always present, telling minor stories, hinting at hidden histories and new becomings.

[59] I Mgbeoji, 'The civilised self and the barbaric other: imperial delusions of order and the challenges of human security' (2006) 27 *Third World Quarterly* 855.

[60] Weber (n 37).

[61] Otto (n 12). See also R Parfitt, 'Fascism, Imperialism and International Law: An Arch Met a Motorway and the Rest is History …' (2018) 31 *Leiden Journal of International Law* 509 for a detailed expansion of how this kind of chronotropic work can reveal unacknowledged 'truths' of international law and legal ordering.

C. Thinking Aion in International Law

This chapter does not seek to untangle the multiple and misaligned temporalities of international law. Chronos and Aion are complementary, not opposites, together forming the totality of temporal movement. As Braidotti notes, sometimes it is necessary to engage in activism and action that is tied closely to predictable, linear temporality.[62] Indeed, while habitual repetition may be limiting, Elizabeth Grosz also argues that predictability is not always a bad thing and within habitual action, there is still potential for transformation and emancipation.[63] In legal terms however, the importance of repetition does not necessary surmount the problem of the suspension of both gender-based and women's rights between 'resistance and compliance' in international legal spheres. The final sections of the chapter ask how thinking the present as a dimension of the past and future allow it to be re-oriented in a way that destabilises that which we have assumed to be fixed and static, and in this sense allows us to think the multidimensionality of gender and international human rights law.

In many respects, this approach has much in common with feminist projects of imagining new futures.[64] Our starting point, however, should be one of caution. The unknown future is not certain – it poses risks that may be beyond those who seek to bring about positive change.[65] Moreover, imagining a new future cannot be done without also carefully attending to the past and present:

> Attempting to resolve issues of justice without recognizing the continuing heavy weight of the past only privileges those who are already powerful enough to evade their responsibilities to the past. While it is tempting to look toward the future, every indication suggests that those who fail to learn from the past are doomed, not to repeat it, but to think that they have escaped it. Is it possible, then, not to dwell in the past; not to be blind to the past and wish only for the future; but to bring all these times together?[66]

Within the framework adopted here, the past cannot be viewed as a single stable object that can be easily reclaimed, because it is an actualisation in the present of the whole of virtual time, and the actualised past that we know and experience will always be smaller than the virtual whole. Instead, by mapping the multidimensionality of international law we can, bring times together without demanding that one dimension of time be collapsed into another.

Attempting to think through multidimensions of gender and international human rights law requires a returning to and acknowledging of the violence of coloniality and racialization that stemmed from the colonial encounter. Alia Al-Saji draws upon Frantz Fanon's argument that 'the racialization and

[62] Braidotti (n 6).
[63] E Grosz, 'Habit Today: Ravaisson, Bergson, Deleuze and Us' (2013) 19(2–3) *Body & Society* 217.
[64] Otto and Grear (n 3).
[65] Braidotti (n 6).
[66] J Tronto, 'Time's Place' (2003) 4 *Feminist Theory* 119, 129.

colonization of the past represses other pasts and rewrites them'.[67] The dichotomization and dualism of the civilized 'self' and barbaric 'other' (which is also a gendered process), becomes the foundation for a universalising (linear) history that progresses in one direction from the dark past to the enlightened future. Race, gender and colonialism combine in multiple ways in the ontological, epistemological and legal frameworks that ordered the colonial past and haunt our 'post-colonial' present.

Thus, the project of imagining new futures must also be one that is attentive to the repression of 'other' pasts. This is done with the knowledge that there are some pasts that cannot be fully known because empire destroyed forms of knowledge production as it conquered.[68] Yet even with this limitation, past, present, and future do not need to be static or linear. The pure past exists as a virtual whole and can always be actualised anew in response to new problems. This actualisation takes multiple forms: it might begin with a line of flight that is not legal, but affective or imaginative. For example, within postcolonial literature, Lorna Burns has argued that the tradition of 'writing back' to empire can go far beyond producing hybrid, revised, or creolised texts, and can instead chart a path that, in repeating the virtual past in new, future oriented forms, charts and crosses new horizons.[69] The question of crossing new horizons is not limited to literature. In developing the tradition of counter histories of empires, Priyamvada Gopal details how anti-colonial resistance shaped Britain and its ideas:

> [T]he possibility that Britain's enslaved and colonial subjects were not merely victims of this nation's imperial history and subsequent beneficiaries of it crises of conscience, but rather agents whose resistance not only contributed to their own liberation but also put pressure on and reshaped about freedom and who could be free.[70]

In re-orienting space, to make clear the temporal horizons and narratives that those spaces make possible, Gopal repositions the relationship between colonised periphery and colonial metropole with respect to the flow of ideas, the emergence of dissent and the way in which diasporic understandings shaped meaning making in the metropolitan centres.

The section above demonstrated how gendered logics resonated through the ontological, epistemological and legal orders of empire. Similarly, wider epistemological and ontological projects of actualising imperial history anew can also be found in *legal* counter histories of empire.[71] For example, continuing with the project of reorienting centre and periphery, Arnulf Becker Lorca's *Mestizo International Law* challenges conventional histories of international

[67] A Al-Saji, 'Too Late: Racialized Time and the Closure of the Past' (2013) 6(5) *Durham University Insights* 2.

[68] R Connell, *Southern Theory* (Polity, 2007).

[69] L Burns, 'Becoming-Bertha: Virtual Difference and Repetition in Postcolonial "Writing Back", a Deleuzian Reading of Jean Rhys's Wide Sargasso Sea' (2010) 4 *Deleuze Studies* 16.

[70] P Gopal, *Insurgent Empire: Anticolonial Resistance and British Dissent* (Verso, 2019) 5.

[71] See H Van Rijswijk and A Vogl, 'Across Islands and Oceans: Re-imagining Colonial Violence in the Past and the Present' (2019) 30 *Law and Critique* 293.

law by presenting a non-Eurocentric mestizo history that traces the investment of non-Western scholars, lawyers and 'semi-peripheral elites' in international law's formation. For Becker Lorca, challenging Western, universalising narratives of the history of international law may allow us to 'clear up space for new and more emancipatory legal practices tomorrow'.[72]

Actualising the past anew is thus more than simply re-reading or revising the past. A future focused repetition of the past is one that re-orients bodies, practices and knowledges in order to open up new ways of being or to reveal new ways of approaching gender and international human rights law. The aim is not hybridity, but new or hidden histories that open space for new futures. In short, past and present cannot be evacuated from the future, but are dimensions of its existence. Most importantly, this adds some nuance to any project of imagining new futures. As Grosz notes, 'how we understand the relations between past and present has direct implications for whatever conceptions of the future, the new, creation, and production we may develop'.[73] Such a project cannot just operate in the time of Chronos: we are interested here in the whole of time – or duration – and this includes the virtual potential that is only known through its different actualisations in the present and future. The virtual past will always give rise to another reading, which will animate the future in different ways. Thus, the project here is not about finding new or correct readings of past and future but attending to the multiplicity of temporality, to the openness of the past and future as dimensions of time in and of themselves rather than projections forwards and backwards from the present instant.

D. Human Rights Futures

The analysis above suggests that while imagination of the future may involve an instinctive leap into duration, this leap is not uncontrolled: it requires careful attendance to multiplicities of past and present. This chapter has insisted upon the importance of postcolonial analysis of the genesis of international law, to show how this history shapes the present of human rights law, gendered statehood and gendered subjectivity. Through this lens, and mindful of Braidotti's discussion of the role of temporality in the formation of unitary subjectivity of individual and state, we might ask how, within a different temporal register, state, subjectivity and international human rights law might be thought differently.

[72] A Becker Lorca, *Mestizo International Law: A Global Intellectual History 1842–1933* (CUP, 2014) 16.

[73] E Grosz, 'Histories of a Feminist Future' [2000] 25 *Signs: Journal of Women in Culture and Society* 1017, 1018.

As the section above suggested, this first requires the exploration of counter-narrative. In particular, there are numerous histories within which individuals and groups acted against gendered colonial norms. These histories range from the involvement of women in peace processes in the early twentieth century,[74] to the histories of women's leadership in human rights and anti-colonial struggles,[75] to non-western gender systems that directly challenged the notion of a universal binary of male/female.[76] They also encompass historical and present queer and trans activists who insist both on the paucity of the male/female binary as a representation of their cultural norms of gender and on their place within those cultures.[77] Yet these histories appear primarily as revisions or additions: important stories that occupy a minor register within the grand narrative of human rights history. This alone would be insufficient: it is not enough to offer a peripheral and hybridised feminist history of international law. Instead, centre and periphery must be upended. We need to question the past to differently configure the future: to engage with our histories in a way that allows for a spatial and temporal reorientation of our foundational subjects and axioms of international law.

It is here that Braidotti's argument that the modern subject is a temporally fragmented subject that gives the appearance of wholeness gains urgency. Within international human rights law, both individual and state subjectivities function as grand narrative, held together across multiple temporalities. From different temporal perspectives, rights operate both as a triumphant narrative of progress and as a hopelessly unsuitable tool for capturing the wholeness of the state, individual subjectivity, or the injustices that rights should work to remedy. The response to this paradox should not be nihilism in the face of the unknowable virtual, but active questioning and engagement with the world. Such paradoxes represent the present making a demand of the past, and thus a moment to leap into duration to reorient past and present, opening up the possibility for a new future. Most often, we progress (legally or otherwise) through time in a habitual fashion – unthinkingly repeating numerous unconscious assumptions, axioms

[74] A O'Donoghue, 'Article 7 of the Covenant of the League of Nations, 1919' in E Rackley and R Auchmurty (eds), *Women's Legal Landmarks: Celebrating the History of Women and Law in the UK and Ireland* (Hart Publishing, 2019); D Otto, The Security Council's Alliance of Gender Legitimacy: The Symbolic Capital of Resolution 1325' in H Charlesworth and J-M Coicaud, *Fault Lines of International Legitimacy* (CUP, 2010) 239.

[75] Gopal (n 70) 202–03 Y Bouka, 'Women, Colonial Resistance, and Decolonization' in O Yacob-Haliso and T Falola (eds), *The Palgrave Handbook of African Women's Studies* (Springer International Publishing, 2020); F Gaer, 'Women, international law and international institutions: The case of the United Nations' (2009) 32 *Women's Studies International Forum* 60; C Johnson-Odim, '"For their freedoms": The anti-imperialist and international feminist activity of Funmilayo Ransome-Kuti of Nigeria' (2009) 32 *Women's Studies International Forum* 51.

[76] See eg T Boellstorff et al, 'Decolonizing Transgender: A Roundtable Discussion' (2014) 1 *TSQ: Transgender Studies Quarterly* 419.

[77] eg N Ayub, 'Transgender Rights in Malaysia: Religion, Politics and Law' in K Lalor et al (eds), *Gender, Sexuality and Social Justice: What's law got to do with it?* (Institute of Development Studies, 2016).

and ways of being in the world. Moments arise that bring these habits from their position of unconscious background repetition, the forefront of action. It is then when we are faced with a choice – to repeat old habits, or to counteractualise the past anew, finding new ways of orienting ourselves and others in the world.[78] The encounter – or the point when we pause in the repetition of habit – is the point when the repetition of the future becomes possible. The challenge is that we cannot anticipate ahead of time when this will be. However, by attending to habitual patterns and to counter narratives that open up minor histories, we might equip ourselves with the tools that mean that when we are faced with the unexpected, our instinct is not towards a return to normal through the 'ritualised incantations' of binarised human rights but to seek an openness to the new.

There are examples of recent work that has undertaken this kind of re-thinking in relation to the state. For example, Davina Cooper, Nikita Dharwan and Janet Newman explore what forms of law and gender are brought into view when the state is understood as networked, rhizomatic and horizontal, rather than top-down and hierarchical.[79] For Cooper, such imaginaries demand new forms of pre-figurative politics: living in the present as if the future has already arrived,[80] or living in a way that renders the past and present as dimensions of an open future. A note of caution is required here however: lines of flight into new becomings do not always succeed.[81] For example, re-thinking the state in a way that that juxtaposed the (masculine) bounded, hierarchical state with the (feminine) networked, rhizomatic state does not necessarily overcome the structuring narrative of masculine/feminine discussed above. However, Cooper's analysis does not simply posit a replacement of a masculine state with a feminist alternative. Instead, it asks important questions of the totality of the state's relationship with gender:[82] whether the relationship between gender and the state might be entirely re-oriented allowing for the emergence of new kinds of state-subject relations.

Cooper's analysis of gender and the state focuses primary on the operation of state power at the national and subnational level – asking, for example, what properties of gender are brought in to view when we consider the possibility of ending the state's power to classify its citizens by gender on their identity documents. These questions could be extended to the supernational – can a masculine/feminine binary offer anything useful to rights, sovereignty or statehood especially in light of how our histories and presents are filled with relations

[78] Williams (n 18) 149, 168.

[79] J Newman and N Dhawan, 'Concluding Reflections' in D Cooper, N Dhawan and J Newman (eds), *Reimagining the State: Theoretical Challenges and Transformative Possibilities* (Routledge 2020) 269.

[80] D Cooper, 'Conceptual prefiguration and municipal radicalism: Reimagining what it could mean to be a state' in Cooper, Dhawan and Newman (ibid).

[81] G Deleuze and C Parnet, *Dialogues 2* (Continuum, 2006) 104.

[82] D Cooper and F Renz, 'If the State Decertified Gender, What Might Happen to its Meaning and Value?' (2016) 43 *Journal of Law and Society* 483.

more complex than a simple binary and include relations with the earth and the non-human? Moreover, what does this tell us about the properties of 'gender' as assembled within international human rights law? Indeed, what does this tell us about the realities of engaging with gendered bodies, rather than just using masculinity or femininity as a metaphor for dominance and submission?

Such an approach brings together the fragmented temporalities of gendered state and subject as they exist in a complex assemblage with the past, present and future of rights. We cannot reclaim lost histories, but we can attempt to make space to attend to the possibility of these lost histories, in order to imagine otherwise. This act of imagining leaves us better able to respond to those moments when we might break old habits to counteractualise new futures. Acting in the time of the future does not ignore past and present – it requires deeply and materially rooted knowledge of past and present, in order to better acknowledge those temporal practices that we take for granted. Within the international context adopted here, this means that we must attend not just to the politics of international human rights law – between resistance and compliance – but gendered roots of international law's founding axioms.

V. CONCLUSION

The urgent question for both scholarship of gender and human rights and for activists and practitioners who must negotiate the tensions of human rights in real time, is whether rights can be usefully re-oriented away from their habitual, colonially embedded iterations. This chapter has taken a perspective that zooms out and approaches human rights from a different scale that encompasses not just women, but gender, and not just rights but the system of sovereign states through which rights are secured. It explores the gendered dimensions of the genesis of international law to expose its habitual repetition in international human rights law's present and future.

Yet this repetition is a grand narrative rather than a fundamental truth. In actualising histories in a way that gives the (masculine) state and (male) subject unity and coherence across time, the limitations of these practices of stabilisation cannot be ignored. The simple binary of identity and its other (masculine/feminine, man/woman, coloniser/colonised, developed/backwards) cannot capture the whole of any subject's reality. As such, approaches that seem to 'add women' to already existing rights regimes, or even to replace a masculine subject with the feminine could only ever be the first step in seeking new futures for international human rights law. Gender and rights are not just peripheral and unevenly acknowledged 'women's' issues, but instead encompass the whole of gender in its intersection with imperialism, coloniality, race, class, security, development and multiple other aspects of experience and identity. This is why the final part of section IV returned to the question of statehood and subjectivity and specifically to how the state might be reimagined in a way that changes how gendered rights could be configured. This is not a re-configuration that replaces masculinity with femininity, nor does it use 'the feminine' as a stand in for the virtual. Instead it asks what possibilities might be brought to bear by thinking gender and state differently and how this would resonate across the whole of international human rights law's temporalities, allowing for the actualisation of new pasts and the opening up of new futures.

There is no certainty in this process, but we also cannot deny the ongoing presence and promise of Aion – and its potential to burst through at unanticipated moments in order to re-orient and re-make what was certain and settled. While these moments cannot necessarily be anticipated, they inhabit both the complexities of activist practice and theoretical debates. Thus, we can prepare for the possibility of the new – in whatever form it comes – by better knowing and facing the temporalities of gendered human rights law, past and present. In this way, unexpected moments might be counteractualised, finding new, and hopefully feminist, futures.

6

International Human Rights Law and Time-Space at Sea: A Rhythmanalysis of Prosecuting Search and Rescue

FADIA DAKKA AND DARIA DAVITTI

I. INTRODUCTION

THIS CHAPTER DRAWS on Lefebvre's *Rhythmanalysis*[1] and *Production of Space*[2] as conceptual, political and metaphorical reservoirs to examine the way in which international protection provisions, as enshrined in international human rights law, are challenged and undermined by current EU migration policies of migration deterrence and containment. In the context of socio-spatial practice, Rhythmanalysis focuses on bodies in space and on their patterns of activities and movements, emphasising the co-existence and co-production of the spatial and the social, of time and space and of place and space in the analysis of the everyday. Within this framework, we examine the political nature of the rhythmic entanglements that connect 'bodies at sea' with 'juridical bodies', represented by EU institutions and policies, and the human rights legal measures, limitations and loopholes that they exploit and reproduce. In particular, we highlight the discrepancy between the stated aims of international human rights law (in our case, the protection of lives at sea and the prohibition against refoulement) and the lived experiences of the people targeted by its provisions, as well as the dislocation between the notion of jurisdiction and the abstracted lives of refugees. This theoretical analysis provides a starting point to reflect on the inherent limitations of international human rights law, its spatio-temporal situatedness vis-à-vis the universality of its ambitions and, too often, its inability to overcome the fundamental spatio-temporal mismatch that we outline in this chapter.

To further clarify and lend strength to the analysis, the chapter takes as a case study the arrest and prosecution of Carola Rackete, the captain of the search

[1] H Lefebvre, *Rhythmanalysis: Space, Time and Everyday Life* (English translation, Continuum, 2004).

[2] H Lefebvre, *The Production of Space* (English translation, Blackwell, 1991 [1974]).

and rescue vessel *Sea Watch 3*, by the Italian authorities in July 2019 for rescuing people at sea and disembarking them in Italy despite the government's closure of all ports to rescue ships operated by non-governmental organisations (NGOs). This case study is emblematic of current migration deterrence and containment policies, and it enables us to focus on the fundamental spatio-temporal mismatch that pits the existence of human bodies in time-space against the tempo of the law. To this end we unpack Lefebvre's theorisation of rhythm and draw attention to its historical and conceptual roots in his antecedent conceptualisation of space. Lefebvre's ideas of abstract space, differential space and alienation are brought to bear on the analysis through the case study. As a magnifying glass, they allow us to outline and acknowledge, in section II, the arrhythmia at the heart of EU migration policies and the way in which they are enabled by, and at the same time constitutive of, international human rights law itself. In our analysis, we also highlight affinities between Rhythmanalysis and Critical Phenomenology, testing their theoretical affordances for critical migration studies and international human rights law.

Crucially, the chapter concludes, Rhythmanalysis enables us to look at the notion of jurisdiction from a different perspective, which challenges the traditional spatial and personal modes with which human rights courts have so far approached the jurisdictional threshold in cases of transnational human rights violations.[3] In Lefebvrian terms, this case study enables us to trace the ways in which the political manipulation of time, space and energy is carved not only into the body of the legislations aimed at ensuring international protection, but also on the human bodies of people on the move. In this chapter, we ultimately seek to demonstrate that arrhythmia is the symptom of a specific type of governmentality, the consequences of which, far from being unintended, are aimed at the deliberate creation of spatio-temporally suspended 'zones of nonbeing'.[4]

The chapter is organised as follows: in section II, we focus on what Rhythmanalysis enables us to see in terms of bodies in space and the relationship between time, space and abstraction. In doing so, we bring international human rights law to the fore as a 'conceived space' and we outline its harmful, 'lived' consequences for people on the move. Section III applies Rhythmanalysis to current search and rescue situations and disembarkation policies in the Mediterranean. This section juxtaposes the lived experiences of bodies at sea with the 'concrete abstraction'[5] of EU migration policies of deterrence and

[3] Various scholars have addressed jurisdiction and its discontents from theoretical and historical perspectives, examining for instance its roots in colonialism and imperialism and its continued racialised present: see eg A Orford, 'A Jurisprudence of the Limit' in A Orford (ed), *International Law and its Others* (CUP, 2006) 1–32; M Pal, *Jurisdictional Accumulation: An Early Modern History of Law, Empires and Capital* (CUP, 2020) especially chs 6 and 7; S Elden, 'Legal Terrain – The Political Materiality of Territory' (2017) 5 *London Review of International Law* 199–224; and N Tzoulava, *Capitalism as Civilisation: A History of International Law* (CUP, 2020) especially ch 5.

[4] F Fanon, *Black Skin, White Masks* (Grove Press/Atlantic Monthly Press, 2007 [1952]).

[5] H Lefebvre, *The Production of Space* (Oxford: Blackwell, 1991 [1974]).

containment. The section also presents the case study of the *Sea Watch 3* to explain the concept of arrythmia and the political manipulation of time, space and energy. It then uses Rhythmanalysis to outline the limitations of the notion of jurisdiction, as it is currently understood in its spatial and personal modes, insufficient as they are to capture the complexity of current transnational measures of migration deterrence and containment adopted by the EU and its member states. The theoretical framings presented in this chapter are useful to understand the production of time-space and the 'willed' abstraction engendered by EU migration measures aimed at continued oppression. Rhythmanalysis is thus ultimately crucial to exposing the spatio-temporal violence of jurisdiction as a key threshold for the applicability of international human rights law.

II. WHAT DOES RHYTHMANALYSIS ENABLE INTERNATIONAL HUMAN RIGHTS LAWYERS TO SEE?

In this section, we situate and contextualise the genesis of Rhythmanalysis within and from Lefebvre's theory and conceptualisation of *space*. This contextualisation is crucial to understand the theoretical relevance of Rhythmanalysis to socio-legal research and, more specifically, to grasp the crucial meaning of 'arrhythmia' that we present as characterising current EU migration policies and the enabling role of international human rights law.

Published posthumously in 1992 and considered de facto the fourth volume of *Critique of Everyday Life*,[6] Lefebvre's Rhythmanalysis can be read as a poetic synthesis and intellectual legacy of the philosopher, social theorist and urbanist's ruminations on space, time and everyday life in modern (Western) societies. It is worth noting how, in Lefebvre's ambition, the rhythmanalytical project should aspire to acquire the status of a 'new science', to be founded on the systematic critique of society – via his trialectic method – and oriented toward the transformation and emancipation of human existence within it. Pivotal in this respect is the understanding of the condition of 'arrhythmia' as a disruption of rhythmic flows. It is here construed as a methodological and political category, whereby bodily and societal disruptions and malfunctions can be detected, acknowledged and potentially addressed.

The central ideas of concrete abstraction, abstract space, differential space and alienation are brought to bear on the analysis through the *Sea Watch 3* case study. The chapter, therefore, argues that arrhythmia is the symptom of a specific type of governmentality, aimed at the deliberate creation of spatio-temporally suspended 'zones of nonbeing'.[7] This, in turn, renders the intractable confrontation with the 'approaching stranger'[8] imperative in its political and humanitarian

[6] H Lefebvre, *Critique of Everyday Life* (Verso, 2014 [1973]).
[7] Fanon (n 4).
[8] K Simonsen and L Koefoed, *Geographies of Embodiment: Critical Phenomenology and the World of Strangers* (SAGE, 2020).

urgency. In this respect, Paolo Novak's work[9] on border rhythms offers an interesting precedent and point of reference for our work, as it grappled with the complexities and unevenness of international migration as a multi-layered, hierarchical social field, from a spatio-temporal perspective. Novak examined concepts such as time-space compression, border biography and refugee cycles to highlight their dynamic interplay, essentially relying on May and Thrift's notion of *timespace*.[10] Novak engaged meaningfully with Lefebvre's rhythm as a substantial and relational energy field, sensing, in the conclusions, its underexplored yet promising ethical and political potential:

> It is thus a concept that allows, in fact forces us, to simultaneously account for the temporalities of borders as depicted above and those of migrants and their journeys (see for example Griffiths et al., 2013). It is the rhythmic encounter between these two sets of temporalities that defines the actual configuration of border openings and closures, of cycles of refugee containment, interdiction and exclusion, of the accelerations and pauses configured by global visa regimes. It is in such encounter that the structural and the experienced mutually configure themselves in discrepant and dynamic ways. It is thus in and through the actual rhythms of such encounter that political action must be conceived and practised, as this is where politics lie.[11]

The intersection where the 'structural and the experienced' configure their mutual arrhythmic relationship represents the novelty of our analysis in this chapter. In other words, we begin where Novak left us, revealing the locus and urgency of political action by demonstrating how its intrinsic rhythmic nature plays out in the contradictions and loopholes that we detect in international human rights law. Compared to Novak, we fully develop and harness the spatial and temporal potential of Rhythmanalysis as a method, critique and, potentially, as an ethics, offering an avenue for research in the cognate fields of international human rights law and migration that has never been pursued before.

A. Bodies in Time-Space

In this chapter, we propose to test the theoretical purchase and affordances of Lefebvre's Rhythmanalysis for socio-legal research. More specifically, we grapple with the political meaning and implications of 'arrhythmia', here introduced as the temporal horizon that characterises EU migration policies and international human rights law. To do so, it is crucial that we first situate and appraise Rhythmanalysis in relation to Lefebvre's conceptualisation of *space*.[12] In fact, Rhythmanalysis' sensitivity to the temporal dimensions of the everyday subsumes

[9] P Novak, 'Border Rhythms' in E Mavroudi, B Page and A Christou (eds), *Timespace and International Migration* (Edward Elgar, 2017).

[10] J May and N Thrift (eds), *Timespace. Geographies of Temporality* (Routledge, 2001).

[11] Novak (n 9) 74.

[12] Lefebvre (n 5 and n 2).

its spatial counterpart, which is to say that lived time always presupposes and implies lived space. Secondly, as we propose to examine, foregrounding it, the nature of the rhythmic clash that pits 'bodies at sea' against juridical bodies, we need to cast them as specific instances and modalities of *co-production of space* endowed with ethical, political and existential implications.

In this respect, Lefebvre's ideas of space as a concrete abstraction, alienation and differential space acquire particular saliency, not least because they are foundational to his subsequent theorisation of rhythm. The idea of 'concrete abstraction' was derived from Hegel's notion of 'concrete universal' and later appropriated and developed by Marx as the dialectical 'forms' of labour, commodity, money and markets in the nineteenth-century capitalist economy.[13] For Marx these are examples of 'abstractions which became true in practice'[14] through the unfolding of three 'moments': universality, particularity and singularity. Concrete abstractions are 'at the same time a universal medium of production, consumption, and distribution; and a commodity, itself produced, consumed, and distributed'.[15] Together they define the internal principle of development and driving force of capitalism.

Let us consider, by way of example, the historical emergence of the concept of labour in eighteenth century Britain. Here, the nascent industry 'required labour to be reduced to its bare features and stripped of the personality of the worker'.[16] The industrial machinery needed labour to be 'malleable, quantifiable, divisible, and measurable by *time*',[17] for efficiency gains, so that under such economic conditions the abstraction of the category 'labour' could become true in practice, separating concrete labour – 'a productive activity of a definite kind and exercised with a definite aim' – from abstract labour, defined as the 'expenditure of human labour in general'.[18] In other words, the abstraction is made (true) in the quotidian process of production. As Marx puts it in the *Contribution to the Critique of Political Economy*:[19]

> The conversion of all commodities into labour-time is no greater an abstraction, and no less real, than the resolution of all organic bodies into air. Labour, thus measured by time, does not seem, indeed, to be the labour of different persons, but on the contrary the different working individuals seem to be mere organs of this labour.

[13] L Stanek, 'Space as Concrete Abstraction: Hegel, Marx, and Modern Urbanism in Henri Lefebvre' in K Goonewardena et al, *Space, Difference, Everyday Life: Reading Henri Lefebvre* (Routledge, 2008).

[14] K Marx, *Grundrisse: Foundations of the Critique of Political Economy* (Penguin, 1993) 25.

[15] L Stanek (ed), *Henri Lefebvre: Toward an Architecture of Enjoyment* (University of Minnesota Press, 2014); Lefebvre, 1973.

[16] Stanek (n 13) 67.

[17] ibid.

[18] ibid.

[19] K Marx, *Contribution to the Critique of Political Economy* (Progress Publisher, 1859), full text available at *Marxist Internet Archive* www.marxists.org/archive/marx/works/sw/index.htm.

Marx's idea of the 'abstraction which became true in practice' was extended by Lefebvre to his conceptualisation of space as another form of concrete abstraction. Space is a concrete, social abstraction with real existence, produced by social relationships and inextricably linked to human practices. In the *Production of Space*,[20] Lefebvre distinguishes three spatial 'moments' or overlapping lenses that translate the physical, mental and social dimensions of space.

The space is at once *conceived* (abstract; representation of space); *perceived* (materially produced and reproduced through spatial practices) and *lived* (imbued with, and enriched through meaning; representational). The conceived space embodies the abstract space of planners, of the state, of the law and, by extension, of capital. The abstract space of capital, mobilised by the state, increasingly dominates perceived and lived spaces, exacerbating a sense of human dispossession and alienation, eventually turning living bodies into *lived abstractions*.[21] To counteract the 'devastating conquest of the lived by the conceived',[22] Lefebvre advocates *differential space* as the space of possibility, difference, *autogestion*, dis-alienation, excess and transformation that might arise from the abstract space. The lived space thus re-appropriated by bodies acknowledged in their mutual existence, otherness, human and non-human entanglements would allow (human) flourishing.

Lefebvre's theorisation of space, alienation and fetishism represents thus the core of his thinking in relation to social domination and a fundamental undercurrent that traverses his subsequent theorisation of rhythm. As previously mentioned, in the first chapter of *Rhythmanalysis*,[23] Lefebvre expresses the ambition that Rhythmanalysis be developed into a new science, with the ultimate aim of subverting the linear rhythms of capital accumulation, exploitation and annihilation via a re-appropriation of the times and spaces of the everyday life and a re-signification of human life as full of meaning and enjoyment.

Both object of the inquiry and instrument for capitalist critique,[24] rhythm is introduced as the basis for a non-essentialist, sensory, process-oriented, new materialist philosophical orientation[25] and as a methodology that asserts the primacy of the body – qua measuring unit – in its plural (perceptual) interrelations, multi-layered existence and re-production. Like a living organism whose ill health is signalled by the sudden disruption (arrhythmia) of an otherwise harmonious flow (eurhythmia), the capitalist society, dominated as it is

[20] Lefebvre (n 2).

[21] C O'Kane, 'Fetishistic concrete abstraction, social constitution and social domination in Henri Lefebvre's writings on everyday life, cities and space' (2018) 42 *Capital & Class* 253–71, 264.

[22] J Wilson, '"The Devastating Conquest of the Lived by the Conceived": The Concept of Abstract Space in the Work of Henri Lefebvre' (2013) 16(3) *Space and Culture* 364–80.

[23] Lefebvre (n 1).

[24] ibid.

[25] See eg Y Chen, *Practicing Rhythmanalysis: Theories and Methodologies* (Rowman & Littlefield, 2017); and D Lyon, *What is Rhythmanalysis?* (Bloomsbury, 2018).

by the linear rhythms of capital accumulation and consumption is increasingly regulating and colonising the times and spaces of human development by superimposing fetishised forms of concrete abstractions that have come to dominate social relations. This has engendered diffused arrhythmias that need to be 'politicised' in order to be effectively counteracted.

For the purposes of our analysis, we set out to demonstrate that the temporal mismatch that pits the human bodies (left) at sea against the tempo of the juridical bodies impeding their rescue, fundamentally subtends – somewhat obfuscating its more nefarious reality – Lefebvrian notions of abstract space and lived abstraction.

In the case study presented later in the chapter, we observe, in the first instance, the political confinement of bodies at sea as a form of triumph of the *conceived space of law over the lived space of human beings*. The obliteration of their human rights effectively maps their juridically suspended space-time (international waters or the rescue ship itself) onto a zone of non-existence.[26] The bodies at sea are therefore turned into lived abstractions in the eye of the law/state. Meanwhile, and, significantly, out of sight, 'bare life'[27] and death continue at sea, rendering arrhythmia all the more apparent.

Juridical Body and *Jurisdiction* are here introduced as prime signifiers of the *conceived space*, mobilised by the state as a form of *practical power* that exerts the violence of abstraction over its subjects, dehumanising them. As dehumanised, lived abstractions whose right to reach a place of safety is stalled or denied, the refugees are de facto discarded as not functional to the logic of capital accumulation. Hence, they cannot be assimilated and re-purposed like economic migrants. The production of space and – crucially – its negation is therefore essential to understand the internal reproductive logic of capitalism as one dominated by forms of fetishistic concrete abstractions.[28] If, in Lefebvre's rendition, the social domination of the conceived over the lived is to be understood as the prime source of human alienation and oppression, the homogeneous yet fragmented space of refugees' confinement (be it the camp or international waters) becomes synonymous with disposability.[29]

As further discussed in the next section, Rhythmanalysis builds on spatial theory adding a temporal dimension and a phenomenological sensitivity visible in the foregrounding of the bodily experience in space-time. The affinity with Critical Phenomenology[30] is further explored to highlight the central role of

[26] WD Mignolo, 'Decoloniality and Phenomenology: The Geopolitics of Knowing and Epistemic/Ontological Colonial Differences' (2018) 32(3) *The Journal of Speculative Philosophy* 360–87. See also WD Mignolo, *The Darker Side of Western Modernity. Global Futures, Decolonial Options* (Duke University Press, 2011).

[27] G Agamben, *Homo Sacer: Sovereign Power and Bare Life* (Meridian, 1998).

[28] O'Kane (n 21).

[29] H Giroux, 'Reading Hurricane Katrina: Race, Class, and the Biopolitics of Disposability' (2006) 33(3) *College Literature* 171–96.

[30] Simonsen and Koefoed (n 8).

embodiment and encounter with the 'other' and the world vis-à-vis the abstraction of law and lived abstraction.

B. Rythmanalysis and Critical Phenomenology: Affinities and Potential for Legal and Political Critique

Lisa Guenther defines Critical Phenomenology as follows:

> By critical phenomenology, I mean both a philosophical practice of reflecting on the transcendental and material structures that make experience possible and meaningful, and also a political practice of 'restructuring the world' in order to generate new and liberatory possibilities for meaningful experience and existence. (…) As a political practice, critical phenomenology is a struggle for liberation from the structures that privilege, naturalize and normalize certain experiences of the world while marginalising, pathologising and discrediting others.[31]

As such, it is a useful starting point to identify its synergy with the rhythmanalytical approach presented in this chapter. The phenomenological orientation of Rhythmanalysis and, in particular, the affinity with Merleau-Ponty's embodied phenomenology[32] has been duly acknowledged and examined by Chen[33] and is, per se, beyond the scope of this chapter. Rather, we are interested in exploring what a cross-fertilisation between critical phenomenology as a *political practice* and rhythm (arrhythmia) as a political method for subversion could offer for the type of legal and political critique that we are advancing.

Following Simonsen and Koefoed,[34] we pay particular attention to three characteristics that define critical phenomenological contributions, in the first place, as critical theories that are centred on *experience*: the emphasis on experiencing the structures of the world, including and especially the oppressive ones, *from within*, and the radical intersubjectivity of our lived experiences find resonance in the rhythmnalytical consideration for the body as a perceptual, metronomic device that orients our existence and lifeworld.

Secondly, critical phenomenology is sensitive to *embodied difference*.[35] Here the debate centres on the idea of self and other as both entangled and divergent, pointing to a *relative* alterity that is always created and revealed in the encounter. This chimes with the deep relationality that characterises Lefebvre's theory

[31] L Guenther, 'A critical phenomenology of solidarity and resistance in the 2013 California prison hunger strikes' in L Dolezal and D Petherbridge (eds), *Body/Self/Other: The Phenomenology of Social Encounters* (State University of New York Press, 2017) 47–74, 49.

[32] See eg M Merleau-Ponty, *The Primacy of Perception* (Northwestern University Press, 1964); M Merleau-Ponty, *The Visible and the Invisible* (Northwestern University Press, 1968); and M Merleau-Ponty, *Humanism and Terror* (Beacon Press, 1969).

[33] Chen (n 25).

[34] Simonsen and Koefoed (n 8).

[35] ibid 10.

of moments, defined as 'a higher form of repetition, renewal and reappearance, and of the recognition of certain determinable relations with otherness (or the other) and the self'.[36]

Finally, and crucially for this analysis, critical phenomenology poses the question of *human co-existence* as a political one that 'ineluctably involves power and conflict as well as reason and communication'.[37] If alterity and plurality constitute the polyrhythmic ensemble of the social, the management of conflict (arrhythmias) and the ensuing question of ethical-political responsibility bring the radical encounter with 'other' and 'otherness' back to the fore. In particular, when lived experience, difference and (human) co-existence are respectively abstracted, suppressed and denied, what forms of (political) action and resistance can be activated to counteract the calculated delay, (deliberate) inaction and/or criminalisation of human solidarity? As the case study in section III will illustrate, the chronography and geography of power[38] that the conceived space of law and jurisdiction produce, essentially aggravate the human condition of people in acute distress while claiming to initiate legal proceedings aimed at ensuring a 'place of safety'. As a result, the tension between stated intentions of the law and practical outcomes that Rhythmanalysis discloses in the *methodological* form of arrhythmia is inevitably transferred and transposed to arrhythmia as a counter-hegemonic project. As we shall see, this explains forms of resistance that act both *within* existing and available 'interstices of law' (eg, the refusal by the judge in the preliminary investigation in Agrigento to confirm Rackete's arrest on the basis of Article 98 of 1982 UNCLOS and the Italian Court of Cassation supporting his decision) and *without*, turning legal breaches into acts of deliberate, political rupture (Rackete's decision to violate the ban to fulfil her duty to rescue people at sea).

That is why introducing Simone De Beauvoir's reasoning on difference and *ambiguity* might help us refine and recalibrate our understanding of legal and political critique. Beauvoir defines the body as a (phenomenal) *situation*: 'it is our grasp of the world and the outline of our projects'.[39] If the body is not a thing (that can be kept at bay or out of sight), but a relation that implies the encounter with the world and the other through the potentiality of action (the outline of our projects), to reject the situation amounts to a nihilistic negation/abstraction of all human existence. And if 'the world is made of the same stuff of the body',[40] the projection of the bodies *onto* the world will determine the agentic capacity of human beings. However, according to De Beauvoir, when considering human efforts, we should start from a philosophical position that acknowledges

[36] Lefebvre (n 5) 638.
[37] Simonsen and Koefoed (n 8) 12.
[38] See eg S Sharma, *In the Meantime. Temporality and Cultural Politics* (Duke University Press, 2014). See also D Massey, *For Space* (SAGE, 2005).
[39] S De Beauvoir, *The Ethics of Ambiguity* (Citadell Press, 1948) 46.
[40] Merleau-Ponty (n 32) (1964) 163.

ambiguity and *failure* as intrinsic to human existence and (political) action.[41] Embodiment and consciousness carry with them irresolvable tensions. Conflict, separation, and relation; violence and the capacity for solidarity co-exist.[42] As the following section III will demonstrate, this condition is mirrored both in the ambiguous perimeter of international human rights law, with its loopholes, and in the unresolved, haunted, Western collective consciousness. The tension between the principle of non-refoulement and the duty to rescue lives at sea, on the one hand, and the threshold and limits of jurisdiction, on the other, clearly encapsulates this ambiguity: while juridically recognising the gravity of the humanitarian emergency and the need for resolute action, the states' failure to assume individual or collective responsibility de facto condemns the 'others' at sea (or in the camp) to a condition of 'absolute otherness'.[43]

III. JURIDICAL BODIES: EU MIGRATION POLICIES OF DETERRENCE AND CONTAINMENT

In this section, we turn to challenge the policies of deterrence and containment that Italy and other EU member states have implemented to criminalise humanitarian organisations assisting migrants, including NGOs carrying out search and rescue operations at sea. It is important to note that this criminalisation of solidarity is by no means isolated in nature, nor the only means through which member states have sought to prevent people on the move from reaching or remaining on the territory of the EU.[44] Similarly, other states in the Global North have pursued similar policies which significantly undermine or circumvent international human rights provisions. By focusing on the case of the *Sea Watch 3* and the arrest of its Captain, Carola Rackete in 2019, we examine the political nature of the rhythmic entanglements that connect 'bodies at sea' with juridical bodies and the policies that they produce.[45] As mentioned above, the *Sea Watch 3* case enables us to focus on the fundamental spatio-temporal mismatch that pits the existence of human bodies in time-space against the tempo of law, making visible the arrhythmia at the heart of such policies of containment and deterrence and, indirectly, of international human rights law itself. As further examined in this section, this case clearly shows the political

[41] De Beauvoir (n 39).

[42] S Kruks, *Simone de Beauvoir and the Politics of Ambiguity* (OUP, 2012).

[43] E Levinas, *Otherwise than Being or Beyond Essence* (Kluwer, 1991).

[44] Push-back and pull-back at sea and on land have been long used by EU member states to prevent arrivals. See eg V Moreno-Lax, 'The Architecture of Functional Jurisdiction: Unpacking Contactless Control – On Public Powers, *S.S and Others v Italy*, and the Operational Model' (2020) 21(3) *German Law Journal* 385–416. See also I Mann, *Humanity at Sea: Maritime Migration and the Foundations of International Law* (CUP, 2016).

[45] For further insightful reflections on rights, sovereignty and nationhood, see L Stonebridge, *Placeless People: Writing, Rights, and Refugees* (OUP, 2018).

manipulation of space-time and the intrinsic ambiguity of the applicable laws, which simultaneously protect and enable the abandonment of people at sea.

A. The Italian Policy of 'Closed Ports' and the *Sea Watch 3* Case

On 29 June 2019, the 31-year-old Captain of the humanitarian rescue ship *Sea Watch 3*,[46] Carola Rackete, guided the ship into the Italian port of Lampedusa. In so doing, to avoid being stopped by the Italian authorities, the *Sea Watch 3* hit an Italian finance police patrol and drove it against the quay. Rackete contravened the express ban to access Italian territorial waters and the order to stop imparted by the Italian authorities. Rackete's decision came after two weeks in international and Italian territorial waters, waiting for being assigned a place of safety (POS) which she had requested from various territorial authorities, to bring to safety approximately 50 migrants that the *Sea Watch 3* had rescued from a drifting rubber dinghy on 12 June 2019. The rescue operation had taken place in Libyan Search and Rescue (SAR), waters 47 miles to the South of the coast of Libya, from where the dinghy had set out. The vessel in distress had been spotted by a French plane of another humanitarian non-governmental organisation, which had proceeded to alert the *Sea Watch 3* as it found itself in close proximity. The Libyan coastguard had immediately declared responsibility for coordinating the rescue mission, but the *Sea Watch 3* had reached the dinghy first and proceeded to transferring the people rescued on board of the humanitarian rescue ship. After requesting to be assigned a POS, the Libyan authorities replied that the *Sea Watch 3* should take the rescued passenger to the port of Tripoli, in Libya. Rackete declined to do so, stating that Tripoli could not be considered a POS. She thus proceeded to request an alternative POS whilst heading North, towards Italy and Malta, the closest ports of safety. Considering Malta's long track record of refusing disembarkation of migrants, the *Sea Watch 3* headed towards Italian territorial waters.

Italy, however, had just adopted new security measures, through decree no. 53 of 14 June 2019, the so-called *decreto sicurezza-bis*.[47] Crucially, the decree introduced two fundamental changes in Italian immigration law. First, it conferred direct powers to the Minister of Interior to issue, in agreement with the Minister of Defence and the Minister of Transport, measures aimed at limiting or banning transit, entry or permanence of vessels in Italian territorial waters for reasons of public order and national security. The new decree was also aimed at

[46] Sea Watch is a German non-governmental organisation (NGO) but at the moment of the events which led to Rackete's arrest the *Sea Watch 3* was carrying a Dutch flag. Under international law, therefore, the responsibility for the conduct of the vessel and its crew, including fulfilling the obligation of rescuing people in distress at sea, was vested upon The Netherlands.

[47] www.giurisprudenzapenale.com/2019/06/18/in-vigore-dal-15-giugno-il-decreto-legge-14-giugno-2019-n-53-cd-decreto-sicurezza-bis/.

preventing foreign vessels seeking to 'load or unload people who are in breach of immigration laws currently in force in the coastal state' (Article 11(1)(3)). Furthermore, the decree amended the Italian immigration law and introduced harsher penalties for vessels that entered Italian territorial waters in breach of an entry ban. The new measures envisaged an administrative sanction of between 150,000 euros and 1 million euros, as well as the immediate confiscation of the vessel after the first breach.

It was on the basis of these new security measures that, on 15 June 2019, the Italian Minister of Interior denied entry to the *Sea Watch 3* which thus remained in international territorial waters adjacent to Italian territorial waters, repeating its request to be assigned a POS. Italian authorities continued to refuse entry but proceeded to evacuate passengers in need of medical care. On 26 June 2019, the *Sea Watch 3* disregarded the orders by the patrol boats of the Italian *Guardia di Finanza* (the Italian finance authority) and, invoking the state of necessity, entered Italian waters directed towards the port of Lampedusa. The NGO ship stopped in the port awaiting authorisation to disembark its passengers, an authorisation that however was not forthcoming. Three days later, on 29 June 2019, the situation on board was rapidly deteriorating and some passengers had started to self-harm. At night, in the absence of a positive response from the Italian authorities and after a failure to obtain an interim measure by the European Court of Human Rights requiring that the applicants be authorised to disembark (*Rackete and Others v Italy*, 32969/19), the *Sea Watch 3* drove to the commercial quay of the port and docked, hitting an Italian patrol in the process as mentioned earlier in this section. Following disembarkation, Rackete was arrested on charges of resisting public authorities (Article 337 of the Italian criminal code) and for resisting and attacking a war ship (Article 1100 of the Italian naval code). The latter charges were based on the aggravating fact that Rackete had repeatedly ignored the explicit orders by the Italian authorities not to enter Italian territorial waters. In what became rapidly a media frenzy, the NGO Sea Watch repeatedly issued statements saying that 'forcibly taking rescued people back to a war-torn country, having them imprisoned and tortured, is a crime that we will never commit'.[48]

On 2 July 2019, the judge in the preliminary investigation (the GIP of Agrigento) refused to confirm the arrest and rejected the request for precautionary measures,[49] put forward by the prosecutor,[50] that Rackete be banned from

[48] R Hughes, 'Carola Rackete: How a ship captain took on Italy's Salvini', *BBC News*, (6 July 2019) www.bbc.com/news/world-europe-48853050.

[49] Ordinanza sulla richiesta di convalida di arresto e di applicazione della misura cautelare, document number N. 3169/19 R.G.N.R. and 2592/19 R.G.GIP, www.giurisprudenzapenale.com/wp-content/uploads/2019/07/Rachete-Carola-Ordinanza-sulla-richiesta-di-convalida-di-arresto.pdf.

[50] Richiesta di convalida dell'arresto e di applicazione di misura cautelare, N. 3169/19 R.G.N.R. Mod. 21, 30 June 2019, www.giurisprudenzapenale.com/wp-content/uploads/2019/07/Richiesta-convalida-arresto-RACKETE.pdf.

residing in the province. In relation to the charges of resisting and attacking a war ship, the GIP of Agrigento referred to the Constitutional Court's decision n. 35/2000 in which it held that patrol boats by the Italian *Guardia di Finanza* can only be considered war ships when they operate in international waters or in foreign ports where no consular authority is otherwise present. Since the patrol boat hit by the *Sea Watch 3* when entering the port of Lampedusa was not operating in such circumstances, it could not be considered a war ship. In relation to the charge of resisting a public authority, the GIP of Agrigento acknowledged that, as per Article 19 of the 1982 United Nations Convention on the Law of the Sea (UNCLOS), states are free to adopt measure to contrast irregular migration by sea. He found, however, that these powers of the state are limited by the duty to rescue vessels and people at sea (Article 18 UNCLOS), a duty that was vested upon Rackete (Article 98 UNCLOS) in relation to the passengers she had rescued and was subsequently requesting to disembark. Her conduct could therefore not be considered criminal in nature since it was carried out while fulfilling such duty of rescue at sea, a duty which could not be considered fulfilled by the captain of a ship until rescued people were disembarked. In this regard, the GIP of Agrigento also noted that under the Search and Rescue 1979 (SAR Convention), coastal states were also under an obligation to collaborate to ensure that the rescue operations are safely completed in the shortest time possible, including by taking the rescued people on board and taking them to a port of safety.

The Court of Cassation, the highest Italian court, was called to consider the prosecutor's appeal that the GIP's decision be annulled, and on 20 February 2020,[51] it rejected the prosecutor's appeal and agreed with the GIP on justifying Rackete's actions because of the obligations vested upon her, including the obligation to deliver the people rescued at sea to a place of safety. The Court of Cassation also confirmed the rejection of the precautionary measures requested against Rackete, reiterating that restrictions to an individual's personal freedom can only be implemented in very exceptional circumstances, not applicable to Rackete's situation. For the purposes of our application of Rhythmanalysis, this case is of significance to highlight the limitations of viewing international human rights law, and relevant notions of jurisdiction and of the right to seek asylum, as linear, progressive and predictable,[52] rather than capable of evolving to respond to developments that are, by their very nature, mutable, unexpected and/or uncontrollable. As further explained in the next section, it is in circumstances like those of the *Sea Watch 3* case that the Lefebvrian notions of abstract space and lived abstraction manifest themselves, in a perverse and ambiguous

[51] Sentenza n. 112 della Corte Suprema di Cassazione, CC – 16/01/2020, registered 20 February 2020, at www.sistemapenale.it/pdf_contenuti/1582492635_sea-watch-rackete-cass-2022020-arresto.pdf.

[52] K McNeilly, 'Are Rights Out of Time? International Human Rights Law, Temporality, and Radical Social Change' (2019) 28 *Social & Legal Studies* 817–38.

game of delayed disembarkation and non-acceptance of responsibility played by EU institutions and member states.

B. *Sea Watch 3*: Arrythmia and the Political Manipulation of Space-Time

Through the *Sea Watch 3* it becomes possible to make visible and acknowledge the arrhythmia at the heart of EU migration policies and of international human rights law itself. Through this emblematic case, we can examine the political manipulation of space-time and its intrinsic ambiguity as they manifest themselves not only into the juridical body – of the applicable laws, simultaneously protecting people at sea and denying them of protection – but also on the human bodies of people rescued at sea. As mentioned earlier in this chapter, the political confinement of bodies at sea and on board of the *Sea Watch 3* represents a form of triumph of the *conceived space of law over the lived space of human beings*. The obliteration of refugees' human rights, any time states refuse to take responsibility for their rescue and for even processing their asylum claims, maps their inhabiting of a legally suspended space (be it international waters or the *Sea Watch 3* vessel while waiting disembarkation) onto a zone of non-existence. The bodies at sea are turned into *lived abstractions* in the eyes of both the law and of the EU institutions and member states. During the *Sea Watch 3* standstill, the refugees awaiting disembarkation were portrayed as a risk, a burden and a threat by both the media and relevant politicians, but their continued living and suffering on board of the vessel was never fully reported or discussed. The decision to keep their lives significantly and deliberately out of sight renders the condition of political arrhythmia apparent in its existential urgency. The juridical body of contradicting legal norms, related for instance to jurisdiction in situations of transnational human rights violations such as the ones continually perpetuated by the Libyan coastguard on behalf of the EU and its member states, is a prime signifier of the *conceived space*, mobilised by the EU and its member states as a form of *practical power* that exerts the violence of abstraction over its subjects by denying their humanity. Within the heightened security context of the current COVID-19 pandemic, these people were presented simultaneously as a health risk and an economic burden, who could not be assimilated and transformed into 'productive subjects'.[53]

[53] See eg A Bhagat, 'Governing Refugees in Raced Markets: Displacement and Disposability from Europe's Frontier to the Streets of Paris' (2020) *Review of International Political Economy*, at doi.org/10.1080/09692290.2020.1844781; L. Turner, '"#Refugees can be entrepreneurs too!" Humanitarianism, race, and the marketing of Syrian refugees' (2020) 46 *Review of International Studies* 137–55; PK Rajaram, 'Refugees as Surplus Population: Race, Migration and Capitalist Value Regimes' (2018) 23 *New Political Economy* 627–39. See also U Krause and H Schmidt, 'Refugees as Actors? Critical Reflections on Global Refugee Policies on Self-Reliance and Resilience' (2020) 33 *Journal of Refugee* Studies 22–41.

The production of space and, crucially, its negation are evident in this case study. The sea and the *Sea Watch 3* itself become a space where the legal obligations pertaining search and rescue are affirmed but also simultaneously negated by a denial of a place of safety and a refusal to disembarkation. At sea and on board of the vessel, however, people continue to live, give birth, hug, fear and die. However denied, the pulsating rhythms of their human existence carry the visible mark of enduring Western colonial practices, placing the West in front of the indicting gaze of the disposable 'Other'.[54]

In the *Sea Watch 3* case, Carola Rackete was criminalised for breaching the ban to access Italian territorial waters, explicitly contravening the order to stop imparted by the Italian authorities. Yet Rackete's decision was justified by a duty to rescue people at sea (Article 18 UNCLOS). In Lefebvrian terms, this not only epitomises the contradictory nature of abstract space, but signals the possibility for a differential space emerging from it. As Wilson aptly observes,

> In Lefebvre's opinion, the increasing political significance of the state-led production of space necessitates a form of revolutionary action that is explicitly oriented against the state and toward the subversion of abstract space, based on the contradiction internal to it. (Wilson 2013, p. 372)

In other words, Rackete's 'revolutionary action' reaffirms the value of the *lived* (bodies) over the violence of the *conceived* (the EU institutions, the member states, the law). Conceptually, this passage can be identified as the trait-de-union between Lefebvre's theorisation of space and his later work on Rhythmanalysis. Arrhythmia, as it delineates itself in the *Sea Watch 3* case, is symptomatic of a very specific type of EU governmentality, aimed at the willful creation of spatio-temporally suspended zones. Against the background of continued criminalisation of humanitarian NGOs and their workers, prolonged stalling in situations of disembarkation, and the presentation of the New Pact on Migration and Asylum in September 2020 (confirming a doubling down of deterrence and containment measures), the identification and subsequent politicisation of arrhythmia remains a key tool for social, legal and political critique. Through it, we can unpack and examine the ethical and political dimension that underpin the spatial and temporal mismatch, in a bid to reaffirm the centrality of the bodily experience of people rescued at sea *against* the violent and ambiguous abstraction of international human rights law. As a clear example of this abstraction, in the next section we focus on the notion of jurisdiction and we examine, in more detail, the need for overcoming this violent positioning of the law.

[54] See eg ET Achiume, 'Migration as Decolonization' (2019) 71 *Stanford Law Review* 1509; LA Flores, *Deportable and Disposable: Public Rhetoric and the Making of the "Illegal" Immigrant* (Pennsylvania State University Press, 2020) especially ch 3; ET Achiume and A Bâli, 'Race and Empire: Legal Theory Within, Through and Across National Borders' (2021) 67 *UCLA Law Review* 1386.

C. Jurisdiction, the Production of Time-space and Violent Abstraction

The importance of reconnecting time and space, and of understanding the production of time-space and abstraction, become crucial to exposing the spatio-temporal violence of a specific legal notion relevant to the *Sea Watch 3* case: the notion of jurisdiction. Jurisdiction is relevant to our case study because much of the contention on disembarkation is due to increased attempts by EU member states to avoid being legally responsible for the rights of people rescued at sea, especially in terms of granting them access to EU territory and to a fair refugee status determination procedure. According to current state practice, this shirking of responsibility seems best achieved by avoiding situations in which state organs come into contact with the migrants[55] and by ensuring that the migrants do not enter the state territory. If we look at migration control in Australia and the United States, we can see that this contactless approach to migration control is not unique to the EU migration context,[56] and relates to the fact that the obligations by state parties to a human rights treaty that contains a jurisdiction clause, such as the European Convention on Human Rights, may also extends to transnational contexts, that is to say outside of a state parties' territory, as long as the threshold criterion for jurisdiction is met.

Whilst the general approach states that jurisdiction is 'primarily territorial' in nature,[57] the threshold criterion for jurisdiction has also been met when states have exercised effective control over a territory (also known as the spatial mode of jurisdiction) or over a person (the personal mode of jurisdiction).[58] A new approach to jurisdiction, however, suggesting that jurisdiction be triggered when the state has 'control over a situation'[59] has been put forward in the case of *SS v Italy*[60] in relation to Italy's collaboration with the Libyan coastguard on migrants' pullbacks at sea.[61] The traditional modes of jurisdiction,

[55] This is also referred to as 'contactless control', see eg M Giuffré and V Moreno-Lax, 'The Rise of Consensual Containment: From "Contactless Control" to "Contactless Responsibility" for Forced Migration Flows' in SS Juss (ed), *Research Handbook on International Refugee Law* (Edward Elgar, 2019) 82–108.

[56] D Scott FitzGerald, *Refuge Beyond Reach: How Rich Democracies Repel Asylum Seekers* (OUP, 2019) especially chs 4 and 5.

[57] *Banković and Others v Belgium*, European Court of Human Rights, Grand Chamber (Admissibility) Application no. 52207/99 (12 December 2001) at hudoc.echr.coe.int. Even more controversially, see *Georgia v Russia (II)*, European Court of Human Rights, Grand Chamber (Merits) Application no. 38263/08 (21 January 2021) paras 81–84.

[58] M Milanovic, *Extraterritorial Application of Human Rights Treaties: Law, Principles, and Policy* (OUP, 2011).

[59] T Altwicker, 'Transnationalizing Rights: International Human Rights Law in Cross-Border Contexts' (2018) 29 *European Journal of International Law* 581–606, 590. See also D Davitti, *Investment and Human Rights in Armed Conflict: Charting an Elusive Intersection* (Hart Publishing, 2019) especially ch 5.

[60] V Moreno-Lax, 'The Architecture of Functional Jurisdiction: Unpacking Contactless Control – On Public Powers, S.S. and Others v Italy, and the "Operational Model"' (2020) 21(3) *German Law Journal* 385–416.

[61] A Farahat and N Markard, 'Places of Safety in the Mediterranean: The EU's Policy of Outsourcing Responsibility' (2020) Heinrich Böll Stiftung Brussels, eu.boell.org/sites/default/

based on control over a territory or over a person, are clearly limited in terms of reflecting the reality on the ground, when states cooperate in carrying out human right violations by proxy, to exploit the legal loophole created when the violation is carried out transnationally by a state on behalf of and with the support of another state.[62] Such approaches to jurisdiction are equally limited in terms of reflecting the lived abstraction experienced by the people rescued at sea and warehoused on board of the *Sea Watch 3* while waiting to be assigned a place of safety. Whilst it will take a few years to know whether the European Court of Human Rights will accept the emergence of a functional approach to jurisdiction in *SS v Italy*, territorial and personal modes of jurisdiction continue to enable egregious violations across the Mediterranean and beyond. In these migration control contexts, the sea becomes an abstract space in which refugees and migrants are kept at a distance and out of sight. Temporally, this deliberate manipulation confirms Sara Sharma's argument that 'the temporal operates as a form of social power and a type of social difference'[63] and that we ought to develop a 'power chronography' that unveils the temporal dimension of power by rendering visible how differentiations operate at a subjective, embodied level.

The spatio-temporal violence of jurisdiction is apparent in the *Sea Watch 3* case, as well as in all the other cases of refused disembarkation and of NGO criminalisation which continue to occur as part of the EU migration control context. The sea and the vessel carrying people rescued at sea, in Lefebvrian terms, are simultaneously conceived (turned into lived abstractions); perceived (materially produced and reproduced through the spatial practice of refused disembarkation) and lived (still imbued with the meanings and hopes shared by the people on board). The conceived space, which embodies the abstract space of the EU member states and the ambiguity of international law on matters of both jurisdiction and disembarkation, is by extension also the space of capital and of human dispossession. This abstract space of capital is enabled by the ambiguity of the law, which facilitates the transnational flow of goods, services and certain 'productive' actors (such as foreign investors and specialised workers), whilst struggling to make sense of situations of transnational human rights harm. By adding a temporal layer to the analysis of space, we make visible the continued violence[64] which take place as part of the stretching of time, intrinsic in the disembarkation debacles played at sea when EU member states claim to uphold the rule of law whilst at the same time refusing disembarkation.

files/2020-02/HBS-POS%20brochure%20web-200219.pdf. See also N Markard, 'The Right to Leave by Sea: Legal Limits on EU Migration Control by Third Countries' (2016) 27(3) *European Journal of International Law* 591–616.

[62] Gammeltoft Hansen and Hathaway (2015); Costello and Mann (2020).

[63] Sharma as cited in E Harris and R Coleman, 'The Social Life of Time and Methods: Studying London's Temporal Architectures' (2020) 29 *Time & Society* 604, 606.

[64] On race, jurisdiction and the concept of free sea, see further R Mawani, *Across the Oceans of Law: The Komagata Maru and Jurisdiction in the Time of Empire* (Duke University Press, 2018) 231–40.

Through these games of delays and rejections, we see at play the temporal suspension of jurisdiction and the politics of ambiguity depicted by De Beauvoir.[65] The non-disembarkation of people rescued at sea exploits the gaps and silences of international human rights law – demonstrating its spatio-temporal unfitness – as well as situations of legal ambiguity which are functional to the creation of architectures of oppression. EU member states, backed by the deliberate silences and constitutive inaction of EU institutions, purport to uphold international human rights law, whilst skilfully taking advantage of its limitations to rely on these architectures of oppression. These in turn, emblematically represent the systems of abstraction at the core of Lefebvre's life-long critique of capital: whilst people rescued at sea are kept out of sight, so that the materiality of their bodies is abstracted and the time-space in which they live is deliberately ignored, their lives continue throughout and in spite of this suspension of time.

IV. CONCLUSION

In this chapter, we have reappraised Lefebvre's theorisation of space and rhythm as political, conceptual and methodological tools to examine and critique current EU migration policies of deterrence and containment. We have contextualised Rhythmanalysis by examining its roots in spatial analysis using Lefebvre's ideas of concrete abstraction, abstract space and differential space to signal the discrepancy and contradictory nature that characterises the stated aims of the EU migration policies and the lived experiences of people targeted by them. We have theoretically grounded, significantly advancing it, Novak's argument that the arrhythmic encounter between the tempo of international human rights law and the lived experience of the refugees at sea has an ambiguous political quality to it, thus introducing a novel way of approaching the fields of international human rights law and migration. One that organically integrates the spatio-temporal dimension of social (re)production, rather than 'cosmetically' applying it.

To theoretically strengthen this position, we have explored the affinities and potential synergies between Rhythmanalysis and Critical Phenomenology *qua* political practices and methodological orientations centred on lived experience, human co-existence and difference. Crucially, we then considered the role of ambiguity and failure that according to De Beauvoir is intrinsic to all human and political existence/action, as the starting point for a resemanticisation of political and legal critique, away from the violence of abstraction associated with the 'certainty' of law.

[65] De Beauvoir (n 39).

To substantiate our claims, we used as illustrative case the arrest and prosecution of the captain of the *Sea Watch 3* by the Italian authorities in July 2019 for rescuing people at sea and disembarking them in Italy despite the government's closure of all ports to rescue ships operated by NGOs. We focussed on the fundamental spatio-temporal mismatch that pits the existence of human bodies in time-space *against* the tempo of law highlighting, in particular, the ambiguous and contradictory remit of jurisdiction. Lefebvre's ideas of abstract space, differential space and oppression were evoked and invoked to demonstrate that the arrhythmia and ambiguity at the heart of EU migration policies and of international human rights law, far from being unintended, are deliberate political aims. On the same basis we invite further reflection to explore novel ways in which arrhythmia and ambiguity could be harnessed, within political and legal research, as counter-hegemonic projects.

7

Human Rights after Fukuyama

MICHELE TEDESCHINI*

THE END OF the Cold War is often considered a key marker in the history of ideology. For many, when the Berlin Wall came down (1989) and the Soviet Union formally dissolved (1991), an ideological conflict came to a halt that had been splitting the world since 1945. Between Western liberal capitalism and the Eastern Bloc's communism, only the former worldview is said to have survived the epochal shift. Francis Fukuyama is perhaps the earliest and most famous proponent of this vision. With his 1989 announcement of the 'end of history',[1] Fukuyama anticipated a certain 'endist Zeitgeist' that would become very popular throughout the 1990s.[2]

Despite recurrent claims that the beginning of the twenty-first century has proved it wrong,[3] Fukuyama's prediction continues being discussed 30 years after its appearance.[4] The reason why it is of interest for the purposes of this collection, lies in three related considerations that I will substantiate in section I. First, even though its explicit scope extends to liberal democracy, speaking of the end of history (EoH) primarily amounts to celebrating the intensification and geographical expansion of capitalist economics at the post-Cold War historical juncture. Secondly, a particular vision of international human rights (IHRs) seems to have attained prominence at that juncture, when debates about legal and moral entitlements were freed from the Cold War dialectic that had previously enmeshed them.[5] Such a vision largely reduces IHRs to civil and political freedoms, which contribute to the smooth functioning of capitalist societies and fall

* For their comments on earlier drafts of this chapter, I am grateful to the editors, Laura Fischer, David Kennedy, Veronica Pecile, Christine Unrau and all my colleagues at the Käte Hamburger Kolleg.

[1] F Fukuyama, 'The End of History?' (1989) 16 *The National Interest* 3.

[2] G Elliott, *Ends in Sight: Marx/Fukuyama/Hobsbawm/Anderson* (Pluto Press, 2008) 34.

[3] J Davis, 'History Didn't End with the Fall of the Berlin Wall – but Only Now Is the New Battleground Clear' *The Conversation* (7 November 2019) theconversation.com/history-didnt-end-with-the-fall-of-the-berlin-wall-but-only-now-is-the-new-battleground-clear-125768.

[4] L Menand, 'Francis Fukuyama Postpones the End of History' *The New Yorker* (27 August 2018) www.newyorker.com/magazine/2018/09/03/francis-fukuyama-postpones-the-end-of-history.

[5] B Rajagopal, *International Law from Below: Development, Social Movements and Third World Resistance* (CUP, 2003) 200.

short of posing any structural threat to existing economic arrangements. When it comes to IHRs scholarship, emblematic of that attitude is a recent monograph authored by Kathryn Sikkink, which I will briefly analyse at the beginning of section II. Thirdly, the EoH construct carries important temporal consequences. Positing capitalism as the high and final point of human civilisation, in fact, that construct does away with the possibility (and desirability) of any non-capitalist future, thereby also constraining IHRs discourse and practice.

Bearing these considerations in mind, this chapter aims to show how certain scholars have attempted to redeem the futural prospects of IHRs, by concurrently countering the EoH understanding of historical time. Importantly, it must be noted that not all the authors I consider cast their investigations as responses to Fukuyama, or see themselves as working in the shade of capital. As will become evident, some are more concerned with structure than others, and some more explicitly so. But even when it is part of a larger set of preoccupations, it seems to me that the pervasiveness and seeming inescapability of EoH economic arrangements is a common concern of the theories under scrutiny. Following up on this intuition, section II will thus identify three temporal constructs that those theories revolve around, also showing what role international human rights law (IHR law) plays in each of those constructs, if any. Costas Douzinas draws on the thought of Ernst Bloch to cast the idea of '*not-yetness*' in a positive light, even though that same idea adopts reactionary undertones in the work of Dipesh Chakrabarty. Stephen Hopgood, Samuel Moyn, and Paul O'Connell all gravitate towards the prospect of a reversal of historical time. For Hopgood, IHRs' best hopes lie in a peculiar return to the epoch of American hegemony. In different ways, both Moyn and O'Connell believe that it is only if they return to embrace socialist challenges to capitalist economics, that IHRs can survive. In any case, the end of IHRs loom large in the works of these three authors. Finally, Upendra Baxi and Kathryn McNeilly emphasise that IHRs always contain an imaginative surplus that exceeds their dominant articulation, thereby remaining potential sources of unpredictable developments including, arguably, beyond the confines of EoH capitalism. Having examined these constructs, the chapter offers some concluding remarks.

I. A TRIANGULAR RELATIONSHIP

Published in 1989, Fukuyama's announcement of the EoH captured a spreading persuasion that the collapse of the Soviet Union marked the triumph of Western ideological values.[6] The core of Fukuyama's claim appears to concern the realm of politics: 'What we may be witnessing is not just the end of the Cold War,' he explained, but 'the end point of mankind's ideological evolution and

[6] Fukuyama (n 1).

the universalization of Western liberal democracy as the final form of human government'.[7] A long time might pass before this ideological evolution fully translates into practice, Fukuyama clarified, but an irreversible process had been set in motion. The demise of worldwide ideological clashes meant that the dialectical movement of history had come to a conclusion. Regardless of how it was cast by its most famous proponent, however, I suggest that it is better to understand the EoH as a thesis positing the success of capitalist economics. In the eyes of some commentators, this is in fact what Fukuyama and those who supported his view were actually celebrating.[8] More importantly, many believe this reading to have proven accurate on the historical plane, given that barriers to the geographical expansion of capital all but disappeared after 1989,[9] while its hold on society also intensified in what had been the Western Bloc.[10] On the ideological front, by contrast, anti-capitalist discourse is alive and well in the twenty-first century.[11]

This summary might raise eyebrows among those who doubt the epistemological value of the label 'capitalism'.[12] But framing the EoH in terms of capitalist triumphalism does not mean seeing capitalist economics as a set of immutable laws. Nor does it signal belief in the existence of one type of capitalism that evenly conquered the world from the 1990s onward. In this chapter, 'capitalism' simply identifies a politico-economic outlook according to which capital accumulation in private hands should be the organising drive of society. In light of this view, markets play a key role in capitalist economics, which favours commodification to the point where even basic means of sustenance (food, shelter, healthcare etc) must be purchased rather than obtained otherwise.[13] Arguably, a capitalist society is defined by much more than these basic working principles.[14] What is more, capitalism is said to constantly change over time, while retaining no more than an operational unity,[15] a unity that I believe the above-mentioned drive captures quite well. But while it seems that EoH capitalism largely coincides with the prevalent political economy of 'neoliberalism',[16] insisting on such a declination is not necessary for my analysis.

[7] ibid 4.

[8] Elliott (n 2) 44–45. For a more general view see M Nowak, *Human Rights or Global Capitalism: The Limits of Privatization* (University of Pennsylvania Press, 2017) Introduction and ch 1.

[9] R D'Souza, *What's Wrong with Rights? Social Movements, Law and Liberal Imaginations* (Pluto Press, 2018) ch 2; T Piketty, *Capital and Ideology* (Belknap Press, 2020) ch 13.

[10] Compare J Whitlow, 'Coming of Age at the End of History' (*Law and Political Economy*, 23 April 2019) lpeblog.org/2019/04/23/coming-of-age-at-the-end-of-history/.

[11] See, for instance, C Douzinas and S Žižek (eds), *The Idea of Communism* (Verso, 2010).

[12] S Moyn, 'Thomas Piketty and the Future of Legal Scholarship' (2014) 128 *Harvard Law Review Forum* 49.

[13] N Fraser and R Jaeggi, *Capitalism: A Conversation in Critical Theory* (Polity Press, 2018) ch 1.

[14] ibid.

[15] M Lazzarato, *The Making of the Indebted Man: An Essay on the Neoliberal Condition* (Semiotext(e), 2012) 107 ff.

[16] H Brabazon, 'Introduction' in Honor Brabazon (ed), *Neoliberal Legality: Understanding the Role of Law in the Neoliberal Project* (Routledge, 2016).

Having said that the expansion of capitalist economics resides at its core, one must acknowledge that this is not all there is to the EoH thesis. In particular, IHRs occupy a central place, among the set of Western values that the demise of the Soviet Bloc is supposed to have vindicated.[17] Moreover, despite recurrent assertions about the indivisibility of IHRs, civil and political freedoms – more congenial to the requirements of capitalist economics than socio-economic entitlements[18] – regained centre stage in political discussions, advocacy, and academic literature after the Cold War.[19] For the purposes of this chapter, it is not important to determine whether IHRs are impotent towards the distributional patterns which obtain under any given historical configuration of capitalism, or whether they are complicit in bringing those patterns about.[20] Instead, what matters is that a certain understanding of IHRs attained prominence at the EoH.[21]

If IHRs *qua* civil-political freedoms entertain a close relationship with what Fukuyama considers the highest and final point of human civilisation, still missing is the link between these two and the question of temporality. That link is easy to spot, for a construct positing the end of historical time necessarily implies the erasure of any epoch that is yet to come.[22] From a macro-temporal perspective, the EoH does away with the very idea of futurity. Progress is linear, everybody is going in the same direction, and some already inhabit history's final destination: this is the scenario Fukuyama depicts.[23] There is no space to conceive of the idea of a different politico-economic order, if capitalist economics and its attendant ideology represent the apogee of human civilisation, an apogee that fits all peoples, and that all peoples either have reached or are in the process of reaching.[24] At this point, one may take note of an argument made by Nancy Fraser, who claims that 'the private appropriation of social surplus [characteristic of capitalism] usurps [human beings of] their ability to determine their future collectively – thereby stunting their relationship to that temporal moment'.[25]

[17] B Kausikan, 'Asia's Different Standard' (1993) 92 *Foreign Policy* 24.

[18] W Brown, '"The Most We Can Hope For …": Human Rights and the Politics of Fatalism' (2004) 103 *The South Atlantic Quarterly* 451.

[19] JR Slaughter, 'Hijacking Human Rights: Neoliberalism, the New Historiography, and the End of the Third World' (2018) 40 *Human Rights Quarterly* 735. See also K Ciupa, 'The Promise of Rights: International Indigenous Rights in the Neoliberal Era' in Brabazon (ed) (n 16).

[20] Paradigmatic of the former opinion is S Moyn, *Not Enough: Human Rights in an Unequal World* (Belknap Press, 2018). Notable works adopting the latter are N Klein, *The Shock Doctrine: The Rise of Disaster Capitalism* (Penguin, 2007), and J Whyte, *The Morals of the Market: Human Rights and the Rise of Neoliberalism* (Verso, 2019).

[21] Whyte (n 20) 238.

[22] F Jameson, 'The End of Temporality' (2003) 29 *Critical Inquiry* 695.

[23] F Fukuyama, *The End of History and the Last Man* (The Free Press, 1992) 46.

[24] F Furet, *The Passing of an Illusion: The Idea of Communism in the Twentieth Century* (The University of Chicago Press, 1999) 502.

[25] Fraser and Jaeggi (n 13) 130. In a somewhat similar vein, Lazzarato argues that the logic of debt, which he identifies as the main rationality of contemporary capitalism, 'locks up possibilities within an established framework', thereby 'stifling our possibilities for action': Lazzarato (n 15) 71.

In other words, given that the surplus value produced by labour – which is to say by a significant portion of the human beings who are alive at any given time – is captured by a few capitalists, that same value is never used towards democratically chosen goals. Instead, it ends up being invested for its own reproduction, which is to say to perpetuate the cycle of capital accumulation. If that is true, it is no surprise that many equate the global spread of capitalism at the EoH with the very cancellation of historical future.

Under this understanding of history, IHRs lose their political thrust to become the moral foundations of society. On the one hand, all evils have to be addressed as violations of IHR law, rather than as symptoms of any structural politico-economic flaw.[26] On the other hand, having one's civil and political rights respected is the essential starting point for achieving a better life by entering the existing economic structure.[27] It thus seems fair to conclude that the EoH, IHRs, and temporality entertain a somewhat triangular relationship. At the EoH, there can be no future in which capitalist economics ceases to be the organising principle of all social life. This erasure of temporality both *affects* IHRs – as their socio-economic dimension is downplayed in line with the Cold War's outcome – and is *effected through* IHRs – as their monopolising moral claims against injustice anchors such claims to the extant socio-economic order.

Such an anchoring reverberates through mainstream IHRs scholarship, as can be seen by briefly considering two contemporary phenomena of global magnitude, and the way in which the problems they raise are commonly approached in specialised literature. The first phenomenon is globalisation. According to Branko Milanovic, '44 percent of the absolute gain [in income from globalisation] has gone in the hands of the richest 5 percent of people globally, with almost one-fifth of the total increment received by the top 1 percent'.[28] A similar imbalance may invite a critical posture towards the very globalising trend, if not an active hostility to its continuation. Most scholars in the field, however, tend to focus on the effectiveness of IHRs mechanisms to confront the new challenges posed by globalisation, as well as on proposing remedies aimed at increasing the influence of the former on the latter.[29] Something similar occurs with respect to the second phenomenon, that of climate change. Several thinkers have made the point that environmental degradation is a necessary feature of capitalist economics, not a side effect that can be eliminated by regulatory means.[30] Mainstream

[26] V Nesiah and A Keenan, 'Human Rights and Sacred Cows: Framing Violence, Disappearing Struggle' in N Gordon (ed), *From the Margins of Globalization: Critical Perspectives on Human Rights* (Lexington Books, 2004).

[27] Brown (n 18).

[28] B Milanovic, *Global Inequality: A New Approach for the Age of Globalization* (Belknap Press, 2016) 24.

[29] See A Brysk, 'Introduction' in An Brysk (ed), *Globalization and Human Rights* (University of California Press, 2002).

[30] See, eg JW Moore, *Capitalism in the Web of Life: Ecology and the Accumulation of Capital* (Verso, 2015).

IHRs commentators, however, appear to ignore 'the view that the climate crisis will fundamentally not be solved by [...] making capital compatible with – if not cashing in on – ecology'.[31] To drive their efforts, instead, is the goal 'to ensure that green economy transition strategies will embrace human rights.'[32]

II. HUMAN RIGHTS AFTER FUKUYAMA?

If most commentators generally accept that a certain idea of IHRs represents the ideology at the EoH,[33] human rights literature also evidences a trend towards portraying IHRs as traversed by a temporal fissure. This trend, which seems to have gained momentum after the 2008 financial crisis, overlays a growing concern with the possibility of imagining non-capitalist futures[34] with the question of what role IHRs may (or may not) play in such futures. In so doing, this scholarly tendency counters a more orthodox perspective whereby IHRs in their currently dominant and allegedly apolitical declination are considered appropriate tools to improve the human condition and redress economic inequality. Emblematic of the latter approach is Kathryn Sikkink's 2017 monograph *Evidence for Hope*, an impassioned defence of IHR law's achievements against injustice.[35] Without aiming to offer a thorough overview of the book, a few elements stand out that place its analysis within what we may call an EoH approach. Sikkink often treats IHRs as if they were external to the politico-economic order, a set of norms and discursive practices which only become relevant after the latter has already been constituted. When she considers the dramatic increase in the number of people displaced by war in the years 2005–14, for example, Sikkink concludes that 'There is no reason to believe that human rights ideas or institutions somehow contributed to the flow of refugees, though better policies could have improved the reception of refugees and diminished their suffering.'[36] In the author's view, IHRs can alleviate this 'crisis of unprecedented proportions',[37] but they have nothing to do with creating the social conditions for its explosion.

Moreover, although Sikkink's view of IHRs is not limited to civil and political freedoms, such freedoms always seem to take precedence over socio-economic

[31] A Kenis and M Lievens, *The Limits of the Green Economy: From Reinventing Capitalism to Repoliticising the Present* (Routledge, 2015) xi.

[32] B Singh and A De Gregorio Leão, 'Where Are the Human Rights in the Green Economy Transition?' (*Oxford Human Rights Hub*, 17 September 2020) ohrh.law.ox.ac.uk/where-are-the-human-rights-in-the-green-economy-transition/.

[33] See, eg C Douzinas, *The End of Human Rights* (Hart Publishing, 2000) ch 1.

[34] See, eg M Hägglund, *This Life: Secular Faith and Spiritual Freedom* (Pantheon, 2019).

[35] K Sikkink, *Evidence for Hope: Making Human Rights Work in the 21st Century* (Princeton University Press, 2017).

[36] ibid 143.

[37] ibid.

entitlements. In her analysis of contemporary trends relating to famine and hunger, the author emphasises that famine is 'the most extreme deprivation of an economic right – the right to food – *that is in turn a violation of the right to life*'.[38] With this move, an event defined by its collective scope is brought within the conceptual horizon of the individual liberty par excellence. And when it comes to promoting IHRs, no large-scale economic reform aimed at redistributing wealth features among the six policy tools proposed by Sikkink.[39] 'Despite some worrisome trends in some areas, such as the rise of economic inequality', Sikkink is satisfied 'that overall there is *less* violence and *fewer* human rights violations in the world than there were in the past'.[40] Based on this assessment, the author does consider the future prospects of IHRs vis-à-vis rising inequality. To do so, she adopts Albert Hirschman's notion of 'possibilism', which requires strengthening existing efforts to achieve improvements by continued commitment.[41] Accordingly, Sikkink points at the 'unexpected ways' in which 'the skills and strategies [that IHRs advocates] have honed in their other struggles' could contribute towards further change.[42] This invitation to adopt a possibilist posture makes clear that there is no rupture with capitalist economics, in Sikkink's imaginative horizon. IHRs can intervene upon the existing political-economic order to make it more humane, including by reducing economic inequality. But overhauling that historically contingent order is not called for, either through IHRs or otherwise.

As I said above, this chapter focuses on some scholars who disagree with analyses like Sikkink's. For them, IHRs often pose little to no resistance to the injustices caused by EoH capitalism, but they can also prove useful to imagine and bring about non-capitalist futures. To be sure: not all the thinkers I will deal with, set as their primary concern the possibility that IHRs help dismantle the extant economic structure. That appears to be the case of Costas Douzinas and Paul O'Connell, whose Marxist moorings require a head-on confrontation with the capitalist base of society. Others, such as Samuel Moyn and Stephen Hopgood, zoom in on the role of civil and political rights in an epoch marked by an intensification of capitalism in the form of neoliberal policies. These two authors' concerns are mainly historiographical in nature, but they also venture to envision a future beyond the crystallisation of the capitalist present into EoH time. For others still, imagining such alternative social realities as IHRs can bring about far exceeds the prospect of dismantling capitalism. Upendra Baxi and Kathryn McNeilly fit this description, but it seems to me that a certain anxiety about the economic structure inhabits their theories too. While acknowledging that it does not function as a main drive,

[38] ibid 147 (emphasis added).
[39] ibid ch 6.
[40] ibid 141.
[41] ibid 19–20.
[42] ibid 220–21.

my purpose is to magnify said anxiety and to show how it relates to the EoH moment in which Baxi and McNeilly are writing.

In any case, while a temporal fissure runs through several IHRs analyses – especially after 2008 – the way in which that fissure operates varies from theory to theory. To show how this is so, I will organise the remainder of this chapter around a few temporal constructs that the works under scrutiny introduce. The first of such constructs revolves around the possible emergence of what is 'not yet'. The second is IHRs endism, with the accompanying theme of the return (or reversal) of history. The third and final construct is the idea that IHRs always exist in excess of their dominant form, which leaves the door open for unpredictable transformations. To be sure, these are not hard and fast categories. They simply represent tentative elucidations of conceptual artifacts that often overlap with one another. For each construct, I will attempt to imagine how it may translate into the more specific field of *international* human rights *law*. This imaginative exercise is made necessary by the fact that not all the authors considered below specifically refer to *international* human rights. But while I claim that the temporal constructs they build can attach to human rights or *international* human rights indifferently, one cannot always transpose them as easily into the legal domain. To preserve simplicity, the following paragraphs consistently use the label 'IHRs' regardless of the specific focus of the scholar at issue.

A. *Not-yetness*

In a 2000 book titled *The End of Human Rights*, Costas Douzinas employs many dichotomies to distinguish the contrasting ways in which IHRs can be understood and practised. To appear particularly relevant here, is the author's assertion that IHRs are torn between a multitude of backward-looking practices based on positive international law, and their enduring potential to serve forward-looking utopian imaginaries.[43] It is interesting that Douzinas explicitly casts the former shape – one that IHRs predominantly adopt in contemporary reality – as a key feature of the anti-utopian climate of the EoH.

> Not only have human rights been hijacked by governments and international committees and their early connection with […] utopianism […] has been severed, but utopia also is not doing too well. It would not be inaccurate to say that our epoch has witnessed the demise of utopian hopes […]. The concept of utopia […] was deleted from the political dictionary with the collapse of communism.[44]

In Douzinas' view, the scope of this EoH declination of IHRs is often limited to the domain of civil and economic freedoms. Moreover, capitalist economics

[43] Douzinas (n 33) ch 12.
[44] ibid 338.

emerges as one of the most prominent rationalities to which such an anti-utopian declination is subjugated.

> As institutional practice, human rights often express the imagination of the one and homogeneous world society, in which the extension of formal equality and negative freedom and the globalisation of Western capitalism and consumerism will equate society with its "ideal" picture drawn by governments and international law experts.[45]

To this arresting practice that contributes to deleting the future, therefore bringing human rights to an end,[46] Douzinas opposes a tradition of turning IHRs into a force *against* the closure of positive law. Victims of injustice, in fact, can always appropriate IHRs, making them carrier of a social utopia in which the atomised subjectivity typical of capitalist economies has been supplanted by a form of collective freedom respectful of the uniqueness of its participants.[47] Drawing on the Marxist philosophy of Ernst Bloch, Douzinas describes this social utopia as 'the prophesying of a future *not yet* and not ever present'.[48] When they are imbued with that social imaginary, IHRs acquire the power to project human beings beyond the historical time of EoH capitalism.

In Douzinas' analysis, therefore, IHRs are traversed by a temporal split between the 'always there' of positive law, and the 'not yet' of social utopia.[49] It is clear what moral connotation each of those poles carries – the former constraining/*bad*, the latter promising/*good*. But this dichotomy can be reversed quite easily. Suffice here to consider Dipesh Chakrabarty's *Provincializing Europe*, also published in 2000, in which the 'not yet' is divested of its Blochian-utopian import, for it symbolises the withholding of self-determination on the part of colonial powers looking down on (and, symbolically, back towards) peoples they kept trapped in an allegedly pre-modern state. By contrast, the colony's insistence on the 'now' of the IHR to self-determination[50] – or, at the EoH, the former colonies insisting on the 'now' of the IHR to development[51] – endows positive law with a certain forward-looking thrust.[52]

Not only does early-2000s scholarship already portray IHRs as ambiguously torn between current positive law and future arrangements yet to come, then. It is the very notion of 'not-yetness', that stands out as an ambiguous temporal construct. It can be understood as a metaphorical utterance, reflecting the

[45] ibid 375.
[46] ibid 380.
[47] ibid 341.
[48] ibid 177 (emphasis added).
[49] ibid 318.
[50] As established by the identical formulation of art 1 in both the International Covenant on Economic, Social and Cultural Rights (adopted 16 December 1966, entered into force 3 January 1976) 993 UNTS 3, and the International Covenant on Civil and Political Rights (adopted 19 December 1966, entered into force 23 March 1976) 999 UNTS 171.
[51] Declaration on the Right to Development, UNGA Res 41/128 of 4 December 1986.
[52] D Chakrabarty, *Provincializing Europe: Postcolonial Thought and Historical Difference* (Princeton University Press, 2000) Introduction.

ways in which IHRs justify a vision of history in which 'the West and the non-West' inhabit non-contemporary temporal dimensions, the latter forever lagging behind the former.[53] As Radha D'Souza has claimed, after all, buying into the EoH narrative comes with a belief that contemporary IHRs violations only (but regularly) occur '"out there" somewhere in Africa, Asia, Latin America'.[54] This 'out there' could also read as a 'back then', the signifier of a rights-infringing historical time that the capitalist West left behind in 1989.[55] From the vantage point of EoH time, in turn, reviving nineteenth century imperialistic practices has often been justified with the pretext of ending violations happening *out there/back then* to restore the IHR to democracy.[56] At the same time, however, the letter of positive IHR law, if properly interpreted, can be seen as embodying the promise of a just international order that is not yet. According to Balakrishnan Rajagopal, this understanding requires setting aside 'The views of both developing and developed countries' – but also of development agencies – which 'seem inconsistent' with the right to development as affirmed by the [General Assembly of the United Nations] in 1986, and subsequently restated by the UN Commission on Human Rights.[57] Instead, argues Rajagopal, it is the practice of grassroots movement in the Third World, that should give content to the right to development. Recognising communities' ability to choose what development means to them, in fact, would have 'the consequence of fundamentally disrupting the capitalistic basis of the international order, which relies on rapid exploitation of resources for profit by replacing traditional practices with modern ones'.[58] Just as it is said to symbolise backward-looking practices disguised as observance of IHR law, then, not-yetness is deemed capable of identifying a multitude of post-EoH, non-capitalist futures that that same law could serve to crack open.

B. End and Reversal

Both Rajagopal and Douzinas believe that the EoH is not the triumph of IHRs, *unless* by 'IHRs' one understands a set of tools wielded by powerful actors to preserve an imbalanced economic order. The growing spread of capitalist

[53] ibid 7.

[54] D'Souza (n 9) 26.

[55] According to Fleur Johns, the institutional rituals of IHRs encourage people 'to locate themselves amid a progressive temporality marked out in human rights terms–to envisage themselves moving away from rights-infringing pasts towards rights-respecting futures': F Johns, 'The Temporal Rivalries of Human Rights' (2016) 23 *Indiana Journal of Global Legal Studies* 39, 56.

[56] A Anghie, *Imperialism, Sovereignty and the Making of International Law* (CUP, 2005). For a critical assessment of the thesis that the right to democracy is a norm of positive international law, see S Marks, *The Riddle of All Constitutions: International Law, Democracy, and the Critique of Ideology* (OUP, 2003) especially ch 2.

[57] Rajagopal (n 5) 220.

[58] ibid 221.

economics at the EoH juncture, by contrast, poses a threat to the survival of IHRs as a force for radical change.[59] Stephen Hopgood's analysis in his 2013 *The Endtimes of Human Rights* follows similar lines, in as much as it identifies two competing declinations of IHRs, and it argues that the prevalence of one of those notions may destroy any hope for a more equal international society. According to Hopgood, it is important to distinguish Human Rights (uppercase initials) from human rights (lowercase initials).[60] The former concept identifies 'a global structure of laws, courts, norms, and organizations' that results from top-down imposition and works to support the global order of capital.[61] The latter, instead, represents a form of activism as varied as the multiplicity of local actors that spontaneously create rights to advance claims against injustice. Historically, what turned human rights into Human Rights was American power ascending to global hegemony and co-opting the language of IHRs for imperialistic purposes. In the author's view, this happened at the EoH juncture: 'The high point of this new world of Human Rights was from 1991 to 2008–the "unipolar moment" of American post-Cold War dominance'.[62]

Hopgood does not specify why he chooses 2008 as the closing of the Human Rights era. Among the many events occurred in that year that he mentions, notably absent is the global economic recession. This is surprising, especially given that a dominant theme of his book is the subordination of Human Rights 'to the end of globalizing neoliberal democracy'.[63] In this sense, one could speculate that the financial crisis, rooted as it was in the United States housing bubble, was one of the major causes of a nascent shift in global power that could not leave Human Rights untouched. Even now that American hegemony is waning, in any case, Hopgood reserves his gloomiest prediction for human rights (lowercase). In his opinion, in fact, IHRs will continue to become more important and less relevant, their advocacy a sign of 'membership in the transnational capitalist class'.[64] Accordingly, it seems that Hopgood agrees with Douzinas, at least in part. When they become the 'signature moral concept' of the EoH,[65] IHRs lose their emancipatory thrust and come to an end. Contrary to Douzinas, however, Hopgood does not stress the need to infuse IHRs with utopian politics, for the purpose of reclaiming their futurity beyond EoH capitalism. On the contrary, and rather bafflingly, he wishes for the United States to achieve

[59] Douzinas (n 33) 380 and passim.

[60] S Hopgood, *The Endtimes of Human Rights* (Cornell University Press, 2013) viii–ix and passim. A very similar dichotomy features in U Baxi, *The Future of Human Rights*, 3rd edn (OUP, 2008), which I will consider in the next section. Hopgood's Human Rights (uppercase) and human rights (lowercase) broadly correspond to Baxi's politics *of* and *for* human rights, respectively.

[61] Hopgood (n 60) ix and ch 8.

[62] ibid xii. See also ch 6.

[63] ibid 95.

[64] ibid 173.

[65] I borrow this formulation from S Moyn, 'A Discussion of Kathryn Sikkink's Evidence for Hope: Making Human Rights Work in the 21st Century' (2019) 17 *Perspectives on Politics* 816, 817.

energetic independence and adopt a more assertive foreign policy based on human rights (lowercase).[66] In other words, a better future lies in the return of American hegemony, but a hegemony used to pursue humanitarian causes rather than imperialistic expansion. In Hopgood's best-case scenario, IHRs are in a state of suspension between a past gone wrong and a return of the most desirable features of that same past, a folding back of time which would rewrite two dialectic struggles – unipolar versus multipolar order, Human Rights versus human rights – in favour of the losing poles to then combine those poles together.

Presumably, one could contextualise the shift Hopgood has in mind by reference to two military interventions of the United States, one which took place and one which did not. A future of human rights (lowercase) would be one in which the Obama administration makes good on its warnings and intervenes in Syria to stop the crimes against humanity committed by the Assad regime, regardless of any retaliatory measures Russia and China may adopt.[67] By contrast, no attack like the invasion of Iraq in 2003 would repeat itself, based as it was 'on deception and lies',[68] as well as causing numerous civilian casualties and IHRs violations.[69] This direction that Hopgood's analysis takes, however, does not seem to envisage much of a radical break with existing structures. It is difficult to imagine a non-capitalist future spearheaded by the United States under the banner of an old vision of IHRs, a vision which has just been cleansed of its elitist drifts. If anything, Hopgood's approach reminds of a certain compulsion identified by Jeanne Morefield, whereby supporters of the liberal transatlantic alliance tend to emphasise on their perception of 'who we are' while downplaying the more important question of 'how we act'.[70] In this sense, depending on the politics of the observer, it may be difficult to see anything beyond the endtimes he predicts, in Hopgood's articulation of IHRs.

As a corollary of his investigations into the twentieth century history of IHRs and of their relationship with economic injustice, Samuel Moyn also considers the problem of the future. In Moyn's view, what I identified as the EoH understanding of IHRs attained dominance in the 1970s,[71] and it proved inadequate to counter a skyrocketing of material inequality which was primarily due to the global spread of neoliberal economics.[72] For him, a just economic future requires the return of redistributive projects of the kinds that used to emanate

[66] Hopgood (n 60) 169 ff.

[67] See J Blake and A Mahmud, 'A Legal Red Line: Syria and the Use of Chemical Weapons in Civil Conflict' (2013) 61 *UCLA Law Review Discourse* 244. See also S Hopgood, 'The Endtimes of Human Rights' in D Lettinga and L van Troost (eds), *Debating the Endtimes of Human Rights: Activism and Institutions in a Post-Westphalian World* (Amnesty International Netherlands, 2014) 18.

[68] D Kellner, 'Lying in Politics: The Case of George W. Bush and Iraq' (2007) 7 *Cultural Studies ↔ Critical Methodologies* 132, 134.

[69] BS Levy and VW Sidel, 'Adverse Health Consequences of the Iraq War' (2013) 381 *The Lancet* 949.

[70] J Morefield, *Empires without Imperialism: Anglo-American Decline and the Politics of Deflection* (OUP, 2014) Introduction.

[71] S Moyn, *The Last Utopia: Human Rights in History* (Harvard University Press, 2010).

[72] Moyn, *Not Enough* (n 20).

from the left of the political spectrum.[73] IHRs could embody such a return[74] – or, at the very least, they could form an alliance with it[75] – in which case they might bring about a more equitable social order. Otherwise, and this is the option Moyn appears to find more credible, those who wish to see a more equal distribution of wealth should direct their energies to some other idea, retaining IHR law as a set of minimal constraints on responsible politics.[76] In Moyn's view of a future beyond the EoH, then, a reversal of the trend towards depoliticising distributional questions is evident. That IHRs can contribute towards this return to history as dialectical opposition between pro- and anti-capitalist economic visions, however, is far from clear.

Political contestation also takes centre stage in Paul O'Connell's analysis of IHRs.[77] Compared to Moyn, though, O'Connell has no doubts about the importance of both civil-political and socio-economic IHRs to the working class' struggle against the growing commodification of social life. Yet, from an avowedly Marxist perspective, O'Connell stresses that only under the current capitalist framework, can IHRs be considered the final form of emancipation.[78] For him, supporting IHRs can contribute to subverting the extant socio-economic order, but the true victory of the working class would amount to transcending said order.[79] In O'Connell's view, then, re-politicising IHRs is necessary to reactivate a historical dialectic. But after this reversal/return lies a radically different future, a non-capitalist order which marks the end of IHR law, if not of IHRs in a narrower sense. This reading is consistent with a Marxist tradition that ultimately stands against the rule of law, as China Miéville has put it. According to that tradition,

> To fundamentally change the dynamics of the system it would be necessary not to reform the institutions but to *eradicate the forms of law* – which means the fundamental reformulation of the political-economic system of which they are expressions. The project to achieve this is the best hope for global emancipation, and it would mean the end of law.[80]

Just like Hopgood, therefore, both Moyn and O'Connell evoke the temporal themes of reversal/return and that of the end of IHRs. Such themes take different shapes in the analyses of these two scholars, however. Moyn leaves open the question of what IHRs may look like, should they become a new political utopia mounting a challenge to the capitalist ideology of the EoH. Based on

[73] ibid 218.
[74] Moyn, *Last Utopia* (n 71) 225–26.
[75] Moyn, *Not Enough* (n 20) 217.
[76] Moyn, *Last Utopia* (n 71) 226 ff.
[77] P O'Connell, 'On the Human Rights Question' (2018) 40 *Human Rights Quarterly* 962.
[78] ibid 967. O'Connell's reference is K Marx, 'On the Jewish Question' www.marxists.org/archive/marx/works/1844/jewish-question/.
[79] O'Connell (n 77) 983 ff.
[80] C Miéville, *Between Equal Rights: A Marxist Theory of International Law* (Brill, 2005) 318.

what one commentator has called Moyn's 'belief in the centrality of politics' and 'America-centric perspective',[81] one may imagine that national legislation would play a much more important role than IHR law, in bringing about such a utopia. According to O'Connell, instead, both civil-economic freedoms and socio-economic rights can acquire a forward-looking thrust. Interestingly, they seem to do so by building what we may call a 'temporal staircase', whereby entitlements such as the freedom of association – including the right to form and join trade unions[82] – offer workers a set of building blocks to fill socio-economic rights with progressive meaning. That meaning would have to emerge by way of collective mobilisation, for instance by pushing governments to accept that IHR law imposes upon states a binding obligation to provide social housing and free healthcare.[83] Achievements such as the latter, in turn, are not goals in themselves, but steppingstones to 'introduce a logic of decommodification' which challenges the existing order with a view to transcending it.[84] Social movements can thus reorient all IHRs towards their own elimination. In this sense, a *double* temporal tension appears to cut across O'Connell's theory. Not only are IHRs torn between impotence towards (or connivance with) capitalist injustice and a more balanced distribution of wealth. They also stand in between an absolute, non-capitalist future which has gone beyond IHRs, and what we may call a welfare-driven 'future anterior' to be transcended with the help of IHRs. Assuming this interpretation is correct, there remains perhaps one IHR that does not partake in this double temporal fissure, namely the right to property articulated by Article 17 of the Universal Declaration of Human Rights (UDHR).[85] This right, whose very elimination lies at the core of orthodox (or revolutionary) communism, may be an unlikely candidate to serve as a tool towards any non-capitalist future. In socialist visions like O'Connell's, nonetheless, the complete elimination of property does not seem to feature, at least not in the transition towards a post-capitalist society. The question of the temporal soul of this right might thus be the thorniest of all.

C. Excess and Unpredictability

Upendra Baxi's *The Future of Human Rights*, first published in 2002, identifies many internal tensions that exist within its field of inquiry. Particularly relevant for this chapter's purposes is the distinction between IHRs' *potentiality* and their *potentiality not to*, which Baxi deems essential for thinking the futurity of

[81] P Alston, 'Book Review: Does the Past Matter? On the Origins of Human Rights' (2013) 126 *Harvard Law Review* 2043, 2073.

[82] International Covenant on Civil and Political Rights (n 50) art 22.

[83] For instance, by virtue of articles 11 and 12 of the International Covenant on Economic, Social and Cultural Rights (n 50).

[84] O'Connell (n 77) 986.

[85] Universal Declaration of Human Rights (adopted 10 December 1948) UNGA Res 217 A(III).

the field. Working through 'the extraordinarily complex constitutive notion of potentiality',[86] Baxi casts IHRs discourse and practice as suspended between a growing set of UDHR-based rights that the reality of politics continually refute (*potentiality not to*), and the utopia of a just future in which the potentiality of IHRs remains capable of unfolding.[87] In Baxi's view, such a utopia must be able to 'decreate' the current hegemonic version of IHRs, a version whose ties to EoH capitalism the author makes clear when speaking of

> the project of contemporary economic globalization, where free trade and commerce (so free as to make the State into a clone of global capital, manifest through the transnational corporate capital) are presented, in the long run, as the harbingers for a secure future for human rights.[88]

In another chapter, Baxi directly addresses Fukuyama's thesis and the endist posture it captured, which often results in 'forms of *endolatry* and even *endomania*.'[89] Even though the rest of the chapter meanders through a wide array of topics loosely kept together by the globalising trend – ranging from nuclear weapons to the rights of corporations – Baxi ultimately returns to display signs of the anxiety I mentioned at the beginning of this section, noting that 'the space created by various modes of activist imagination and social praxis is largely pre-determined by the space of contemporary globalization'.[90] Based on this difficulty to escape the imaginative and practical boundaries imposed by dominant economic structures, the author poses a fundamental question that frames his analysis against its EoH context. 'Is the contemporary human rights mode of resistance to globalization historically adequate to retrieve the movement from the market?'[91]

Having taken stock of these concerns about the present, it is easy to see how Baxi's vision of IHRs' futures partially overlaps with some of the theories that were encountered above. His idea of a utopia negating the present echoes Douzinas' claim that IHRs are suspended between backward-looking positive law and forward-looking utopian appropriations. That the future of IHRs lies in decreating IHRs as they exist at the EoH, moreover, reminds of O'Connell's Marxist warning that IHR law should be used to build a society in which IHRs themselves have been transcended. There is, however, an important difference between O'Connell and Baxi, for the latter does not wish to put current IHR law to work to eliminate itself. On the contrary, he envisions a new revolutionary beginning in which an imaginative surplus comes to the fore that is always immanent within the language and practice of IHRs.[92] In so doing, perhaps more than Douzinas and certainly more than O'Connell – but it is a matter of degree rather

[86] Baxi (n 60) 2.
[87] ibid ch 1.
[88] ibid 40.
[89] ibid 244.
[90] ibid 275.
[91] ibid.
[92] ibid 3.

than absolute difference – Baxi turns the utopian dimension of IHRs into the domain of unpredictability. As they imagine a socialist future or point towards a time that is not yet, in fact, both O'Connell and Douzinas primarily build on 'the suffering of the past and the injustices of the present'.[93] Baxi's notion of *potentiality*, by contrast, evokes an 'alteration of time' marked by the eruption of 'not one but many futures.'[94] And even the idea of 'not-yetness', for all its indeterminacy and open-endedness, seems somewhat insufficient to capture this expected fracture in the linear progression of time.

Excess and unpredictability reappear in Kathryn McNeilly's theorisation of IHRs as a performative politico-legal activity oriented towards the future. In her 2017 *Human Rights and Radical Social Transformation*, indeed, McNeilly depicts IHRs as a discourse which always exists in excess of its dominant articulation.[95] Given that such an articulation calls for constant reassertion in order to remain dominant, activists and radical thinkers can always challenge it by inventing unorthodox, emancipatory ways of performing IHRs. This performative activity aims to recreate the world and social relations, striving towards ever newer resignifications of IHRs. In line with Judith Butler, McNeilly reminds us that performative doings escape easy predictions for their being unpredictable and always out of control.[96] Echoing Baxi, the author thus envisages many futures for IHRs, a multitude of social arrangements in which diverse utopian visions come to fruition, without ever exhausting the imaginative surplus that IHRs always retain within themselves. Clearly, the realm of political economy is not the primary site in which McNeilly would look for those visions. When elaborating on the possibilities for action that her theory may create, the author pays particular attention to issues of gender and to feminist work.[97] But her analysis takes aim at 'dominant ways of viewing the world' more generally, including 'neoliberalism and the interests of the political elite in the contemporary period'.[98] Approvingly nodding at some post-2008 rebuffs to Fukuyama's announcement,[99] McNeilly calls for re-filling the meaning of IHRs with political contestation against extant hegemonic structures.[100] And if one shares my view that capital economics is one of the major hegemonic structures of our historical moment – if not *the* major hegemonic structure – it becomes possible to read McNeilly's theory as projecting IHRs beyond its EoH time.

To conclude this analysis, it bears noting how the categories of excess and unpredictability make it quite complicated to bring the legal element into focus and move from IHRs to IHR law. Indeed, it is no coincidence that McNeilly

[93] Douzinas (n 33) 380.
[94] Baxi (n 60) 3, 26.
[95] K McNeilly, *Human Rights and Radical Social Transformation: Futurity, Alterity, Power* (Routledge, 2017) ch 2.
[96] ibid 40.
[97] ibid ch 8.
[98] ibid 2 and 5.
[99] ibid Introduction, note 2.
[100] ibid 5.

objects to conceptualising rights as static legal provisions, portraying IHRs as a performative doing aimed at remaking the world. What that *doing* may be from time to time must resist prescription and fixation by the letter of the law. Its consequences in the legal domain are bound to remain uncertain. This seems to sit well with Douzinas' hostility towards the 'always there' of positive law, to which he opposes the 'not yet' of utopian IHRs. And even Rajagopal, whom I mentioned as a believer in the emancipatory potential of the positive IHR law of development, acknowledges how that law can become 'simply a right of states to pollute rivers, displace people, and create development refugees.'[101] Such a drift is a result of imbuing IHR law with a well-defined (and somewhat infamous) goal, or temporal destination: capitalist development as a marker of the Western idea of modernity. Under this guise, IHR law seem useless to efforts aimed at changing current politico-economic arrangements, for it can only lead more and more people straight into the EoH historical time.

III. CONCLUSION: OF CONCRETENESS AND SEMANTICS

The EoH narrative celebrates capitalist economics as the organising rationality of the apogee of human civilisation. Under that linear vision of history with a finish line where all world societies become one, IHRs largely mean civil and political freedoms, a set of minimum moral standards allowing individuals to engage in market transactions. It is thus not surprising that, in their assessments of the futural prospects of IHRs, the authors I have considered link such prospects to the possibility of opening alternatives to capitalism – albeit some more forcefully and more explicitly than others. In so doing, these authors broach various temporal constructs that stand in clear opposition to the capitalist triumphalism of EoH time. Having attempted to pin down a few of those constructs, while acknowledging that significant overlaps link them together, I would like to conclude with two sets of reflections.

First, I believe it has become apparent that the more one strives to form concrete images of politico-economic future(s) and the more one tries to focus on IHR law, the more difficult it becomes to think of a radical historical break with EoH capitalism. This clearly emerges from the capitalist undertone that the 'now' of the right to development easily assumes. It also stands out as soon as we think of Hopgood's longing for a return of American hegemony, or O'Connell's use of IHR law as a mere steppingstone towards socialism and the elimination of IHR law itself. At the end of this spectrum, one would meet Jürgen Habermas and his definition of human rights as a 'realistic utopia', which he juxtaposes to the 'deceptive images of a social utopia' painted by thinkers like Bloch.[102] For Habermas, the utopian break is behind us, having occurred when (and where)

[101] Rajagopal (n 5) 220.
[102] J Habermas, 'The Concept of Human Dignity and the Realistic Utopia of Human Rights' (2010) 41 *Metaphilosophy* 464, 476.

human rights were incorporated in national constitutions as positive law.[103] On the other hand, the more the emphasis shifts to unpredictability and the imaginative excess of IHRs discourse, the more difficult it gets to imbue theory with content and to imagine what the futurity of IHRs might look like[104] – not to mention what role IHR law may have within (or in bringing about) such a futurity, if any role at all. Relatedly, it seems to me that causal links get blurrier and blurrier, as we pull away from the fixedness of IHR law and from the utopian futurity one struggles towards. In O'Connell's view, for instance, civil-political freedoms are necessary to claim socio-economic rights and proceed along a decommodification path, a path that leads to transcending IHRs altogether and to achieving full human emancipation. By contrast, whenever one dares to imagine – actually, invoke – more open-ended departures from the extant socio-economic order, it gets trickier to determine to what extent IHRs would be a cause, and to what extent a result, of those departures, and even more difficult does it become to bring IHR law into view.

Secondly, one must bear in mind the obvious consideration that the EoH is just an intellectual construct.[105] More: that there is something – a set of legal provisions, a moral code, a powerful discourse – responding to the name of 'international human rights' is also a construct. Law's boundaries are porous, morals are subjective and subject to change. Discourse, as McNeilly notes, is open to resignification as well as to endless counter-resignification. Accordingly, to remain unclear is why the label of IHRs in all its monolithic unity would stand, when an alteration of historical time – a 'not yet' becoming already, or the unpredictable actualisation of potentiality – have disrupted and refuted the linear narrative of the EoH. If that happened, one may suspect that the way we describe the world and our practices in it would also change, along with the terms we use to stake our (often collective) claims. For why would we continue using the same signifiers in vogue at the EoH, when socio-economic relations all around us have been fundamentally rearranged, perhaps in a variety of ways that differ from region to region, exploding the idea of one historical time that is common to the whole of humanity? Borrowing the words of Gloria Anzaldúa, who also dealt with an (admittedly different) 'internal strife' in which a 'counterstance refutes the dominant culture's views and beliefs', it seems admissible to imagine that 'perhaps we will decide to disengage from the dominant culture, write it off altogether as a lost cause, and cross the border into a wholly new and separate territory'.[106]

103 ibid 465 and passim.

104 Illan Rua Wall makes precisely this point in his review of McNeilly's monograph: 'McNeilly has refused to set out any particular horizon of social transformation. […] She does this, because to determine a specific sense would foreclose the futural openness that she has been describing. But without this sense of a trajectory, the question becomes whether we can think about radical practice.' I Rua Wall, 'Kathryn McNeilly: Human Rights and Radical Social Transformation (Book Review)' (2018) 26 *Feminist Legal Studies* 219, 222.

105 Compare FB Berardi, *After the Future* (AK Press, 2011) 18.

106 G Anzaldúa, *Borderlands: La Frontera*, 2nd edn (Aunt Lute Books, 1999) 100–01.

8

Queer Temporalities and Human Rights

ANTHONY J LANGLOIS

THE TURN TO human rights as an international mechanism for the protection of people from violence and discrimination based on sexuality and gender identity is very recent, particularly with respect to its formal institutionalisation. The thickening and spread of legal and institutional mechanisms – at the United Nations, and in various regions – is conventionally depicted as part of the progressive unfolding of a rights triumph over time.[1] The extension of human rights protection to lesbian, gay, bisexual, transgender, intersex and queer (LGBTIQ)[2] people is celebrated as an overdue culmination of the global human rights project. Those of us identifying in these ways can now more confidently hope to be 'free and equal', as declared by the UN's dedicated media campaign.[3] The 2016 establishment by the UN Human Rights Council of an Independent Expert on Sexual Orientation and Gender Identity (SOGI), and the role's renewal in 2019, is the most visible example of this significant and consequential trajectory in the expansion of formal human rights mechanisms.

Notwithstanding the undeniable benefit that is brought to many people through the application of human rights to sexual orientation and gender

[1] K Sikkink, *The Justice Cascade: How Human Rights Prosecutions Are Changing World Politics* (WW Norton & Company, 2011); R Normand and S Zaidi, *Human Rights at the UN: The Political History of Universal Justice* (Indiana University Press, 2008); Ş İlgü Özler, 'The Universal Declaration of Human Rights at Seventy: Progress and Challenges' (2018) 32 *Ethics & International Affairs* 395.

[2] The LGBT acronym comes in many forms, with additional letters: I for Intersex, Q for Queer (and another for questioning), A for asexual (and another for allies), and often simply '+' for your preferred extension. The UN standardly uses LGBT or LGBTI. It also uses the SOGI (or SOGIE) nomenclature: Sexual Orientation and Gender Identity (and Expression), as discussed below in the context of the UN SOGI Independent Expert. My preference is to use LGBTIQ or SOGIE, with consideration given to the usage in source material and context. Consequently, various versions of these acronyms will appear in the text. For reasons which will become obvious (connected to the below discussions of the political role of Hillary Clinton and the analytical work of Cynthia Weber), I also maintain the use of 'gay rights' and 'the gay rights holder' as both shorthand and as an analytical reference.

[3] UNFE, 'UNFE Report 2019' (Geneva, United Nations Free and Equal, 2019) www.unfe.org/about-2/.

identity, the very success and visibility of this development raises intriguing – and often troubling – questions. In this chapter I examine the ways in which these rights – as human rights – are positioned in time, the relationships between their chronopolitics and geopolitics, neoliberalism and the time of homonormativity, and the possibility of maintaining an emancipatory rights politics through a refusal to forget the time before 'gay rights' were human rights.

Section I gives an overview of recent developments at the United Nations, through which people of diverse and non-normative sexualities and gender expressions have been clearly and unambiguously identified as human rights subjects, deserving of protection from violence and discrimination. In section II, we start to consider the temporalities commonly associated with this change, a change conventionally designated as a development, an advance, an overdue extension, the culmination of a long battle, the long-awaited unfolding of justice. A closer look, however, suggests queerer temporalities than those denoted by the standard liberal progress narrative of justice gradually unfolding in time. In section III, the 'arc of history' is diffracted through the prism of our neoliberal times. The resulting rainbow is splintered: the 'last utopia' of human rights for queers is disrupted, its optimism rendered cruel, as it fractures along geopolitical and homonormative lines.[4] In section IV, I argue for a remedy. Human rights for queers had their long-ago origins in gay liberation. Against the fracturing that contemporary rights normalisation in some (predominantly global north) jurisdictions feeds, I argue the need to stay with the absence of rights: a painful past some would forget, but also a present most must endure. Into this absence must be retrieved, and retained where it has not been lost, a politics of liberation. With this, 'gay rights' – indeed all human rights – can avoid normalisation and co-optation into the designs of power and capital against which, to be an emancipatory politics, they must fight.

I. ACQUIRING HUMAN RIGHTS

In 2013, the then Secretary General of the United Nations, Ban Ki-moon, declared that the struggle for the protection of the rights of lesbians, gays, bisexual and transgender people was 'one of the great, neglected challenges of our time'.[5] At the heart of the international human rights regime, change was afoot. After decades of refusal and invisibility,[6] LGBTI rights advocates were being

[4] S Moyn, *The Last Utopia: Human Rights in History* (Belknap Press of Harvard University Press, 2010); L Berlant, *Cruel Optimism* (Duke University Press, 2011).

[5] United Nations, 'Ban Ki-Moon: Struggle for LGBT Right One of the Great, Neglected Human Rights Challenges of Our Time' (International Conference on Human Rights, Sexual Orientation and Gender Identity (Oslo, 15–16 April 2013) www.youtube.com/watch?v=7uaHZWCgGss&feature=youtube_gdata_player.

[6] AJ Langlois, 'Making LGBT Rights into Human Rights' in M Bosia, SM McEvoy, and M Rahman (eds), *The Oxford Handbook of Global LGBT and Sexual Diversity Politics* (OUP, 2019) 75–88.

heard.[7] A major sign of this was the launch by the UN of a global education campaign, Free and Equal,[8] 'aimed at promoting equal rights and fair treatment of LGBTI people'[9] – complete with a Bollywood style video clip (focussed on gay marriage), and an array of explainers and advocacy materials.

More important politically and institutionally, however, were developments at the Human Rights Council (HRC), the peak body of the UN human rights system. A resolution to establish an Independent Expert on Protection Against Violence and Discrimination based on Sexual Orientation and Gender Identity, under the UN's Special Procedures System, was filed on 17 June 2016.[10] It was brought by seven Latin American states: Argentina, Brazil, Chile, Colombia, Costa Rica, Mexico and Uruguay. Under the leadership of Mexico, and with the backing of members of a group of LGBTI supportive states knows as the Core Group (which includes 29 member states, mostly from the West or Latin America) and their allies, the resolution eventually prevailed against concerted opposition at the HRC.[11] Vitit Muntarbhorn, an international human rights law expert from Thailand, with extensive experience in SOGI matters, became the inaugural SOGI Independent Expert (2016–17); he was followed by the incumbent, Costa Rican jurist Victor Madrigal-Borloz. The value to the global LGBTI community of the Independent Expert (particularly in the continuing absence of any formal instrument specifically focused on sexuality and gender rights) was demonstrated by the vigorous campaign to have the mandate renewed after its original three year term, with support by 1312 non-governmental organisations (NGOs) from 174 states and territories around the world. In July 2019 the HRC renewed the mandate of the SOGI Independent Expert with an increased level of support, although not without significant opposition.[12]

As a UN Special Procedure, the mandate holder is able to utilise the resources and expertise of the UN in a wide range of activities.[13] These activities are designed to establish the ways in which existing human rights instruments do or can address the elimination of violence or discrimination based on SOGI, with attention to best practice and gaps. It has long been the complaint of LGBTIQ activists and theorists that they have been invisible to the norms and structures of human rights[14] – that, in effect, non-normative sexuality and gender

[7] E Jordaan, 'The Challenge of Adopting Sexual Orientation Resolutions at the UN Human Rights Council' (2016) 8 *Journal of Human Rights Practice* 298.

[8] United Nations, Born Free and Equal: Sexual Orientation and Gender Identity in International Human Rights Law, HR/PUB/12/06 (New York, United Nations, 2012).

[9] United Nations, 'UN Free & Equal', www.unfe.org/.

[10] HRC, 'Protection against Violence and Discrimination Based on Sexual Orientation and Gender Identity', 30 June 2016, ap.ohchr.org/documents/dpage_e.aspx?si=A/HRC/RES/32/2.

[11] ARC International and ILGA, 'Compilation of the Adoption of the 2016 SOGI Resolution' (ARC International/ILGA, 25 August 2016), ilga.org/compilation-adoption-2016-sogi-resolution/.

[12] ARC International, ILGA World, and ISHR, '#RenewIESOGI', 2019, arc-international.net/wp-content/uploads/RenewIESOGI_report.pdf.

[13] A Nolan, R Freedman, and T Murphey, *The United Nations Special Procedures System* (Brill, 2017).

[14] P EeNam Park Hagland, 'International Theory and LGBT Politics: Testing the Limits of a Human Rights-Based Strategy' (1997) 3 *GLQ: A Journal of Lesbian and Gay Studies* 357.

discounts one's human status, thus rendering the whole edifice of the regime redundant, unable to address the impact of violence and discrimination against queer people. Indeed, before the advent of the SOGI Independent Expert, the level of frustration was such that sympathetic human rights legal experts and professionals took matters into their own hands, convening an independent forum designed to demonstrate how *existing* human rights instruments *should* protect the sexuality and gender diverse. The outcomes of their deliberations – known as the Yogyakarta Principles,[15] remain a critical resource (even when critically received[16]) in the fight for human rights recognition and protection. The Principles were recently updated and expanded to mark their tenth anniversary.[17]

The larger story of what the Yogyakarta Principles represent remains salient now, as LGBTI/SOGIE rights become increasingly recognised and institutionalised within the global human rights regime. Beyond the UN, these rights have support from a range of inter- and non-governmental organisations and regimes across different regions.[18] A number of states, including the US and UK, have prioritised LGBTI rights in foreign policy, as has the European Union in its enlargement practices.[19] International Financial Institutions such as the World Bank and the IMF have practiced forms of 'gay conditionality' in their development assistance programs.[20]

This is a story of power and visibility, the significance of gaining either or both for one's standing within the international political system, and how their temporal valance functions and might be understood. What does it mean to live in a time when making rights claims extends to LGBTI – and even Q – rights?[21] Here – and this is a, if not the, critical point – the consequences of the success of meeting Ban Ki-moon's challenge, of getting noticed, of moving from *neglect* at the furthest margins of the global political stage, to regular episodes in the central spotlight, turns out to be more complex than simply arriving at a point

[15] Yogyakarta Principles, 'The Yogyakarta Principles' (Yogyakarta Principles, 2007) www.yogyakartaprinciples.org/; RR Thoreson, 'Queering Human Rights: The Yogyakarta Principles and the Norm That Dare Not Speak Its Name' (2009) 8 *Journal of Human Rights* 323.

[16] cf M Waites, 'Critique of "Sexual Orientation" and "Gender Identity" in Human Rights Discourse: Global Queer Politics beyond the Yogyakarta Principles' (2009) 15 *Contemporary Politics* 137.

[17] M O'Flaherty, 'The Yogyakarta Principles at Ten' (2015) 33 *Nordic Journal of Human Rights* 280.

[18] RR Thoreson, *Transnational LGBT Activism: Working for Sexual Rights Worldwide* (University Of Minnesota Press, 2014).

[19] K Slootmaeckers, H Touquet and P Vermeersch (eds), *The EU Enlargement and Gay Politics: The Impact of Eastern Enlargement on Rights, Activism and Prejudice* (Palgrave MacMillan, 2016); C Lennox and M Waites, *Human Rights, Sexual Orientation and Gender Identity in the Commonwealth: Struggles for Decriminalisation and Change* (Human Rights Consortium, Institute of Commonwealth Studies, 2013); PM Ayoub, *When States Come Out: Europe's Sexual Minorities and the Politics of Visibility* (CUP, 2016); M Bosia, SM McEvoy and M Rahman (eds), *The Oxford Handbook of Global LGBT and Sexual Diversity Politics* (OUP, 2019); OG Encarnación, 'Clinton's Legacy on Gay Rights', Foreign Affairs (16 June 2016) www.foreignaffairs.com/articles/2016-06-16/clintons-legacy-gay-rights.

[20] R Rao, 'Global Homocapitalism' (2015) 194 *Radical Philosophy* 38.

[21] K Zivi, *Making Rights Claims: A Practice of Democratic Citizenship* (OUP, 2011).

in time where (at least some) queer people have their rights recognised. As well as providing rights protection, for at least some, this transition also imbricates gay rights holders into the broader rights *politics* of our times in complex and consequential ways. Subsumption into that politics *also* incorporates the gay rights holder into the rights politics associated with the formal institutional rights regime globally, complete with its temporal, spatial and geopolitical elements – when we may acquire and exercise 'our' rights, where they might be claimed, and under or by who's power and authorisation. As Shakhsari says, 'Even as the claims of having, giving, and exporting rights mark the difference between the "civilised" and the "uncivilised" countries in the international order of rights, cultural and political citizenship are not enjoyed equally by those who are excluded from normative race, sexuality, and gender in "civilised countries." The inconsistency in the value of the life of different populations and their disposability calls for an analysis of the chronopolitics and geopolitics of rights.'[22]

The balance of this chapter will consider precisely such considerations: what changes for the politics of sexuality and gender with the advent of political attention to, even advocacy for, 'gay rights as human rights'? Because significant elements of the argument will be drawing out critical consequences from what, on the face of it, is a triumph of the extension of human rights, I conclude this opening section by citing from the prefatory statement of the most recent SOGI Independent Expert thematic report. Part of the challenge of the time of the gay rights holder is how we theorise reconciling the gains of inclusion in the system with the losses and compromises that necessarily go along with such recognition. I cite these remarks, then, to emphasise and affirm the very real value of formal recognition and inclusion within human rights systems of SOGI matters, critical considerations to come notwithstanding, for those so long wilfully excluded from its remit:

> In the report, the Independent Expert provides an overview of violence and discrimination based on sexual orientation and gender identity. Such acts are committed in all corners of the world, and victims are presumed to be in the millions, every year. These acts extend from daily exclusion and discrimination to the most heinous acts, including torture and arbitrary killings .... The Independent Expert also explores the root causes of violence and discrimination based on sexual orientation and gender identity, including deeply entrenched stigma and prejudice reinforced by discriminatory laws and regulations that foster a climate where hate speech, violence and discrimination are condoned and perpetrated with impunity.[23]

[22] S Shakhsari, 'The Queer Time of Death: Temporality, Geopolitics, and Refugee Rights' (2014) 17 *Sexualities* 1010.

[23] UN HRC and V Madrigal-Borloz, 'Report of the Independent Expert on Protection against Violence and Discrimination Based on Sexual Orientation and Gender Identity' (United Nations, 11 May 2018).

II. TEMPORALITIES

LGBTI rights receive support within both the Human Rights Council and the UN General Assembly, particularly through the advocacy of the above-mentioned LGBTI Core Group. The coalition of support is not constant, however, nor overwhelming.[24] While equality and freedom for sexuality and gender identity do have increasing purchase on standard interpretations of human rights norms and procedures, levels of contestation remain high, as the need to fight for the renewal of the SOGI Independent Expert Mandate in 2019 clearly showed.[25] The emergence of LGBTI rights as human rights – in keeping with the way in which the history of human rights itself is popularly told[26] – is one of incremental, evolutionary, hard fought gains. It is an unfolding over time of ethical consciousness into the structures of contemporary international politics via the institutions of the international human rights regime. In many versions, these international developments follow triumphs in national and regional contexts (North America, Western Europe, Australia, etc).

The achievement of gay rights thus appears to happen in linear time – one incremental gain happening after another. As many activists would attest, however, it is more like one thing not happening after another: constant deferrals, refusals and setbacks; long gaps, interminable stretches between the steps which have finally led to key achievements. Partly as a consequence, the achievement, when related by advocates and supporters, is expressed with triumph, joy, relief, vindication. And indeed, for many people, this success means that a level of personal safety, communal solidarity and political legitimacy can be hoped for with more certainty. It provides optimism; the ability to imagine and hope for a future, a time in which one's being is not denominated by the certainty of abjection, but through the possibility of wellbeing and fulfilment. 'And not before time …!' This exclamation, with the sense that these developments are long overdue, should, indeed, have been a part of the human rights project from the outset, can be imagined in the voice of many a human rights defender or abuse survivor.

This phrase 'not before time' is also useful analytically, because it prompts a range of critical questions about why sexuality and gender took time to be incorporated into the human rights corpus, and what this temporal displacement from the origins of the human rights project signifies, the meanings it generates, the suffering it represents.[27] LGBTIQ rights have crashed the party that is the international human rights regime (they were manifestly not invited), and as they have done so, along with other minority rights, they raise questions about

[24] cf F D'Amico, 'LGBT and (Dis)United Nations: Sexual and Gender Minorities, International Law and UN Politics' in M Lavinas Picq and M Thiel (eds), *Sexualities in World Politics: How LGBTQ Claims Shape International Relations* Routledge, 2015) 54–74.

[25] ARC International, ILGA World, and ISHR, '#RenewIESOGI'.

[26] eg M Ishay, *The History of Human Rights: From Ancient Times to the Globalization Era* (University of California Press, 2008).

[27] cf Lavinas Picq and Thiel (n 24).

political time. The rhetorical claim made by human rights – to be universal, applicable in all times and all places – is temporally displaced by the need to suddenly declare that human rights now apply to more people – this time, to queer people. The puzzle of this political temporality is only emphasised by the way in which high profile political advocates articulate these 'wins' as being 'on the right side of history' – a claim we will presently examine and unpack.

In this, we may see the interplay of two different kinds of time, distinguished by the ancient Greeks as chronos and Kairos. In chronos we have the ordinary, normal time: 'a quantitatively infinite, divisible medium within which finite lives are lived out …'. Kairos, by contrast, is exceptional: it is linked 'to a qualitative event that creates, arrests or changes time, rather than endures it.'[28] In many tellings, the advent of human rights are a clear breaking into 'normal time' of something exceptional: the political time of human rights re-shapes the field of normal time, rupturing and critically reorienting normative expectations of collective human behaviour. The 'never again' response to the carnage and holocaust of World War II, the outrage this represented against the conscience of humankind, signalled a new time, a new order:

> Whereas disregard and contempt for human rights have resulted in barbarous acts which have outraged the conscience of mankind, and the advent of a world in which human beings shall enjoy freedom of speech and belief and freedom from fear and want has been proclaimed as the highest aspiration of the common people …[29]

Such major changes in world order are couched in the language of time and temporality – as is certainly the case with World War II and the creation of new institutions and new forms of international relations in its wake. It is also characteristic of the end of the Cold War and of our contemporary ruminations about the rise of China – not to mention the advent of the COVID-19 global pandemic, as I write.

'Time', Kimberly Hutchings comments in her magisterial survey of the use of time in international relations theory, 'emerges in the role of both analysand and the analyser …'.[30] The outcome of such analyses throws into doubt the simple progress narrative in which the unfolding or development of the human rights regime is regularly packaged. Even preliminary scrutiny of the operation of the international human rights regime shows, rather, that political actors and theorists alike do not have the heroic capacity presupposed by the progress narrative in which rights are commonly situated, and to which their proclamations and analyses often lay claim: the capacity to 'hold and direct the arrow of time', and inaugurate 'a better world'.[31]

[28] K Hutchings, *Time and World Politics: Thinking the Present* (Manchester University Press, 2008) 5.

[29] UN General Assembly, 'Universal Declaration of Human Rights', 1948, www.un.org/en/universal-declaration-human-rights/.

[30] Hutchings (n 28) 14.

[31] ibid 24.

Consider, 'never again': the failure of this aspiration, the inability to correct human action through the vision of an imagined human rights future. It is true that rights norms and institutions have proliferated beyond expectation – even to encompass the perverse and queer homosexual!! Notwithstanding this normative and regulatory spread of rights, and despite the cry of 'never again', the common experience of human rights is as a reporting regime for their absence, an eternal return of broken promises, as power (state and capital) routinely goes about its business, claims of justice notwithstanding. From this point of view, the whole human rights project, including its putative extension to gay rights holders, may be thought to be a form of what Lauren Berlant terms *cruel optimism* – a 'relation of attachment to compromised conditions of possibility'.[32] Because rights are 'the last utopia'[33] without which there is only hopelessness, our faith in them persists, notwithstanding, as Ratna Kapur observes, 'the persistence of the illusion that the pursuit and accumulation of more rights will offer more freedom, despite material evidence to the contrary'.[34]

III. HOMONORMATIVE TIMES

The Human Rights Council of the United Nations has now, for over a decade, regularly been involved in institutional developments which have profiled the consequences of violence and discrimination against LGBTI persons.[35] The establishment and then renewal of the SOGI Independent Expert is testament to the success of sustained political lobbying within the UN system, and within the domestic political systems of supporting states. Early momentum toward these outcomes was generated through a high profile speech by Hillary Clinton. In Beijing in 1995 (then) First Lady Clinton had addressed the UN's Fourth World Conference on Women, insisting that women's rights are human rights.[36] In 2011, in her role as US Secretary of State, she reprised her formulation in an agenda setting speech for international LGBTI advocacy, famously declaring that 'gay rights are human rights and human rights are gay rights'.

Clinton continued:

> It is a violation of human rights when people are beaten or killed because of their sexual orientation, or because they do not conform to cultural norms about how men and women should look or behave. It is a violation of human rights when governments declare it illegal to be gay, or allow those who harm gay people to go

[32] Berlant (n 4) 24.

[33] Moyn (n 4).

[34] R Kapur, *Gender, Alterity and Human Rights: Freedom in a Fishbowl* (Edward Elgar Publishing, 2018) 171.

[35] Langlois (n 6).

[36] H Clinton, 'Remarks for the United Nations Fourth World Conference on Women' (Speech, UN Fourth World Conference on Women, Beijing, China, 5 September 1995) www.un.org/esa/gopher-data/conf/fwcw/conf/gov/950905175653.txt.

> unpunished. It is a violation of human rights when lesbian or transgendered women are subjected to so-called corrective rape, or forcibly subjected to hormone treatments, or when people are murdered after public calls for violence toward gays, or when they are forced to flee their nations and seek asylum in other lands to save their lives. And it is a violation of human rights when life-saving care is withheld from people because they are gay, or equal access to justice is denied to people because they are gay, or public spaces are out of bounds to people because they are gay. No matter what we look like, where we come from, or who we are, we are all equally entitled to our human rights and dignity.[37]

Clinton places her powerful advocacy of gay rights as human rights in a clear temporal frame: our recognition of these rights is part of the great narrative of human progress to which the human rights story itself bears witness. She starts with the original deliberations of the delegates who drafted the Universal Declaration on Human Rights, and tells a story of the nations who have, over time, 'made great progress in making human rights a human reality. Step by step, barriers that once prevented people from enjoying the full measure of liberty, the full experience of dignity, and the full benefits of humanity have fallen away. In many places, racist laws have been repealed, legal and social practices that relegated women to second-class status have been abolished, the ability of religious minorities to practice their faith freely has been secured.' Carefully, she introduces another group of people whose rights continue to be denied, an 'invisible minority', the 'LGBTs' – people born free and equal but yet still denied.

Clinton's speech is widely thought to have been a major symbolic turning point in the global recognition of LGBT rights, and particularly, for their advocacy at the UN. It is therefore worth taking the time to examine what this moment can show us about the coming into being of the gay rights holder within the international rights regime. To unpack the role of time and temporality in this text, and their consequential connections with broader politics of rights, I turn to a masterful analysis of Clinton's speech by Cynthia Weber.[38]

Weber's reading of Clinton is situated within a broader study of sexuality and gender in International Relations, a study which examines the way in which states are normalised or pathologised according to sexualised orders. Weber says, 'In contemporary international relations, answers to the question, Which states are "normal states" and which states are "pathological states"? are increasingly tested against a specific figure in international relations – the "gay rights holder" …. [This figure] is a variation of the entrepreneurial neoliberal subject who is (re)productive in/for capitalism on behalf of the nation ….'[39] In her reading, Weber traces three forms of temporality that are deployed to

[37] H Clinton, 'Remarks in Recognition of International Human Rights Day' (Archive, Palais des Nations, Geneva, Switzerland, 6 December 2011) 2009-2017.state.gov/secretary/20092013clinton/rm/2011/12/178368.htm.

[38] C Weber, *Queer International Relations* (OUP, 2016).

[39] ibid 105.

introduce and vindicate this new kind of rights holder, 'the gay rights holder', or 'the LGBT' (it should be noted that Clinton never uses the term *homosexual*, a calculated elision of great political salience given the West's own deep historical antipathy to so-identified subjects). The three forms of temporality that Weber traces within and uses to analyse Clinton's case for the legitimacy of the gay rights holder, are identified as *universal*, *progressive* and *historical*.

Universal temporality is the now conventional and familiar view that all people have human rights, and that they have them in all places and all times. That states or other agents have not recognised these rights is the principal problem, and what we come to see with the inclusion of gay rights is the gradual amelioration of that problem. But progress is being made: and so we move from consideration of universal temporality to progressive temporality, the recognition of incremental and linear evolutionary change. While all states change and evolve over time, it is clear that some states are further along the spectrum to recognising the universal nature of human rights, progress to the goal which also clearly allows them to claim advanced moral standing. This progress and moral standing is then tied into the third dimension of temporality, that it is historical – where historical, for Clinton, is not just about events unfolding over time, but is also about an evaluative view of history, linked to one's support of change, which then also authorises moral judgements. 'History has a "right side" and a "wrong side". "The right side of history" is always the side of the progressive implementation of universal moral imperatives; "the wrong side of history" is the side of obstructing such progress.'[40]

On the use of this phrase, Rahul Rao observes:

> The phrase seems to assert the speaker's clairvoyance in being able to see all the way to the end of history, secure in the knowledge that things will turn out their way, obviating the need to make a substantively persuasive argument. A proleptic declaration of triumphalism, it invites the audience to join what will turn out to be the winning side, the side which gets to write History.[41]

In a range of rhetorical moves which link the gay rights holder, 'the LGBT', to other national and international campaigns to end injustice and bring equality to all in the social domain, Clinton and similar advocates powerfully assert that the time has come for the international human rights regime to demand an end to discrimination and violence against LGBTs. The sexuality and gender diverse are added to a long roster of groups found not to have been treated with equal respect: women, the indigenous, ethnic and racial minorities, children, the disabled, and workers among them.

Here the gay rights holder appears as a universal figure, both out of time – having been stripped of all identifiable particularities (including, perhaps, their specific 'gay-ness') – and paradoxically newly introduced into time as a

[40] Weber (n 38) 126.
[41] R Rao, 'Queer Questions' (2014) 16 *International Feminist Journal of Politics* 199, 212.

neglected victim of prejudice, but whom we have recently come to understand as worthy of sexual self-determination and justice. Here, the 'gay' rights holder encompasses the broad range of people now commonly referred to using one or another version of the LGBT+ acronym, or – more queerly perhaps – by reference to sexual and gender diversity in all its forms.

However, as Weber reminds us, 'universal figures are never as universal as they may at first appear …'.[42] This is particularly the case for the gay rights holder, who only yesterday was the perverse homosexual, the deviant, degenerate, undeveloped – indeed undevelopable – figure, unworthy of rights, commonly denied even human status. This perverse figure, often transcribed in an international political context as the racialised other, the unwanted immigrant, the terrorist, is (*apparently*) absent in the new discourse of the LGBT, the gay rights holder, who is now advanced as the vanguard figure of the human rights denominated (neo)liberal international order.

There is also the question of the gay rights holder's defender: Clinton is not just any rights advocate, but in her role as Secretary of State, and while addressing the UN, is spokesperson for *the* hegemonic state of the early twenty-first century, one with military bases in every region of the world, global economic supremacy (notwithstanding continued suggestions of the imminent demise of this status) and a long history of racialising and sexualising states in the pursuit of its imperial ambitions.[43] Clearly, a new found fondness for the hitherto perverse homosexual is unlikely to be played purely for its normative desirability. In the same way that the rights regime in general, and specific aspects of it in particular, have been played for geopolitical advantage by the US and other actors (think, for example, of the role of economic rights during the Cold War), LGBT rights are optionable in a similar way – in fact, quite fashionably so.[44] As Aeyal Gross comments, 'Once LGBT rights are incorporated into global governance, they can be appropriated to reinforce or strengthen the political and/or economic power of Northern states over states in the global South, and potentially harm vulnerable populations.'[45]

The assimilation of human rights in general to state and imperial power, and to the interests of global capital, has been much remarked in recent critical literature on human rights.[46] In the case of LGBT rights, such concerns mean any

[42] Weber (n 38) 137.

[43] JK Puar, *Terrorist Assemblages: Homonationalism in Queer Times* (Duke University Press Books, 2007); N Hoad, 'Arrested Development or the Queerness of Savages: Resisting Evolutionary Narratives of Difference' (2000) 3 *Postcolonial Studies* 133; R Rao, *Out of Time* (OUP, 2020).

[44] K Franke, 'Dating the State: The Moral Hazards of Winning Gay Rights' (2012) 44 *Columbia Human Rights Law Review* 1.

[45] A Gross, 'Homoglobalism: The Emergence of Global Gay Governance' in D Otto (ed), *Queering International Law: Possibilities, Alliances, Complications, Risks* (Routledge, 2018) 148–70, 154.

[46] S Hopgood, *The Endtimes of Human Rights* (Cornell University Press, 2013); S Hopgood, JL Snyder and L Vinjamuri, *Human Rights Futures* (CUP, 2017); J Whyte, *The Morals of the Market: Human Rights and the Rise of Neoliberalism* (Verso, 2019).

good faith engagement requires a capacity and framework to discern between activities and associations which align with the normative and emancipatory ideas at the core of practices of 'gay liberation', and those which are in various ways instrumentalised and politicised. As Gross says, this places advocates in 'a familiar double bind': 'the draw of harnessing powerful global institutions to the LGBT cause on the one hand, thereby doing a lot of good, and the risk of co-option on the other, which can result in considerable harm'.[47]

Once factors such as these are brought into the picture, a very different interpretative frame can be placed upon the arrival of the gay rights holder within the international human rights regime. Added to the good behaviour bond that the hegemon expects of its client states is a form of *gay conditionality*[48] which fundamentally complicates our understanding of the role that human rights denominated in sexuality and gender come to play in international politics. When the gay rights holder, the LGBT, is particularised into specific people in particular nation states – the US itself, Russia, India, Uganda, Iran, Indonesia, Malaysia, or those fleeing states as refugees or asylum seekers – the behaviour of powerful LGBT rights advocating states similarly becomes very specific and particular. In all cases, as with any number of other rights issues, state behaviour does not proceed on the basis of universal moral concerns, but evinces very special attention to material and political interests. As Dean Spade has put it with reference to the US:

> Clinton's speech evinces a relatively new logic in US imperialism: that the US, regardless of failures to protect queer and trans people from state violence at home, will now use gay rights to exert pressure on countries where the US has some ulterior motive. Clinton uses lesbian and gay rights to bolster the notion that the US is the world's policing arm, forcing democracy and equality globally on purportedly backward and cruel governments. Gay rights operates as a new justification for this imperial role – a justification that fits well within the anti-Arab and anti-Muslim framings that have been developed during the War on Terror and portray Arab and Muslim countries as more sexist and homophobic than the US, European countries and Israel .... These declarations of gay rights aim to distract from and justify – to pinkwash – the brutal realities of US politics and policy.[49]

At this point then, turning back to the three forms of temporality that Weber picks out of Clinton's speech and re-reading them, different interpretive trajectories are opened up. Here, the universal can be read as a very temporally specific take on what it means to be LGBT that is then naturalised and depicted as universal for the regulation and maintenance of a certain form of global order. This is what Weber describes as 'the normal homosexual', a figure

[47] Gross (n 45) 158.

[48] Rao (n 43); Rao (n 20); R Rao, 'On "Gay Conditionality", Imperial Power and Queer Liberation' (*Kafila* (blog), 2012) kafila.org/2012/01/01/on-gay-conditionality-imperial-power-and-queer-liberation-rahul-rao/.

[49] D Spade, 'Under the Cover of Gay Rights' (2013) 37 *NYU Review of Law & Social Change* 79, in Weber (n 38) 139–40.

unthreatening to and able to be imbricated within the political status quo of international (neo)liberalism. The temporality of progress is no longer read in relation to measuring distance from moral standards, but rather via co-optation within political and legal strategies which signal conformity to and support for the neoliberal order. And historical temporality is that time within which states take symbolic and practical actions to orient their behaviour to support LGBT rights, as this becomes a pathway materially associated with their interests within the international order.

In all of this 'the normal homosexual' is the key figure. International Relations – the academic discipline – is not very good at discussing sexuality, notwithstanding that tropes of sexual barbarism, sexual development, and the like, are pervasive in depictions of the relations between Western, modern, developed states and their (used advisedly) less developed counterparts. In a curious way, the advent of the gay rights holder, the LGBT, allows for the open discussion of sexuality and diverse sexual subjects within the international system – but does so while carefully cordoning off the terrain. The West's long denigration of the perverse homosexual, and the sustained use of this trope in the sexual politics of imperialism, colonialism and developmentalism, is not so much overturned by the discovery of gay rights, as it is put to one side for specific purposes only, while the gay rights holder, the LGBT, is propelled into the spotlight as the – potentially – new near-ideal model subject of a global order organised according to the principles and goals of neoliberalism.

The 'normal homosexual' is the LGBT (although Ts are routinely excluded, even while being rhetorically included) who is able to take their place as a normally sexualised figure, the gay version of which, like their straight counterpart in the global north, is 'on its way to maturing into a (usually) white, Christian, bourgeois, ableised, cisgendered, heterosexual, reproductive family that functions as the biological and social engine of reproduction for the Western state'.[50] Lisa Duggan famously depicts this 'normal homosexual' as the key figure in a new form of sexual politics, one which 'does not contest dominant heteronormative assumptions and institutions, but upholds and sustains them, while promising the possibility of a demobilised gay constituency and a privatised, depoliticised gay culture anchored in domesticity and consumption'.[51] The coinage Duggan produces for this new sexual politics is homonormativity, a politics which enables the perverse and denigrated homosexual to enter into a new time, a temporality in which they are accepted – or even, as per Clinton, celebrated – as the bearers of human rights. There is a catch however, as there is with all subjected who are imbricated into the international human rights regime. Perversity and denigration must be traded for devotion to and incorporation within the newly welcoming order. The rights holder must embrace modes of being that comport

[50] Weber (n 38) 108.

[51] L Duggan, *The Twilight of Equality? Neoliberalism, Cultural Politics, and the Attack on Democracy* (Beacon Press, 2003) 50; cf Weber (n 38) 108.

with their new status as an ideal neoliberal subject: domesticity, consumption, depoliticisation, docile patriotism. As Ratna Kapur similarly puts it, 'These normative alignments involve marriage, parenthood and material success – all of which are made possible through the acquisition of rights within the alluring cartography of the neoliberal market .... Ultimately, such recognition ends up simulating the standard heterosexual model.'[52]

As Weber then elaborates, the locus of perversity shifts – no longer is the homosexual necessarily perverse, if they can be incorporated into the general political and ideological project:

> Homonormativity shifts the axis of perversion from same-sex sexual desires to desires around neoliberal domesticity and consumption. The 'homosexual' who shares these neoliberal desires, who organises his life around them, and who becomes depoliticized as a result of living in proper domesticity and consumption is no longer perverse. *What is perverse is a desire for a different political, economic, and social life that is incompatible with neoliberalism.* The 'new normal' sexual subject in 'the new homonormativity', then, is the 'homosexual' whose desires for domesticity and consumption are the same as those of the 'straight' neoliberal subject. (Emphasis added).[53]

In this new time of LGBT rights, then, the homosexual – that is, the *normal* homosexual, is no longer perverse. What of those who don't want to be, aren't, or can't be, 'normal'? There are remainders left over in this politics.[54] As Kapur puts it:

> The assimilative pull of human rights has decanted an entitled, legible, respectable, desirable queer subject while simultaneously producing its opposite – the unsuccessful sexual subaltern/non-subject; the silent or vocal queer dissident navigating the existential pressures of stigmatized criminal deviance, unable/unwilling to comply with the prescriptions of [liberal] freedom .... Who aspires to equality, legibility and grievability but does not/cannot participate in the frameworks that bring about recognition through this set of arrangements.[55]

The homonormative critique of the 'new sexual politics', a politics which has supported and facilitated the realisation of LGBT rights in domestic societies in the West, and their eventual incorporation into the international human rights regime, threatens a disillusionment with the fight for international human rights protection for people of diverse sexualities and genders.[56] If co-option and politicisation are the outcome – whether inevitable or contingent – then what is to be done? How does one position oneself in a politics that takes advantages of what human rights can offer, without contributing to or underwriting

[52] Kapur (n 34) 70.

[53] Weber (n 38) 110.

[54] cf B Honig, *Democracy and the Foreigner* (Princeton University Press, 2003).

[55] Kapur (n 34) 79.

[56] AJ Langlois, 'International Political Theory of LGBTQ Rights' in C Brown and R Eckersley (eds), *The Oxford Handbook of International Political Theory* (OUP, 2018).

the forms of co-optation? Such forms easily multiply, as work by a range of scholars analysing various domains that come under scrutiny with respect to how homonormativity functions politically within them shows, leading in turn to the coinage of various 'homo-isms': homonationalism,[57] homocolonialism,[58] homocapitalism,[59] homoglobalism[60] and homomunicipalism.[61]

At the same time, and as I have argued elsewhere, the coincidence of rights politics, and even the subjectivities which rights politics enable, within formations such as neoliberalism, does not make them the culprit or cause. Such a reaction too quickly removes complexity from our analysis, and also, as Weber points out, narrows our options for meaningful resistance.[62] While there is no question that human rights can be co-opted and politicised in the ways that homonormative analysis identifies, there remains within rights discourse a normative element which can speak back – it is precisely this normative element which enables even the cynical among us to see it as a mis-use or bastardisation in some way of what rights 'are supposed to' be and do. And as Karen Zivi has argued, the making and performance of rights claims may well operate within certain social and political contexts, reflecting norms and power structures – but they also routinely and regularly have a power that pushes beyond the intended or 'authorised' use of rights talk. That rights could come to be claimed for perverse figures like the homosexual bears witness to this dynamic.[63]

IV. TEMPORAL DISJUNCTURES: THE FUTURE OF QUEER RIGHTS IS THEIR PAST

> At one point in my life as a scholar of queer culture and theory, I thought the point of queer was to be always ahead of actually existing social possibilities. On this model, it seemed that truly queer queers would dissolve forms, disintegrate identities, level taxonomies, scorn the social, and even repudiate politics altogether .... Now I think the point may be to trail behind actually existing social possibilities: to be interested in the tail end of things, willing to be bathed in the fading light of whatever has been declared useless .... For queer scholars and activists, this cultural debris includes our incomplete, partial, or otherwise failed transformations of the social field.[64]
>
> It may ... seem shaming to hold onto an identity that cannot be uncoupled from violence, suffering, and loss. I insist on the importance of clinging to ruined identities

[57] Puar (n 43).
[58] M Rahman, *Homosexualities, Muslim Cultures and Modernity* (Palgrave Macmillan, 2014).
[59] Rao (n 20).
[60] Gross (n 45).
[61] A Gross, 'Gay Governance: A Queer Critique' in JE Halley, P Kotiswaran and R Rebouché (eds), *Governance Feminism: Notes from the Field* (University of Minnesota Press, 2019) 344–74.
[62] Weber (n 38) 117–18; AJ Langlois, 'Human Rights in Crisis? A Critical Polemic Against Polemical Critics' (2012) 11 *Journal of Human Rights* 562.
[63] Zivi (n 21).
[64] E Freeman, *Time Binds: Queer Temporalities, Queer Histories* (Duke University Press, 2010) xiii.

> and to histories of injury. Resisting the call of gay normalization means refusing to write off the most vulnerable, the least presentable, and all the dead.[65]

Elizabeth Freeman captures for me the tensions carried by someone working critically in the queer human rights space. On the one hand, there is the normative impetus to challenge injustice and – as human rights advocates in the UN system and in countless domestic political contexts do and have done – push for justice using any and every avenue that might be available through the mechanisms of the international human rights regime. The vision of LGBTIQ rights as human rights in many places remains, in Freeman's language, *ahead* of actually existing social possibilities: this much is clear from the quote at the head of this chapter from the UN's SOGI Independent Expert's recent report. While queer organisations the world over have been striving against the odds for decades to achieve such recognition, at precisely the time that these efforts produce material institutional change, queer critique and scholarship points to how these changes are often co-opted by state power and capital. The critical analysis of homonormativity is arguably precisely what Freeman's evocative words speak of here: to trail behind the changes that have become socially possible, and to speak of the way in which they manifest in the world – including the experiences of failure, co-optation, refusal and betrayal.

Freeman's interest in the 'tail end of things', the incomplete, partial and failed transformations, fits well with one of the most paradoxical characteristics of human rights: their capacity to work as an aid to social change and transformation, as a call for justice, at precisely those times when they are most denied and least welcome. *Remembering* – especially for those of us now in rights respecting jurisdictions – the *absence* of rights, may be what is critical to preventing the future of rights from being taken from us.

Remembering is what Heather Love insists on, with her evocative discussion of the need to *feel backward*, to carry the past with us, in order to create an alternative kind of politics in the present. Love notes that 'The origin story of gay liberation describes how on one particular night an underground bar turned into the front line of a struggle for freedom and civil rights', and reflects that the 'powerful utopianism' of this movement is alive and well today in the global advocacy for LGBTIQ rights and its future orientation.[66] Rights have subsequently been won in many places, particularly in the global North, and this has enabled many to conclude that 'the worst difficulties of queer life are behind us'.[67] But, Love argues, 'The discomfort that contemporary queer subjects continue to feel in response to the most harrowing representations from the past attests to their continuing relevance. The experience of queer historical

[65] H Love, *Feeling Backward: Loss and the Politics of Queer History* (Harvard University Press, 2007) 30.
[66] ibid 28.
[67] ibid 32.

subjects is not at a safe distance from contemporary experience; rather, their social marginality and abjection mirror our own.'[68]

Love cuts against the grain of recent tendencies in queer theory and history to drop and leave the pain of our past, when we can, and to celebrate and champion the possibilities of an optimistic present and future. Her project is explicitly set against such optimism, futurity and forgetting: the seduction of 'gay normalisation' in a remarkable time when at least some queers can be 'mainstream' and – well, perhaps, *unremarkable*. In the context of any achievement of such mainstreaming, Love's insistence that we remember the persecution, hate and humiliation, is a critical political practice. We must *feel backward*. Yes, she says, 'we can turn shame into pride, but we cannot do so once and for all: shame lives on in pride, and pride can easily turn back into shame'.[69]

This admonition is critical at a juncture when in many of those states that have won pride, there are increasing indications of a reversal in the political and material fortunes of the movement. Globally, however, the '*history* of injury' for sexuality and gender diverse people is very much a *present* of marginalisation and abjection. *This* temporal shift or re-alignment, derived by changing our spatial focus from the West or North to the whole globe, places a different gloss on the analysis Love presents, making it less parochial, more urgent and more universality comprehensible:

> What counts as political in the contemporary context is … out of touch with the longer history of queer experience. Rather than disavowing the history of marginalization and abjection, I suggest that we embrace it, exploring the ways it continues to structure queer experience in the present. Modern homosexual identity is formed out of and in relation to the experience of social damage. Paying attention to what was difficult in the past may tell us how far we have come, but that is not all it will tell us; it also makes visible the damage that we live with in the present.[70]

V. CONCLUSION

The suggestion from Heather Love that we embrace the long history of marginalisation and abjection experienced by queers, and look at how it structures our experience in the present, now finds institutional support within the international human rights regime through the establishment of the UN SOGI Independent Expert. Love's terms seem to perfectly encapsulate the Independent Expert's job description: paying attention to the past in order to work toward overcoming discrimination and violence based on sexual orientation and gender identity.

As I write, the present is riven by COVID-19; as in the past, those considered perverse often get the blame for such bewildering tragedies, and their own

[68] ibid 32.
[69] ibid 28.
[70] ibid 29.

suffering is made worse by concomitant exclusions.[71] Incumbent Independent Expert Victor Madrigal-Borloz has acted expeditiously to develop a set of guidelines for addressing the specific concerns of SOGI people through the time of the pandemic. This rapid response builds on investigations that Madrigal-Borloz had already been pursuing. His 2019 report to the UN General Assembly details a focus on issues of social, cultural and economic inclusion, taking up the day-to-day concerns which comprise the material substance of what Love referred to as the 'history of injury': access to (or more often, exclusion from) education, employment, housing, health, public spaces, and religious and political discourse.

In other critical work, Madrigal-Borloz has been investigating the long-standing and invidious matter of so-called 'conversion therapy', a practice which seek to 'de-gay' people who identify non-normatively, to make them heterosexual and cisgender. This practice has no medical justification and is a severe threat to the health and human rights of targeted individuals. Madrigal-Borloz has also investigated the diversity of global understandings of gender identity, and the way in which the failure of states to recognise gender identity diversity, and in particular the formal pathologisation of some forms of gender identity, has been a contributing factor to violence, discrimination and injury.[72]

This work, as well as much like it that is being done by other agencies, civil society organisations, academics, and activists, can help us to stay cognisant of 'the damage that we live with in the present', as Love puts it. Why is this so critical? Because without it, we risk losing sight of an emancipatory politics, drifting (or being co-opted) into the politics of 'the normal homosexual' – the pinup boi of human rights chronopolitics and geopolitics, in which LGBT rights are only for the 'non-perverse', and are often instrumentalised by state power and capital, captured for sectoral and state interests.

While not wishing to discount the genuine status improvement that gay rights as human rights brings to some queer subjects, nor wishing to reduce all human rights advocacy or politics to the play of power, the new status afforded the 'gay rights holder' has fundamentally changed the dynamics of global sexuality and gender politics, and an emancipatory politics must reckon with the full extent of these changes. The material and social gains this means for some (and that these gains can *only* be utilised or reached by *some*) cannot be separated from the homonormative framing these rights trajectories are commonly situated within, and which directly affect the wellbeing of others. As an advocate of human rights and a believer in their capacity to change the world, but also as a critical theorist with a queer view of the world, I suggest that practising a politics of what Love

[71] For eg. V Pillai, 'Blaming LGBT People for Covid-19 Is Spreading Fast' (*Queer Lapis* (blog), 5 April 2020) www.queerlapis.com/blaming-lgbt-people-for-covid19/.

[72] Annual reports detailing these investigations can all be found on the UN SOGI Independent Expert webpage: www.ohchr.org/en/issues/sexualorientationgender/pages/index.aspx.

calls *feeling backward* will help maintain a radical and emancipatory core for LGBTIQ rights as human rights. We must dwell on what it means to be vulnerable, unpresentable, and even to have lost out to death. Here we might find the reflective resources needed to hold together queer and critical imperatives with the compromised but real opportunities afforded by these new developments for LGBTIQ people in the chronopolitics of human rights.

9

Against the Eternal Law(s) of Human Rights: Towards a Becoming-Chaotic of Time

CHRISTOS MARNEROS

I. INTRODUCTION

THE NOTIONS AND question(s) of time and truth – or in better terms, the Truth – are closely intertwined. Indeed, since the period of antiquity, this close relation between Truth and time is, usually, manifested in a form which is akin to two parallel lines that always face each other but, nonetheless, they do not intersect. This is because, Truth, for the ancients, was to be conceived of as something eternal and as such, something which can be understood as *timeless* or something which is universal and unchangeable for all times that *are* and for those *to come*.[1] On the other hand, time was understood in terms of movement (or temporality) and as such, time was considered to be something that counts movement (eg in terms of years). For example, Aristotle in his *Physics* defines time as 'the number of movement'.[2] To that extent, the Truth, in its understanding as an absolute transcendent entity, *transcends* every form of movement and thus, it is manifested as eternal or timeless.

While, in modern philosophy, and especially with Immanuel Kant's contribution, we witness some effort to 'liberate' time from its subordination to movement,[3] this mode of thought tends to remain entrapped in that understanding of time as a measure to movement (eg the understanding of a linear conception of past, present and future) and immobility (eg the *eternal*). My hypothesis in this chapter is that human rights, and in particular human rights law (in its international, regional and national manifestation) fosters a mode of thinking which thinks in such an eternal or an *atemporal* manner and as such,

[1] DW Smith, 'Temporality and Truth' (2013) 7(3) *Deleuze Studies* 377, 377.

[2] Aristotle, *Physics* trans, with Intro and Notes CDC Reeves (Hackett Publishing, 2018) 219b5–10.

[3] For Kant's definition of time see, I Kant, *Critique of Pure Reason: Unified Edition (with all the variants from 1781 and 1787 Editions)* trans WS Pluhar (Hackett Publishing Company, 1996) 85–90.

they *transcend* our time and mode(s) of life, remaining, fundamentally, out of touch with (our) time.

Indeed, such a view, with regards to human rights and how they form a notion of transcendent, eternal values was held by one of the most important French philosophers of the twentieth century, the late Gilles Deleuze. In his ferocious, yet brief (and relatively overlooked) critique of human rights, Deleuze states that philosophical thought has become 'barren' and that human rights are responsible for this 'uncreative' stalemate because they 'provide our eternal values'.[4] A central difficulty that results from these remarks is the fact that Deleuze does not clarify whether he criticises a particular human rights discourse, tradition, philosophical system, laws or the idea of human rights *as such*. Nonetheless, Deleuze states that 'human rights and their *declarations* are never made as a function of the people who are directly concerned'[5] and from this particular comment we can infer that human rights law does not escape such criticism. As such, not only rights, and to that extent human rights law, are 'out of time' but they are also 'out of touch' with life, its particularities and the predicaments of the so-called subjects of their protection. This is because, and due to their conception as eternal, they fail to account for a different mode of being, an *ethos*, which thinks its place within the world in a temporal manner, characterised by never-ending *becomings*, that are not to be reduced in purely historical events and a linear understanding of time as a measure to movement or an eternity of Truth.[6]

While the multiple developments of human rights law since Deleuze authored the above critique may suggest that such claims by Deleuze could be characterised as 'outdated',[7] I would argue that this is not the case. Indeed, if we take as an example the debates around the potential evolution and ever-expanding, interpretations of 'the right to life'[8] in the jurisprudence of the European Court

[4] G Deleuze with A Dulaure and C Parnet, 'On Mediators' in *Negotiations* trans M Joughin (Columbia University Press, 1995) 121–22.

[5] G Deleuze and C Parnet 'What it means to be on the Left' in *Gilles Deleuze A to Z* (Semiotext(e) DVD, 2004) [emphasis added].

[6] The Deleuzian notion of becoming is, usually, examined through the prism of Bergsonian thought. Indeed, Deleuze develops the concept influenced by the philosopher Henri Bergson. See, G Deleuze, *Bergsonism* trans H Tomlinson and B Habberjam (Zone Books, 1991). Alexandre Lefebvre touches upon Deleuze's critique of human rights and tries to (re)think human rights through an ethical framework, as *a way of life*, with Bergson being the main figure of his analysis. See A Lefebvre, 'Human Rights in Deleuze and Bergson's Later Philosophy' in L De Sutter and K McGee (eds), *Deleuze and Law* (Edinburgh University Press, 2012); *Human Rights as a Way of Life: on Bergson's Political Philosophy* (Stanford University Press, 2013). My approach and analysis of the Deleuzian becoming takes a different approach. In particular, as I argue below, in order to better grasp the temporal, ethical aspect of the notion, we should focus on Deleuze's reading of Friedrich Nietzsche and the latter's understanding of becoming which originates from the pre-Socratic philosopher Heraclitus of Ephesus. As such, I focus on Deleuze's *Nietzsche and Philosophy* (Columbia University Press, 2006).

[7] P Patton, 'Immanence, Transcendence, and the Creation of Rights' in L De Sutter and K McGee (eds), *Deleuze and Law* (Edinburgh University Press, 2012) 17.

[8] I discuss the expansion of the meaning of the right to life in section III. See eg P Tiensuu, 'Whose Right to What Life: Assisted Suicide and the Right to Life as a Fundamental Right' (2015) 15 *Human*

of Human Rights – for example, the extension of the right 'beyond the absence of death',[9] or incorporation of conditions that are paramount for the continuation of life, but also questions about the legal status of foetuses – some may go as far as to interpret these novelties as signs of 'progress' and an inclusive vision of a dynamic human rights law. If we pay closer attention to Deleuze's critical comments towards rights, they do not seem to refute the ability of rights and their laws to expand, change or regress. What seems to be the issue with the predominant rights-oriented mode of thought is that it is based on presupposed, eternal or timeless values that lead back to the aforementioned problem between the eternal and Truth. As such, while we could witness several changes of rights and their laws, these changes occur within a predetermined framework, that significantly *lacks* creativity and thus, it is entrapped within these presuppositions of a notion of the eternal.

On the other hand – and this is the main hypothesis of this chapter – Deleuze's understanding of temporalities (which is not reduced to a simple measure to movement or non-movement) as a notion of pure becoming and never-ending variation and change could, potentially, lead to a (re)thinking about our relation with, but most importantly *beyond* human rights and their laws that do not stand above or 'out of time' as eternal Truth(s). It is in that sense, that I will refer to a *becoming-chaotic* of time, where chaos can be thought as a constant variation, 'an infinite speed' that 'take[s] shape and vanish[es]'.[10] Thus, this notion of a *becoming-chaotic* should be thought as something creative that questions any supposed truthfulness of eternal values. Ultimately, this exploration not only aims to bring together the question of human rights law and temporality but also to question these *eternal laws of rights*, through this *untimely* notion of becoming, which is, as I argue, closer to life and its *temporalities*.

II. HUMAN RIGHTS AND THEIR 'ETERNAL VALUES'

What Deleuze identifies as problematic with human rights as a mode of thought or a 'culture', as Alain Badiou calls it,[11] can be incorporated within the philosopher's broader distaste for a way of existing and thinking in terms of transcendence.[12] While transcendence as a notion has a multiplicity of meanings

Rights Law Review 251; FC Ebert and RI Sijniensky, 'Preventing Violations of the Right to Life in the European and the Inter-American Human Rights Systems: From the Osman Test to a Coherent Doctrine on Risk Prevention' (2015) 15 *Human Rights Law Review* 343; A Plomer, 'The Foetal Right to Life – The Case of *Vo v France*' (2005) 5 *Human Rights Law Review* 311; S Joseph, 'Denouement of the Deaths on the Rock: The Right to Life of Terrorists' (1996) 14 *Netherlands Quarterly of Human Rights* 5.

[9] E Wicks, 'The Meaning of "Life": Dignity and the Right to Life in International Human Rights Treaties' (2012) 12(2) *Human Rights Law Review* 199, 199.

[10] G Deleuze and F Guattari, *What is Philosophy?* trans G Burchell and H Tomlinson (Verso, 1994) 42.

[11] A Badiou, *The Communist Hypothesis* trans D Macey and S Corcoran (Verso, 2010) 2.

[12] Deleuze criticises a transcendent mode of being and thinking throughout his corpus as a dogmatic and hierarchical way of existing. For a short introduction of what he means and why

within the broader (Western) philosophical and theological tradition(s), Deleuze understands transcendence as a mode of existing and thinking which is infused by dogmatic principles and fixity.[13] This happens because, according to the philosopher, transcendence initiates a mode of thinking that 'thinks' in terms of foundational and eternal principles. Deleuze identifies as the origin, and the subsequent dominance of such a mode of thought, the introduction of the Platonic concept of Ideas or Forms. He states the following:

> [Plato] will have to invent a transcendence that can be exercised and situated within the field of immanence itself. This is the meaning of the theory of Ideas. As modern philosophy will continue to follow Plato in this regard, encountering a transcendence at the heart of immanence as such. The poisoned gift of Platonism is to have introduced transcendence into philosophy, to have given transcendence a plausible philosophical meaning (the triumph of judgment of God).[14]

In other words, Deleuze identifies as the dominant position of Western philosophy, since Plato, a way of thinking that 'thinks' in terms of primary sources, in terms of beginning(s) and end(s). As the primary source in a vertical sequence, Platonic Ideas or Forms are used as *a measure* in order to determine which things are closer to their qualities, in other words, which things possess more 'reality' than others.[15] As a consequence, a hierarchy of beings is formed, where some beings are more *authentic* or hold more *perfection* compared to others. Ultimately, we witness a formation of 'the One', in terms of a unity,[16] or 'eternal notion of Truth'. The eternal being(s) *stands out of time* or movement, as it is unchangeable, and judges the rest of beings according to their 'obedience' to its eternal principles (eg an idea of 'the good' – 'the good citizen').

But how does this relate to the idea of human rights and their laws? In an interview with Antoine Dulaure and Claire Parnet, Deleuze professed his

he finds this mode of being problematic see G Deleuze, 'To Have Done with Judgment' in *Essays Critical and Clinical* trans DW Smith and M Greco (Verso, 1998). For a more detailed account see his two books on Baruch Spinoza: G Deleuze, *Expressionism in Philosophy: Spinoza* trans M Joughin (Zone Books, 1992); G Deleuze, *Spinoza: Practical Philosophy* trans R Hurley (City Lights Publishers, 2001).

[13] G Deleuze, 'To Have Done with Judgment' in *Essays Critical and Clinical* (n 12) 126–35.

[14] G Deleuze, 'Plato, The Greeks' in *Essays Critical and Clinical* (n 12) 137.

[15] For Plato, the world of Ideas is a non-material but substantial realm which manifests the most accurate form of reality. Hence, an Idea can be said to be the essence of the beings we encounter in the material world. However, all the material beings are but 'shadows' of the real Ideas. These real Ideas transcendent the notion of time as they are 'eternal' refusing any sort of mutation. As a consequence, a hierarchy of beings is formed, where some beings hold 'more reality' than others depending on the beings' proximity to an Idea. For example, something will be judged as good or bad according to its proximity to the Idea of 'the Good'. For a dialogue where Plato explains this notion see, 'Republic' book VII, the 'Allegory of the Cave' in CDC Reeve (ed), *A Plato Reader: Eight Essential Dialogues* (Hackett Publishing, 2012) 514a–20a, 463–68.

[16] G Deleuze, 'Zones of Immanence' in *Two Regimes of Madness* trans A Hodges and M Taormina (Semiotext(e), 2007) 261.

disappointment for the decadent state of philosophy at the time (the interview took place in 1985). As he states:

> And yet in philosophy we're coming back to eternal values, to the idea of the intellectual as custodian of eternal values [...] These days, *it's the rights of man that provide our eternal values*. It's the constitutional state and other notions everyone recognizes as very abstract. And it's in the name of all this that thinking's fettered, that any analysis in terms of movements is blocked. But if we're so oppressed, it's because our movement's being restricted, not because our eternal values are being violated. In barren times philosophy retreats to reflecting 'on' things. If it's not itself creating anything. What can it do but reflect on something? So it reflects on eternal or historical things, but can itself no longer make any move.[17]

Despite its briefness, this part is rich and thought-provoking and at the same time enigmatic, due to the peculiar use of certain terms such as 'movement' or 'thought'. Here, Deleuze suggests, that the central problem that threatens communities and people is not that they have to face a constant violation of inalienable human rights and their eternal principles, but, instead, it is human rights that create pendency and an inability to think otherwise and to create, leading to a situation of static permanence – a stagnant position. In this rather bleak situation, human rights not only are unable to *save us* but, according to Deleuze, because they contribute to the (re)introduction of eternal values into people's way(s) of thinking, they are to be blamed for this impasse.

In order to better understand how this is happening, we need to disentangle what is meant by 'movement' and 'thought'. With the use of these terms, Deleuze does not want to refer to the simple, every-day understanding of movement as a physical exercise. Similarly, thought is not limited to the exercise that we tend to call 'thinking' in everydayness. Here movement is something that happens constantly and it refers to our becoming(s) (as I will elaborate further in the third section of this chapter). It engages with *how* we affect and we are affected by a particular situation, by *our temporalities* – how we change our modes of existing after we encounter a particular situation, body, an idea, a thought, a smell and so forth. In order to be able to capture and let this movement flow, however, we have to be attentive and to be characterised by an openness and willingness to analyse and question this movement or transformation that traverses us. Thus, this is an openness characterised by a will to examine different possibilities in life. However, what happens with the (re)introduction of 'eternal values' into thought and our way(s) of existing more broadly via human rights is the eventual 'blocking' (or even 'a blindness') of attentiveness to this constant transformation. This is because our attention is solely focused on finding the 'true nature' of our eternal values, instead of focusing on the particularities and specificities of a situation, the *here and now*. As a result, human rights tend to become 'uncreative' in the sense that we tend to turn all of our

[17] Deleuze with Dulaure and Parnet (n 4) 121–22 [emphasis added].

attention to this 'quest' for Truth. To that extent, any potential for human rights to create something innovative and radical that takes into account our temporalities as ongoing becomings vanishes. All that remains is the articulation of human rights' demands in terms of values that became 'barren', 'inefficient' and completely 'empty abstractions'.[18]

The results of our preoccupation with these eternal values and our incapacity to create are catastrophic, according to Deleuze. As he explains in another instance to Claire Parnet, human rights are impotent in addressing the predicaments of vulnerable people because not only their values are 'out of touch' with time and the specific temporalities of these people, but these eternal values also hide an insidious 'hatred for life'[19] because they try to negate anything 'new' and 'creative' as 'inauthentic' or counter to their indisputable Truth. As he states:

> Listen, this respect for the 'rights of man' – this really makes me want to say, almost to make some odious statements. It belongs so much to this weak thinking of the empty intellectual period that we discussed earlier. It's purely abstract, these 'rights of man'. What is this? It's purely abstract, completely empty.[20]

Ultimately, then, it is this mode of thought that leads back to a certain engagement with 'empty' questions that, merely, reflect on 'new forms of transcendence, new universals, restoring reflective subject as the bearer of rights, or setting up communicative intersubjectivity'.[21] As Deleuze laments the situation is 'not much of a philosophical advance'.[22]

The immediate question that arises is whether we can accept this criticism as something that, efficiently, reflects the position and (im)possibilities of human rights and their laws in our age. In other words, can we say that Deleuze's critique is 'outdated'[23] if we take into account that human rights and their laws, in particular, are a subject of 'progressive interpretation' that leads to the expansion (and sometimes regress as well) of the scope of these laws and of a particular right?

In section III, by examining the expansion of the scope of 'the right to life' in the context of European Human Rights jurisprudence, I will argue that human rights law is still *symptomatic* of a mode of thinking which is infused by eternal values. As a consequence, this mode of thinking remains unchangeable, monolithic and thus, 'out of touch' with time and the temporalities of life. For the purpose of this chapter, my focus will be on the way that the right to life is identified by the European Convention on Human Rights (hereafter ECHR or 'the Convention')[24] and the development of its interpretation through the

[18] ibid 121.
[19] Deleuze, *Nietzsche and Philosophy* (n 6) 122.
[20] Deleuze and Parnet (n 5).
[21] G Deleuze with R Bellour and F Ewald, 'On Philosophy' in *Negotiations* (n 4) 152.
[22] ibid.
[23] Patton (n 7) 17.
[24] Convention for the Protection of Human Rights and Fundamental Freedoms (European Convention on Human Rights, as amended) (ECHR) (adopted on 4 November 1950, entered into force 3 September 1953).

jurisprudence of the European Court of Human Rights (hereafter ECtHR or 'the Court'). The choice of examining the legal framework of a particular right is, in my view, a good way to bring closer this Deleuzian critique of rights to the 'realities' of human rights laws of our age. This is because the fundamental position of life, as one of the most celebrated rights of human rights jurisprudence (and also the way that life is understood by human rights treaties and case law) constitutes a good example of the problematic way of thinking that human rights law fosters and which 'thinks' in terms of eternal, timeless principles. It should be stressed, however, that Deleuze's critique of rights should be understood as one which points towards an understanding of a mode of thinking of human rights as 'a totality' or 'a framework' – a framework that includes, of course, their laws and for our purposes the law(s) of the 'right to life'. In other words, my engagement with the regional (European) human rights law on the right to life should be read as an example that aims to give more 'substance' and to manifest how human rights are symptomatic of this 'attachment' to eternal values which lead to an 'uncreative' stalemate.

III. 'THE RIGHT TO LIFE': A SUPPOSEDLY OPEN-ENDED INTERPRETATION OF 'LIFE' WHICH IS STILL DICTATED BY ETERNAL VALUES

The first time that the 'right to life' appeared in international human rights instruments was in 1948, with the drafting of the Universal Declaration of Human Rights (UDHR)[25] and the American Declaration of the Rights and Duties of Man (ADRDM).[26] More specifically, Article 3 of UDHR and Article 1 of ADRDM confirm the right's universal application,[27] whilst they, also, point towards an inherent connection between the notion of life and those of 'liberty' and 'security'. Nonetheless, it is with the introduction of the European Convention on Human Rights, which came into force in 1953, that we witness the first steps towards an effort to take legally binding measures for guaranteeing the universal, legal, enforcement of the right to life.

Article 2(1) of the ECHR states that 'everyone's right to life shall be protected by law. No one shall be deprived of his life intentionally save in the execution of a sentence of a court following his conviction of a crime for which this penalty is provided by law'. Further to that, Section 2 of the Article declares the situations where life can be deprived without contradicting the purposes of Article 2.

[25] Universal Declaration of Human Rights (adopted 10 December 1948 UNGA Res 217 A(III) (UDHR).

[26] American Declaration of the Rights and Duties of Man, OAS Res XXX adopted by the Ninth International Conference of American States (1948) reprinted in Basic Documents Pertaining to Human Rights in the Inter-American System OEA/Ser L V/II.82 Doc 6 Rev 1 at 17 (1992).

[27] In particular, Article 3 of the UDHR manifests right to life's universal application by stating that: '*Everyone* has the right to life, liberty and security of person'. Article 1 of ADRDM states: '*Every human being* has the right to life, liberty and the security of his person.'

For example, situations where deprivation of life takes place as an absolutely necessary means against 'unlawful violence', such as in cases of 'riot and insurrections.' The first point that we can infer from Article 2 is that similarly to the aforementioned declarations, the European Convention recognises the universal duty of the law to protect everyone's right to life. However, what is interesting about the wording of Article 2 is the fact that life becomes a 'pre-existing concept'[28] that the law ought to, universally, protect. As a result, the Article (without clarifying what the concept 'life' entails for the scope of its protection) seems to consider life as a concept which can be acknowledged as something possessed by every human being. Despite the obscurity on the meaning or nature of life, the Convention and the ECtHR, through its jurisprudence and publication of guiding principles[29] on Article 2, have stressed that:

> Article 2 ranks as one of the most fundamental provisions in the Convention, one which in peace time, admits of no derogation under Article 15. Together with Article 3, it enshrines one of the basic values of the democratic societies making up the Council of Europe'.[30] 'As such, its provisions must be strictly construed.[31]

The importance is given to the right to life is unquestionable. The right to life is elevated to a status of one of the fundamental values shared by 'the democratic societies making up the Council of Europe'. This signifies that the understanding of life, according to human rights law, is deeply influenced, but not exhausted,[32] by liberal values, in particular, the centrality and importance that the individual human enjoys in liberal thought[33] (in particular, the right to life as a protection of individuals against other individuals is paramount for liberals[34]). As a result, the meaning or the nature of the life of an individual is taken as 'a common sense' – hence, the lack of clarifications – while, at the same time its importance remains fundamental. Evidently then and according to this mode of thought, this common and universal understanding of life – as something possessed by the individual and its subsequent importance that demands law's unqualified

[28] Wicks (n 9) 201.

[29] Council of Europe, 'Guide on Article 2 of the European Convention on Human Rights' (updated on 31 August 2019).

[30] *Giuliani and Gaggio v Italy* [2011] ECHR 513, para 174.

[31] *McCann and Others v the United Kingdom* A 324 (1995); 21 EHRR 97, para 147.

[32] Efforts to 'liberate' human rights from this liberal language and the subsequent effort to use rights as an emancipatory project, often rely on 'eternal' principles and dogmatic values (this is common in Marxist accounts). See eg of such a case P O' Connell, 'Human Rights: Contesting the Displacement Thesis' (2018) 69(1) *Northern Ireland Legal Quarterly* 19.

[33] See eg M Ignatieff, *Human Rights as Politics and Idolatry* (Princeton University Press, 2003) 72–76; D Miller, 'Grounding Human Rights' (2012) 15(4) *Critical Review of International Social and Political Philosophy* 407, 412–13.

[34] The most famous example supporting this rationale is, possibly, T Hobbes, *Leviathan* (Penguin Classics, 1986). This importance of the protection of an individual against another is manifested by the situations where the deprivation of life is permissible according to Article 2 and, specifically, in a case where killing is the only measure of self-defence or protection of another's life in situations of 'riots and insurrections'.

and efficient protection – forms something akin to what I defined above as a transcendent, eternal, value that stands out of time.[35] Life, as a fundamental right (even as a matter of an objective Truth) acts as a foundation for the values enshrined in human rights law. Hence, it could be argued that the right to life's eternal principles act as the framework that shapes accordingly the changes that take place within the law – changes that happen only within boundaries of law. To that extent, as I will demonstrate below, the expansions and clarifications on the nature and meaning of life, protected by the ECHR, through the ECtHR's jurisprudence are unable to move away from these eternal principles that the right to life entails. As a result, these developments on the interpretation of the right to life, according to human rights law, are not sufficient to take into account the ever-changing character of our temporalities and, as such, they end up being unable to be attentive to our becomings.

An example of such an expansion is the development of the interpretation of the obligation of the states to protect life under Article 2. The Court in *McCann and Others v the United Kingdom* moved beyond the interpretation of life as a mere prohibition of arbitrary killing by a state agent. In the case, the Court recognised 'that a general legal prohibition of arbitrary killing by the agents of the state would be ineffective, in practice, if there existed no procedure for reviewing the lawfulness of the use of lethal force by State authorities'.[36] Thus, the Court stresses that the state has an obligation to make sure that there are procedures and effective measures that are used to investigate the lawfulness of the deprivation of life by its agents. Further, in *Osman v the United Kingdom* the ECtHR highlighted that state authorities have a duty to take positive measures in the sense that 'the state [is responsible] not only to refrain from the intentional and unlawful taking of life but also to take appropriate steps to safeguard the lives of those within its jurisdiction'.[37] These two points signify that the right to life for the ECHR entails an obligation from the state authorities not only to avoid depriving their subjects of their lives but, in addition, they should make sure 'human life [is] respected by the avoidance of death where possible and the investigation of its cause where not possible'.[38] While, it could be argued that these are positive developments, with the Court imposing an obligation on the state to investigate and also scrutinise whether it acted appropriately in avoiding a deprivation of life, what they do in terms of interpreting life is, simply, to interpret the notion in a static, a-temporal manner. Subsequently, and despite these supposed expansions, the meaning of life which is protected within the scope of Article 2 seems to continue to be taken for granted. More explicitly, what we

[35] For a similar view on the right to life's 'hierarchical' position, see P Tiensuu, 'Whose Right to What Life: Assisted Suicide and the Right to Life as a Fundamental Right' (2015) 15 *Human Rights Law Review* 251, 252.

[36] *McCann* (n 31) para 161.

[37] *Osman v the United Kingdom* Application No. 23452/94 [1998] ECHR 101, para 115.

[38] Wicks (n 9) 202.

witness is a situation where the Court, by taking life's meaning 'for granted', intensifies the right to life's timeless foundations as a notion of 'common sense' – a common sense which is, nonetheless, 'common' only to this (predominantly liberal) ideology which dictates right to life's understanding.

This 'mentality' of human rights law becomes more evident once we pay attention to the way that the Court responded to the question of the 'beginning of life'. The case of *Vo v France*[39] is an example where the Court, in its effort to avoid answering the controversial question of when life begins and which 'life' falls within the scope of Article 2, manifested that its rationale is symptomatic of an understanding of the living human being in a normative way, infused by eternal values. In particular, this is manifested in the Court's understanding of the 'everyone' of Article 2 as a human subject, which can be characterised as 'a person'. In the case, the Court refused to decide whether Article 2 is fully applicable to an unborn child, by stating that 'it is neither desirable nor even possible as matters stand, to answer in the abstract the question of whether the unborn child is a person for the purposes of Article 2'.[40] Instead, the Court added that responding to the matter whether a foetus enjoys the full protection of the Article was 'unnecessary' for the examination of the facts of the case. The Court justified this by stating that 'even assuming that the provision was applicable, there was no failure on the part of the respondent state to comply with the preservation of life in the public-health sphere'.[41] By adding this second part, the Court seemed ready to accept that it is possible that the foetus can qualify as something 'as possessing life' – and in fact, it, directly, said that the foetus has the 'capacity to become a person' – yet it is a life that does not qualify for the full protection of Article 2.[42] Despite the fact that the foetus does not fully qualify as a person (or as the 'everyone' of Article 2), it requires some protection, according to the Court, 'in the name of human dignity'.[43]

Having examined the development of case law and in particular the *Vo* decision, there are two striking points that we need to take into account, in order to understand how international human rights law, and in particular the right to life in the European context, is dictated by eternal values. First, the equation of 'everyone' of Article 2 with a notion of 'personhood' signifies an understanding of the human subject as one which holds an identity characterised by a certain degree of fixity. So even if the Court, in future cases, decides that the foetus should enjoy the full protection of Article 2 because it qualifies as a person, then this change will still be based on a certain understanding of the human subject in terms of unity and totality. In that sense, human rights become the rights of, what Deleuze calls, 'a reflective subject'.[44] This is an understanding of a human

[39] *Vo v France* 2004-VIII; 40 EHRR 12.
[40] ibid para 85.
[41] ibid.
[42] Wicks (n 9) 209 argues the same but for different purposes.
[43] *Vo* (n 39) para 84.
[44] Deleuze with Bellour and Ewald (n 21) 152.

being as 'a closed entity', which is not subjected to change and to that extent, it is considered to be the possessor of an eternal Truth. As such, this way of thinking about the subject as a closed entity, a unity is unable to take into account our temporalities or becoming(s). Secondly, the Court, by being ready to accept some protection for the foetus, solely, 'in the name of human dignity' manifests further this rationale. This happens because the Court seems to ground the importance of preserving life as a matter of human dignity. The grounding of the right to life and its importance on abstract and eternal notions such as 'dignity',[45] further points towards the symptomatic mode of thought of rights, identified by Deleuze. This is because if we accept that the right to life (and potentially human rights in their totality) are based on foundational principles such as dignity, we automatically concede that rights hold a fundamental Truth (similarly to the Platonic Idea as mentioned above).

In other words, such a mode of thought necessitates the incorporation of (moral) eternal values for the justification of what a right is or could be. To that extent, any potential development of rights' interpretation by human rights law is susceptible to thinking in these terms. Then, we have to ask the following: Is there a potential for human rights law to move beyond this mentality of grounding its rationale in eternal principles? Furthermore, if human rights law is unable to foster a way of think otherwise then how can we move beyond this problematic thinking by existing and thinking in terms of a mode of being (ethos) which is characterised by an openness towards our ever-changing temporalities? In the next section, by elaborating on the Deleuzian concept of 'becoming', I aim to point towards this 'thinking otherwise' in terms of an ethos which exists in terms of constant movement and variations, something that I call a becoming-chaotic of time.

IV. HOW IS A DELEUZIAN BECOMING?

According to Martin Heidegger, the predominant tradition of Western philosophy tends to understand 'a becoming' or 'becoming' as a transformative process which is, nonetheless, entrapped within two fixed points (eg something is becoming something else and as such in its past it was one thing and in its present another).[46] Becoming, then, becomes the mere process that simply vanishes once the transformation is complete and as such our tendency is to think of the notion as secondary to the fixed points. This leads immediately to a certain difficulty of grasping a Deleuzian becoming as a term. This is because

[45] For an example of how 'dignity' is often understood as a fundamental grounding principle of human rights see, J Griffith, 'First Steps in an Account of Human Rights' (2001) 9(3) *European Journal of Philosophy* 306.

[46] M Heidegger, 'World and Life as 'Becoming' in DF Krell (ed), *Nietzsche: Volumes Three and Four* trans. J Stambaugh, DF Krell and FA Capuzzi (HarperCollins Publishers, 1987) 64.

once becoming is given a definition or once we respond to 'what a becoming is' automatically the notion loses its dynamism as it becomes enclosed within the boundaries of a fixed identity. Deleuze's becoming is not about 'naming' (giving an essence of a thing). It is rather 'about the *circumstances of the emergence of a thing*'.[47] However, despite the refusal of a becoming to respond to the traditional philosophical question (what is it?), it calls us to think about its sense or the sensibilities that it has the potentiality to cause – that is a call to be attentive to becoming(s). It is in a sense the un-thought (or undefinable) that, yet must be thought. It is more appropriate, then, to ask the question of how a becoming is because a becoming is to be thought of as a force of transformation that calls for an openness. Such an openness suspends any notions of the eternal. It is, therefore, a tool to be used in order to suspend or disorient this unity of the foundational and timeless principles of human rights and their laws.

Indeed, while Deleuze refuses to fall into the trap of giving becoming a fixed identification, he, explicitly, explains what becoming *is not*. Writing with Félix Guattari, they state the following:

> becoming is certainly not imitating, or identifying with something; neither it is regressing-progressing; neither is it corresponding, establishing corresponding relations; neither is it producing, producing filiation or producing through filiation. Becoming is a verb with a consistency all its own; it does not reduce to, or lead back to, 'appearing', 'being', 'equalling' or 'producing'.[48]

It becomes clear that for Deleuze becoming is not to be thought of as secondary to being. Becoming, as Deleuze and Guattari write, is characterised by 'self-sufficiency' as 'a verb with consistency all its own'. But how are we to grasp this consistency of constant change? Deleuze seeks this dynamism of ever-changing becoming(s) by examining 'a different story' of Western philosophical tradition. In particular, he recognises Friedrich Nietzsche and the Pre-Socratic philosopher Heraclitus of Ephesus as the two figures who resisted a mode of thought that 'thinks' in terms of foundational and timeless principles.

Heraclitus is known as the philosopher of 'flux' and of becoming, in brief, of constant change. As one of his fragments on how the world is one of becoming reads 'that which always, and is, and will be everliving fire, the same for all, the cosmos, made neither by god nor man, replenishes in *measure* as it burns away'.[49] The fragment suggests that the world is, indeed, one of becoming (it burns away) and it becomes, constantly by the force that it traverses it ('the everliving fire'). However, this becoming happens in measure, it is not chaos pure and simple, but instead, it is in constant strife with chaos in order to produce

[47] CV Boundas, 'Deleuze's Difference' in his (ed), *Deleuze and Philosophy* (Edinburgh University Press, 2006) 11.

[48] G Deleuze and F Guattari, *A Thousand Plateaus* trans B Massumi (Bloomsbury Revelations, 2015) 279.

[49] Heraclitus, *Fragments* trans B Haxton (Penguin Classics, 2003) 15 [emphasis added].

change and to constantly create a new, yet, consistent world. Nietzsche, recognising Heraclitus' influence upon his thought, praises him because Heraclitus 'rejected the [...] evidence [of higher Truths] because they showed things as if they had duration and unity [...]'.[50] To that extent, Nietzsche objects to an understanding of the world as a universe which is dictated by a notion of an objective, eternal Truth, characterised by permanence. He, instead, suggests that becoming is something of 'this world' that does away with any notion of hierarchies, which reduce life to a mere stage of a quest towards the Truth. Becoming, instead, affirms this life and this world – the only world and thus, it is what makes life goes.[51] Similar to the Heraclitean 'everliving fire', the Nietzschean becoming is the driving force that does not cease to traverse the world and all of the beings, something which can be equated with his notion of the *will to power*. Thus, contrary to the quest for an eternal Truth, permanence and stability, which becomes *the* goal of the world and dominates the modes of existence of the West, Nietzsche objects and fights this eschatology and hierarchical mode of thought based on eternal principles.[52]

Deleuze revisits the Nietzschean and Heraclitean notion of becoming in his *Nietzsche and Philosophy* and he manages to give the notion a new impetus.[53] The way he treats becoming in these passages is as an ethical mode of existing which is characterised by 'innocence' and 'playfulness', as opposed to the subjugation of our existence to eternal principles. Innocence, as Deleuze writes, 'is the game of existence of force and of will'.[54] As such, a game is something that is defined by movement and force, where game-players are not static, even if they do not physically move. They think, they imagine and they try to be creative and thus, they, actively, participate in their game. In analogous terms, innocence calls for an affirmative participation in life, away from eternal, dogmatic truths and values. In Deleuze's words; 'we create grotesque representations of force and will, we separate force from what it can do, setting it up in ourselves as "worthy" because it holds back from what it cannot do, but as "blameworthy" in the thing where it manifests precisely the force that it has'.[55] Such an objection to eternal values that dictate our modes of being, leads Deleuze to examine Heraclitus. According to him, 'Heraclitus denied the duality of worlds, [and to that extent], he denied being itself'.[56] But in denying being, Heraclitus showed that there is a second element in his thought, distinct, yet inseparable from the denial of being,

[50] F Nietzsche, *The Twilight of the Idols or How to Philosophise with a Hammer* trans and Intro D Large (Oxford Classics, 1998) 16–17.
[51] See C Cox, *Nietzsche: Naturalism and Interpretation* (University of California Press, 1999) 185–93.
[52] F Nietzsche, *Will to Power* trans and ed W Kauffman (Vintage Books, 1968) 546.
[53] Deleuze, *Nietzsche and Philosophy* (n 6).
[54] ibid 23.
[55] ibid.
[56] ibid.

'like ciphers'.[57] This second element manifests becoming as that which affirms being, that is 'being is affirmed in becoming'.[58]

> For there is no being beyond becoming, nothing beyond multiplicity; neither multiplicity nor becoming are appearances or illusions. But neither are there multiple or eternal realities which would be, in turn, like essences beyond appearance. Multiplicity is the inseparable manifestation, essential transformation and constant symptom of unity.[59]

These rather enigmatic statements want, in our view, to present a denial of being – as long as being is to be understood as a unified, eternal entity – but such a denial is not a negative or a merely polemical one. The denial of being takes place through an affirmation of such being that happens in a process of becoming, that is an affirmation of being's fragmented condition as a multiplicity, an affirmation of being that is open to change and movement. The denial of the unity of being, as the true indestructible and unchangeable entity, is an affirmation of this unity through multiplicity. The unity of our principles or even our existence then, is only affirmed through its multiplicity. Thus, there are no eternal or unchangeable principles or beings that stand 'out of time'. Further to that, Deleuze suggests that becoming(s) or multiplicities are not 'illusions', they may not be corporeal or 'actual', but they are real and in their realities, they ensure that being is affirmed.

Subsequently, being is justified simply by its openness, by the fact that there is no higher Truth or realm that it must arrive at, there is only *this* life. And paying attention to the becoming(s) of life suggests active participation, as opposed to the alienation caused by the stability of the eternal. Becoming, then, should be understood as a chaotic constant change, as something *untimely*,[60] something that takes place constantly and it *returns*. As Deleuze reads Nietzschean 'eternal return', what returns is not the same but what is produced by repetition is difference.[61] Thus, 'the eternal return as law of becoming'.[62] What this means is that the eternal return points towards a refutation of the understanding of becoming as a mere 'passage' from a state of being to another, it rather suggests that everything returns in its difference:

> it is not some one thing which returns but rather returning itself is the one thing which is affirmed of diversity or multiplicity. In other words, identity in the eternal return does not describe the nature of that which returns but, on the contrary, the fact of returning for that which differs.[63]

[57] ibid.
[58] ibid.
[59] ibid 23–24.
[60] For an example of how this notion of the 'untimely' is used to question human rights relation with temporality and time, see K McNeilly, 'Are Rights Out of Time? International Human Rights Law, Temporality and Radical Social Change' (2019) 28(6) *Social & Legal Studies* 817. McNeilly focuses on the notion of the Nietzschean 'untimely' as it was developed by Elizabeth Grosz (823–25).
[61] ibid, 48.
[62] ibid 24.
[63] ibid 48.

To that extent, becoming constantly returns in its multiplicity and difference, in a manner that is not reduced by actual historical events or changes of state of beings that happens within the boundaries of countable time and thus it is untimely. In a passage from the *Logic of Sense* this untimeliness of becoming becomes evident when Deleuze writes that:

> When I say that 'Alice becomes larger', I mean that she becomes larger than she was. By the same token, however, she becomes smaller than she is now. Certainly, she is not bigger and smaller at the same time. She is larger now; she was smaller before. But it is at the same moment that one becomes larger than one was and smaller than one becomes. This is the simultaneity of a becoming whose characteristic is to elude the present.[64]

A becoming, then, has no beginnings nor ends, it rather operates 'in between',[65] always escaping its capture ('it eludes the present') by a fixed, timeless framework. Thus, an *ethos* and a politics (including law) attentive to becoming(s) are ones which dissolve the eternal, permanence and stability. It is an *ethos* and politics of 'pure temporality' – a *becoming-chaotic* of time. Chaos here, should not be understood in a negative sense of 'anything goes' but it signifies a notion of constant movement and creativity. A mode of being and thinking that embraces this chaos is characterised by its refusal to remain static, to accept certain principles as eternal and thus, objectively true. To that extent, a *becoming-chaotic* requires an *ethos* which is open and attentive to its temporalities, in the sense that, and similar to Heraclitean everliving fire, one which is in constant *strife* with chaos, assessing the multiplicity of potentialities that it encounters.[66]

V. CONCLUSION: *BEYOND* HUMAN RIGHTS AND THEIR ETERNAL LAWS(?)

Can human rights and their laws, in their international, regional or national manifestation, 'think' in terms of this *becoming-chaotic* of time? Can they become attentive to our temporalities or is this 'human rights culture' a framework which always 'thinks' and it is shaped by foundational and eternal principles? In those terms, are human rights our modern 'eternal values', as Deleuze has it, hence they are and they will always be 'out of time'? In this chapter, I tried to address these questions. By investigating some of Deleuze's critical comments on human rights, I demonstrated how his understanding of rights suggests that human rights and their laws are based on (and they become themselves) eternal values. This timeless mode of thought, as I argued, leads

[64] G Deleuze, *Logic of Sense* trans CV Boundas, M Lester and CJ Stivale (Bloomsbury 2015) 1.
[65] Deleuze with Dulaure and Parnet (n 4) 121.
[66] See E Grosz, *The Incorporeal: Ontology, Ethics and the Limits of Materialism* (Columbia University Press, 2017) esp ch 4.

to a stalemate and a blocking of creative, new modes of being with its ultimate consequence 'a hatred towards life'. I further demonstrated how such a mode of thought operates and dictates the way human rights laws are created. In particular, by focusing on the European Convention on Human Rights and the European Court of Human Rights' jurisprudence on the 'right to life', I argued that the right and its developments are symptomatic of foundational and timeless principles, such as a notion of 'personhood' and a normative understanding of what life is. Finally, by examining the Deleuzian notion of 'becoming', I offered some insights on how a *thinking otherwise* about time and our temporalities is possible. In particular, I proposed a mode of being and thinking characterised by an *ethos* of a *becoming-chaotic* of time. That is an *ethos* which is attentive to our temporalities, characterised by a strife for ever-changing creation. Such an *ethos* always questions the supposed eternal Truth(s) aiming and, to that extent, it suspends and disorients their permanence.

What remains to be seen is whether human rights and their laws are able to accommodate this *thinking otherwise*. In my part, I am highly sceptical of such a possibility. Perhaps, and if we are to take our temporalities – *our here and now* – seriously, we should be careful that the creation of law and rights is not to 'be left to judges' (and here we should add any form of 'wise authority').[67]

[67] G Deleuze and A Negri, 'Control and Becoming' in *Negotiations* (n 4) 169.

10

From Crisis to Quotidian: Countering the Temporal Myopia of Jus Cogens

MARY H HANSEL

I. INTRODUCTION

THE DOCTRINE OF *jus cogens* has a paradoxical relationship with crisis. In a sense, the doctrine is impervious to crisis due to the non-derogable nature of *jus cogens* norms: States cannot suspend their obligations with respect to such norms during an emergency. Notwithstanding, the doctrine seems to be constituted and governed by a crisis temporality. Indeed, this chapter argues that *jus cogens* instantiates international human rights law's well-established prioritisation of crisis and is underpinned by the discipline's myopic temporal scheme. The chapter then proposes and applies an alternative temporal approach to inform the doctrine and support the identification of 'everyday' *jus cogens* norms, not dictated by crisis.

The chapter builds on and is situated within a series of foundational works. Hilary Charlesworth's 2002 article 'International Law: A Discipline of Crisis' describes how international law's fixation on crisis obscures many of the issues that most affect women's lives.[1] Recognising that such issues are 'seen as part of the status quo and not truly the business of international law', this article concludes with an invitation for further exploration: 'What might an international law of every day life look like?'[2] In a 2014 follow-up article, Charlesworth and Benjamin Authers examine international human rights law's focus on crisis and resultant marginalisation of economic, social and cultural (ESC) rights, the category of rights correlated with 'every day life'.[3] Expanding upon these articles, my previous scholarship demonstrates that international law's preoccupation

[1] H Charlesworth, 'International Law: A Discipline of Crisis' (2002) 65 *Modern Law Review* 377, 389–92. The term 'women' is understood to include any individual who identifies as a woman.

[2] ibid 389, 391.

[3] See B Authers and H Charlesworth, 'The Crisis and the Quotidian in International Human Rights Law' (2014) 44 *Netherlands Yearbook Of International Law* 19, 28–37.

with crisis (termed the 'crisis model'), which marginalizes systemic, quotidian issues, is defined by the role of time and sustained by a linear, reactive temporal scheme.[4] My scholarship proposes an alternative temporality that would centre quotidian issues and, in turn, ESC rights and many feminist priorities.[5]

Throughout this chapter, I seek to apply and reify these analytical frameworks in the context of *jus cogens* – perhaps the epitome of the crisis model and its dominant temporal scheme. Section II provides a background summary of the crisis model and its obfuscation of quotidian issues, with profound implications for ESC rights and feminist priorities. It then reiterates the myopic temporal scheme, termed 'emergency time', underpinning the crisis model. Section III turns to *jus cogens* as a case study of the crisis model and its temporal dimensions. Indeed, the recent list of *jus cogens* norms by the UN International Law Commission (ILC) shows a bias in favour of norms linked to crisis and governed by emergency time, at the expense of norms reflecting quotidian issues. Section IV sets forth alternative temporal approaches derived from the feminist literature; monikered 'The Four Rs', these approaches are the times of Regression, Redemption, Rupture and Repetition. Time as Repetition is identified as particularly germane due to its associations with the everyday. This temporality, as applied to *jus cogens*, would foster an iterative approach, such that norms linked to quotidian issues would be candidates for *jus cogens* status. Also, such issues would be recognised as falling within the contours of currently recognised *jus cogens* norms. Section V offers concluding reflections on the importance of surfacing time as a potent force in human rights and a tool for both subjugation and emancipation.

II. THE TEMPORALITY OF CRISIS

This section provides a summary of relevant scholarship, including the aforementioned works, establishing the crisis model of international human rights law, its marginalisation of quotidian issues and the dominant temporal approach underpinning the model. Subsequent sections will discuss how the existing frameworks apply to the identification and construction of *jus cogens* norms.

A. The Crisis Model of International Human Rights

The existing literature demonstrates that international human rights law devotes an inordinate amount of attention and resources to events and situations

[4] See generally MH Hansel, 'Feminist Time and International Law of the Everyday' in *The Future of Women's Engagement with International Law* (Edward Elgar, 2019) 379–98.
[5] ibid.

characterised as crises.[6] Pursuant to this crisis model, crises seem to spontaneously erupt without warning, demanding attention and, often, intervention by the international community.[7] International legal treatment typically begins with this eruption and subsides as the crisis loses apparent urgency – flitting on to the next crisis.[8] As Gerry Simpson has observed, '[b]y the time we have put some distance between ourselves and a particular human tragedy, we have moved on to the next "international incident"'.[9]

Crisis is central to how international human rights are given value and meaning.[10] The crisis label places events and situations in the category of anomaly, deviation from the status quo.[11] Rendering events or situations as exceptions to the norm can obscure and shield state failures from criticism.[12] Meanwhile, 'the less individuated and cyclical systems that are at the root of those failures are presented as beyond fault and ultimately to be protected'.[13] These cyclical systems – the status quo human rights violations – do not receive comparable attention and resources. As Diane Otto has explained, governing by crisis has 'legitimate[d] the adoption of short-term, quick-fix responses that ignore the larger historical context of causation and individualize responsibility … depicting everyday structural inequalities and injustices as given'.[14] The absence of a crisis rubric makes everyday human rights concerns, including ESC rights and many feminist priorities, appear less urgent and less deserving of redress than human rights issues driven by crisis.[15]

ESC rights are rarely depicted as the subjects of crisis and generally relegated to the periphery of international human rights. According to Charlesworth and

[6] See eg Charlesworth (n 1) 382 ('Crises are not of course the only catalyst for the development of international law, but they dominate the imagination of international lawyers').

[7] See S Pahuja, '"Don't Just Do Something, Stand There!" Humanitarian Intervention and the Drowning Stranger' (2005) 5 *Human Rights & Human Welfare* 51, 52. See also C O'Rourke, 'International Law, COVID-19 and Feminist Engagement with the United Nations Security Council: The End of the Affair?' (2020) 28 *Feminist Legal Studies* 321, 325 (noting that the purported facts of crises, which are treated as 'uncontroversial and ripe for picking', often break down upon scrutiny).

[8] See A Orford, 'Muscular Humanitarianism: Reading the Narratives of the New Interventionism' (1999) 10 *European Journal of International Law* 679, 689–92; Charlesworth (n 1) 384.

[9] Charlesworth (n 1) 384, citing G Simpson, 'Kosovo Imprints: International Law at the Fault-Line' 1 (unpublished, on file with author).

[10] Authers and Charlesworth (n 3) 21.

[11] See ibid 23–24. This holds true even when crises have effectively become the status quo – several scholars, including Dianne Otto, have observed the liminal phenomenon of sustained crisis. See eg D Otto, 'Remapping Crisis Through a Feminist Lens' in *Feminist Perspectives on Contemporary International Law: Between Resistance and Compliance?* 81–82 (Hart Publishing, 2014).

[12] Authers and Charlesworth (n 3) 23.

[13] ibid.

[14] D Otto, 'Decoding Crisis: A Queer Feminist Perspective on the Productivity of Crisis for International Law and its Resistive Possibilities' in *International Law and Its Discontents: Confronting Crisis* (CUP, 2015) 116. 'Crisis governance, assisted by sexual and gender panics, inaugurates a more repressive paradigm for the management of life, wherein the structures of privilege are protected and strengthened by ignoring structural injustices, individualizing responsibility and vigorously silencing dissent.' ibid 129.

[15] Authers and Charlesworth (n 3) 21.

Authers, this relegation stems from 'a crisis-driven hierarchy of urgency', which artificially distinguishes between civil and political rights and ESC rights and casts the latter as less important and deferrable.[16] Indeed, crises are often associated with breaches of civil and political rights, which are endowed with great exigency and often deployed to respond to statist crises.[17] Violations of ESC rights, by contrast, are seen as 'situations of unexceptional daily life that are easily swept aside in times of crisis or emergency'.[18] The distinction between these two categories of rights, and their relevance to apparent crises, is illustrated by their respective implementation: The International Covenant on Civil and Political Rights (ICCPR) requires immediate implementation, while the International Covenant on Economic, Social and Cultural Rights (ICESCR) calls for progressive realisation subject to the availability of state resources.[19] As Authers and Charlesworth point out, this dichotomy is exacerbated by the work of human rights organisations, which tend to emphasise civil and political rights.[20]

The crisis model likewise marginalises and diminishes many feminist priorities, particularly those related to everyday gender-based harms.[21] As Charlesworth emphasises, 'systemic violence, or structural discrimination against women, do not constitute a crisis for international lawyers' but are seen as 'part of the status quo'.[22] Similarly, the model obscures persistent issues that have gendered impacts (many of which implicate ESC rights), such as climate

[16] ibid 30–37. This hierarchy persists notwithstanding that the 1993 World Conference on Human Rights established that '[t]he international community must treat human rights globally in a fair and equal manner, on the same footing, and with the same emphasis'. Office of the United Nations High Commissioner for Human Rights, Vienna Declaration and Programme of Action (1993), para 5.

[17] Authers and Charlesworth (n 3) 32–37.

[18] ibid 32. This view is somewhat ironic given that, unlike the International Covenant on Civil and Political Rights (ICCPR), the International Covenant on Economic, Social and Cultural Rights (ICESCR) does not provide for derogation in times of emergency. B Saul, D Kinley and J Mowbray, *The International Covenant on Economic, Social and Cultural Rights: Commentary, Cases and Materials* (OUP, 2014) 258 (stating that the ICESCR's lack of an express derogation provision means that no derogation is permissible). Occasionally, violations of ESC rights attract the rhetoric of crisis, particularly in the context of famine and natural disasters; however, for these violations, 'the sense of crisis dissipates the longer the situation endures'. Authers and Charlesworth (n 3) 30–37. The COVID-19 pandemic may be an example of such a crisis, as it implicates various ESC rights.

[19] Compare International Covenant on Civil and Political Rights (adopted 16 December 1966, entered into force 23 March 1976) 999 UNTS 171, art 2 [hereinafter, 'ICCPR'] with International Covenant on Economic, Social and Cultural Rights (adopted 16 December 1966, entered into force 23 March 1976) 993 UNTS 3, art 2 [hereinafter, 'ICESCR']. 'The lines of accountability for breaches of civil and political rights appear more straightforward than for economic, social and cultural rights and thus more susceptible to a crisis analysis.' Authers and Charlesworth (n 3) 35.

[20] Authers and Charlesworth (n 3) 35–36.

[21] This is in part because ESC rights, which are relegated to the periphery, are linked to the daily lives of women. See D Otto, 'Handmaidens, Hierarchies and Crossing the Public–Private Divide in the Teaching of International Law' (2000) 1 *Melbourne Journal of International Law* 3, fn 7 ('the normative hierarchy between civil and political rights (many of which have achieved a customary, even jus cogens, status) and economic, social and cultural rights (largely still soft law) reflects social hierarchies of class, race and gender').

[22] Charlesworth (n 1) 389. For a discussion of the myriad other ways in which the crisis model marginalises the experiences of women, please refer to Hansel (n 4).

justice, family violence, poverty, lack of access to healthcare and barriers to education. Notably, as Karen Engle, Vasuki Nesiah and Otto explain, successful feminist engagements with crisis-based legal interventions, including laws addressing armed conflicts, have contributed to the 'crowding out' of alternative feminist perspectives, 'particularly those that take aim at the often-quotidian forms of violence based in structures of colonialism, racism, gender normativity, and gross economic inequality – as well as their overlap'.[23]

Quotidian human rights issues, including ESC rights and many feminist priorities have been eclipsed by the allure of sporadic, yet dramatic, crises. In short, '[c]risis imbues some human rights violations with drama, making others recede drably into the background'.[24] The following section delves into the temporal assumptions driving this dynamic.

B. The Crisis Model's Temporal Underpinnings

Despite the centrality of crises in international human rights law, there is a scarcity of literature exploring what crises are and are not – what criteria are used to make such determinations, explicitly or implicitly, consciously or unconsciously.[25] While the gravity of an event or situation may be a necessary criterion for crisis, gravity alone is not sufficient to explain why some phenomena are deemed crises and others are not.[26] Metrics used to assess gravity, such as loss of life, structural damage, extent of violence or economic cost, are not reliable indicators of what constitutes a crisis.[27] Sonja Starr brings this point into sharp relief: '[F]or instance, compare a single day's massacre of 200 people to a regime's systematic extrajudicial killing of tens of thousands, one by one, over

[23] K Engle, V Nesiah and D Otto, 'Feminist Approaches to International Law' in J Dunoff and M Pollack (eds), *International Legal Theory: Foundations and Frontiers* (CUP) (forthcoming).

[24] Authers and Charlesworth (n 3) 30.

[25] 'Crisis' is a 'malleable and ambiguous' term, 'a generic term for a type of transition, one framed by particular urgency'; Authers and Charlesworth have pointed out that '[i]t is precisely its lack of definition that gives the idea of crisis its discursive force'. Authers and Charlesworth (n 3) 23–24. See also K Loevy, 'What Is an Emergency? The Legal Politics of Defining the "Un-Definable"' (2015) 22 *ILSA Journal of International & Comparative Law* 155, 158 ('It is common knowledge that emergencies are unexpected events and therefore essentially un-definable. They resist, as it is often claimed, precise definitions.').

[26] For a compilation of factors international bodies have found to be relevant in assessing gravity, please refer to R Lopez, 'The Law of Gravity' (2020) 58 *Columbia Journal of Transnational Law* 565, 599–615.

[27] See eg Charlesworth (n 1) 391 (questioning why international law fixated on the 1999 Kosovo crisis, while contemporaneous global epidemics, such as extreme poverty, lack of sanitation, disease and gender-based violence, received far less international legal attention); M Koskenniemi, '"The Lady Doth Protest Too Much" Kosovo, and the Turn to Ethics in International Law' (2002) 65 *Modern Law Review* 159, 172 (comparing the number of civilian casualties during the Kosovo crisis with the much higher number of children dying from malnutrition – an issue deemed 'a "social", "cultural" or "economic" condition of law which therefore cannot be touched by law.').

the course of a decade' – the former would likely be deemed a crisis, while the latter would not, even though 'all crimes against humanity that take the form of a sudden onslaught [are not] worse than those committed slowly'.[28] Crises, as Starr's example highlights, seem to be defined by temporality.

Indeed, events and situations are considered crises when there is a perceived (or even manufactured) dearth of time.[29] Crises are characterised by the present, the urgent, the right now; in essence, they are defined by emergency. Thus, the temporal scheme that governs the crisis model is termed 'emergency time'.[30] This term was coined by Jérome Bindé of the UN Educational, Scientific and Cultural Organization in his critique of the international community's abdication of responsibility for enduring societal problems.[31] Bindé explains that emergency time is afflicted by a form of temporal myopia, 'leav[ing] no time for either analysis, forecasting, or prevention' and impelling 'an immediate protective reflex rather than a sober quest for long-term solutions'.[32]

This temporal approach underpins the crisis model's salient features. It is responsible for international human rights law's peripatetic tendency to address each crisis at the point of eruption and then abruptly move on to the next, once the emergency seems to be quelled.[33] Moreover, the temporal myopia of emergency time serves to obscure issues that do not seem to require urgent attention, including quotidian issues involving ESC rights and many feminist priorities. Because these issues do not present as urgencies, they are marginalised within the crisis model.

The burgeoning literature on 'slow death' helps to elucidate this dynamic. The slow death paradigm refers to harms that happen gradually over time and are often undetected or overlooked.[34] As Lauren Berlant explains, '[s]low death prospers not in traumatic events, as discrete time-framed phenomena like military encounters and genocides can appear to do, but in temporal environments whose qualities and whose contours in time and space are often identified

[28] S Starr, 'Extraordinary Crimes at Ordinary Times: International Justice Beyond Crisis Situations' (2007) 101 *Northwestern University Law Review* 1257, 1277. 'Nor have all of the specific crisis crimes addressed by tribunals thus far – presumably, those crimes that the international community has deemed the most serious – caused more suffering than have the world's worst systemic crimes.' ibid.

[29] See generally Hansel (n 4); MH Hansel, 'International Law, Crisis and Feminist Time' in *Feminist Perspectives on Transitional Justice* (Intersentia, 2013).

[30] This concept is similar to what Fleur Johns has described as international law's 'temporal fitfulness'. See F Johns, 'The Temporal Rivalries of Human Rights' (2016) 23 *Indiana Journal of Global Legal Studies* 39, 41.

[31] J Bindé, 'Toward an Ethics of the Future' (2000) 12 *Public Culture* 51, 52.

[32] ibid. ('It neglects the fact that situations have to be put in perspective and that future events need to be anticipated.').

[33] International law's adherence to emergency time is of course fuelled by media fickleness and sensationalism. See M Short, 'Taking Back the Trash: Comparing European Extended Producer Responsibility and Take-Back Liability to U.S. Environmental Policy and Attitudes' (2004) 37 *Vanderbilt Journal of Transnational Law* 1217, 1247.

[34] S Lee, 'Family Separation As Slow Death' (2019) 119 *Columbia Law Review* 2319, 2327–33.

with the presentness of ordinariness itself ....'[35] Other scholars have observed that systemic discrimination 'can lead to the slow death of a person's soul or psyche'.[36] 'Slow' harms stand in contrast to extraordinary bouts of violence, which are 'those that can be appreciated immediately in the moment'[37] and provide 'a spectacular, immediately sensational, and instantly hypervisible image of what constitutes a violent threat'.[38] Broad structural conditions, which seem to move slowly, barely register as they are obfuscated by the spectacular. 'In other words, slow death is by its very nature taken for granted.'[39]

The prioritisation of crises over systemic, quotidian issues 'contribut[es] to the dominance within the mainstream agenda of issues peripheral to the lives of most people in the world today'.[40] In particular, the crisis model of international human rights is at the expense of ESC rights and many feminist priorities. As the next section describes, *jus cogens* epitomises the model, along with its deleterious impacts, and is afflicted by the same temporal myopia as the broader discipline.

III. *JUS COGENS* TYPIFYING THE TEMPORAL BIAS OF INTERNATIONAL HUMAN RIGHTS

The determination of *jus cogens* norms instantiates the crisis model's temporal approach. The ILC's recent reports identifying confirmed and candidate *jus cogens* norms demonstrate the doctrine's prioritisation of crisis and narrow construction of norms – to the exclusion of quotidian issues. The crisis-driven nature of *jus cogens* can be attributed to emergency time, which, as explained above, permeates international human rights law and fuels the crisis model.

A. The International Law Commission's Determination of *Jus Cogens* Norms

It is difficult to overstate the unrivalled potency of *jus cogens* status. A *jus cogens* norm is 'a norm accepted and recognised by the international community of states as a whole as a norm from which no derogation is permitted and which

[35] L Berlant, 'Slow Death (Sovereignty, Obesity, Lateral Agency)' (2007) 33 *Critical Inquiry* 754, 759.

[36] AK Wing and M Nigh Smith, 'Critical Race Feminism Lifts the Veil?: Muslim Women, France, and the Headscarf Ban' (2006) 39 *U.C. Davis Law Review* 743, 777. See also Lee (n 34) 2327–33 (explaining that many marginalised communities live '[u]nder a regime of crisis ordinariness').

[37] Lee (n 34) 2327.

[38] R Nixon, *Slow Violence and the Environmentalism of the Poor* (Harvard University Press, 2011) 13.

[39] Lee (n 34) 2327–33, citing Berlant (n 35) 759.

[40] See R Wilde, 'Casting Light on the "Legal Black Hole": Some Political Issues at Stake' (2006) 5 *European Human Rights Law Review* 552, 556–57.

can be modified only by a subsequent norm of general international law having the same character'.[41] As a legal matter, *jus cogens* norms are hierarchically superior to all other international norms and override conflicting domestic laws, treaties and even UN Security Council resolutions.[42] Yet much of the doctrine's power derives not from its practical effects but from its symbolic importance.[43] Indeed, *jus cogens* norms are seen as 'guarding the most fundamental and highly-valued interests of international society'[44] and an 'expression of a conviction, accepted in all parts of the world community, which touches the deeper conscience of all nations'.[45] As a result of their profound legal and symbolic impacts, *jus cogens* norms are not merely reflective, they are constitutive; they help dictate the international human rights agenda.[46] Accordingly, the issue of which norms are deemed to be *jus cogens* is of stunning consequence.

Acknowledging the privileged position of *jus cogens* norms within the international order, the ILC set out to formulate an authoritative list of such norms several years ago. In 2019, the ILC Special Rapporteur on peremptory norms of general international law (*jus cogens*) submitted a report identifying a list of norms that have attained *jus cogens* status, pursuant to a positivist methodology.[47] In assessing the *jus cogens* status of each norm, the report compiles the evidence in support of each norm, including international court decisions, state declarations and scholarly analyses.[48] The plenary ILC adopted the Special Rapporteur's list of norms in its subsequent report (which is awaiting state inputs before finalisation).[49] The two ILC reports provide the most

[41] Draft Conclusions on Peremptory Norms of General International Law (Jus Cogens), Report of the International Law Commission, Seventy-first Session, General Assembly Official Records (A/74/10), Draft Conclusion No. 2 [hereinafter, 'ILC Plenary Report']. This definition is mirrored by art 53 of the Vienna Convention on the Law of Treaties. Vienna Convention on the Law of Treaties, 1155 UNTS 331 (1969).

[42] See eg ILC Plenary Report, Draft Conclusion Nos 3, 10; A Cassese 'For an Enhanced Role of Jus Cogens' in A Cassese (ed), *Realizing Utopia: The Future of International Law* (OUP, 2012) 162; D Tladi, 'The International Law Commission's Draft Conclusions on Peremptory Norms of General International Law (jus cogens): Making Wine from Water or More Water than Wine' (2020) 89 *Nordic Journal of International Law* 244, 256–57.

[43] H Charlesworth and C Chinkin, 'The Gender of Jus Cogens' (1993) 15 *Human Rights Quarterly* 63, 66 ('The "most essential" human rights are considered part of the jus cogens.').

[44] ibid, citing G Christenson, 'Jus Cogens: Guarding Interests Fundamental to International Society' (1998) 28 *Virginia Journal of International Law* 585, 587.

[45] Charlesworth and Chinkin (n 43) 66, citing U Scheuner, 'Conflict of Treaty Provisions with a Peremptory Norm of General International Law and its Consequences' (1967) 27 *Zeitschrift Fur Auslandisches Offentliches Recht und Volkerrecht* 520, 524.

[46] J Paust, 'The Reality of Jus Cogens' (1991) 7 *Connecticut Journal of International Law* 81, 85.

[47] See Fourth Report of the Special Rapporteur on Peremptory Norms of General International Law (Jus Cogens) (Dire Tladi) (A/CN.4/727) (2019), para. 122 [hereinafter, 'Fourth Report'].

[48] See ibid., paras 62–121. For a critique of the methodology used to assess the *jus cogens* status of each norm, please refer to MH Hansel, '"Magic" or Smoke and Mirrors? The Gendered Illusion of Jus Cogens' in D Tladi (ed), *Peremptory Norms of General International Law (Jus Cogens): Disquisitions And Disputations* (Brill, 2021).

[49] ILC Plenary Report, Annex. As of December 2020, states are in the process of submitting comments on this report prior to its finalisation. See Resolution adopted by the General Assembly on 15 December 2020, A/RES/75/135, para 6.

rigorous and influential *jus cogens* identifications to date; therefore, this chapter relies on them as a point of reference in examining the temporal dimensions of such identifications.

The ILC reports delineate three categories of norms: those with confirmed *jus cogens* status (the 'confirmed norms'), those that may be candidates for but have unconfirmed *jus cogens* status (the 'candidate norms') and those that have decidedly not attained *jus cogens* status (the 'excluded norms'). The confirmed norms are: the prohibition of aggression or aggressive force, the prohibition of genocide, the basic rules of international humanitarian law, the prohibition of crimes against humanity, the prohibition of torture, the prohibition of slavery, the right to self-determination and the prohibition of apartheid.[50] The candidate norms are: the prohibition of enforced disappearances, the principle of non-refoulement, the right to life, the prohibition against arbitrary arrest, the right to due process and the prohibition of terrorism.[51] The excluded norms are: the prohibition of gender discrimination (and seemingly the general principle of non-discrimination) and the duty to protect the environment.[52] Although the lists of confirmed and candidate norms are non-exhaustive, the reports make clear that the excluded norms are not viable candidates for *jus cogens* status.[53]

B. The Time of *Jus Cogens*

The ILC's authoritative *jus cogens* determinations conform to the crisis model and reflect the emergency time that underpins the model. Each of the confirmed and candidate norms address or relate to a discrete urgency – what slow death scholars have referred to as 'a spectacular, immediately sensational, and instantly hypervisible image of what constitutes a violent threat'.[54] Further, the construction of these norms underscore their crisis-driven nature. Meanwhile, the excluded norms do not address issues deemed to require immediate attention. The doctrine's prioritisation of crisis obscures and marginalises quotidian issues, including ESC rights and feminist priorities not operating on emergency time.

The majority of the norms recognised by the ILC, as either confirmed or candidate *jus cogens* norms, directly relate to crisis. These include the prohibition of aggression or aggressive force, the prohibition of genocide, the basic rules of international humanitarian law, the prohibition of terrorism, the prohibition of

[50] Fourth Report, para 137. The Fourth Report explains that the prohibition of apartheid subsumes the prohibition of racial discrimination but only insofar as the latter rises to the level of apartheid. Ibid, para 91. Presumably, systemic racial discrimination that does not amount to apartheid does not qualify for *jus cogens* status.

[51] ibid, paras 122–34.

[52] ibid, para 134.

[53] ibid, paras 122, 137.

[54] Nixon (n 38) 13.

crimes against humanity, the prohibition of torture, prohibition of slavery, the prohibition of apartheid, the prohibition of enforced disappearances, the principle of non-refoulement and the right to life. As a facial matter, these norms address various international human rights crises (including genocide, armed conflict, acts of terrorism).[55] Underscoring their linkage to crisis, each of these norms also constitutes a rule of international criminal law. As Starr explains, '[i]nternational criminal law is broadly seen as a mechanism for responding to crises that threaten international security – specifically, mass atrocity and war'.[56] Indeed, the crime of aggression; the crime of genocide; war crimes in violation of international humanitarian law, which subsume acts of terrorism;[57] and crimes against humanity comprise the list of crimes over which the International Criminal Court has jurisdiction.[58] Further, crimes against humanity are defined by certain enumerated acts that rise to the level of a crime against humanity 'when committed as part of a widespread or systematic attack directed against any civilian population, with knowledge of the attack'.[59] Such enumerated acts include those prohibited by many of the other *jus cogens* norms: torture, slavery, apartheid, enforced disappearances, refoulement and murder and extermination (in violation of the right to life).[60]

The remaining confirmed and candidate norms identified by the ILC primarily relate to civil and political rights, which, as explained above, are prioritised within the crisis model. The prohibition against arbitrary arrest, the right to due process and the right to self-determination are all rights enshrined in the ICCPR (in Articles 9, 14 and 1, respectively).[61] Notably, several of the norms linked to crisis are also linked to civil and political rights and contained in the ICCPR. For example, the prohibition of torture is set forth in Article 7; the prohibition of slavery is set forth in Article 8; the right to life is set forth in Article 6; and, although not a discrete 'right' per se, the prohibition of apartheid finds footing in Article 26.[62]

[55] Due to spatial constraints, this chapter does not detail the connection between each of these norms and crisis; however, these connections are apparent from the general subject matter of the norms.

[56] Starr (n 28) 1260–1271 'Taking into account the ad hoc and hybrid tribunals (whose jurisdiction limits them to specific crises), the overall picture is stark: out of many hundreds of prosecutions brought in eight international or hybrid criminal tribunals, including thousands of charges, nobody has ever been charged with a crime unconnected to a crisis, and it does not look like it will happen soon' ibid 1271. Their criminal nature also reflects the crisis model's focus on individual responsibility at the expense of systemic reforms. See Otto (n 14) 129.

[57] UN General Assembly, Rome Statute of the International Criminal Court (last amended 2010), 17 July 1998 [hereinafter, 'Rome Statute'], art 8(2)(b), (e). The crisis-driven nature of the prohibition of terrorism is beyond dispute, particularly in light of the paradigmatic terrorist crisis of 9/11. See Otto (n 11) 78 (The language of "crisis" has become ubiquitous in international law and politics. Rising to a crescendo with the 9/11 crisis of international terror, "emergencies" now dominate global intercourse.').

[58] Rome Statute, art 5.

[59] ibid, art 7.

[60] ibid.

[61] ICCPR, arts 1, 9, 14.

[62] ibid, arts 6–8, 26. Article 26 of the ICCPR provides: 'All persons are equal before the law and are entitled without any discrimination to the equal protection of the law. In this respect, the law

As the ILC's norm identifications prioritise crisis and civil and political rights, they marginalise quotidian issues, ESC rights and many feminist priorities. Although a few of the confirmed and candidate norms may reflect quotidian issues (the right to due process, for example), the rights that make up the fabric of everyday life are conspicuously absent from *jus cogens* consideration. Not one of the confirmed or candidate norms is (exclusively[63]) an ESC right. The only norm mentioned that is primarily considered to be an ESC right is the duty to protect the environment, and the ILC reports expressly exclude this norm from *jus cogens* status. Likewise, the prohibition of gender discrimination, a norm reflecting feminist priorities, is also expressly excluded from *jus cogens* status.

Not only are norms linked to quotidian issues largely omitted from *jus cogens* recognition but also such issues are omitted from how recognised *jus cogens* norms are conceptualised. The ILC construes the confirmed norms narrowly – as discrete crises. This construction is apparent from the evidence set forth in support of each norm's *jus cogens* status. The evidence only includes items that involve paradigmatic, crisis-driven understandings of each norm. The reports include minimal evidence reflecting quotidian issues. For example, the evidence for the prohibition of torture does not include judicial decisions or scholarly works establishing that state failures to prevent and redress domestic violence may amount to torture.[64] *Jus cogens* norms are understood through the narrow lens of crisis.

The identification and construction of *jus cogens* norms are governed by the emergency time that pervades the discipline and underpins the crisis model. In turn, crisis-driven norms are prioritised, while norms that implicate more enduring issues are relegated to the margins. The ILC's recognition of *jus cogens* norms is consistent with the crisis model of international human rights: The norms are crisis-driven or reflect civil and political rights, at the expense of quotidian issues, ESC rights and many feminist priorities. Disrupting the crisis model calls for the invocation of alternative temporal approaches, explored in the next section.

IV. ALTERNATIVE TEMPORAL APPROACHES TO INFORM *JUS COGENS*

To counter the temporal bias of *jus cogens*, this section presents alternative temporal approaches from the feminist literary arena. (Invoking feminist temporalities is particularly appropriate given the gendered nature of *jus* cogens identifications and the crisis model.) Monikered the 'Four Rs', these approaches

shall prohibit any discrimination and guarantee to all persons equal and effective protection against discrimination on any ground such as race, colour, sex, language, religion, political or other opinion, national or social origin, property, birth or other status.'

[63] The right to self-determination is set forth in art 1 of the ICESCR, as well as art 1 of the ICCPR.

[64] See Fourth Report, paras 69–77. Similarly, '[a]lthough crimes against humanity and genocide can be committed outside armed conflict, they are often lumped, at least rhetorically, into the category of "war crimes"'. Starr (n 28) 1268.

are the times of Regression, Redemption, Rupture and Repetition. This section sets forth brief summaries of the Four Rs and then focuses on Time as Repetition as an approach that could subvert the crisis model and correct the temporal bias of *jus cogens*. The application of this temporality would yield a set of *jus cogens* norms untethered from crisis and linked instead to systemic, quotidian issues.

A. The 'Four Rs' of Feminist Time

The Four Rs were coined by Rita Felski in the context of literary scholarship and provide a useful distillation of the predominant feminist temporal approaches.[65] All of these temporalities stand in contrast to the emergency time characterising the crisis model. Thus, as my prior work demonstrates, these approaches have broad relevance across international law.[66] The following summaries of the Four Rs provide context for the introduction and application of Time as Repetition.[67]

Time as Regression. Time as Regression looks to and finds value in the past.[68] Indeed, '[a]n attachment to the past can throw critical light on the present, allowing us to question the smugness of the now and the sovereignty of the new'.[69] The past serves not only as a cause or precursor to the present, but also as its latency, its potential for being otherwise.[70] According to Elizabeth Grosz, an examination of the past is invaluable to the creation of a future in which women's experiences are included and feminist goals are actualised.[71] Applied to the crisis model, Time as Regression would promote a more retrospective approach and greater consideration of root causes, including systemic inequalities, that precede the eruption of a crisis.[72]

Time as Redemption. The temporality of redemption is forward looking, hopeful about the future and marked by a sense of progress. 'Progress', here, refers to the divergence of expectation from experience and the possible emergence of improved conditions, rather than the connotations of 'teleology, historical evolution, meta-narratives, and the ideological baggage of Western claims to supremacy'.[73] A sense of progress is inherent in much of feminist thought;[74] feminism itself is a long-term, interconnected project with

[65] See R Felski, 'Telling Time in Feminist Theory' (2002) 21 *Tulsa Studies in Women's Literature* 21.
[66] See eg Hansel (n 4) 379–98.
[67] For further expansion and detail of these four temporal approaches, please refer to Hansel (n 4).
[68] Felski (n 65) 24.
[69] ibid 25.
[70] E Grosz, 'Histories of a Feminist Future' (2000) 25 *Signs* 1017, 1018–20.
[71] ibid.
[72] Hansel (n 29) 136–37.
[73] Felski (n 65) 22–23.
[74] '[A]s a project that acts on the present in order to enact a different future, feminism necessarily operates in a different temporality from that of the nation.' V Hesford and L Diedrich, *Feminist Time Against Nation Time: Gender, Politics, and the Nation-State in an Age of Permanent War* (Lexington Books, 2008) 9.

an aspirational future.[75] As Felski states, 'as a social movement and political philosophy, feminism constantly gestures toward the future. It crafts plans and projects, offers prescription and policy'.[76] In the crisis model, Time as Redemption would urge international human rights to craft such forward-looking plans and policies, focusing on the long term rather than the next crisis.[77]

Time as Rupture. Time as Rupture 'is an attempt to imagine the new outside of teleology, stripped of all evolutionary or gradualist garb'.[78] This is a temporality of disruption, disjointedness, post-structuralism.[79] It stands out from the other 'Rs' in its suspicion of narratives claiming to be continuous and coherent, and stems from a deep-seated frustration with the status quo and the present.[80] Proponents of Time as Rupture contend that actualising feminine difference requires temporal alterity, a radical departure from existing notions of time.[81] Time of Rupture creates space for feminism to seek out imaginary horizons for itself, beyond mere extrapolation from the past and present.[82] Applied to the crisis model, Time as Rupture might support Dianne Otto's 'counter-crisis strategy' to 'question the certainties of the crisis paradigm and explore possibilities for disrupting the neoliberal agendas that are being served'.[83]

Time as Repetition. The final temporality, Time as Repetition, is cyclical and infinitely recurrent. The feminist roots of this approach are manifold. Julia Kristeva's innovative work *Women's Time* links feminine subjectivity to the eternal repetition of cyclical time, positing that this temporality derives from bodily rhythms.[84] Kristeva explains that 'there are cycles, gestation, and the eternal recurrence of a biological rhythm which conforms to that of nature and imposes a temporality whose stereotyping may shock, but whose regularity and unison with what is experienced as extra-subjective time, cosmic time, occasion vertiginous visions and unnamable *jouissance*'.[85] A long line of feminist theorists have reiterated the connection between temporal cycles and physiological rhythms.[86] Time as Repetition has also been associated with women's traditional roles in society.[87] Because, for the most part, women have been traditionally relegated to the home and repetitive chores of quotidian life, '[r]epetition is linked to the

[75] See eg Felski (n 65) 21–22.
[76] ibid 23.
[77] Hansel (n 4) 385.
[78] Felski (n 65) 26.
[79] ibid.
[80] ibid.
[81] See ibid.
[82] See Hesford and Diedrich (n 74) 10; E Grosz, *Time Travels: Feminism, Nature, Power* (Duke University Press, 2005) 73–74.
[83] Otto (n 14) 131.
[84] J Kristeva, 'Women's Time' in *The Kristeva Reader* (Columbia University Press, 1986) 191.
[85] ibid.
[86] Felski (n 65) 25–26.
[87] ibid 26.

everyday, and the everyday to women'.[88] This linkage has been identified as both a problem and source of strength in feminist literature. Simone de Beauvoir, for example, lamented the fact that women have often been trapped in domestic monotony, unable to create, invent or break out of the grip of endless cyclical time.[89] In contrast to the mundane, rote existence de Beauvoir describes, Felski points out that innovation and creativity can actually stem from the routines of everyday life.[90] For repetition is necessary to shore up identity and is used to organise the world and stave off chaos.[91] As Felski explains, '[q]uite simply, we become who we are through acts of repetition'.[92]

Repetition and cyclical time do not preclude the possibility of gradual change, movement or historical time.[93] Time as Repetition is iterative and supports the notion of evolution, advancement and reform. This temporality is applied in the next section to counter the temporal bias of *jus cogens* and its marginalisation of systemic, quotidian issues.

B. Time as Repetition Applied to *Jus Cogens*

Applied in the context of *jus cogens*, Time as Repetition would reorient the doctrine's crisis focus and support the promotion of norms that reflect everyday human rights concerns. This approach would supplant, or at least supplement, emergency time. As a result, the identification and construction of *jus cogens* norms would prioritise quotidian issues.

Indeed, Time as Repetition would prompt recognition of norms addressing quotidian issues, in lieu of crises. Accordingly, *jus cogens* norms would include those linked to ESC rights and everyday feminist priorities, rather than only international crimes and civil and political rights. For example, the two norms that the ILC excludes from *jus cogens* status, the prohibition of gender discrimination and the duty to protect the environment, could be recognised as *jus cogens*.[94] Additional rights that may be prioritised in this way include the right to family;[95] the right to an adequate standard of living, including adequate food, clothing and housing;[96] the right to health;[97] and the right to education,[98] given that they are ESC rights with profound gendered impacts.[99]

[88] ibid 25.
[89] ibid; S de Beauvoir, *The Second Sex* (Picador, 1988) 610.
[90] Felski (n 65) 26.
[91] R Felski, *Doing Time: Feminist Theory and Postmodern Culture* (New York University Press, 2000) 84.
[92] ibid.
[93] ibid.
[94] The general principle of non-discrimination may also be recognised as *jus cogens*.
[95] See ICESCR, art 10.
[96] See ibid, art 11.
[97] See ibid, art 12.
[98] See ibid, art 13.
[99] As Bruno Simma and Philip Alston have said of *jus cogens*, 'it must be asked whether any theory of human rights law which singles out race but not gender discrimination, which condemns

Moreover, the application of a Time as Repetition approach would broaden the construction of each *jus cogens* norm. The ILC's compilations of evidence in support of each norm is telling: They seem to only include evidentiary items that involve paradigmatic, crisis-driven understandings of each norm. Application of this new temporality would compel understandings of the recognised norms that include everyday human rights issues. In effect, everyday issues would be better mainstreamed throughout norm constructions. For example, state failures to prevent and redress domestic violence might be recognised as paradigmatic violations of the prohibition of torture. Various sources of international law have found that such failures may amount to torture, yet, as noted above, the ILC does not acknowledge these sources in its evidentiary compilations.[100] If these failures were broadly understood as torture, they might be higher on the international legal agenda as violations of *jus cogens* norms.

It might be argued that Time as Repetition lends support for the ILC's current approach to *jus cogens* identification, which is grounded in positivism. Positivism is 'the idea that the rules constituting international law flow from particular sources of law such as treaties or customary international law, and that these sources provide the content of international law regardless of their moral or ethical content'.[101] Pursuant to a positivist approach to *jus cogens*, the doctrine reflects and recapitulates existing state practice and preferences, thereby adhering to a kind of cyclical temporality. As noted above, however, Time as Repetition is iterative and would move *jus cogens* toward greater inclusivity and likely away from a positivist approach.

In sum, the Four Rs offer alternative temporalities to inform and complicate *jus cogens*. Time as Repetition, in particular, would offset the crisis model and its observance of emergency time, such that *jus cogens* norms would include those linked to systemic, quotidian issues. Norms reflecting ESC rights and many feminist priorities could attain *jus cogens* status and the construction of existing *jus cogens* norms would highlight everyday issues. Ultimately, *jus cogens* recognition would not be limited to and driven by crisis.[102]

arbitrary imprisonment but not death by starvation, and which finds no place for a right of access to primary health care is not flawed in terms both of the theory of human rights and of United Nations doctrine'. B Simma and P Alston, 'The Sources of Human Rights Law: Custom, Jus Cogens and General Principles' (1992) 12 *Australian Year Book of International Law* 82, 94.

[100] See eg UN Committee Against Torture, General Comment No. 2, para 18; *Opuz v Turkey*, Application no. 33401/02, Council of Europe: European Court of Human Rights, 9 June 2009; R Copelon, 'Recognizing the Egregious in the Everyday: Domestic Violence As Torture' (1994) 25 *Columbia Human. Rights Law Review* 291, 296 (arguing that 'when stripped of privatization, sexism and sentimentality, private gender-based violence is no less grave than other forms of inhumane and subordinating official violence that have been prohibited by treaty and customary law and recognized by the international community as *jus cogens*, or peremptory norms.').

[101] J David Ohlin, 'In Praise of Jus Cogens' Conceptual Incoherence' (2018) 63 *McGill Law Journal* 701, citing MV Totaro, 'Legal Positivism, Constructivism, and International Human Rights Law: The Case of Participatory Development' (2008) 48 *Virginia Journal of International Law* 719.

[102] Prioritisation of everyday issues is also consistent with TWAIL critiques. See eg L Eslava and S Pahuja, 'Beyond the (Post)Colonial: TWAIL and the Everyday Life of International Law' (2012)

V. CONCLUSION

By definition, *jus cogens* norms are non-derogable and thus, in a sense, immune to crisis. Paradoxically, however, they are governed by the emergency time that pervades international human rights and fuels the crisis model. Indeed, *jus cogens* identification appears to be underpinned by this temporal scheme, as the norms that have achieved such status are directly linked to crisis.[103] Alternate, feminist temporalities, particularly Time as Repetition, could inform the doctrine such that norms reflecting everyday issues would be recognised as *jus cogens*. Accordingly, ESC rights and feminist priorities could be elevated to *jus cogens* status. Further, pursuant to Time as Repetition, the quotidian dimensions of each *jus cogens* norm would be included in each norm's construction.

Teasing out and questioning the temporal assumptions on which international human rights law is predicated (as well as rejecting notions of temporal secularism) is a critical project in ensuring that systemic, quotidian issues are not marginalised by crisis. As one slow death scholar has explained, 'I feel like our opponents own time .... And when we give into their timelines, we lose.'[104] Time can be used to disempower and disenfranchise[105] – and also for emancipatory ends. This chapter invites further examination of the temporal foundations of international human rights and further exploration of the approaches set forth above.

Verfassung und Recht in Übersee VRÜ 45, 217 ('[I]nternational law should be understood as a field of material practice. Approaching international law in this way implies the examination and contestation of sites, procedures, artefacts and forms of being that operate at the mundane and quotidian level and that tie together a vast raft of heterogeneous phenomena in a specific kind of way.').

[103] Although this chapter focuses on the temporal underpinnings of norm identification and construction, there are other temporal aspects of *jus cogens* deserving of exploration. William Conklin has raised a few examples of these temporal aspects by asking, 'Since the weight of time seems to be a relevant factor, how many years or months must transpire before a sense of obligation and state behaviour manifest a peremptory norm? If a peremptory norm may lose its weightiness through calendar time, why is it described as peremptory?' WE Conklin, 'The Peremptory Norms of the International Community' (2012) 23 *European Journal of International Law* 837, 841.

[104] C Ahmann, '"It's Exhausting to Create an Event Out of Nothing": Slow Violence and the Manipulation of Time' (2018) 33 *Cultural Anthropology* 142, 146.

[105] Michel Foucault has explained how power is '"articulated directly onto time," thereby making time a useful method of subjugation.' M Olmsted, 'Are Things Falling Apart? Rethinking the Purpose and Function of International Law' (2005) 27 *Loyola L.A. International & Comparative Law Review* 401, 419–21, quoting M Foucault, *Discipline and Punish* (Penguin Books, 1977) 160.

11

Human Rights Futures

PAUL O'CONNELL

I. INTRODUCTION

OURS IS THE age of human rights.[1] Conventional wisdom has it that this age was inaugurated with the adoption of the Universal Declaration of Human Rights (UDHR), although recent historical accounts have cast doubt on this neat narrative.[2] Whichever account one finds most persuasive about the historical origins of human rights, it is indisputable that the language of human rights is pervasive today.[3] The proliferation of human rights treaties, both international and regional, since 1948 (and particularly from the mid-1960s onwards) has seen the growth of international, regional and national monitoring bodies as well as human rights non-governmental organisations (NGOs). Another way of putting this, is to say that now is the time of human rights. But, of course, time and temporality are not singular. The macro-temporality of human rights, evinced in the core texts of the international human rights regimes and competing scholarly accounts, is shaped by competing narratives about the past, present and future of human rights, and how these intersect with each other. Dominant accounts stress a progressive movement through stages, from a neglectful past, through an improved present and on to a brighter human rights future. Some contemporary scholars have even marshalled a body of data to provide evidence for hope in this promised human rights future.[4]

[1] N Bobbio, *The Age of Rights* (Polity, 1995).

[2] S Moyn, *The Last Utopia* (Harvard University Press, 2010); S-L Hoffmann, 'Introduction: Genealogies of Human Rights' in Hoffmann (ed), *Human Rights in the Twentieth Century* (CUP, 2011) 1; C McCrudden, 'Human Rights Histories' (2015) 35(1) *Oxford Journal of Legal Studies* 179; S-L Hoffmann, 'Human Rights and History' (2016) 232 *Past and Present* 279; L Hunt, 'The Long and the Short of the History of Human Rights' (2016) 232 *Past and Present* 323.

[3] As Sen puts it, the 'rhetoric of human rights is omnipresent in the contemporary world'. A Sen. 'The Global Reach of Human Rights' (2012) 29 *Journal of Applied Philosophy* 91, 91.

[4] K Sikkink, *Evidence for Hope* (Princeton University Press 2017); G Dancy and K Sikkink, 'Human Rights Data, Processes, and Outcomes: How Recent Research Points to a Better Future' in S Hopgood, J Snyder and L Vinjamuri (eds), *Human Rights Futures* (CUP, 2017) 24; A Brysk, *The Future of Human Rights* (Polity, 2018).

The aim of this chapter is to contest this rosy narrative, and to posit, instead, an understanding of the temporality of human rights which points towards a likely grim future, unless serious, radical and sustained remedial action is taken. To begin with, section II situates discussions of the time and temporality of human rights within the broader, overarching regulative framework of capitalism. While there are multiple times and temporalities of human rights, it will be argued here that these are fundamentally shaped by the deeper laws of motion of capital accumulation, and that the past, present and future are not infinitely open, but, rather, constrained by concrete regulative tendencies that are characteristic of the capitalist mode of production. Having established the importance of situating discussions of the times and temporality of human rights within a broader understanding of capitalism, section III then looks at the dominant narratives on human rights, focussing in particular on the optimistic accounts of a hopeful human rights future. In this regard it is argued that the optimism is, in large part, a product of not understanding the ways in which capitalism regulates and constrains social life in general, and human rights in particular. Section IV then sets out a picture of the likely future of human rights, informed by an emphasis on the role of capitalism, and argues that the dynamics of capital accumulation and development point towards a particularly stark human rights future, unless a serious politics of rupture is able to disrupt the extant order.

II. CAPITAL, TIME AND TEMPORALITY

With the advent of Judeo-Christian modernity, and its subsequent generalisation via the aegis of Western colonialism and imperialism, it has been commonplace to view the movement of time as linear.[5] In due course this common sense has been contested, as both time and temporality have been problematised, and the comforting idea of a straight line has been displaced by competing accounts of the overlapping, recursive, and uneven temporalities of social life.[6] The opening up of an emergent vista of multiple temporalities invites us to consider how 'past, present and future relate to one another, for instance through repetition and cyclical temporalities or ruptured and discontinuous temporalities, and through experiences and expectations'.[7] Temporality, in this context, can be 'described as a form of experience and thought among historical actors, and it can be applied as a category of analysis through which the historian today understands certain developments in the past',[8] as well as the present and future.

[5] V Morfino and P Thomas, 'Introduction: *Tempora multa*' in V Morfino and P Thomas (eds), *The Government of Time: Theories of Plural Temporality in the Marxist Tradition* (Brill, 2018) 1, 3–9.

[6] See P Pierson, *Politics in Time: History, Institutions and Social Analysis* (Princeton University Press, 2004); E Grosz, *Time Travels: Feminism, Nature, Power* (Duke University Press, 2005).

[7] V Ogle, 'Time, Temporality and the History of Capitalism' (2019) 243 *Past and Present* 312, 314.

[8] ibid 314–15.

This opening up of the temporal frame is important, because it disrupts convenient historical narratives, unsettles perceptions of a staid present, and opens the horizon to myriad possible futures. The conceptual shift around temporality has, potentially, important implications for how we think about any number of discrete issues, from environmental change, through changing relations of racialised and gendered oppression, through to human rights. One implication of breaking with static, linear temporality is to reopen debates about our understandings of history, and of potential futures – in this sense the turn to time and temporality can re-cast the social world as radically open, capable of producing any number of possible futures, out of shifting and contested pasts and presents.

This impulse, however, needs to be tempered. Certainly, breaking with linear notions of progress or teleology is valuable for revealing alternative accounts of past, present and future, but it does not follow that this theoretical rupture means that anything and everything is possible. The great value of the insight that what 'happened in history was never a necessary outcome', has to be complemented with an understanding that 'at least retrospectively, we can identify logics of political and economic power which drove particular processes, which proscribed some outcomes and made others possible'.[9] As such, a materialist understanding of temporality is crucially important – in particular, an account which situates the myriad temporal horizons within the overall context of the capitalist mode of production, with its attendant laws of motion. With regard to this, Harry Harootunian makes the crucial point that capitalism is 'the temporal dominant of modern society'.[10] As such, the capitalist mode of production, according to István Mészáros, has an 'inexorable tendency toward an all-embracing, structurally embedded determination of all aspects of societal reproduction'.[11]

While making no claims to linearity, and accepting entirely that myriad, complex and overlapping temporalities are, indeed, a truer reflection of reality, capitalism remains as the metronome in the background, conditioning and shaping all of these possible temporalities at a fundamental and decisive level.[12] Harootunian draws out the implications of this point well when he observes that,

> capitalism itself is, among other things, an immense conceptual organization of time that seeks to regulate and thus dominate a system of 'social metabolic' control capable

[9] B Dunn, *Global Political Economy* (Pluto, 2009) 5.

[10] H Harootunian, *Marx After Marx* (Columbia University Press, 2015) 22.

[11] I Mészáros, *Social Structures and Forms of Consciousness: Volume II* (Monthly Review Press, 2011) 9.

[12] This point is made, in a roundabout way, by Marx in the *Grundrisse*, where he notes that while production, exchange and distribution are notionally distinct and temporally consecutive, they are, in fact, intimately connected and coterminous, with the imperative of valorising capital providing 'a general illumination' which colours all of these distinct instances: K Marx, *Grundrisse* (Penguin, 1993) 94–107; see also S Tombazos, *Time in Marx: The Categories of Time in Marx's Capital* (Brill, 2014).

> of penetrating every aspect of society ... this view matches precisely the contemporary experience of capitalism as an all-encompassing temporal rhythmology dedicated to ordering the differing tempos of time with an unrelenting and inescapable circularity, which, accordingly, has truncated history itself, if not bracketing it altogether, and appears now to constitute the exclusive material of the construction of life.[13]

It is crucially important to grasp this point. The capitalist mode of production, which prevails at a global level, instantiates a particular temporality of its own. This, in turn, shapes our understandings of time and temporality, and, importantly, sets firm limits on alternative accounts.

Or, to put it slightly differently, while we may conceive of different temporal arcs, capitalism and the social-metabolic relations of capital accumulation, set firm, material limits on what, in fact, is possible. This perspective does not entail the re-imposition of 'iron laws' of history or of crude determinism,[14] rather it is about understanding the firm, material limits that capitalism as a mode of production and system of social metabolic reproduction,[15] imposes on us. The point is well made by Anwar Shaikh, who notes that,

> the capitalist economic system generates powerful ordered patterns that transcend historical and regional particularities, the forces that shape these patterns are neither steely rails nor mere constellations of circumstance. They are, rather, moving limits whose gradients define what is easy and what is difficult at any moment of time. In this way they channel the temporal paths of key economic variables. Indeed, these shaping forces are themselves the results of certain immanent imperatives ... It is not a matter of contrasting ahistorical laws to historically contingent outcomes. Agency and law coexist within a multidimensional structure of influences. But this structure is itself deeply hierarchical, with some forces (such as the profit motive) being far more powerful than others.[16]

Contesting the hitherto dominant narrative of linear time and static temporalities is important, but while this theoretical leap can be productive, it is fundamentally bounded by imperatives imposed by capitalism. This does not mean that alternative readings of the past and present, or alternative futures, are not possible, but simply that in framing and constructing them we do not operate with an entirely free hand, under conditions of our own choosing.

[13] Harootunian (n 10) 22.

[14] See S Marks' useful discussion of the difference between determinism and determination: S Marks, 'False Contingency' (2009) 62 *Current Legal Problems* 1, 5–10.

[15] I Mészáros, *The Necessity of Social Control* (Monthly Review Press, 2015) 199–217.

[16] A Shaikh, *Capitalism: Competition, Conflict, Crises* (OUP, 2016) 5. Shaikh's argument echoes a similar stance advanced by Engels: 'in the real world ... metaphysically polar opposites exist only in a crisis ... instead the whole great process takes place solely and entirely in the form of interplay – if of very unequal forces of which the economic trend is by far the strongest, the oldest and the most vital'; F Engels, 'Letter to Conrad Schmidt, 27 October 1890' in *Marx-Engels Collected Works: Vol. 49* (Lawrence & Wishart, 2010) 57, 63.

As well as conditioning competing temporalities, capitalism articulates, by implication, its own temporal horizons. This is well captured by Marx, who, commenting on the intellectual 'prize fighters' of capitalism,[17] noted that,

> When the economists say that present-day relations – the relations of bourgeois production – are natural, they imply that these are the relations in which wealth is created and productive forces developed in conformity with the laws of nature. These relations therefore are themselves natural laws independent of the influence of time. They are eternal laws which must always govern society. Thus there has been history, but there is no longer any. There has been history, since there were the institutions of feudalism, and in these institutions of feudalism we find quite different relations of production from those of bourgeois society, which the economists try to pass off as natural and as such, eternal.[18]

The temporality of capitalism, then, is a bounded one. It is a temporality that, in Harootunian's words, annihilates history and posits the 'eternality of the present'.[19] In contrast to the radical openness of multiple temporalities, and hence multiple possible futures, the temporality of capitalism insists that there is no alternative to the recurrent present. This rendering of capitalism as not only the best of all possible worlds, but the only possible one, has serious implications for how we think about the possible futures of human rights, and it is to that which we no turn.

III. THE TIMES OF HUMAN RIGHTS

In contrast to the bounded temporality of capitalism, international human rights law proclaims, both explicitly, and by implication, a forward looking, progressive conception of time and temporality. Inscribed in the Preamble to the UDHR, the founding document of the international human rights regime, is the story of international human rights law reflecting a turning point from a barbarous past, to a better future in which human rights are the 'highest aspiration' and 'a common standard of achievement' which all peoples and nations will aspire to and work towards.[20] In a similar vein, the International Covenant on Economic, Social and Cultural Rights (ICESCR), one of the sister covenants which gave legal teeth to the aspirations of the UDHR, commits states to the progressive realisation of the rights enshrined in the treaty.[21] While the concept of progressive realisation has come in for much valid criticism, in the context

[17] K Marx, *Capital – Volume 1* (Penguin, 1990) 97.
[18] K Marx, 'The Poverty of Philosophy' in *Marx-Engels Collected Works: Vol. 6* (Lawrence & Wishart, 2010) 105, 174.
[19] Harootunian (n 10) 22.
[20] Universal Declaration of Human Right U.N. Doc A/810 (1948).
[21] International Covenant on Economic, Social and Cultural Rights U.N. Doc A/6316 (1966), art 2(1).

of the general neglect of socio-economic rights,[22] the general thrust of the obligation coheres with the overall perspective of the international human rights regime in being one that imagines, or assumes, a progressive, teleological development of human rights protection on a global scale.

This approach is of a piece with historical and sociological accounts of the development of human rights over time. Whether it is Micheline Ishay's charting of embryonic human rights norms and principles from antiquity, through millennia of human history, carried forward by 'human rights couriers over time'.[23] Or, as is more common, with Lynn Hunt's identification of human rights as emerging with the modern bourgeoisie in the eighteenth century, and progressing forward from there.[24] The British sociologist TH Marshall captures the general theme well, in his influential account of the expansion of citizenship, mirrored by a steady expansion in the protection of individual rights, starting with civil rights in the eighteenth century, political rights in the nineteenth and social rights in the twentieth century.[25] Cumulatively, all of this speaks to a dominant understanding of the story of human rights, which leans heavily on a progressive, forward moving teleology. This is summed up by Stephen Hopgood, Jack Snyder and Leslie Vinjamuri, who note that,

> The most influential narrative sees post-Enlightenment European revulsion with torture and slavery at the heart of a linear account of liberal progress, this 'revolution in moral sentiment' then globalized in the name of civilization through the vector of empire. Its culmination came in the period immediately following World War II and the Holocaust, when human rights were embedded through a series of bold institutional developments such as the Nuremberg trials, the Charter of the United Nations, the Universal Declaration of Human Rights, the Genocide Convention, and the revised Geneva Conventions.[26]

This dominant account illustrates well the 'definite' and 'dominant' progressive linearity which underpins international human rights law.[27]

However, in recent years this account has come under strain: with a spate of academics declaring the twilight, or endtimes of human rights.[28] Other accounts have problematised the standard history of human rights, and posited competing accounts which throw into question the linear progressive narrative about

[22] See K Young, 'Waiting for Rights: Progressive Realization and Lost Time' in K Young (ed), *The Future of Economic and Social Rights* (CUP, 2019) 654.

[23] M Ishay, *The History of Human Rights: From Ancient Times to the Globalization Era* (University of California Press, 2008) 2.

[24] L Hunt, *Inventing Human Rights* (WW Norton and Co, 2008).

[25] TH Marshall, *Citizenship and Social Class and Other Essays* (CUP, 1950) 14.

[26] S Hopgood, J Snyder and L Vinjamuri, 'Introduction: Human Rights Past, Present and Future' in S Hopgood, J Snyder and L Vinjamuri (eds), *Human Rights Futures* (CUP, 2017) 1, 5.

[27] K McNeilly, 'Are Rights Out of Time? International Human Rights Law, Temporality, and Radical Social Change' (2019) 28 *Social & Legal Studies* 817, 820.

[28] E Posner, *The Twilight of Human Rights* (OUP, 2014); S Hopgood, *The Endtimes of Human Rights* (Cornell University Press, 2013).

the development of international human rights law and practice.[29] In turn, these academic accounts find support in reports from international NGOs about a 'crisis in human rights',[30] which argue that, according to one set of metrics, human rights are being eroded in the majority of countries around the world today.[31] In contrast, then, to the forward looking and progressive view of international human rights law, there is now a substantial body of opinion which sees the future of human rights as 'much more one of ambivalence, ineffectiveness, failure and even irrelevance'.[32] Or, as Kathryn McNeilly puts it, there are strong arguments that international human rights law 'are out of time, that their time as an emancipatory vision for the future is up and that they are no longer the discourse of the moment that we are living in'.[33]

There has, of course, been pushback against this pessimistic account of human rights. Kathryn Sikkink has argued forcefully that 'we may have too much critique and despair at the moment and not enough hope, resilience, or belief that we can make a difference'.[34] To counter this, and to bolster the human rights project, Sikkink draws on a range of data sets to argue that there has been improvement in human rights protection across the world, by no means uniform or perfect, but clear and important.[35] As such, Sikkink argues that far from being in the endtimes of human rights, we are living through 'a period of vibrant dynamism in human rights movements, laws and institutions'.[36] Building on this, Geoff Dancy and Kathryn Sikkink state that,

> The future we foresee is one that involves continued fights over rights and heightened outrage at bloody and brazen acts of violence. Rent-seeking state leaders, militaristic warlords, and exclusionary nativists will continue to use violence, and will seek to evade accountability. They will issue threats, and they will challenge people's resolve. Meanwhile, networks of individuals, which will penetrate more and more deeply into unreached populations, will continue to resist abuses of power, will adapt the law and discourse of human rights to their advantage using innovative tactics, and will translate rights-based ideals into local practices. Political and economic rights issues will merge more closely together, and conditions will improve – slowly, and in fits and starts.[37]

[29] Moyn (n 2); J Whyte, *The Morals of the Market* (Verso, 2019). Although it should be noted that while these newer histories disrupt the neat consensus on the past(s) of human rights, they do not depart, as such, from a general idea of the linear progression of human rights.

[30] W Bordell and J Robbins, '"A Crisis in Human Rights": New Index Reveals Global Fall in Basic Justice' *The Guardian* (31 January 2018).

[31] World Justice Project, *Rule of Law Index 2017–2018* (World Justice Project, 2018) 5.

[32] Hopgood, Snyder and Vinjamuri (n 26) 2.

[33] McNeilly (n 27) 818.

[34] Sikkink (n 4) 226–27.

[35] ibid 181–221, 227–30.

[36] ibid 247.

[37] Dancy and Sikkink (n 4) 52.

For Sikkink, then, human rights are not out of time, rather the 'concept of human rights, though not infallible, has proven itself effective in the past. It should be trusted to continue to effect change into the future'.[38]

Alison Brysk advances a similar set of arguments, both building on and complementing the data sets and arguments that underpin Sikkink's *Evidence for Hope*. Brysk notes that human rights 'are poised on the knife's edge between hope and despair, beloved and beleaguered, inspiring and ignored'.[39] In view of the theoretical, empirical and political challenges to human rights, Brysk urges a doubling down on the human rights enterprise, as she puts it,

> This is not the end of the human rights journey; it is the beginning of a new stage, as we are bound together across stormy waters in a leaky, listing, but ultimately sound craft. This is no time to abandon ship – it is a time for 'all hands on deck' to navigate the storm and plot a new course. The way forward is dialectical, dynamic, and strategic. The future of human rights is to construct a practice of global citizenship in a troubled world.[40]

Thus, while acknowledging the myriad challenges and critiques human rights face at present, Brysk concludes that we 'can affirm that human rights remain the last best hope of the global order'.[41]

The approach of Sikkink and others takes on board the criticisms of human rights and the pessimism about the future of human rights but reasserts the progressive teleology of the international human rights regime, with some caveats. Others, such as Kathryn McNeilly, reject the pessimistic accounts, but from a different perspective. Unlike Sikkink, McNeilly does not ground her account in statistical models, nor does she purport to re-establish hope or certainty in the future of human rights. Rather, by problematising the idea of linear progression and introducing the idea of multiple times and temporalities of human rights, McNeilly argues, building on the work of Elizabeth Grosz, for an understanding of human rights as 'untimely'. In other words, an approach which does not see human rights subsumed within one, particular history, nor locked into a foreseeable future – whether a positive future, à la Sikkink, or one of the more pessimistic accounts. Instead, the future of human rights is 'unsettled and unknowable, capable of moving forwards, backwards or in another direction in response to contingent contexts'.[42] From this perspective, the 'future for rights … cannot be known',[43] which in turn is productive and potentially positive, because it leaves the future radically open to new possibilities. This approach does not reproduce the *Evidence for Hope* that Sikkink offers, but more modestly 'offers

[38] Sikkink (n 4) 230.
[39] Brysk (n 4) 2.
[40] ibid 16.
[41] ibid 96.
[42] McNeilly (n 27) 828.
[43] ibid.

hopeful possibility',[44] grounded in a non-linear understanding of the times and temporalities of international human rights.

Commenting on the 60th anniversary of the UDHR, Robert McCorquodale argued that notwithstanding the many limitations and setbacks of the international human rights system, one of the positive 'effects of the UDHR has been to include human rights in everyday discourse at local, national, regional and international levels' and that this, in turn, evidenced 'a pull towards human rights being recognized as relevant to daily life'.[45] McCorquodale's central contention is of course irrefutable, the language of human rights is pervasive today, and the optimistic tone that imbues McCorqudale's intervention chimes with the forward looking, optimistic, and linear (albeit with bumps in the road) account at the heart of dominant accounts of international human rights law. But as we have seen here, this is not the only account of the past, present and future of international human rights law. There are critical and pessimistic accounts which both contest the past and doubt the future of human rights, these in turn are contested by scholars and activists who acknowledge the shortcomings of the human rights enterprise, but insist that there is sufficient empirical evidence, and political reason, to insist on a positive future for international human rights. Others, still, argue that the future cannot be gainsaid, but there are a range of radical possibilities, which in turn can be a basis for pursuing and developing human rights claims and work.

Each of these approaches has some merit – critical accounts rightly burst the bubble of self-satisfaction often evident in the human rights industry, and the misplaced faith and assumptions that underpin dominant accounts of human rights, but Sikkink is also right that we need to 'move beyond' mere critique.[46] McNeilly offers one way of doing this, by positing a radical, progressive critique that does not rely on a promised future, but instead embraces the disruptive possibility of many possible human rights futures. In the next section, I will argue that while all of these accounts have something to offer, they also all share a crucial absence: namely an understanding of the place and role of capitalism, with its distinct temporal rhythm, in shaping the potential futures of human rights. As such, it will be argued that there is much truth in the critical accounts of human rights, but not for the reasons that the critics often focus on; further, Sikkink's *Evidence for Hope* is dependent on blindness to the deeper, structural dynamics of capitalism, and how they militate against the protection of human rights. It will also be argued that while there is much to recommend McNeilly's approach, it too fails to take account of the material processes and relationships that make some futures far more likely than others.

[44] ibid 830.

[45] R McCorquodale, 'A Future for Human Rights Law' in M Baderin and M Ssenyonjo (eds), *International Human Rights Law: Six Decades After the UDHR and Beyond* (Ashgate, 2010) 541, 552.

[46] Sikkink (n 4) 51.

IV. HUMAN RIGHTS FUTURES

The foregoing discussion demonstrates a fundamental tension at the heart of understandings about the temporality of human rights. The dominant discourse of international human rights law, and attendant scholarship, presumes and promises a brighter human rights future. In practice, however, this promised future is forever deferred – to borrow from Barbara Stark's discussion of international economic law and distributive justice, the promises of the international human rights regime are, much like the Queen's promises of jam in *Alice's Adventures in Wonderland*, forever deferred to tomorrow.[47] This gap between promise and reality provides fertile ground for myriad critiques of the past, present and future of human rights.[48] One problem, however, is that both champions and detractors of the human rights enterprise rarely pay attention to what Harootunian referred to as the 'temporal dominant' that shapes our social world, and conditions any possible future for human rights: capitalism.[49] As was argued above, capitalism has its own dominant temporality, one which erases the past and locks us into the inevitability of the recurrent, capitalist present. Crucially, the contradiction in differing accounts of the potential futures for human rights and the preeminent temporal drive of capitalism entail not merely duelling concepts, but rather contradictions that emerge from real, material relations.[50]

Economic inequality[51] is central to understanding the material basis for the gap between promise and reality in the field of human rights, and for the material basis of the temporal closure imposed by capitalism. In recent years the issue of inequality has gained increasing prominence, due to the work of Thomas Piketty and others.[52] So much so that we can now say that inequality will shape and 'inform all politics for the foreseeable future'.[53] In thinking about the potential futures of human rights, understanding how capitalism systematically produces inequality, how this systematicity is central to the temporality of capitalism as a recurrent (and inescapable) present and how this tendency towards generating and increasing inequalities fundamentally undermines the possibility of realising human rights, is absolutely central.

[47] B Stark, 'Jam Tomorrow: Distributive Justice and the Limits of International Economic Law' (2010) 30 *Boston College Third World Law Journal* 3.

[48] For McNeilly and others, this gap may provide the basis for some hopeful optimism about possible human rights futures: McNeilly (n 27).

[49] Harootunian (n 10) 22.

[50] Marx (n 12) 90.

[51] While there is much ongoing debate about inequality, its measurement, and its wider relationship to poverty, the term economic inequality will be used here to cover both inequality in terms of wealth and income share, and the broader picture of both relative and extreme poverty.

[52] T Piketty, *Capital in the Twenty-First Century* (Harvard University Press, 2013); B Milanovic *Global Inequality* (Harvard University Press, 2016).

[53] M Yates, *The Great Inequality* (Routledge, 2016) 4.

The first point to note is that economic inequality on a global scale has now reached alarming levels. A report published in 2020 by Credit Suisse shows that the top one per cent of the world's population now owns almost 50 per cent of the world's total wealth.[54] The charity Oxfam puts the same general picture in slightly different terms, noting that at present a mere 2,153 billionaires own more wealth than 4.6 billion people, and this general inequality further reinforces gendered and racialised vectors of inequality and marginalisation.[55] Thomas Piketty and his colleagues at the World Inequality Lab have reported, with the most comprehensive data set to date, that inequality has been rising in virtually every region and country across the world since the 1980s.[56] Although trends are moving at different speeds, this includes a general record of and tendency towards increasing inequality both within and between countries, attributable, for the authors, in large part to the demise of the post-World War II golden era/compromise between labour and capital.[57] The data supports the central claim of Piketty's much bought, but little read, book on inequality, and the general tendency (or law) which he identifies: namely that because returns on wealth always outstrip returns on annual income (r>g) inequality will tend, over time, to increase.[58] Indeed, a report published by the UK House of Commons in 2018 warned that, in light of current trends, the top one per cent of the world's population were on course to own as much as two-thirds of all global wealth by 2030.[59]

Notwithstanding the oft-repeated mantra of a rising tide raising all boats,[60] the available data instead speaks to an era – the halcyon days of globalisation – in which inequality has both been entrenched and increased over time.[61] This, of course, has serious implications for human rights.[62] As Asbjørn Eide noted some years ago, the 'most dramatic obstacle to the enjoyment of economic and social rights is the steep increase in income-specific inequality, both among nations and within nations, and the spread of poverty in the midst of plenty'.[63] What was

[54] Credit Suisse, *Global Wealth Report 2020* (October 2020) 25.

[55] Oxfam, *Time to Care: Unpaid and Underpaid Care Work and the Global Inequality Crisis* (Oxfam International, 2020).

[56] *World Inequality Report 2018* (World Inequality Lab, 2017) 9–15.

[57] ibid.

[58] Piketty (n 52).

[59] M Savage, 'Richest 1% on Target to Own Two-Thirds of All Wealth by 2030' *The Guardian* 7 April 2018).

[60] M Wolf, *Why Globalization Works* (Yale University Press, 2004); D Griswold, 'Globalization, Human Rights and Democracy' (*eJournal USA*, 11 August 2006).

[61] As Robinson and Baker note 'Capitalist globalization has resulted in unprecedented social polarization worldwide … just 1% of humanity [own] over half of the world's wealth and the top 20% own 94.5 of that wealth, while the remaining 80% had to make do with just 4.5% … What is more, this polarization continues to intensify'. W Robinson and Y Baker, 'Savage Inequalities: Capitalist Crises and Surplus Humanity' (2019) 9(3) *International Critical Thought* 376, 377.

[62] See the recent special issue of *Humanity*, edited by Brinks, Dehm and Engle: D Brinks, J Dehm and K Engle, 'Introduction: Human Rights and Economic Inequality' (2019) 10(3) *Humanity* 363.

[63] A Eide, 'Obstacles and Goals to Be Pursued' in A Eide, C Krause and A Rosas (eds), *Economic, Social and Cultural Rights: A Textbook*, 2nd edn (Martinus Nijhoff, 2001) 553, 555.

true of socio-economic rights for Eide, is equally true for the entire corpus of human rights, which are, in complex ways, hollowed out by conditions of deepening, structural inequality. As the former UN Special Rapporteur on Extreme Poverty and Human Rights, Philip Alston, put it 'extreme inequality and respect for the equal rights of all persons are incompatible'.[64] While Alston and many other human rights and liberal scholars focus on extreme inequality or extreme poverty it is in fact inequality and poverty per se that sap at the social and democratic foundations of any society, and the dynamics that generate inequality that undermine the possibility of human rights being advanced or enjoyed in any meaningful, sustainable sense.

Economic inequality, then, undermines the enjoyment of human rights – denying individuals, communities and in some instances whole nations the capacity to meet basic material needs, thus undermining the entire panoply of socio-economic rights. But inequality also threatens and undermines the foundations of civil and political rights. In the first instance, inequality does not impact abstract entities, but rather concrete individuals and social groups – more specifically inequality in capitalist society reflects and reinforces inequalities of class and class power. As Eric Schutz puts it, the 'real heart of the issue of inequality' is 'the problem of class.[65] Michael Yates picks up this theme and notes that,

> Inequality has its roots in unequal power. Those with more assets have more power than those who do not; that is, they can compel us to do what we would be unlikely to do otherwise. Here I do not mean the power of any particular person, although in a specific circumstance, this might be important. Critical is what is best-called class power.[66]

What Piketty almost comprehends but shies away from because of his pre-commitment to the postulates of neoclassical economics,[67] is that the tendency of wealth to outstrip income, and thus to generate inequality, is another way of saying that one class, the capitalist class of owners, grows richer at the expense of another, those who rely solely or primarily on income, namely workers and peasants. The growth of inequality within and between countries over the last forty years is a product not of some aberration within the extant global order, but of its normal and proper functioning.

In other words, the tendency towards increasing inequality, and in turn the tendency of such inequality to undermine and deny the realisation of human rights, is not an aberration, but rather the result of the dynamics of a properly functioning capitalist economic and social order. As Yates puts it,

> the essence of the capitalist system drives inequality. The default position of such a system is an unregulated drive to accumulate capital, and this accumulation cannot

[64] P Alston, *Report of the Special Rapporteur on Extreme Poverty and Human Rights*, Human Rights Council, Twenty-ninth session, Agenda item 3, A/HRC/29/31 (27 May 2015) para 48.
[65] E Schutz, *Inequality and Power: The Economics of Class* (Routledge, 2011) 1.
[66] Yates (n 53) 6.
[67] For a valuable critique of the conservatism of Piketty's project see S Kaufmann and I Stützle *Thomas Piketty's Capital in the Twenty-First Century: An Introduction* (Verso 2017).

> transpire without the exploitation of workers. If the working class is able to exert sufficient power, this exploitation can be mitigated. However, it, and the resulting inequality, cannot be eliminated unless capital's control is eliminated altogether.[68]

In similar terms, William Robinson and Yousef Baker, reflecting on the spiralling inequality produced by the era of capitalist globalisation, note that 'polarization is inherent to the capitalist system since capitalists own the means of producing wealth and therefore appropriate as profits as much wealth as possible that society collectively produces'.[69] Understanding that inequality poses a fundamental challenge to the enjoyment of human rights is crucial – understanding the systemic nature of that inequality even more so. Because it brings to the fore the fact that the violation of human rights results not just from this or that bad government or inadvisable policy, but rather from 'wider systemic processes, dynamics and institutions'.[70]

The structural antagonism between labour and capital, the motor-force of the capitalist mode of production, is the deep source of growing inequalities in the world today. With the ascent of neoliberalism from the late 1970s onwards, masquerading at different times under the banner of globalisation or the Washington Consensus, the limited compromises made between labour and capital in the wake of World War II have been displaced. In place of this limited compromise, we have had the restoration of an unadulterated version of the labour-capital relation,[71] this relationship is described well by Marx, who argued that,

> in proportion as capital accumulates, the lot of the labourer, be his payment high or low, must grow worse … It establishes an accumulation of misery, corresponding with accumulation of capital. Accumulation of wealth at one pole is, therefore, at the same time accumulation of misery, agony of toil slavery, ignorance, brutality, mental degradation, at the opposite pole, i.e., on the side of the class that produces its own product in the form of capital.[72]

The growing inequality characteristic of the last four decades is the inevitable product of a system of global capitalism, as capitalists and corporations extract as much value as they can from workers in their own countries. Alongside this, capital in core countries, through global value chains, exploit even more value from workers in the Global South, re-inscribing and sustaining relations of imperialism that are integral to capitalism in the contemporary world order.[73]

[68] Yates (n 53) 18.

[69] Robinson and Baker (n 61) 377.

[70] S Marks, 'Four Human Rights Myths' in D Kinley, W Sadurski and K Walton (eds), *Human Rights: Old Problems, New Possibilities* (Edward Elgar, 2013) 217, 231.

[71] Robinson and Baker (n 61); D Harvey, *A Brief History of Neoliberalism* (OUP, 2005); M Li, 'The End of the "End of History": The Structural Crisis of Capitalism and the Fate of Humanity' (2010) 74(3) *Science & Society* 290.

[72] Marx (n 17) 709.

[73] EM Wood, *Empire of Capital* (Verso, 2003); J Smith, *Imperialism in the Twenty-First Century* (Monthly Review Press, 2016); U Patnaik and P Patnaik, *A Theory of Imperialism* (Columbia University Press, 2017).

Of course there are other dynamics at play, and trade and tax policy could, in principle, mitigate to some extent the inequality producing tendencies of capitalist accumulation, but the social and political power of capital,[74] means that, for the most part, existing regimes serve to reinforce and legitimate the inequalities produced by the extant global order.[75]

Economic inequality, then, is integral to the system of global capitalism. It is part of the inevitable, recurrent present that characterises the temporal horizons of capitalist development. With respect to human rights, this facet of the capitalist system fundamentally undermines the possibility of human rights being enjoyed or advanced for the vast majority of the world's population. Economic inequality overlaps with poverty to deny people the basics of food, shelter, education, health care and safe, stable working conditions.[76] This material inequality is reinforced nationally and internationally by the social relations of inequality that it creates, hollowing out democracy and reducing democratic politics to an elite charade.[77] As Yates puts it, a 'nation with significant and growing inequality cannot be a democracy'.[78] While governments consistently fall short on their obligations to meaningfully tackle poverty and inequality, they 'continue to pour money into repressive practices and carceral systems, while depriving poor communities of basic rights such as decent healthcare, housing, and education'.[79]

This prioritising of mechanisms of control and discipline reinforces the concerns expressed by Robinson and Baker of the emergence and consolidation of a global police state, which they argue is characterised by three overlapping developments,

> First is the ever more omnipresent systems of mass social control, repression and warfare promoted by the ruling groups to contain the real and the potential rebellion of the global working class and surplus humanity. In this regard, global police state is centrally aimed at *coercive exclusion* of surplus humanity. Second is how the global economy is itself based more and more on the development and deployment of these systems of warfare, social control, and repression simply as a means of making profit and continuing to accumulate capital in the face of stagnation – what Robinson has termed *militarized accumulation*, or *accumulation by repression* – and that now goes well beyond military Keynesianism. And third is the increasing move towards political systems that can be characterized as twenty-first century fascism, or even in a broader sense, as totalitarian.[80]

[74] Robinson and Baker (n 61); Schutz (n 65).

[75] See Stark (n 47) and J Linarelli, M Salomon and M Sornarajah, *The Misery of International Law* (OUP, 2018).

[76] P Alston, *The Parlous State of Poverty Eradication: Report of the Special Rapporteur on Extreme Poverty and Human Rights*, Human Rights Council, Forty-fourth session, Agenda item 3 A/HRC/44/40 (3 July 2020).

[77] P Mair, *Ruling the Void* (Verso, 2007).

[78] Yates (n 53) 9.

[79] Alston (n 76) para 2.

[80] Robinson and Baker (n 61) 387.

In this way the systemic inequality produced by capitalism also undermines the entire catalogue of civil and political rights, by necessitating an expansion of the coercive capacity of states to police opposition to the extant order. But also, by creating the conditions that give rise to the very sorts of reactionary populism that so exercises liberal human rights defenders, and which they imagine emerged out of thin air with the election of Trump as US president in 2016.

On the issue of inequality and how it relates to human rights, Dancy and Sikkink make a telling observation when they argue that 'Economic and social conditions are imperfect and continue to be substandard for many people around the world, but they are generally improving across time and space, with the important exception of income inequality, which remains nearly constant over the last three decades'.[81] This view is, of course, at complete variance with the preponderance of available evidence, and with the inherent tendencies of global capitalism. Along similar lines Brysk argues that to advance human rights in the future 'we need systematically to embrace the contradictions of capitalism and embrace the role of business as defenders of rights that create positive conditions for their activities'.[82] Similar arguments have been advanced by David Kinley and others.[83] Such authors can envisage a potentially bright future for human rights, primarily because they do not understand the root causes of human rights violations in the contemporary global order. For these liberal proponents of human rights, capitalism is simply a given, and the challenge of human rights within that given is technical tweaks to ameliorate some of the worst excesses. This, however, surrenders any possible future to the Sisyphean task of earnestly pursuing the promise of jam tomorrow, while never grasping why it is that it never materialises.

Understanding the dynamics of capitalism and how it shapes the potential futures of human rights also casts a different light on the arguments of McNeilly and others. While it is absolutely right to pursue the radical possibilities of a very different future, and this indeed is central to developing any sort of emancipatory politics, it is essential to be aware that all such possibilities are fundamentally bounded. As Susan Marks rightly notes, while we should reject the false necessity of liberal complacency, we must also note 'the equally important progressive point that possibilities are framed by circumstances. While current arrangements can indeed be changed, change unfolds within a context that includes systematic constraints and pressures'.[84] As noted above, this is not about the imposition of deterministic, iron laws of history, but rather of understanding and taking cognisance of capitalism and how it both sets 'the outer limit of political possibility',[85] and ultimately makes some courses of development far more likely than others.[86]

[81] Dancy and Sikkink (n 4) 33.
[82] Brysk (n 4) 14.
[83] D Kinley, *Necessary Evil: How to Fix Finance By Saving Human Rights* (OUP, 2018).
[84] Marks (n 14) 2.
[85] T Eagleton, *Why Marx Was Right* (Yale University Press, 2011) 157.
[86] Dunn (n 9).

In this regard, the critical and pessimistic accounts of human rights and their likely future(s) would seem to be the more likely, but perhaps not for the reasons that many of the critics imagine. As things stand, the inequality engendered by global capitalism operates to fundamentally undermine the entire corpus of human rights. The global health pandemic occasioned by COVID-19, and the impending global depression will further exacerbate and reinforce these inequalities,[87] with all the attendant deleterious consequences for human development and flourishing. It is, however, crucial that 'the crisis we are living through should not be allowed to mask another that is infinitely more important'.[88] The tendencies that have hitherto sustained the chasm between the promise of human rights and the lived reality of billions around the world is not the result of COVID-19, nor is it the product of neoliberal capitalism, financial-ised capitalism, or any form of capitalism with prefix or euphemism. It is the deep rhythms of capitalism *as such*, along with its temporality of a recurrent, inevitable present, that has shaped the history of human rights and will be the determining force in shaping the future of human rights. As things stand, that future looks bleak.

V. CONCLUSION

In one of his many asides on time and temporality, Marx argued that it was for the revolutionaries of his age to write the poetry of the future.[89] The same can now be said for those committed to human development today – but in order to write the poetry of our future we must first understand cadence, meter and rhyme; in other words, we must understand how the 'temporal dominant' of our age, capitalism, works. This point is made forcefully by István Mészáros, who argues that,

> without understanding the true character of the hierarchically articulated structural determinations of capital's increasingly more destructive societal reproductive order, with its organic system in which the parts sustain the whole, and vice versa, in their now paralyzing circular reciprocity, there can be no significant improvement in the time still available to us.[90]

All possible futures of human rights are conditioned by the broader, determining role of capitalism and its attendant laws of motion. Capitalism systemically produces inequality that undermines the entire corpus of human rights, and on the current evidence the dynamics and relations of power of the contemporary global order do not portend a hopeful future for human rights.

[87] Alston (n 76).
[88] L Althusser, *On the Reproduction of Capitalism* (Verso, 2014) 15.
[89] K Marx, 'The Eighteenth Brumaire of Louis Bonaparte' in *Marx-Engels Collected Works Vol. 11* (Lawrence & Wishart, 2010) 90, 105.
[90] Mészáros (n 11) 14.

This, however, is not set in stone. There are other possible futures, but to realise any future that might be more promising for the protection of human rights will require understanding and reckoning with the systemic character of global capitalism, its temporality of a recurrent present alongside a future glimpsed but denied, and its rights denying tendencies. As Yates puts it 'attacking inequality will require nothing less than attacking capitalism itself',[91] it is of course important to make short-term demands for redistribution, tax reform and myriad other immediate steps – but these reformist approaches are ultimately insufficient, in large part because they fail to grasp the systemic nature of the challenge. Failing to understand the systemic nature of the challenge results either in surrendering to human rights as ideological apologia for the extant social order, or into sterile criticism. With an understanding of capitalism as the fundamental threat to any positive human rights future, it may be possible to radicalise the international human rights framework,[92] but ultimately advancing human rights will require 'ending the rule of capital over humans'.[93] This, in turn, will require the jettisoning of all liberal and idealist illusions, and a fundamental rethinking of the nature of international human rights regime, its relationship to capitalism, and the role of human rights in movements for emancipatory social change.

[91] Yates (n 53) 23.
[92] Brinks, Dehm and Engle (n 62) 370.
[93] B Rajagopal, 'Greece: Welcome to the Third World and Here Are Some Lessons' *Huffington Post* (13 July 2015).

Afterword: Between the Times

SAMUEL MOYN

HUMAN RIGHTS HAVE most frequently been posited as eternal principle that transcends time. When history has been accepted as something that happens to them, however, they have been caught between the two temporal poles of beginnings and conclusions. Yet like existence as such, human rights are always *in medias res*, neither an essence that never changes nor at the absolute beginning or final stage of their trajectory.

Whenever you think they were announced or prized, there has always been a strong temptation for partisans of human rights to deny their historicity, and even their temporality altogether. Like gravity or relativity, the fact that they were discovered after being unknown hardly means they were not there. American and French revolutionaries, while citing historical grievances for their uprisings, insisted that the authority for them ultimately depended on applicable principle that had no history.

In writing the Declaration of Independence of 1776, Thomas Jefferson – so explained Abraham Lincoln later – had 'the coolness, forecast, and capacity to introduce into a merely revolutionary document, an abstract truth, applicable to all men and all times'.[1] 'The values enshrined in the Universal Declaration of Human Rights are as relevant and timeless today as they were 70 years ago', agrees a recent Human Rights Watch statement.[2]

This very fact, ironically, once made human rights seem ineligible as master principles for a modern age seen as defined by acceptance rather than denial of inexpungeable human temporality. There were no human rights except as lived in human time, in which no appeal to the eternal was credible any more. Reflecting on the Universal Declaration of Human Rights at just the moment existentialism made being in time more plausible than beliefs in changeless essences, the Italian philosopher Benedetto Croce wrote that there were only 'human rights in history'.[3] This meant that the only question about human rights was what to do to and with them in the course of our historical evolution and transformation.

Yet in the recent phase of debate, aside from seeing the return of the belief that human rights must be rooted outside time, most contention has raged about

[1] A Lincoln, letter to H Pierce, 6 April 1859, *Collected Works*, ed R Basler, 11 vols (Rutgers University Press, 1953) vol 3, 376.

[2] Human Rights Watch, '70 Years of the Universal Declaration of Human Rights' (28 February 2018).

[3] B Croce, 'The Future of Liberalism' in J Maritain et al, *Human Rights: Comments and Interpretations* (Columbia University Press, 1949).

the chronology of origins of human rights, on the one hand, and how far they are into an apocalyptic endtimes, on the other.

Part of this is my fault. Addressing proposals by my fellow historians to find the first annunciation of human rights in *The Last Utopia: Human Rights in History* (2010), I helped kick off a debate about locating chronological beginnings that shows no signs of abating – even though part of my agenda was to attack the whole idea of what the great French medievalist Marc Bloch called 'the idol of origins'.[4] The argument since has indirectly cast a great deal of light (and shed no little heat) on even more important topics, such as how to define human rights in the first place such that they could emerge in history at one point or another, what the causal factors were that allowed that emergence, and whether it was an uplifting breakthrough for progress in the future or depressing concession to the failure of hope.

More prominent still than the search for inception, given the continuation of history and the setbacks and surprises of time, has been the debate over whether human rights are at or nearing the chronological end of their vicissitudes. In his catastrophising book *The Endtimes of Human Rights*, Stephen Hopgood has affirmed that they are – to much consternation from those who not long before associated human rights with the dawn of a new age.[5] But even Hopgood, by distinguishing what he calls 'Human Rights' in their imperial and neoliberal mode from 'human rights', left open whether the curtain of time is falling on them as such, or only on the premature foreclosure of human rights in the version than ascended with the 'end of history' in 1989.

It was the monotheistic salvation religions in general, and Christianity in particular, that created these scripts, with their commitment to 'meaning in history', and the idea that time is organised as a meaningful plot with a beginning or end.[6] It is not clear how easy, or even possible, it is to escape such preconceptions. For everyone with a script of history, what they see as starting can be reconfigured as ending, and vice versa. But for the moment perhaps it makes sense for those interested in human rights to think less than they have about first genesis or immaculate conception, on the one hand, or eschatological finale or last days, on the other. Perhaps, rather, it is time to recognise that human rights endure as part of our own middle ages, caught somewhere 'between the times', a phase which turns out to last indefinitely, much as it did in Christian history.

What would this mean precisely, either as a conceptual or political matter? Human rights express some parts of the aspiration to human emancipation, but only in an indefinite and provisional way. This was what Croce thought. He was a follower of GWF Hegel who believed the unfolding of freedom was more *in medias res* than his predecessor (or some of his followers at the end of

[4] M Bloch, *The Historian's Craft* trans P Putnam (Manchester University Press, 1992) 24–28.

[5] S Hopgood, *The Endtimes of Human Rights* (Cornell University Press, 2011).

[6] See eg, K Löwith, *Meaning in History* (University of Chicago Press, 1949) or F Kermode, *The Sense of an Ending* (OUP, 1967).

the Cold War) accepted. It helped that the 1940s when the Universal Declaration was born were the very apogee of philosophical existentialism – whose most famous claim challenged being and substituted becoming as what made humans most distinctive. There could be no human rights in the timeless sense, on this view, because nothing about human beings is immune from time. Neo-Hegelians merely hoped that, compatibly with the new discovery that time goes all the way down, we could rescue some sense of the rise of freedom and equality over the millennia. If so, human rights would not mark a departure from time but a moment or stage in our understanding of what we are becoming next.

In mainstream philosophical circles, such existentialist and neo-Hegelian perspectives are out of fashion. Most regularly, human rights are considered as reflecting eternal moral truths about permanent human interests, though some are more coy about this belief than others. Advocates of human rights have often inclined to this view, albeit more strategically, out of their fear that their fledgling project will suffer if any doubt is expressed about the eternal applicability of its norms – even when these same advocates go on to propose new rights and redefine old ones in an inevitably temporal process. But when human rights are beset by claims of 'relativism', the thought goes, it is better to pretend they have been applicable, even if not known, everywhere and always.

The alternative view admits that nothing human exists beyond time, a perspective that some have taken in a quietistic and others in a revolutionary direction. Human rights, so long as they are applicable and meaningful, are subordinate to human becoming. And if the list of basic entitlements and the organisation of movements seeking their enforcement change over time, it is not a problem – let alone a surprise – but a reflection of the only permanent fact about humanity and perhaps the universe: that everything changes sooner or later.

The fact that some have appealed to the temporality of culture and history cynically, as a way of lifting the requirements of human rights as they are understood now, is hardly a strike against the need to integrate those rights into an account of human becoming. Indeed, such cynicism is generally linked, not to an embrace of the openness of time, but rather a nostalgia for an earlier stage when roles were fixed and repression was normal. At the same time, resistance to human rights itself is part of the story of their temporalisation – and if that story is one of emancipation in history, it also means radical new possibilities about the place of rights can emerge, including their obsolescence, singly or as a set of norms. Of these new possibilities, in our era when the credibility of human rights remains certain for as long into the future we can imagine, the most startling has been the modern realisation that the social framework for freedom presupposes conditions for the enjoyment of rights that movement activists and political regimes must secure to make the entitlements meaningful.

The politics that follow from this conceptual understanding of a temporalised human rights as norms that are not static but tentative and not etched in stone but open to revision can therefore still be an emancipatory one. Indeed,

I believe it is. That this evolving understanding has so often pointed beyond rights, seeking the conditions for their enjoyment, only reinforces the point.

In saying that human rights are part of an indefinitely long evolution and necessarily tentative political agenda, I can still suggest that we can expect them to be crucial for a long time. Of course, no one can decree in advance that human rights will remain central to or even present in the moral and political lexicon as more and more is discovered and enacted about their enjoyment, and about the meaning of emancipation in time, any more than we can know how long it will take for that discovery or enactment to take place. We only know for the moment that human rights matter greatly, even if we also know now that they matter in the mix of a broader emancipatory agenda, in part for the sake of enjoying rights rather than just insisting people deserve them.

This existentialist and temporalised understanding of a human rights imagination and practice in history is disturbing only to those who assume either that norms, to be real, must exist beyond time, or that a freedom bound to time is fated to be so evanescent and shifting that it could not accommodate central values cherished and pursued over long duration. Both views are mistakes. For others, the existentialist understanding alone can make human rights an intellectually and credible project, beyond the myth of the eternal or the equation of the temporal with chaos and instability.

From the perspective that views human rights as part of emancipation in time, the recent tempests among scholars concerning the origins or endtimes of human rights look, now, like attempts to take stock on the premature declaration of the end of history in 1989. Not that locating when in the past human rights came to matter to so many was pointless or that decreeing their endtimes did not usefully indict complacency. But the effect of these intellectual campaigns as events in time was principally to shake self-satisfaction for the sake of better and more securely placing human rights in a prospective agenda of emancipation in time.

The result, for the moment, is that human rights are between the times. The laws and movements that seek to protect human rights have new possibilities, not just new threats, before them now that the norms those laws and movements care about are more and more generally embraced as the horizon of emancipation in time. But human rights also face a future, not only of greater enjoyment of the entitlements we know and understand now, but also of a search for emancipation we cannot yet fully understand, let alone know when and how it can come.

Index

www.ingramcontent.com/pod-product-compliance
Ingram Content Group UK Ltd.
Pitfield, Milton Keynes, MK11 3LW, UK
UKHW020805290926
15470UKWH00003B/972

9 781509 9499